Citrix XenDesktop® Cookbook

Third Edition

Over 40 engaging recipes that will help you implement a full-featured XenDesktop® 7.6 architecture and its main satellite components

Gaspare A. Silvestri

[PACKT] enterprise 🀰
PUBLISHING   professional expertise distilled

BIRMINGHAM - MUMBAI

Citrix XenDesktop® Cookbook
Third Edition

First published: January 2013

Second edition: January 2014

Third edition: August 2015

Production reference: 1260815

Published by Packt Publishing Ltd.
Livery Place
35 Livery Street
Birmingham B3 2PB, UK.

ISBN 978-1-78217-517-9

www.packtpub.com

Disclaimer

Credits

Author
Gaspare A. Silvestri

Reviewers
Erik Bakker
Jack Cobben
René Lindeboom
Florian Zoller

Commissioning Editor
Ashwin Nair

Acquisition Editor
Meeta Rajani

Content Development Editor
Shweta Pant

Technical Editor
Anushree Arun Tendulkar

Copy Editor
Charlotte Carneiro

Project Coordinator
Sanjeet Rao

Proofreader
Safis Editing

Indexer
Tejal Soni

Production Coordinator
Manu Joseph

Cover Work
Manu Joseph

About the Author

Gaspare A. Silvestri is an IT specialist with 10 years of experience in the information technology market. During his career, he covered a set of different infrastructural roles, including the important role of CTO for an ICT company, based in Italy. He considers his job to be the most enduring of all his passions, with a particular preference in the areas of virtualization and Unix.

He is always curious and in search of new IT projects on which he performs his research activities.

Gaspare has been involved in the design, tuning, and consolidation of physical and virtual infrastructures for the important system integration companies that are based in Italy.

Gaspare is also the author of *Citrix XenDesktop 5.6 Cookbook* and *Citrix® XenDesktop® 7 Cookbook*, published by Packt Publishing.

Thanks to Viola and Manuela, the shining stars of my life.

Thanks to my parents for the road of life they have given me.

Thanks to my entire family for the support and the strength they have given me.

Thanks to Roberto, who gave me the opportunity to start working on the Citrix® platforms some years ago.

A special thanks to Steven Wright, a wonderful person who allowed me to use his fantastic software (WrightSMS2—*Chapter 10, Configuring the XenDesktop® Advanced Logon*).

Thanks to the coffee, Miles Davis, and Pino Daniele, who have been my main fellowship during the working hours.

Special thanks to the entire Packt staff and the technical reviewers for the exceptional work that they have done with me.

About the Reviewers

Erik Bakker is a freelance consultant/architect, based in the Netherlands, with a strong focus on Microsoft and Citrix® virtualization technologies (SBC and VDI). He has specialized in designing and troubleshooting large Citrix® and Microsoft environments using the latest available technologies.

He's been adept at Citrix® since the early WinFrame product and has since been certified in the complete Citrix® suite up, to the latest released products, as a CCE-V^{SM} for XenDesktop® 7.6. Besides working with the product, he's also a subject-matter expert for Citrix® regarding the Citrix® Virtualization Exams, where he helped design the exams.

Next to everything related to Citrix®, he's also an expert in Microsoft technologies. He has broad knowledge of almost every Microsoft product that has been released and is also certified in all the major Microsoft products as an MCSE/MCITP.

Erik can be contacted on Twitter at `@bakker_erik`, or you can contact him by sending him a message using LinkedIn at `https://nl.linkedin.com/in/bakker123`.

Jack Cobben has over 13 years of systems management experience. He is no stranger to the challenges that enterprises can experience when managing large deployments of Windows systems and Citrix® implementations. In his spare time, Jack writes for his own blog at `www.jackcobben.nl` and is active on the Citrix® support forums. He loves to test new software and share knowledge in any way he can. You can follow him on Twitter via `@jackcobben`.

Jack has reviewed several other books such as *Citrix XenDesktop® 7 Cookbook, Getting Started with Citrix® Provisioning Services 7.0, Getting Started with XenDesktop® 7x*, and other titles for Packt Publishing.

Although he works for Citrix®, Citrix® didn't help with, or support, this book in any way or form.

A big thanks to my wife and twins for letting me have the time to review this book.

René Lindeboom lives in Almere, the Netherlands, with his wife and two little dogs.

He is (and has been for the past 15 years) a specialist in the field of server-based computing, Virtual Desktop Infrastructure, and other related application delivery technologies. He is also skilled in VMware View, Horizon, and end user computing technologies such as XenMobile®, RES Workspace Manager, and others.

René works for Platani Nederland as a senior IT specialist, and is experienced in designing, implementing, and troubleshooting or reviewing larger customer environments, based upon a sound and pragmatic approach. He likes transferring knowledge to those who are eager to get acquainted with new technologies, and he is fascinated by the speed in which technology evolves in this fast-moving world.

Platani Nederland offers specialized knowledge and expertise in all the current technologies, delivered to customers by experienced senior consultants in a quality-driven fashion, using common sense and lessons learned. Find out more at `http://www.platani.nl`.

Follow René on Twitter at `@renelindeboom` or see his LinkedIn profile here at `http://nl.linkedin.com/in/renelindeboom`.

Florian Zoller works as a lead IT architect at msg services, a consulting company based in Germany.

He has several years of experience in designing and implementing the Citrix® Infrastructures for midsize and large customers. Besides his expert knowledge of XenApp®, XenDesktop®, XenMobile®, and NetScaler®, he focuses on software distribution and automation technologies such as Frontrange Desktop and Server Management.

www.PacktPub.com

Support files, eBooks, discount offers, and more

For support files and downloads related to your book, please visit www.PacktPub.com.

Did you know that Packt offers eBook versions of every book published, with PDF and ePub files available? You can upgrade to the eBook version at www.PacktPub.com and as a print book customer, you are entitled to a discount on the eBook copy. Get in touch with us at service@packtpub.com for more details.

At www.PacktPub.com, you can also read a collection of free technical articles, sign up for a range of free newsletters and receive exclusive discounts and offers on Packt books and eBooks.

https://www2.packtpub.com/books/subscription/packtlib

Do you need instant solutions to your IT questions? PacktLib is Packt's online digital book library. Here, you can search, access, and read Packt's entire library of books.

Why subscribe?

- ▶ Fully searchable across every book published by Packt
- ▶ Copy and paste, print, and bookmark content
- ▶ On demand and accessible via a web browser

Free access for Packt account holders

If you have an account with Packt at www.PacktPub.com, you can use this to access PacktLib today and view 9 entirely free books. Simply use your login credentials for immediate access.

Instant updates on new Packt books

Get notified! Find out when new books are published by following @PacktEnterprise on Twitter or the *Packt Enterprise* Facebook page.

Table of Contents

Preface

Introduction

The way to work is changing. Jobs and workplaces are evolving; tasks can be accomplished anytime, anywhere, and from any device, thanks to the evolution of technologies and higher network connectivity levels.

In the era of mobile and BYOD (Bring your own Device), Citrix® has still improved its products in terms of integration, performance, usability, and user experience. Moving a step forward in this market by powering its desktop and application virtualization platforms, Citrix® integrates the ability to publish virtual and physical desktops with the ability to assign applications and content in a secure manner, with all the products strongly focused on the mobile and mobility markets. This is XenDesktop® 7.6.

In this book, we will discuss the evolution of the XenDesktop® platform, discussing how implementing and optimizing the new mobile world-oriented features is done. Also, we will learn how separating personal data from company working spaces is achieved by using a personal device. We will discuss the changes in the component's releases, such as StoreFront™ or NetScaler®, plus integrating the practical steps of the XenMobile® and the EMM (Enterprise Mobility Management) platforms provided by Citrix®.

After reading this book, readers will be able to understand how to implement a full XenDesktop® 7.6 architecture from its core components to its satellite features, which will allow them to receive a stronger user experience with an improved security of the personal information.

What this book covers

Chapter 1, XenDesktop® 7.6 – Upgrading, Installation, and Configuration, will discuss in detail the way to upgrade to the latest release from the previous XenDesktop versions for both the MCS and PVS architectures. Moreover, we will install and configure the main platform components, such as the database (the Microsoft SQL Server 2012 platform), StoreFront™, and the Licensing Services.

Chapter 2, Configuring and Deploying Virtual Machines for XenDesktop® 7.6, will show you how to interface XenDesktop® with hypervisor's hosts for Farm and the VM-BASE image creation. All the recipes will be based on the latest releases of the supported hypervisors.

Chapter 3, Master Image Configuration and Tuning, is focused on the configuration and optimization operations that are realized on the base desktop, server, or the physical workstation images for future deployments.

Chapter 4, User Experience – Planning and Configuring, will discuss how to implement the profile management techniques, the virtual desktop agent versions (Server, Desktop, and the Remote PC), and the main version of the Citrix Receiver™ component (agent and HTML5 agentless).

Chapter 5, Creating and Configuring a Desktop Environment, will perform the implementation and optimization activities for the infrastructural satellite components, such as Citrix Merchandising Server™ or the CloudBridge™ platform.

Chapter 6, Deploying Applications, will explain in detail how to deploy and migrate applications with the integrated XenApp® platform: the Hosted applications, the Local Access App, Microsoft App-V, and the AppDNA® platform.

Chapter 7, XenDesktop® Infrastructure Tuning, will perform optimization activities to enrich the quality level of the VDI with the use of the XenDesktop® policies and printers.

Chapter 8, XenDesktop® Component Integration, will explain the setup and the configuration phases of the main infrastructural Citrix® components that are required to enrich the XenDesktop® offering (CloudBridge®, NetScaler Gateway®, and XenMobile®).

Chapter 9, Working with PowerShell, will be an advanced guide to Powershell modules. With these, we will realize the high level configurations by using the command line.

Chapter 10, Configuring the XenDesktop® Advanced Logon, will explain the operations to implement the secure and strong authentication for the XenDesktop® 7 architecture.

What you need for this book

The software required to perform the component's installation are:

- Windows Server 2008 R2 SP1 (the Standard, Enterprise, Datacenter editions) or Windows Servers 2012 / 2012 R2 (the Standard, Datacenter editions)

- Microsoft .NET Framework 3.5 SP1 (only for Windows Server 2008 R2), Microsoft .NET 4.0

- SQL Server 2008 R2 SP2 (the Express, Standard, Enterprise, Datacenter editions), SQL Server 2012 SP1 (Express, Standard, Enterprise), SQL Server 2014 (Express, Standard, Enterprise)

- Microsoft Internet Information Services (at least edition 7.0)

- 100 MB of disk space for the Delivery Controller

- 75 MB of disk space for the Citrix Studio® component

- 50 MB of disk space for the Licensing and Director components

Who this book is for

If you are a system administrator or an experienced IT professional who wants to refer to a centralized container of procedures and advanced tasks in XenDesktop®, this is the book for you. If you are an IT technician approaching this technology for the first time and want to integrate a more theoretical formative process with step-by-step installation and configuration activities, this book will also help you. You will need to have experience of the virtualized environment, and an understanding of the general concepts of desktop, and application virtualization (VDI).

Sections

In this book, you will find several headings that appear frequently (Getting ready, How to do it, How it works, There's more, and See also).

To give clear instructions on how to complete a recipe, we use these sections as follows:

Getting ready

This section tells you what to expect in the recipe, and describes how to set up any software or any preliminary settings required for the recipe.

How to do it...

This section contains the steps required to follow the recipe.

How it works...

This section usually consists of a detailed explanation of what happened in the previous section.

There's more...

This section consists of additional information about the recipe in order to make the reader more knowledgeable about the recipe.

See also

This section provides helpful links to other useful information for the recipe.

Conventions

In this book, you will find a number of styles of text that distinguish between different kinds of information. Here are some examples of these styles, and an explanation of their meaning.

Code words in text, database table names, folder names, filenames, file extensions, pathnames, dummy URLs, user input, and Twitter handles are shown as follows: "This is the `dbscript.exe` utility, located under the default installation path."

Any command-line input or output is written as follows:

```
echo staticmax=$staticmax
```

New terms and **important words** are shown in bold. Words that you see on the screen, in menus or dialog boxes for example, appear in the text like this: "In the **Firewall** section, let XenDesktop configure the required firewall exceptions by selecting the **Automatically** radio button, then click on **Next** to continue.".

> Warnings or important notes appear in a box like this.

> Tips and tricks appear like this.

Reader feedback

Feedback from our readers is always welcome. Let us know what you think about this book—what you liked or may have disliked. Reader feedback is important for us to develop titles that you really get the most out of.

To send us general feedback, simply send an e-mail to feedback@packtpub.com, and mention the book title via the subject of your message. If there is a topic that you have expertise in and you are interested in either writing or contributing to a book, see our author guide on www.packtpub.com/authors.

Customer support

Now that you are the proud owner of a Packt book, we have a number of things to help you to get the most from your purchase.

Downloading the example code

You can download the example code files for all Packt books you have purchased from your account at http://www.packtpub.com. If you purchased this book elsewhere, you can visit http://www.packtpub.com/support and register to have the files e-mailed directly to you.

Downloading the color images of this book

We also provide you with a PDF file that has color images of the screenshots/diagrams used in this book. The color images will help you better understand the changes in the output. You can download this file from http://www.packtpub.com/sites/default/files/downloads/5179EN_ColoredImages.pdf.

Errata

Although we have taken every care to ensure the accuracy of our content, mistakes do happen. If you find a mistake in one of our books—maybe a mistake in the text or the code—we would be grateful if you could report this to us. By doing so, you can save other readers from frustration and help us improve subsequent versions of this book. If you find any errata, please report them by visiting http://www.packtpub.com/submit-errata, selecting your book, clicking on the **Errata Submission Form** link, and entering the details of your errata. Once your errata are verified, your submission will be accepted and the errata will be uploaded to our website or added to any list of existing errata under the Errata section of that title.

To view the previously submitted errata, go to `https://www.packtpub.com/books/content/support` and enter the name of the book in the search field. The required information will appear under the **Errata** section.

Piracy

Piracy of copyright material on the Internet is an ongoing problem across all media. At Packt, we take the protection of our copyright and licenses very seriously. If you come across any illegal copies of our works, in any form, on the Internet, please provide us with the location address or website name immediately so that we can pursue a remedy.

Please contact us at `copyright@packtpub.com` with a link to the suspected pirated material.

We appreciate your help in protecting our authors, and our ability to bring you valuable content.

Questions

You can contact us at `questions@packtpub.com` if you are having a problem with any aspect of the book, and we will do our best to address it.

1

XenDesktop® 7.6 – Upgrading, Installation, and Configuration

In this chapter, you will cover the following recipes:

- ▶ Upgrading from XenDesktop 5.6/7.x to XenDesktop 7.6
- ▶ Preparing the SQL Server 2012 database
- ▶ Installing and configuring the Citrix Licensing Services (11.12.1)
- ▶ Installing XenDesktop 7.6 components
- ▶ Installing and configuring StoreFront 2.6
- ▶ Installing and configuring Provisioning Services 7.6

Introduction

XenDesktop 7.6 is the latest release of the Citrix desktop and application virtualization platform, strongly oriented to the mobile world and the **Bring Your Own Device** way to work. It also manages different types of Cloud deployments. This gives the customer the ability to use their personal devices, with no loss in terms of security and data isolation. All the new functionalities introduced with this latest version have been discussed in the book's introduction.

In this chapter, we will discuss the implementation of the **Machine Creation Service** (**MCS**) and the **Provisioning Services** (**PVS**) architectures. We will also discuss how to upgrade from XenDesktop Version 5.6 to Version 7.6, including the Provisioning Services 7.6 component. After this, you will learn how to install a XenDesktop 7.6 infrastructure from scratch, configuring the most important and required components such as the database server, the licensing components, and the web access portal for users, **StoreFront 2.6**. StoreFront 2.6 is the evolution of the previous existing StoreFront releases, and it is also the substitute of the old Citrix Web Interface platform.

The following are the prerequisites to install and configure a fully functioning XenDesktop 7.6 architecture:

- Operating Systems: Windows Server 2008 R2 SP1 (Standard Edition, Enterprise Edition, and Datacenter edition), Windows Server 2012 (Standard and Datacenter editions), and Windows Server 2012 R2 (Standard and Datacenter Editions).

> For the Citrix Studio and the Virtual Delivery Agent, Windows 8 / 8.1 and Windows 7 (Ultimate, Professional, and Enterprise) are also supported as operating systems.

- Microsoft .NET Framework 3.5 SP1 (Windows Server 2008 R2) and Microsoft .NET Framework 4.5.1 and 4.5.2.
- Windows PowerShell 2.0 (included in Windows Server 2008 R2) and Windows PowerShell 3.0 (included in Windows Server 2012 and 2012 R2).
- Visual C++ 2005, 2008 SP1 and 2010 Redistributable packages.
- Required disk space: At least 100 MB for the Delivery Controller, at least 75 MB for the Studio platform, at least 50 MB for the Citrix Director, and at least 40 MB for the License Server.
- At least Microsoft Internet Information Services (IIS) 7.0 Version as Web or application server.

Citrix customers can choose between two deployment mechanisms: MCS, which consists of hosted desktops and applications published to users based on given accessibility permissions, or PVS, which consists of a single desktop or a pool of them, booted over a network and streamed on demand to end users.

In both cases, information is stored in a Citrix database repository, based on Microsoft SQL Server. It is used and populated with data coming from the main architectural components. In this book, we will discuss in detail about all of them.

> Starting from the XenDesktop 7 edition, you can deliver both desktop and server operating system images, virtually or physically, thanks to the union with the XenApp platform and its changes, which are now based on the **Flexcast Management Architecture** (**FMA**) rather than the **Independent Management Architecture** (**IMA**).

Configured resources such as virtual desktops can be accessed by end users through a web portal called **StoreFront**, the substitute of the old **Citrix Web Interface**, which permits publishing online stores with the applications and the desktops published to the end users.

MCS and PVS architectures can be combined together and used within the same company for different desktop distribution areas. This is the implementation of the **Flexcast** technique, the methodology that applies different Citrix products and configurations together, based on the requirements of specific company areas or customized architectures for specific teams.

> As generic reference, for a number of delivered virtual desktops nearer to or greater than 500, you should always consider using PVS architecture in order to avoid global performance and maintenance issues.

The main goal of this recipe is for you to understand the differences between the two main kinds of architectures: MCS and PVS. Once you have understood this, you will be able to better comprehend what and how to implement a consistent XenDesktop installation in line with your user/company requirements.

Starting from the database server and licensing configuration, along the chapter we will walk through XenDesktop components, StoreFront, and the configuration of provisioning service architecture.

The first implementable deployment is MCS. Its most important part is based on hosted virtual desktops.

How can we choose if MCS is the better solution for us? We have a set of main parameters to decide listed here:

- MCS is the right solution if we only want to deploy a virtualized desktop infrastructure, both client and server operating systems.
- As a general reference, we should choose MCS with a number of deployed desktops lower than 500.
- It is better to use MCS when we need to frequently upgrade base images. Despite the complexity of the operations required with the use of the PVS architecture, this is a quite simple process in terms of operations for machine creation platforms.

> Cons for the MCS configuration are I/O intensive, more storage per single VM despite the PVS infrastructure, and higher time to update images in the presence of an elevated number of desktops.

▶ Consider implementing this architecture when you have a shared storage like **Network File System** (**NFS**) or **Storage Area Network** (**SAN**); especially in the second case, it's preferable to have MCS architecture, thanks to its large **Input/Output Operations Per Second** (**IOPS**) capacity.

To implement a pure MCS architecture, you need the following XenDesktop components:

▶ Director
▶ Delivery Controller
▶ Studio
▶ StoreFront
▶ Licensing Service
▶ SQL Server database

> Even if not explicitly specified, you need a Hypervisor platform to create the virtualized resources.

The second kind of XenDesktop infrastructure is PVS, a Citrix implementation fully based on desktop streaming technology.

PVS is the right choice in the following cases:

▶ When you need to provide the users with not only hosted desktops, but also streamed physical workstations.
▶ In the case of physical machines, PVS is the only available solution.
▶ When we have more than one site with a number of desktops per location between 500 and 1,500 per PVS server.
▶ When we do not have a shared storage or we are faced with low performance storage areas. In this case, we will take advantage of PVS memory caching activity.
▶ When we have many users logging on or logging off simultaneously. This is known as the **I/O boot storm** phenomenon; choosing PVS, we can avoid this problem by passing storage constraints.

Cons for the PVS infrastructure are possible network boot storm, and network traffic have to be separated and isolated from the company network traffic to avoid bottlenecks.

To implement PVS instead of MCS, you must configure these components in your architecture:

- Director
- Delivery Controller
- Studio
- StoreFront
- Licensing Services
- Citrix Provisioning Services
- Provisioning Service database

You should consider combining MCS and PVS together, especially in cases where your architecture has the right balance of RAM quantity and storage performance. This is what Citrix calls **Flexcast** approach, a way to combine different architectures to satisfy all the requirements for a set of different end user's topologies.

Upgrading from XenDesktop® 5.6/7.x to XenDesktop® 7.6

If you already have an existing and configured XenDesktop 5.6 site or any XenDesktop 7.x release, you have the ability to upgrade it to this latest release. In this recipe, we will discuss in detail all the required steps to perform a fully functioning migration while preventing the loss of production data.

If you are using the XenDesktop Express edition, you cannot upgrade the platform; you have to obtain a valid non-express license to proceed with the upgrade process.

Getting ready

You can perform a direct upgrade to XenDesktop 7.6 from one of the following XenDesktop components versions:

- Virtual Desktop Agent (5.0 SP1, 5.5, 5.6, 5.6 FP1, 7.x) to the Virtual Delivery Agents 7.6
- Delivery Controller (5.0, 5.0 SP1, 5.5, 5.6, 5.6 FP1, 7.x) to the Delivery Controller 7.6
- Director (1.0, 1.1, 2.x) to the Citrix Director 7.6
- XenDesktop SQL Server database.

Before starting the upgrade process, be sure you have considered the following points:

- In presence of a single Desktop Controller, this will be not available during the upgrading process
- Be sure that all the users have been logged off by the involved desktop resources
- Be sure you have backed up the system critical components, such as database and controller platforms
- If using the NetScaler platform, be sure your running version is compatible with the XenDesktop 7.6 platform (at least 10.1 release)

How to do it...

To perform a correct and functioning XenDesktop resources upgrade, you have to execute the following steps in the right order:

1. Connect to your XenDesktop 5.6/7.x director machine with domain and XenDesktop administrative credentials.

2. After downloading the ISO file from your personal Citrix account, burn it or mount it as virtual CD (if performing the installation with a virtual machine, for example). Double-click on the **AutoSelect** executable file on the installation media. In the XenDesktop 7.6 welcome screen, click on the **Start** button in the XenDesktop section to proceed:

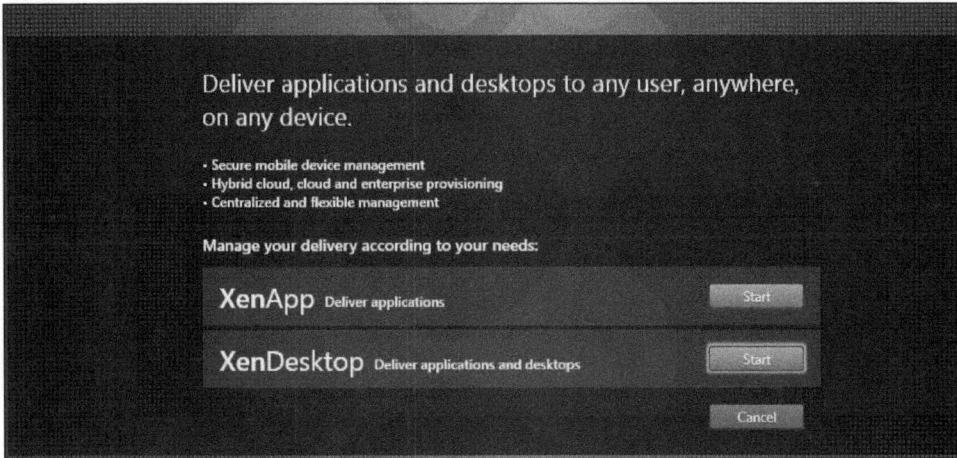

3. In the XenDesktop 7.6 installation menu, navigate to the **Upgrade | Studio and Server Components** section:

4. Accept **Software License Agreement** and click on the **Next** button.

> **Downloading the example code**
>
> You can download the example code files for all Packt books you have purchased from your account at `http://www.packtpub.com`. If you purchased this book elsewhere, you can visit `http://www.packtpub.com/support` and register to have the files e-mailed directly to you.

5. Carefully read the **Ensure a Successful Upgrade...** tasks list, then flag the **I'm ready to continue** option and click on **Next**:

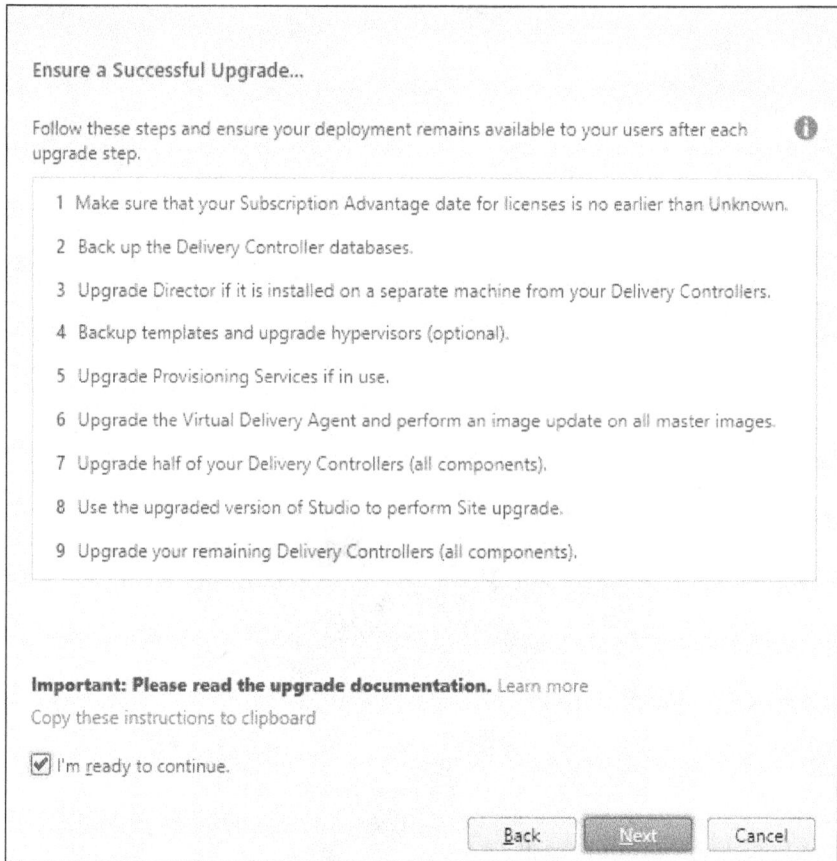

Ensure a Successful Upgrade...

Follow these steps and ensure your deployment remains available to your users after each upgrade step.

1 Make sure that your Subscription Advantage date for licenses is no earlier than Unknown.

2 Back up the Delivery Controller databases.

3 Upgrade Director if it is installed on a separate machine from your Delivery Controllers.

4 Backup templates and upgrade hypervisors (optional).

5 Upgrade Provisioning Services if in use.

6 Upgrade the Virtual Delivery Agent and perform an image update on all master images.

7 Upgrade half of your Delivery Controllers (all components).

8 Use the upgraded version of Studio to perform Site upgrade.

9 Upgrade your remaining Delivery Controllers (all components).

Important: Please read the upgrade documentation. Learn more

Copy these instructions to clipboard

☑ I'm ready to continue.

[Back] [Next] [Cancel]

6. In the **Firewall** section, let XenDesktop configure the required firewall exceptions by selecting the **Automatically** radio button, then click on **Next** to continue.

7. In the **Summary** screen, if all the information are correct, click on the **Upgrade** button to proceed.

8. After completed, in case of a positive upgrade, you will see a screen as shown in the following screenshot. Flag the **Launch Studio** option and click on the **Finish** button:

Finish Installation

The installation completed successfully.   ✓ Success

Core Components
  ✓ Delivery Controller   Upgraded
  ✓ Studio   Upgraded
  ✓ Director   Upgraded
  ✓ License Server   Upgraded
  ✓ StoreFront   Upgraded

Post Install
  ✓ Component Initialization   Initialized

☑ Launch Studio

Back   Finish

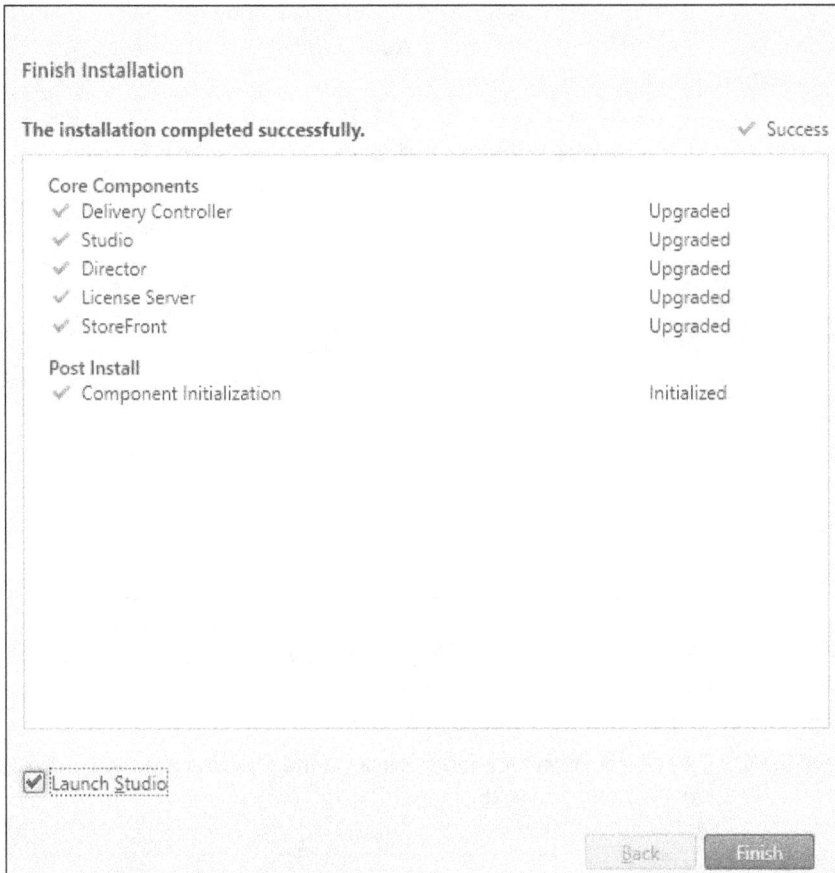

9. After you started the studio console, you have to upgrade the existing site configured
    for XenDesktop 5.6/7.x and the relative database. In the **Mandatory upgrade** page,
    click on the **Start the Site upgrade automatically** option. When required, flag the
    I am ready to upgrade option and click on **Next**. At the end of the procedure (**Site
    Upgrade Complete** screen), click on the **Finish** button.

10. In the **Upgrade Successful** section, select the **Finish upgrade** and return to the **Site
    overview** option to come back to the Citrix Studio console.

> If you want, you can manually update the database component by running
> the following PowerShell and SQL scripts, in the indicated order within the
> specified environment:
>
> `DisableServices.ps1`: XenDesktop controller
>
> `UpgradeDatabase.sql`: DB Server with SQL Server Management Studio
>
> `EnableServices.ps1`: XenDesktop controller

11. The last operation to perform is upgrading the VDA component on the instance machines. To perform this, select the **Virtual Delivery Agent** for Windows Desktop OS option from the installation menu.

12. In the **Environment** section, select **Create a Master Image** and click on **Next**. We will discuss the **Enable Remote PC Access** option later in this book:

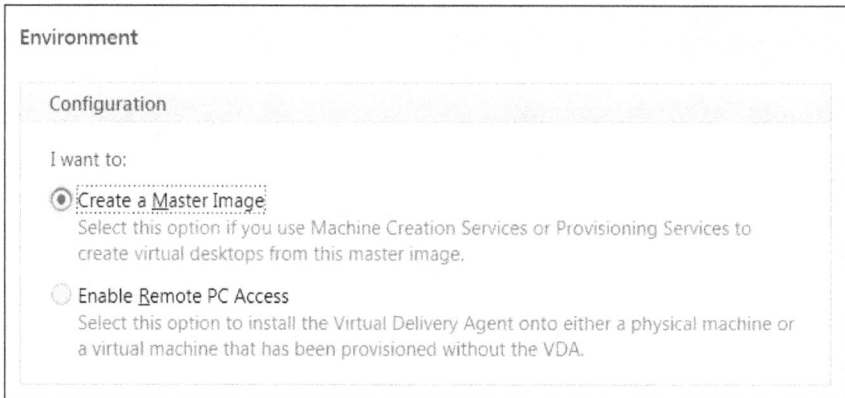

Environment

Configuration

I want to:

◉ Create a Master Image
   Select this option if you use Machine Creation Services or Provisioning Services to create virtual desktops from this master image.

◯ Enable Remote PC Access
   Select this option to install the Virtual Delivery Agent onto either a physical machine or a virtual machine that has been provisioned without the VDA.

13. In the **Firewall** screen, configure the firewall rules **Automatically**, and then click on **Next** to continue. If the information in the **Summary** screen are correct, click on the **Upgrade** button to proceed with the VDA upgrade activities.

14. At the end of the installation procedure, click on the **Finish** button to complete the entire infrastructure upgrade task.

How it works...

The process we illustrated is known as upgrade in-place procedure. This is a kind of upgrade procedure based on the evolution of an already installed and running system to a newer version; this is the only way to perform the upgrade from XenDesktop 5.6/7.x to XenDesktop 7.6.

> In the presence of a XenDesktop 4.x architecture, the operation will be no more based on an upgrade in place procedure, but it will be in the form of a platform migration. Please refer to the Citrix link at `http://support.citrix.com/proddocs/topic/xenapp-xendesktop-76/xad-migrate-xd4-intro.html`.

The steps required to successfully complete the procedure are given as follows:

- ▶ Upgrade the License Server platform
- ▶ Upgrade the Provisioning Services platform

> In case you want to maintain a hybrid infrastructure, with both XenDesktop 5.6 and XenDesktop 7.6, you should have two PVS infrastructures, for both releases.

- ▶ Upgrade the installed client agents, both for MCS (VDA) and PVS
- ▶ Upgrade the Controller components
- ▶ Manually/automatically upgrade the XenDesktop 5.6/7.x database

> Before running the database upgrade, you should consider to backup your database(s) in order to avoid unexpected loss of data.

After verifying all the prerequisites, we started the XenDesktop 7.6 installation setup from the resource media. At this point, we selected the platform installation option, in the form of upgrading the existing XenDesktop 5.6/7.x systems. The procedure flow goes on automatically, upgrading all or part of the components installed on the machine you are running the procedure on. Next, the most important operation in this procedure is upgrading the existing site including its database. This operation can be performed in two ways: automatically, using the Citrix Studio GUI and selecting the upgrade site option, or manually by executing already generated scripts (Powershell plus SQL), which directly operate on the Citrix services and data repository. These scripts can be generated by choosing the **Manually upgrade this site** option in the Citrix Studio console **Mandatory upgrade** section.

At the end, you have to upgrade the template image and client components, such as Virtual Delivery Agent and Citrix Receiver. Also in this case, the procedure is based on the automatic upgrade allowed by the XenDesktop setup agent, which detects the presence of an installed agent on the target machine and performs an upgrade operation instead of a normal installation task.

> In the presence of a VDA component installed on a Windows XP or Windows Vista operating system, you cannot perform a direct upgrade. To be able to complete the upgrade tasks, please refer to the Citrix article at `http://support.citrix.com/article/ctx140941`.

There's more...

To completely move from XenDesktop 5.6 to XenDesktop 7.6, it is important to upgrade the Provisioning Services component.

Despite the illustrated procedure for the XenDesktop core components, PVS requires you to uninstall the PVS software components on the infrastructural server completely and then reinstall them at this latest release. At this point, the only thing you have to do is select the **Join a farm**, an already configured option.

The part that requires you to pay more attention is the database upgrade; this can be performed using the PVS GUI or alternatively running a specific GUI tool.

This is the `dbscript.exe` utility, located under the default installation path (in our case the path is: `C:\Program Files\Citrix\Provisioning Services`). In order to generate an upgrading database script, you have to choose the **Upgrade database** option in the software GUI, and then you have to assign a name to the script you are going to generate, selecting the `PVS database` name that you want to upgrade at the end. Now, click on the **OK** button, as shown in the following screenshot:

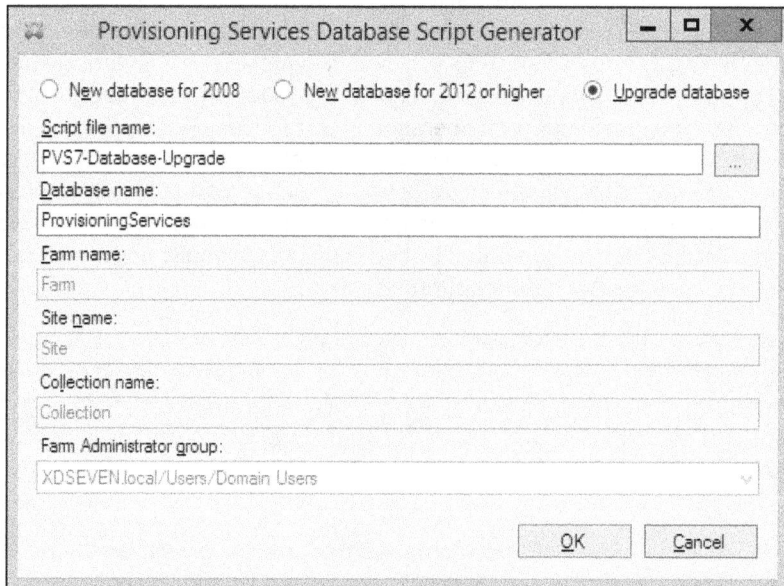

You are now ready to perform the database upgrade task by running the script on the appropriate database server.

- ▸ The *Configuring a target device – PVS architecture* recipe in *Chapter 3, Master Image Configuration and Tuning*

Preparing the SQL Server 2012 database

The evolution of the XenDesktop platform is not only in terms of Citrix core components, but also for collateral technologies used to implement its architecture. For this reason, we decided to implement all the latest releases of the software required by XenDesktop 7.6. This is also the case for the database component, which will be installed and configured in this recipe on Microsoft SQL Server 2012 edition.

> Even if the latest release of the SQL Server product is 2014, we preferred to work on the more supported and documented 2012 version.

Getting ready

XenDesktop 7.6 supports the following versions of Microsoft SQL Server:

- ▸ SQL Server 2008 R2 SP2 (Express, Standard, Enterprise, and Datacenter editions)
- ▸ SQL Server 2012 SP1 (Express, Standard, and Enterprise editions)
- ▸ SQL Server 2014 (Express, Standard, and Enterprise editions)

> SQL Server high availability supported features are: clustered instances, mirroring, and AlwaysOn Availability groups.

How can we choose the right database version? It depends on the required level of performance and availability. For standalone installations (integrated with the XenDesktop Controller server) within a test or POC environment, the Express Edition should be the right choice. In the presence of a huge number of clients and users, with a great number of processed data, if you want to create a clustered database instance, you should implement the non-Express version of SQL Server.

For a separate database installation, we need to perform the common installation operations, as explained in the following section.

How to do it...

Perform the following steps to generate SQL Server Database, which will be used by XenDesktop:

1. From the SQL Server installation media, launch the executable setup file. If you want, you can launch **System Configuration Checker** from the **Planning** section, to perform a preinstallation test and verify that all the requirements are met:

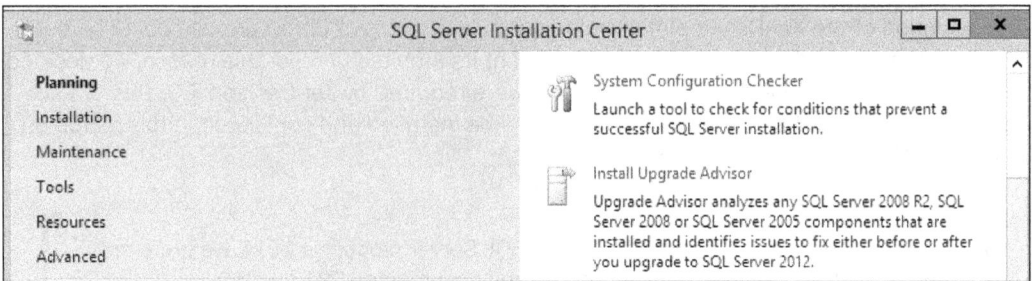

2. Click on the **Installation** tab, which you can see in the left-hand side menu and select **New SQL Server stand-alone installation or add features to an existing installation** option. For the purpose of this book, we won't execute all the steps required to complete the database installation:

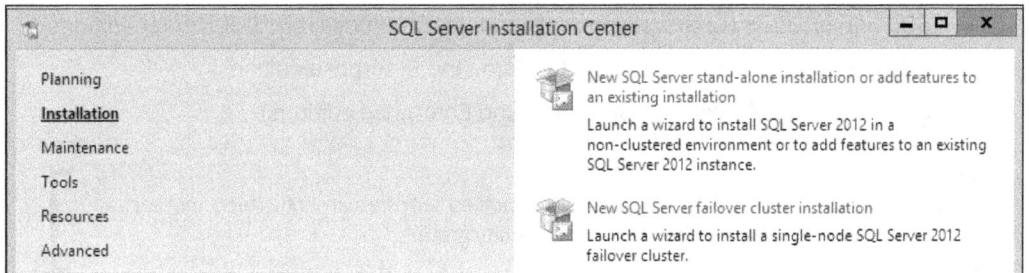

3. If you have available resources, you can select to create a new named instance, not using the default SQL Server instance (MSSQLSERVER).

4. On the database server, create a database on the desired instance (preferably having a dedicated instance for Citrix, as previously seen) with the following parameters:

    ❏ Create a new database instance on the database server, setting the Collation sequence parameter to Latin1_General_CI_AS_KS

    ❏ Configure the authentication method only as Windows authentication

❏ Configure the **Permissions** settings, as shown in the following table:

Activity	Server role	Database role
Database creation	dbcreator	
Schema creation	securityadmin	db_owner
Controller addition	securityadmin	db_owner
Controller removal		db_owner
Schema update		db_owner

5. This permission will be granted to the operating system user, who will perform configuration activities through XenDesktop.

> Using a separate instance is not mandatory, but it is better (more isolation, more security).

How it works...

We configured the most common format for the collation sequences (the same used by Citrix), and also restricted the way to log on to the database at Windows authentication, because XenDesktop does not support SQL or Mixed mode. For the collation, you are free to use not only the indicated version, but also the most important thing is that you will choose a version one that is member of the ***_CI_AS_KS** category (collation family is case and accent insensitive, but kanatype sensitive).

You must be careful when increasing the size of database logging; despite the normal data component (you should expect to have a database size of 250 MB with some thousands of clients), logs can unexpectedly increase in 24 hours in the presence of thousands of desktops. Based on the following table for MCS architectures, we will be able to calculate the database log and data files occupation:

Component	Data/log	Occupation
Registration information	Data	2.9 kB per desktop
Session state	Data	5.1 kB per desktop
Active Directory computer account info	Data	1.8 kB per desktop
MCS machine info	Data	1.94 kB per desktop
Transaction log for idle desktop	Log	62 kB per hour

> For a more detailed SQL Server installation, please refer to official Microsoft online documentation at `http://msdn.microsoft.com/en-us/library/ms143219.aspx`.

There's more...

In case of necessity to redeploy one or more Desktop Delivery Controller servers configured in your VDI infrastructure, the first action to perform is cleaning the XenDesktop configured database. To perform this task, you have to set all the Citrix components' database connection to null, using the custom PowerShell running the following commands:

```
Set-ConfigDBConnection -DBConnection $null

Set-AcctDBConnection -DBConnection $null

Set-HypDBConnection -DBConnection $null

Set-BrokerDBConnection -DBConnection $null
```

Once you finished these operations, you can proceed with the manual deletion and the recreation of the SQL Server database.

> Later in this book, we will explain how to use the PowerShell cmdlets available with XenDesktop 7.

See also

▶ The *Retrieving system information – Configuration Service cmdlets* recipe in the *Chapter 9, Working with PowerShell.*

Installing and configuring the Citrix® Licensing Services (11.12.1)

Among the XenDesktop updated components for the 7.6 release customers can also find the licensing platform: customers can easily convert their existing licenses to the XenDesktop 7.6 Version without any additional effort in terms of money and work. In this recipe, we will discuss how to allocate and manage licenses for the 11.12.1 release.

Citrix permits users to buy XenDesktop in different versions, as given in the following list:

▶ XenDesktop Trial Edition: a 90 days-99 users edition, which allows you to test the platform without any cost in the available time period.

▶ XenDesktop VDI Edition

- ▸ XenDesktop Enterprise Edition
- ▸ XenDesktop Platinum Edition

The choice is based on personal needs; in this book, when we refer to XenDesktop 7.6, it will be about Platinum Edition, with the ability to show and implement the full functionality of the platform.

Getting ready

The associated version of license server for XenDesktop 7.6 is Version 11.12.1.

System requirements for the latest version of the License Server are as follows:

- ▸ Windows Server 2008, 2008 R2, Windows Server 2012 or Windows Server 2012 R2 versions; as an alternative, you can also use Windows 7 and Windows 8 / 8.1 (both 32 or 64 bits)
- ▸ 55 MB for licensing components and 2 GB for user and/or device licenses
- ▸ At least .NET Framework 3.5
- ▸ A compatible browser (at least Internet Explorer 10, at least Firefox 14, at least Chrome 14, and at least Safari 5.1)

How to do it...

In this section, we are going to perform the required operations for the Citrix license server installation and configuration, based on the Windows Server 2012 R2 operating system platform:

1. After downloading the XenDesktop 7.6 installation media from your personal Citrix account, run the `CTX_Licensing.msi` installer, located under the following installation media path: `x64\Licensing`. Accept the **Citrix License Agreement** option and click on the **Next** button.

2. Select a destination folder's path for the program as default—we selected: `C:\Program Files (x86)\Citrix\`—then click on the **Install** button. Click on the **Finish** button when license server is successfully installed.

3. On the first configuration screen, you must assign port numbers for the **License Server Port**, **Vendor Daemon Port**, **Management Console Web Port**, and **Web Services for Licensing port** fields, as shown in the following screenshot, then click on the **OK** button:

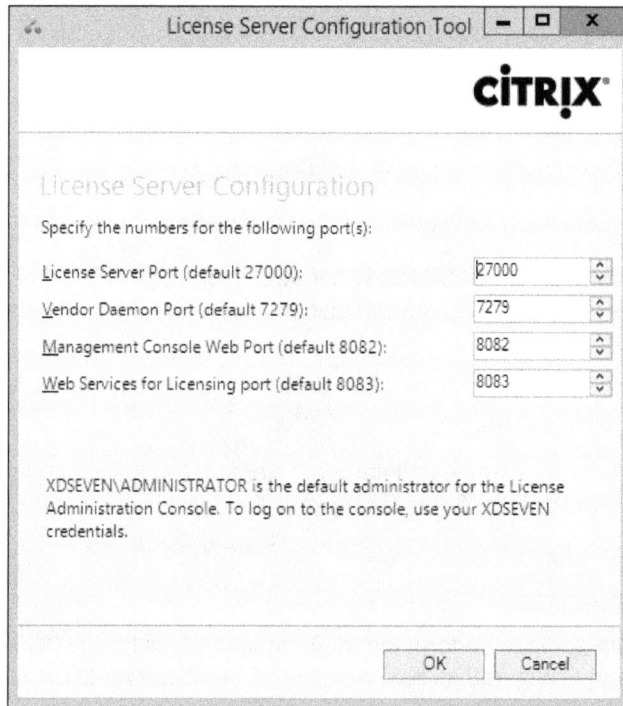

4. You can decide to leave default ports for these three options or change them. In any case, the ports you will decide to use must be opened on Windows Server's personal firewall.

5. To generate the license file for importing to our license server, run a web browser installed on your client machine, connect to `www.citrix.com/MyCitrix`, and log in using your credentials.

6. Go to **Activate and Allocate Licenses** and click on **Allocate Licenses**.

7. Insert the exact hostname of your license server and select the number of licenses you want to allocate. Generate the license file by clicking on the **Allocate** button.

8. Now, you will be able to save the file. When prompted for the location, select the path on which the license manager will read the file with the `.lic` extension, as `C:\Program Files (x86)\Citrix\Licensing\MyFiles`.

[XenDesktop license server is case sensitive. Be careful when you insert server hostname. You have to respect all uppercase and lowercase characters.]

9. Then to configure the license server, search for the **Citrix License Administration Console** link (using the Windows + *C* key combination or by clicking on the **Search** icon), and then click on it.

10. You'll see the summary dashboard; click on the **Administration** button and insert the administrative credentials for your machine (domain or local admin account):

11. After a quick look in the **Summary** tab, click on the first button on the left-hand side menu—the **User Configuration**.

12. Add a new user account to differentiate from standard administrative machine credentials; we can decide to create this account as **Locally Managed Admin**, **Domain Administrator**, or **Domain Administrator Group**. After these operations, click on **Save**.

> You can decide to force the user to change the password in the next logon, by enabling the relative flag, as showed in the earlier picture.

13. Now, it is time to configure alerting. Depending on our needs, we can set up critical and important alerts. It is preferable to leave them as default settings, and click on **Save** to archive the options.

> You should take care with the following licensing alerts: **Out of activatable licenses**, **Out of concurrent license**, and **Concurrent license expired**.

14. In the **Server Configuration** menu, configure the port for the web server (default is
    8082) and session timeout period (default is 30 minutes, but if possible you should
    reduce this value, so you can avoid inactive sessions locking unused resources).
    For security reasons, it is a good practice enabling SSL (port 443) and eventually
    using a personal certificate for strong authentication (as shown in next screenshot).

15. The available port range is from 27000 to 27009, on which the License Server is
    configured; the default port is 27000.

Server Configuration

Web Server Configuration

Secure Web Server Configuration

☑ Enable HTTPS (Default 443)

*HTTPS Port:
0

*Certificate File:
conf\server.crt

*Certificate Key File:
conf\server.key

Certificate Chain File:

☑ Redirect non-secure web access to secure web access

License Server Configuration

Logging

User Interface

Save   Cancel

16. At the end comes the most important part, **Vendor Daemon Configuration**. After
    that, this license file has been generated. Click on **Import License**, browse for the file
    location, and upload it by clicking on the **Import License** button. If everything is ok,
    you will receive a confirmation message about the success of the loading operation.

17. Click on **Vendor Daemon** (in our case, the default daemon is called Citrix), then and
    click on **Reread license file**, to make sure that everything is correct.

> Never manually edit the license file! If vendor daemon configuration
> returns you an error, probably you have to reallocate licenses and
> regenerate file, but do not correct it with any text editor.

How it works...

The XenDesktop license file is generated on the personal area on the MyCitrix Web portal. When you generate a `.lic` file, it must be generated and registered with the hostname of the license server on which you are going to use the file. This means that, if for any reason you need to reinstall the server or change its name, you must reallocate the license currently assigned, reassigning it to the new server and always referring to its FQDN; the license file must be regenerated and reimported, as seen previously.

> Until the 11.11.x License Server release, if using XenDesktop for test purposes or in case of a license server's fault, Citrix gives you a graceful period of 30 days. With this latest release, you have an additional 15 days. This is not covered with the License Server VPX version. More information about the VPX version can be found here: `http://support.citrix.com/proddocs/topic/licensing-1110/lic-vpx-import-configure.html`

Moreover, with the License Server 11.12.x edition, you have the ability to monitor the following alerts within the **Citrix Director** platform:

- Expired licenses
- Licenses about to expire
- Expired period of grace
- Activation of an additional 15 days period of grace

> We will discuss about Citrix Director later in this book.

There's more...

It is also possible to install the license server from a command line, using Windows command, `msiexec`, with the following parameters:

- ► `/I`: This is the installation option.
- ► `/qn`: This is for a silent installation.
- ► `INSTALLDIR`: This is used to specify the path of the installation folder (if not specified, default is `C:\Program files\Citrix\Licensing` for a 64-bit system or `C:\Program files(x86)\Citrix\Licensing` for a 32-bit system).
- ► `LICSERVERPORT`: This is the port that the license server will listen to, for connections (default is 27000).

- ► `ADMINPASS`: This is the administrative password for user admin on the licensing console. In the presence of Active Directory, you have to use administrative domain credentials.
- ► `VENDORDAEMONPORT`: This is the port of the vendor daemon component (default is 7279).
- ► `MNGMTCONSOLEWEBPORT`: This is the administrative license console port (default is 8082).

Therefore, for example, if we install Licensing in a silent way, using the `LICSERVER` folder on port 27004 and assigning `TestCase01` as the administrative password, the following will be the required string to run:

```
msiexec /I ctx_licensing.msi /qn INSTALLDIR=C:\LICSERVER
LICSERVERPORT=27004 ADMINPASS=TestCase01
```

See also

- ► The *Managing the Citrix® Desktop Controller and its resources – Broker and App-V cmdlets* recipe in *Chapter 9, Working with PowerShell*

Installing XenDesktop® 7.6 components

After illustrating how to upgrade from the older version of XenDesktop and implementing the database and licensing components, it is time to install and configure all the XenDesktop 7.6 core components from scratch.

Getting ready

In order to be able to install all the necessary components, you need to have domain administrative credentials on the server machine(s) on which you are going to implement your infrastructure.

How to do it...

The following are the steps by which we will perform the installation of the core components of the XenDesktop platform, including the Desktop Delivery Controller:

1. After downloading the ISO file from your personal Citrix account, burn it or mount it as a virtual CD (if performing the installation with a virtual machine, for example).

> On Windows Server 2012 R2/Windows 8.1 you can directly mount the ISO within the operating system by right-clicking it and selecting the **Mount** option.

2. Double-click on the CD-ROM icon or browse the mounted media and run the `AutoSelect.exe` file, then launch the XenDesktop installation by clicking on the **Start** button in the welcome screen, XenDesktop section, as shown in the following screenshot:

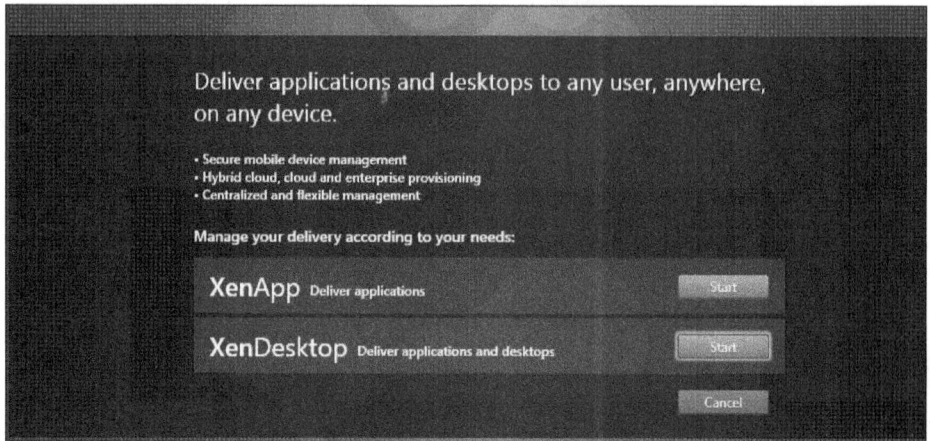

Deliver applications and desktops to any user, anywhere, on any device.

- Secure mobile device management
- Hybrid cloud, cloud and enterprise provisioning
- Centralized and flexible management

Manage your delivery according to your needs:

XenApp Deliver applications   Start

XenDesktop Deliver applications and desktops   Start

Cancel

3. In the installation menu screen, click on the **Get Started** section button to proceed with the setup procedure:

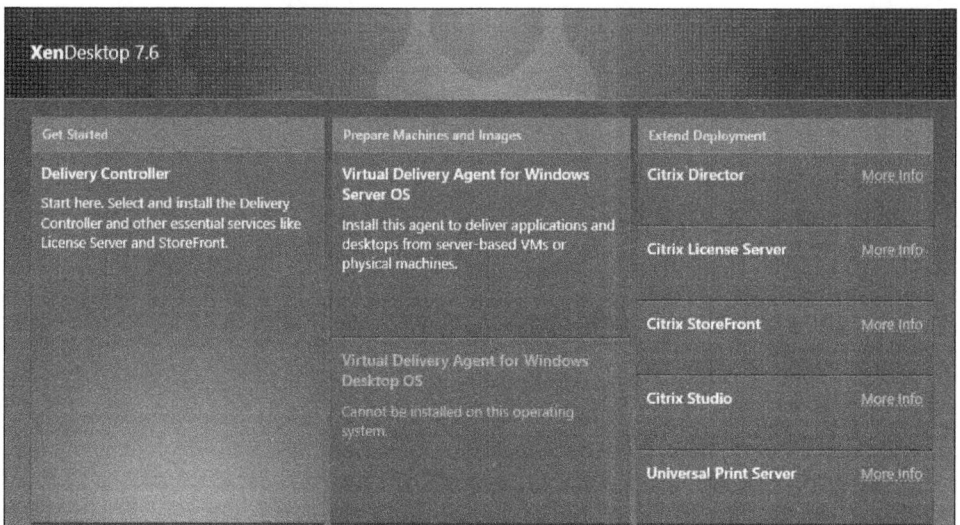

XenDesktop 7.6

Get Started	Prepare Machines and Images	Extend Deployment	
Delivery Controller	**Virtual Delivery Agent for Windows Server OS**	Citrix Director	More Info
Start here. Select and install the Delivery Controller and other essential services like License Server and StoreFront.	Install this agent to deliver applications and desktops from server-based VMs or physical machines.	Citrix License Server	More Info
		Citrix StoreFront	More Info
	Virtual Delivery Agent for Windows Desktop OS		
	Cannot be installed on this operating system.	Citrix Studio	More Info
		Universal Print Server	More Info

4. After the setup initialization, accept the licensing agreement, and then click on the **Next** button.

5. At this point, select the components that we need to install (**Delivery Controller**, **Studio**, and **Director**).

6. It is also possible to change the installation folder, by clicking on the **Change** button on the right top of the screen. If the path is correct, click on the **Next** button to proceed with the installation.

> Do not check both the **License Server** and **StoreFront** options. The first has already been installed on a separate server, the second will be explained and configured in the next recipe.

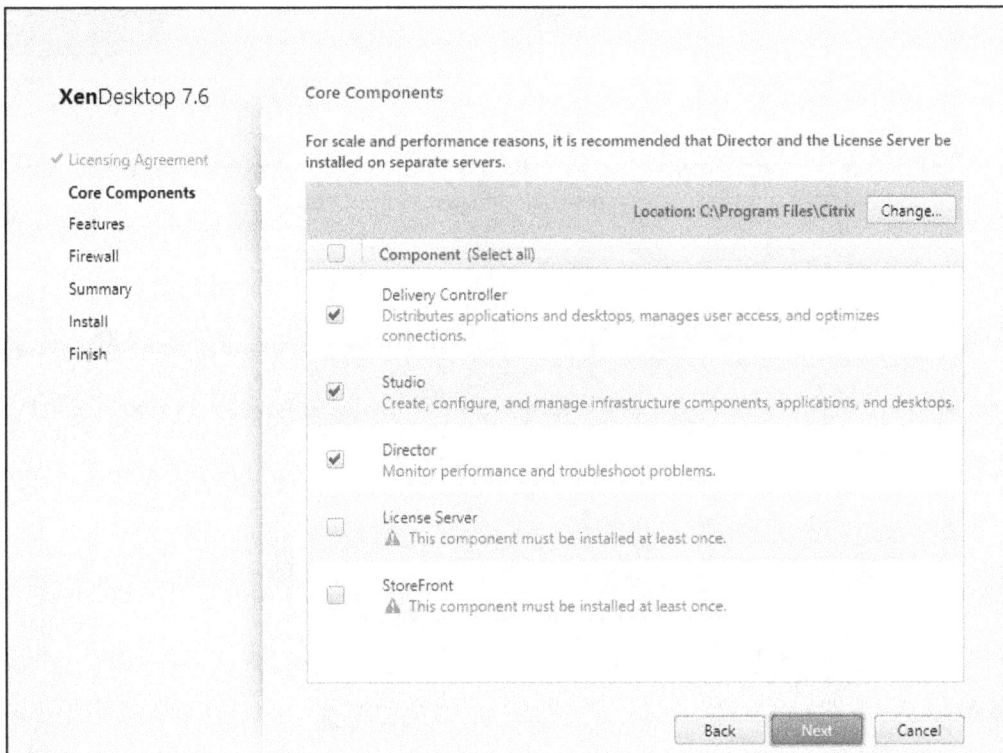

XenDesktop 7.6

Core Components

✓ Licensing Agreement

For scale and performance reasons, it is recommended that Director and the License Server be installed on separate servers.

Core Components

Features

Location: C:\Program Files\Citrix   Change...

Firewall

☐ Component (Select all)

Summary

☑ Delivery Controller
Distributes applications and desktops, manages user access, and optimizes connections.

Install

Finish

☑ Studio
Create, configure, and manage infrastructure components, applications, and desktops.

☑ Director
Monitor performance and troubleshoot problems.

☐ License Server
⚠ This component must be installed at least once.

☐ StoreFront
⚠ This component must be installed at least once.

Back   Next   Cancel

7. In the features screen, you have to select the **Install Windows Remote Assistance** option, and in case you do not need to use a full SQL Server version, select the **Install Microsoft SQL Server 2012 Express** voice. Click on **Next** to proceed.

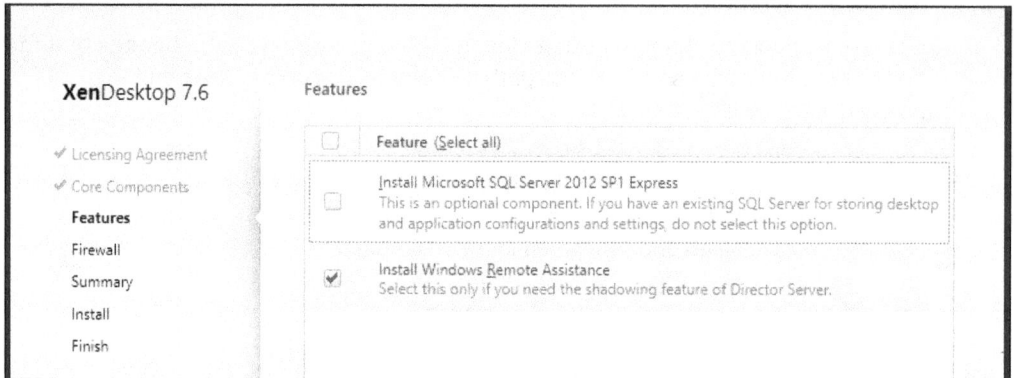

XenDesktop 7.6   Features

✓ Licensing Agreement

✓ Core Components

Features

Firewall

Summary

Install

Finish

☐ Feature (Select all)

☐ Install Microsoft SQL Server 2012 SP1 Express
This is an optional component. If you have an existing SQL Server for storing desktop and application configurations and settings, do not select this option.

☑ Install Windows Remote Assistance
Select this only if you need the shadowing feature of Director Server.

8. In the **Firewall** section, you can let XenDesktop automatically open the required network ports on the Windows firewall (TCP 80/443), or as an alternative, you can operate on it manually. After this click on **Next** to continue.

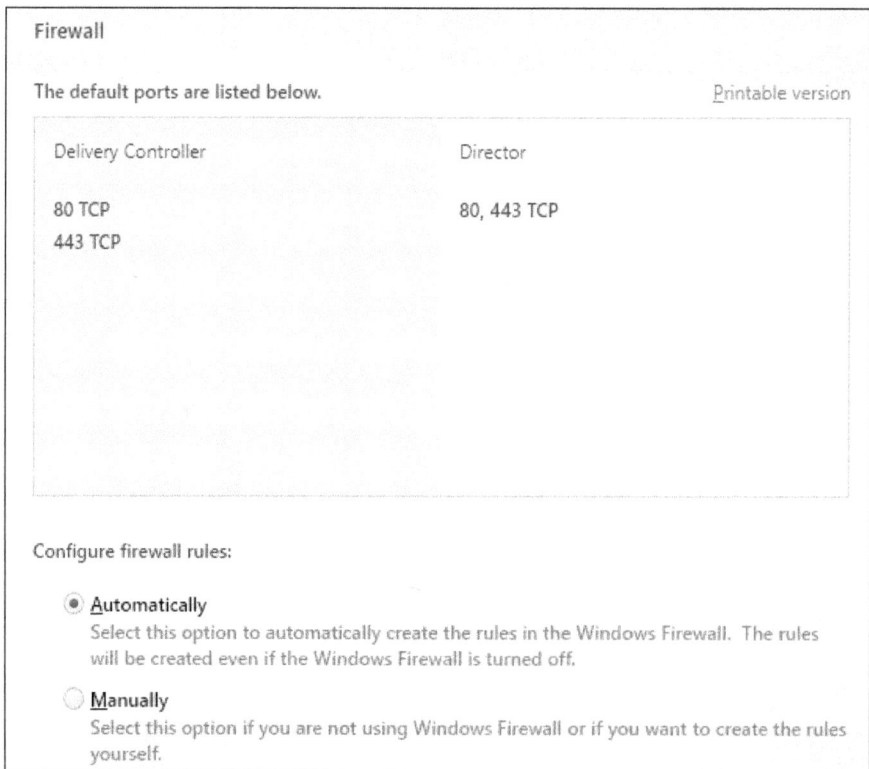

Firewall

The default ports are listed below.   Printable version

Delivery Controller	Director
80 TCP	80, 443 TCP
443 TCP	

Configure firewall rules:

⦿ Automatically
Select this option to automatically create the rules in the Windows Firewall. The rules will be created even if the Windows Firewall is turned off.

◯ Manually
Select this option if you are not using Windows Firewall or if you want to create the rules yourself.

9. You will be presented with the **Summary** window. If you agree with the summary details, click on the **Install** button to proceed.

10. At the end of installation, leave the **Launch Studio** checkbox checked, in order to verify the correct execution of the installed platform:

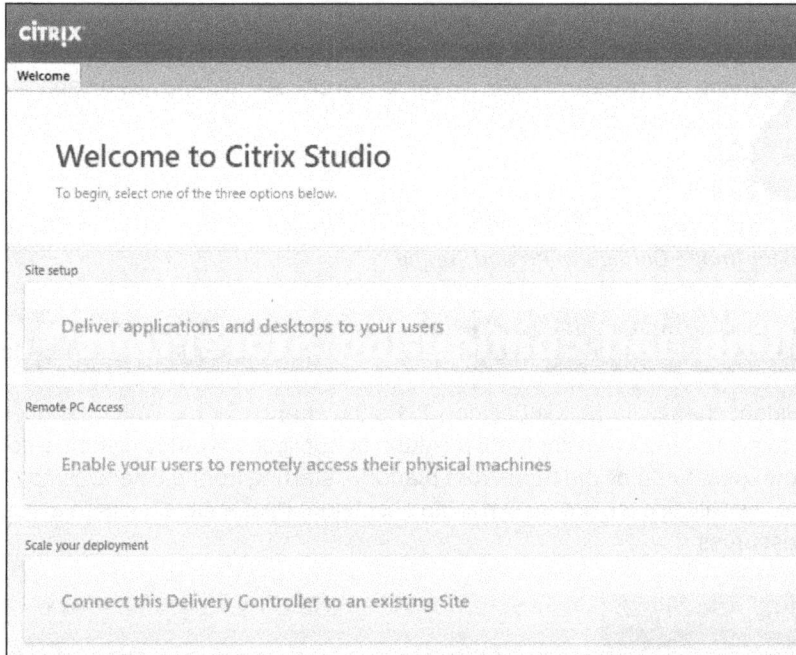

How it works...

XenDesktop 7.6 is the evolution of the 7.x release, in terms of functionalities and integration with other Citrix products. It combines the consolidated XenDesktop architecture with the XenApp platform, permitting end users to manage all the necessary deployments from a single management point (desktop OS, server OS, physical machines remote access, or published applications).

Users access their resources using the Citrix Receiver, installed on the device from which they established the connection; the Receiver points to the configured store within the StoreFront platform, which can be considered a stronger evolution of the Citrix Web Interface, an infrastructural component used with the previous XenDesktop releases. The delivery of all the resources is managed by the Delivery Controller component, also known as **Broker**, which regulates the association between the users and their resources. Once that this task has been accomplished, the Broker stops its intermediary channel activities, and a direct communication is established between the user's physical workstation and the requested desktop or application.

There's more...

With the release of the XenDesktop 7.6 Platform, the software activation procedure interacts with KMS, thanks to the ability to use a Microsoft KMS Server to release licenses for the operating systems and the Microsoft Office suites installed on the virtual desktops. This permits a better management of the licensing, especially for those environments configured in a non-persistent way, that is, any deployed desktop asks for a license activation code in a unique way, allowing the Microsoft KMS Server to identify any instance as a separate object.

See also

▶   The *Configuring and optimizing a Desktop OS Master Image* recipe in *Chapter 3, Master Image Configuration and Tuning*

Installing and configuring StoreFront™ 2.6

The most evident change in the XenDesktop 7.6 is the change for the Web Interface portal component to access their own contents (desktop or applications). This historical component has been now substituted by the StoreFront platform, starting from the XenDesktop 7 release. In this recipe, we will discuss how to install and configure it, to enable users to access their published resources.

Getting ready

StoreFront can be installed on both Windows Server 2008 R2 SP2 (Standard, Enterprise, and Datacenter Editions), Windows Server 2012 (Standard and Datacenter Editions), and Windows Server 2012 R2 (Standard and Datacenter Editions).

The following ports need to be opened on the firewalls within your network:

▶   TCP ports 80 and 443, in order to access the StoreFront Web Portal

▶   TCP port 808, used to the intercommunications between StoreFront servers

▶   TCP port 8008, used by the Citrix Receiver to communicate with the HTML5 store version

Moreover, you need to configure the **Internet Information Service** (**IIS**) role (Web Server) on the Windows Server machine dedicated to StoreFront.

After this configuration is completed, remember to bind the IIS Web Server address to the HTTPS connection, by clicking on the **Bindings** link in the right-side menu of the IIS control panel—**Default Web Site** view.

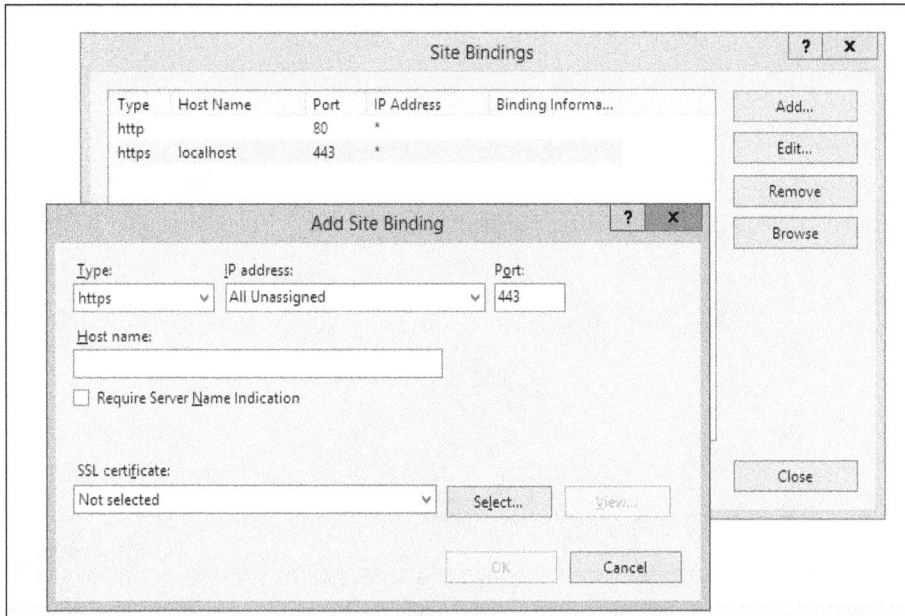

Be sure that you are installing the software on a domain-joined machine within the same forest of the XenDesktop components earlier installed.

How to do it...

Follow the detailed step required to install and configure the StoreFront 2.6 platform:

1. After downloading the software from your personal Citrix account, run the `CitrixStoreFront-x64.exe` installer, located under the following installation media path: `x64\StoreFront`.

> In case of a Windows 2008 R2 environment, you will be prompted to install the .NET 3.5.1 framework.

2. Accept the **Citrix StoreFront License Agreement** and click on the **Next** button.

3. Accept to install the missing Web Server IIS components and click on **Next** to continue.

4. After that, all the required components have been installed. Click on the **Install** button on the **Ready to Install** screen to proceed. After the installation is completed, click on **Finish** to start automatically the StoreFront administration console.

5. After the console has been opened, click on the **Create a new deployment** button in the StoreFront main menu.

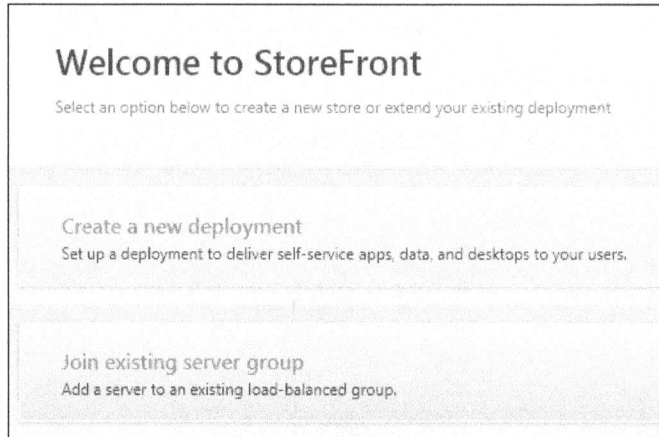

Welcome to StoreFront

Select an option below to create a new store or extend your existing deployment

Create a new deployment
Set up a deployment to deliver self-service apps, data, and desktops to your users.

Join existing server group
Add a server to an existing load-balanced group.

6. In the **Base URL** screen, assign a valid URL to which the StoreFront server will be available to the end users, and then click on **Next** and wait until the end of the deployment.

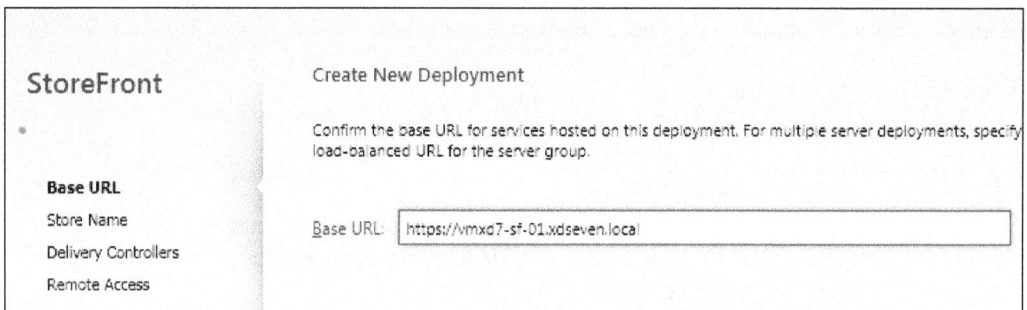

StoreFront

Create New Deployment

Confirm the base URL for services hosted on this deployment. For multiple server deployments, specify load-balanced URL for the server group.

Base URL
Store Name
Delivery Controllers
Remote Access

Base URL: https://vmxd7-sf-01.xdseven.local

7. In the **Store Name** field inside the **Store Name** category, enter a name of the store you are going to create, then click on **Next**.

8. In the **Delivery Controllers** section, click on the **Add** button to open the **Add Delivery Controller** menu.

9. In the **Add Delivery Controller** menu, perform the following configuration steps:

  ❑ Assign a name to the controller by populating the **Display name** field.

  ❑ Select the controller type by clicking on the specific radio button option (**XenApp 7.5 (or later) or XenDesktop**, **XenApp 6.5 (or earlier)**, **AppController**, or **VDI-in-a-box**).

  ❑ In the **Servers (load balanced)** field, click on the **Add** button and enter the name of your configured Delivery machine.

  ❑ Select the relative transport type and port (**HTTP/80** or **HTTPS/443**).

  ❑ After completion, click on the **OK** button. Then, click on **Next** to continue with the procedure.

> To be able to use the HTTPS connection, you need a valid SSL certificate on the Delivery Controller server.

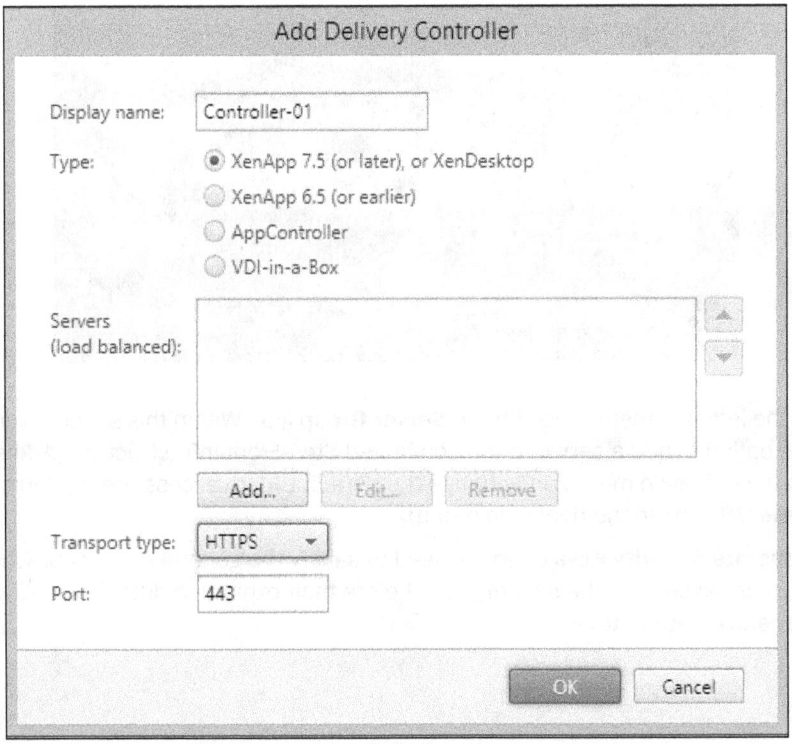

Add Delivery Controller

Display name: `Controller-01`

Type:
- ● XenApp 7.5 (or later), or XenDesktop
- ○ XenApp 6.5 (or earlier)
- ○ AppController
- ○ VDI-in-a-Box

Servers (load balanced):

Add... Edit... Remove

Transport type: `HTTPS`

Port: `443`

OK Cancel

10. In the **Remote Access** section, select the option you want to configure (**None, No VPN tunnel**, or **Full VPN tunnel**).

> In this case, you can select the **None** option. We will configure the secure gateway later in this book.

11. To complete the configuration process, click on the **Create** button. At the end of the store creation, click on **Finish**.

12. To check the configuration of your StoreFront platform, type the configured address in a compatible browser, in the form of `https://FQDN/Citrix/<storename>`.

> Before being able to use the web platform, you have to install the Citrix Receiver on the machine from which you want to use the web store.

Install Citrix Receiver to access your applications

☑ I agree with the Citrix license agreement

Install

Security details | Log on

13. In the left-side menu, click on the **Server Group** link. Within this section, you will have the option to add a server to the configured StoreFront infrastructure (**Add server** link on the right-side menu) and change the default URL to access the platform (**Change Base URL** link in the right-side menu).

14. **Generate Security Keys** option is used to satisfy the general security practices, you can regenerate the security keys before their expiration date, by clicking on the **Generate Keys** button.

Generate Security Keys

Generate Security Keys

Regularly generate new security keys as part of security best practice.

⊘ Current keys expire: 8/15/2015 12:31:24 PM

Generate Keys   Cancel

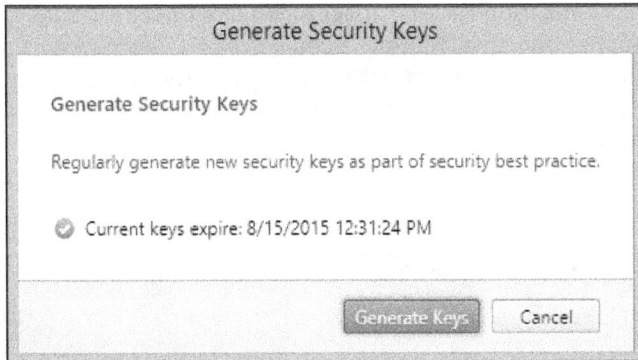

15. Click on the **Authentication** link in the left-side menu and configure the following options:

- **Authentication** section | **Add/Remove Authentication Methods**: Select the authentication methods you want to configure for the login on your infrastructure.

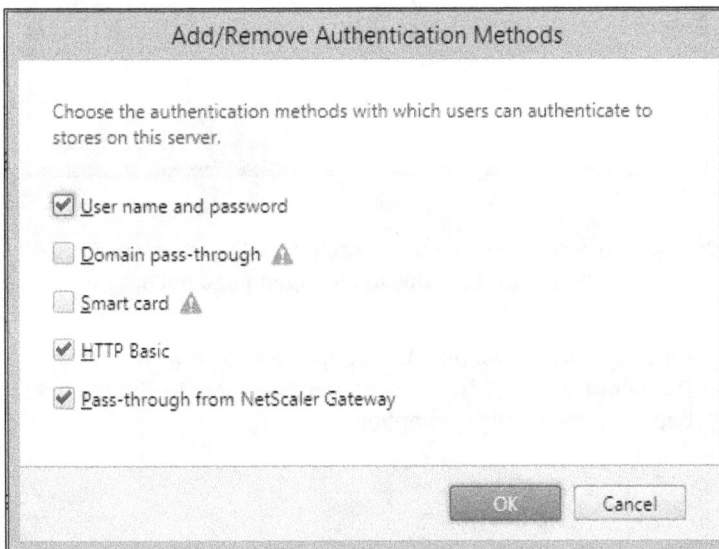

Add/Remove Authentication Methods

Choose the authentication methods with which users can authenticate to stores on this server.

☑ User name and password

☐ Domain pass-through ⚠

☐ Smart card ⚠

☑ HTTP Basic

☑ Pass-through from NetScaler Gateway

OK   Cancel

At the end of this book, we will discuss about the XenDesktop 7.6 advanced logon.

❑ **Authentication** section | **User name and password sub**section | **Configure Trusted Domains**: With this option, it is possible to restrict the domains from which users can perform the login phase. The Trusted Domain section will also avoid users to specify the domain for their user every time they log on to Storefront. Instead of typing it, they will choose the domain from the drop-down list of trusted domains. Click on the **OK** button to complete the configuration.

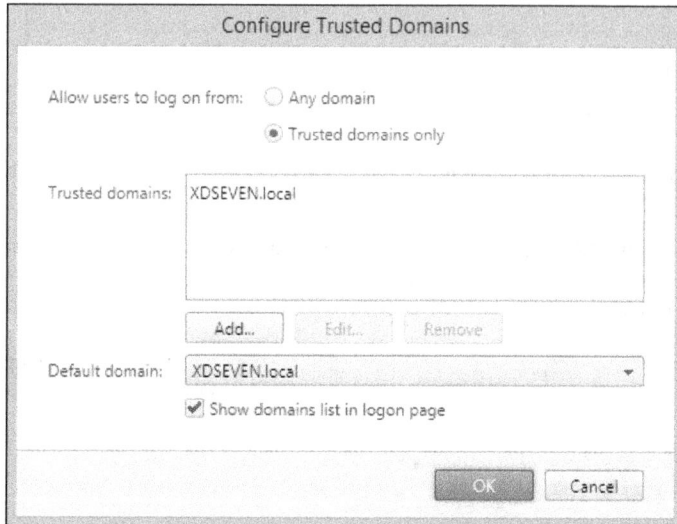

In order to enable the Default domain option, remember to flag **Show domains list in logon page** option.

❑ **Authentication** section | **User name and password** subsection | **Manage Password Options**: This section permits users to change their password based on the configured option.

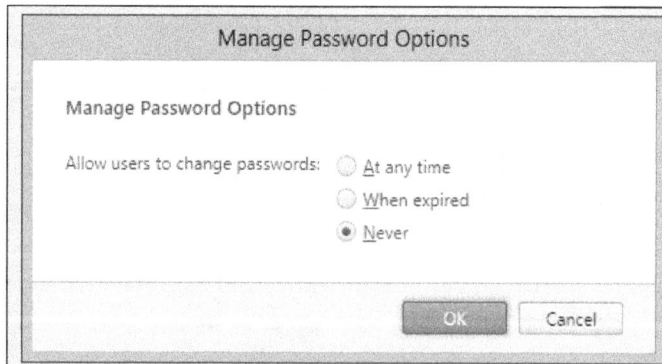

16. Click on the **Stores** link in the left-side menu and configure the following options:

    ❏ **Stores section | Create store**: This options permits you to create a new store in the StoreFront infrastructure.

    ❏ **Stores section | Export Multi-Store Provisioning File**: This section permits you to export all the configured stores to the store configuration file to be used by the end user devices on which you have installed the Citrix Receiver. The file will be saved with the `.cr` extension.

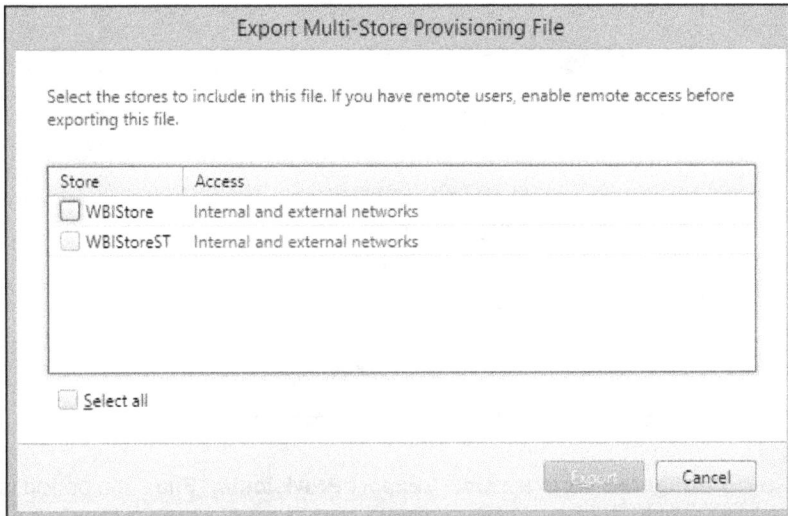

Export Multi-Store Provisioning File

Select the stores to include in this file. If you have remote users, enable remote access before exporting this file.

Store	Access
☐ WBIStore	Internal and external networks
☐ WBIStoreST	Internal and external networks

☐ Select all

Export   Cancel

    ❏ **Configured store section | Manage Delivery Controllers**: With this link, you can **Add**, **Edit**, or **Remove** the Delivery Controllers configured within your farm.

    ❏ **Configured store section | Enable Remote Access**: This option is used to configure external remote access using a NetScaler Gateway appliance.

    ❏ **Configured store section | Disable User Subcriptions**: By enabling this link, users will receive all the applications configured within StoreFront and not only the apps that they selected and enabled.

❑ **Configured store section | Integrate with Citrix Online**: This option permits you to include the three main Citrix online applications in your configured store.

❑ **Configured store section | Export Provisioning File**: This option is similar to the multistore export earlier seen, with the difference that this is related only to the current used store.

❑ **Configured store section | Configure Kerberos Delegation**: This option enables StoreFront to use single-domain Kerberos delegation when authentication is performed to delivery controller(s).

> More information about Kerberos Delegation parameter can be found at the following Citrix link:
>
> http://docs.citrix.com/en-us/storefront/2-6/dws-manage/dws-manage-store/dws-configure-kcd.html

❑ **Configured store section | Configure XenApp Services Support**: This option activates the retro compatibility access for old Citrix legacy clients. In the previous releases, this option was called **Configure Legacy Support**.

❑ **Configured store section | Remove Store**: With this option, customers have the ability to remove configured stores.

17. Click on the **Receiver for Web** link in the left-side menu and configure the following options:

   ❏ **Configured store section | Choose Authentication Methods**: This option lets customers decide which kind of authentication enables the Web version of the store.

   ❏ **Configured store section | Add Shortcuts to Websites**: This interesting option permits you to add a StoreFront shortcut to a specified websites, to make access to your published resources quicker.

   ❏ **Configured store section | Change Store**: By clicking on this link, you can change the store to which the Web Receiver is configured.

   ❏ **Configured store section | Set Session Timeout**: By clicking this option, you can configure the time period after which inactive logged on users are disconnected.

- **Configured store section | Deploy Citrix Receiver**: In this section, you can choose how to deploy the Citrix Receiver to end users.

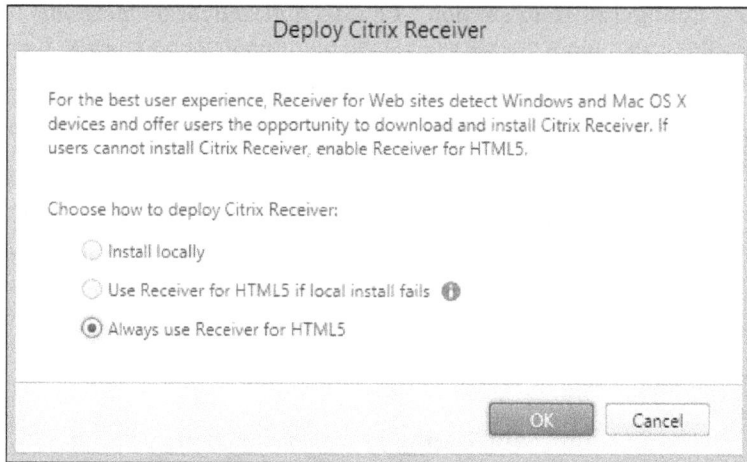

Deploy Citrix Receiver

For the best user experience, Receiver for Web sites detect Windows and Mac OS X devices and offer users the opportunity to download and install Citrix Receiver. If users cannot install Citrix Receiver, enable Receiver for HTML5.

Choose how to deploy Citrix Receiver:

○ Install locally

○ Use Receiver for HTML5 if local install fails ⓘ

◉ Always use Receiver for HTML5

OK   Cancel

- **Configured store section | Remove Website**: This option must only be used in case you want to remove a configured Receiver Website.

> The options **NetScaler Gateway** and **Beacons** will be discussed in the *Chapter 8, Installing and Configuring NetScaler Gateway™ 10.5*.

How it works...

StoreFront 2.6 is the latest version of this platform used with XenDesktop to access published resources. It is structured in the form of a catalog, which is able to deploy resources like desktops and applications from heterogeneous Citrix software (XenDesktop, XenApp, XenMobile, and so on).

StoreFront offers the same login methodologies used by the Web Interface. Customers can access their contents using simple authentication, smart card, or smart card pass-through; in addition, it is also possible to access the Citrix farm with the pass-through from the NetScaler Gateway.

The great step forward with the use of this platform is given in the new features listed as follows:

- StoreFront no longer needs to use an external database, now it can use its local repository for users' subscriptions.
- The high availability has been improved, thanks to the Storefront's capacity to replicate its database content among all the StoreFront machines within a configured site.

▶ StoreFront gives you a choice in how to access the resources, through the use of the Citrix Receiver or using the new HTML5 web client.

> When using the Citrix Receiver to access your StoreFront server, you can use a configured e-mail address to directly access your store. This is the **e-mail-based account discovery** feature.

▶ StoreFront is able to apply a sync between all the configured StoreFront servers used by customers to access their resources, this permits to do not apply again for application subscription.

▶ StoreFront 2.6 permits you to change the password of your Active Directory account used to connect to the store.

▶ With StoreFront 2.6 release, you can configure unauthenticated access. This means that users accessing a StoreFront store will insert accessing credentials directly within the application and not twice (StoreFront + application). This is particularly useful for mission critical applications, such as medical software.

▶ With StoreFront 2.6, applications can be organized in folders, using the Receiver for Web store.

> We will discuss in more detail unauthenticated access and folder views in the *Chapter 6, Deploying Applications*.

▶ The Citrix Receiver installed on the end user workstations can be easily configured using the exported Store configuration file also in multistore mode. This means that it is possible to export and configure all the available stores configured in the infrastructure on a client device.

▶ In a configured store, the Citrix online application is already available to be deployed to the end users (Citrix GoToMeeting, GoToWebinar, and GoToTraining).

There's more...

Also in case of StoreFront installation, users can perform this task by the use of the command line. You have to execute from a command prompt shell the same executable file used for the graphical installation (`CitrixStoreFront-x64.exe`), followed by one or more of these options:

▶ `-silent`: This option executes all the required steps in silent way.

▶ `-INSTALLDIR`: This option specifies the destination folder on which StoreFront 2.6 is installed.

▸ -WINDOWS_CLIENT: This option will make the Citrix Receiver installation files for Windows available on the StoreFront server.

▸ -MAC_CLIENT: This option will make the Citrix Receiver installation files for Mac available on the StoreFront server.

See also

▸ The *Configuring Citrix Receiver™* recipe in *Chapter 4, User Experience – Planning and Configuring*

Installing and configuring Citrix Provisioning Services 7.6

In this book, we decided to give particular importance to both the possible resource deployment ways (MCS and PVS) as we did earlier in the previous XenDesktop cookbooks. In this recipe, we will explain the step-by-step way to install and configure the Provisioning Services 7.6 platform.

Citrix Provisioning Services 7.6 eliminates the need of external PXE and TFTP platforms, thanks to the empowered **Boot Device Manager** feature.

> Thanks to the BDM feature, you can avoid using any IP helper (DHCP relay) within your network, because of the absence of PXE systems that eliminates the boot problems across different networks. Moreover, BDM also introduces the chance of centrally manage PXE and TFTP in a more dynamic way.

Getting ready

The Provisioning Services 7.6 can be implemented on the following platforms:

▸ PVS Server—Operating Systems: Windows Server 2008 and 2008 R2 (Standard, Enterprise, Datacenter editions), and Windows Server 2012 and 2012 R2 (Essential, Standard, and Datacenter editions).

> For a number of vDisks equal or greater than 250, the minimum RAM requirement for the server machine changes from 2 GB to 4 GB of RAM.

▸ Databases: Microsoft SQL Server 2008 and 2008 R2 (Express, Standard, Enterprise Editions), Microsoft SQL Server 2012 (Express and Standard Editions), and Microsoft SQL Server 2014.

▶ Target Devices—Operating Systems: Windows Server 2008 R2, Windows Server 2012, Windows XP SP2 and SP3, Windows 7 SP1 (Ultimate Edition supported only in Private Image mode), and Windows 8/8.1.

> In case of Master Images deployed with the latest XenDesktop Virtual Desktop Agent installed, Windows XP is not supported.

How to do it...

In this recipe, we are going to execute all the steps required to install and configure the Citrix Provisioning Services platform, as follows:

1. Download the PVS 7.6 ISO software from the Citrix website, using your credentials on www.citrix.com/MyCitrix. It is necessary to install .NET Framework 3.5; if not present on your PVS server, you can install it from **Windows Server Features**.

> In presence of Windows Server 2012 / 2012 R2, you have to install the .NET Framework 3.5 from the Windows installation media, by following this guide: `http://blogs.msdn.com/b/sql_shep/archive/2012/08/01/windows-2012-and-net-3-5-feature-install.aspx`

2. Run `Autorun.exe` from the installation media.

3. From the **Provisioning Services** installation screen, select **Server installation**.

4. In the missing prerequisites screen, click on **Install** to add all the pending components to the system:

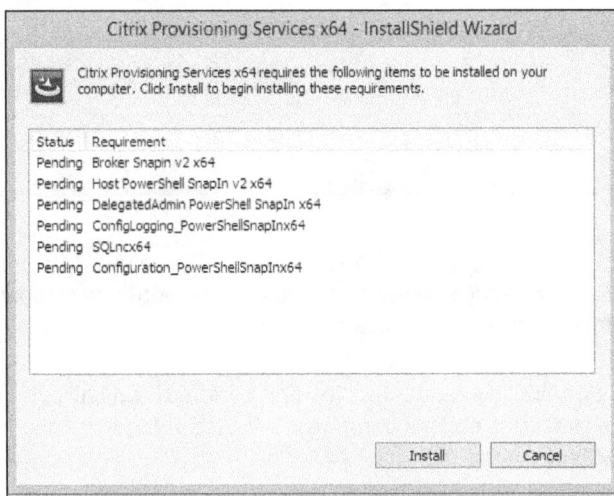

5. In the Welcome screen, click on **Next** to proceed. Accept the **Citrix License Agreement** and click on the **Next** button. After this, insert a valid **User Name** and **Organization** values, and choose if installing the application for **Anyone who uses this computer (all users)** or **Only for me (Windows User)**. Then click on **Next**.

6. In the **Destination Folder** screen, accept the proposed installation path (default path is `C:\Program Files\Citrix\Provisioning Services\`) or modify it by clicking on the **Change** button. After completion, click on the **Next** button to proceed.

7. In the **Ready to Install** program screen, click on the **Install** button to start the installation process.

8. After completion, click on the **Finish** button, then proceed with the configuration operations. In the **Welcome** screen, click on the **Next** button to proceed.

9. In the **DHCP Services** screen, select the **The service that runs on another computer** radio button. Then click on **Next**.

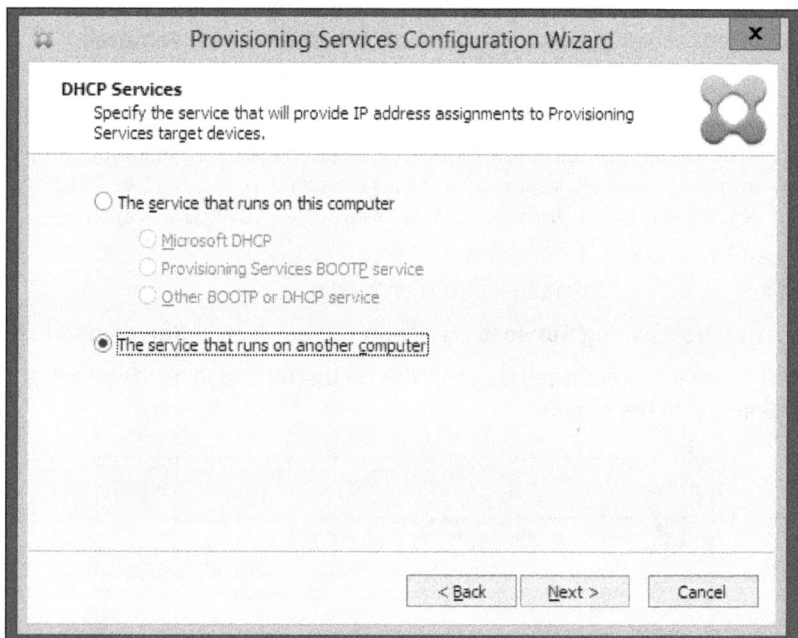

The best choice is to install DHCP server on a machine different from the Provisioning Service server. You should always separate components for better performance and roles isolation.

10. On the **PXE Services** screen, select the first option to configure the PXE component (**The Service that runs on this computer | Provisioning Services PXE service**), and click on **Next** to continue.

11. In the **Farm Configuration** section, select the **Create farm** radio button, and then click on the **Next** button.

> To better convey the differences between the MCS and PVS architectures, we will always use two different farms to accomplish tasks for both architectures.

12. In the **Database Server** section, populate all the required fields to make the PVS server able to connect to the database server. After completed, click on **Next**.

> You should always consider separating the database server from the PVS machine. Separating roles will assure you separation, isolation, and better load balancing and security.

13. In the **New Farm** screen, populate all the required fields. Then choose the configured **Use Active Directory groups for security** option. After completion click on the **Next** button:

14. In the **New Store** screen, assign a name to the store, select a **Default path**, and click on the **Next** button to continue with the installation process.

15. In the **License Server** section, populate the **License Server name** and **Licenser Server port** fields with the values of an existing Citrix Licensing Server. Then, click on **Next** to proceed.

> To check the validity of your License Server with the PVS 7.6 platform, flag the **Validate license server version and communication** option.

16. In the **User account** screen, specify a valid account for the **Stream and Soap Services**. You can choose between the **Network service account** or a **Specified user account**. After the user account is configured click on the **Next** button.

17. In the **Active Directory Computer Account Password** you can automate the computer account password updates by enabling this option, configuring the interval in days after which the passwords will be updated. To continue with **Provisioning Services Configuration Wizard**, click on **Next**.

18. The **Network Communications** screen allows users to be able to configure the network components in the PVS console component, in terms of streaming NICs and communication ports. Click on **Next** to continue.

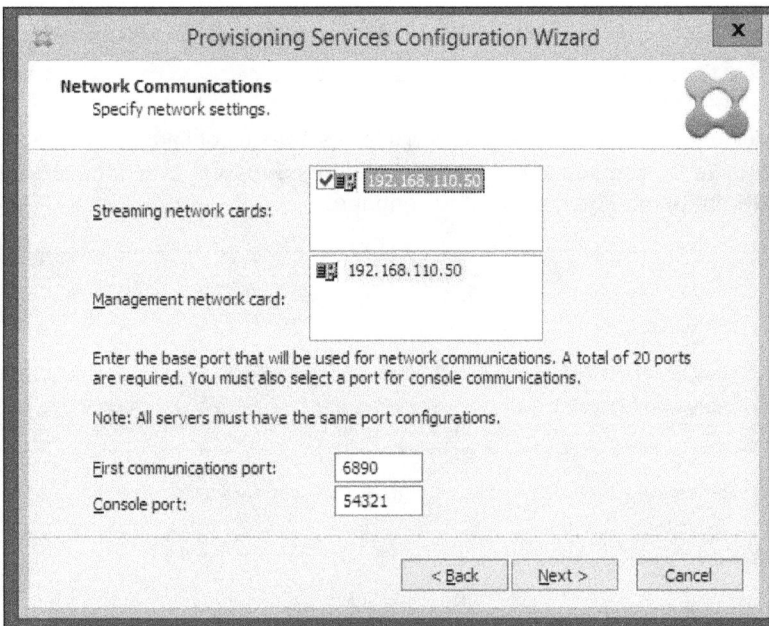

19. In the later screen, flag the **Use the Provisioning Services TFTP Services** option to enable the use of the PVS 7.6 TFTP feature and browse for a disk path, on which locating the installed resources (in our case the BIN files have been located under C:\ProgramData\Citrix\Provisioning Services\Tftpboot). Click on the **Next** button to continue.

20. In **Stream Servers Boot List**, users can configure up to four boot servers, specifying their network configurations.

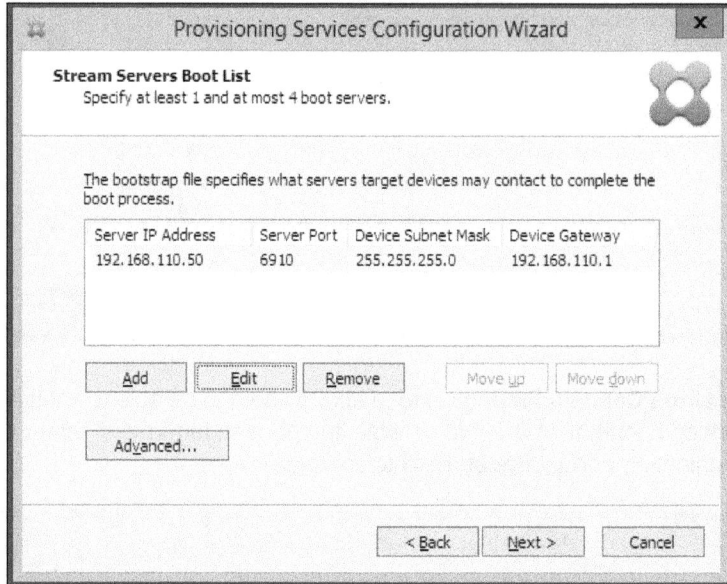

21. By clicking on the **Advanced...** button, it's possible to configure advanced options, such as **Verbose mode** and **Advanced Memory Support**. After completion, click on the **OK** button and then on **Next** to continue.

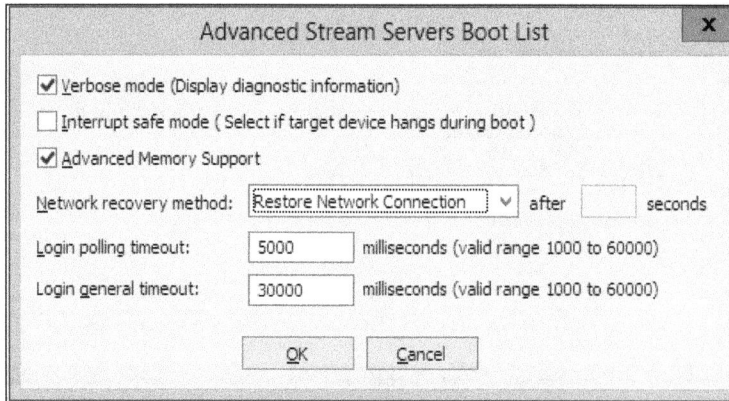

The verbose mode is particularly useful when executing a problem analysis. Consider this as a PVS debug mode.

22. At the end of this procedure, flag the **Automatically Start Services** option and click on the **Finish** button. Then, click on **Done** after all the configurations have been completed.

> Remember that active Windows Firewall may be a problem for your installation process. You have to open required ports or turn them off. The ports are UDP 6890-6909 (Inter-Server communication), TCP 1433 (SQL Server database), TCP 389 (Active Directory communication), UDP 67 (DHCP), UDP 67 and 4011 (PXE Services), UDP 69 (TFTP), UDP 6910 (Target Device logon), UDP 6910-6930 (vDisk Streaming), and TCP 54321 and 54322 (SOAP Service).

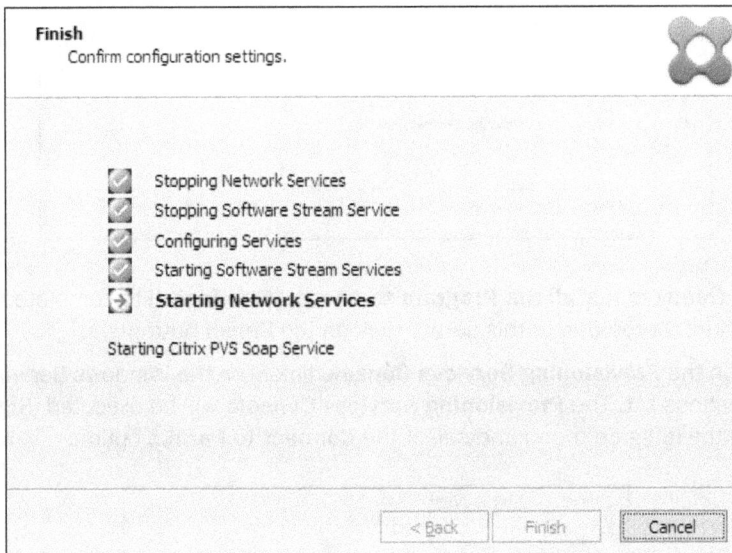

Finish
  Confirm configuration settings.

- ☑ Stopping Network Services
- ☑ Stopping Software Stream Service
- ☑ Configuring Services
- ☑ Starting Software Stream Services
- ▣ **Starting Network Services**

Starting Citrix PVS Soap Service

`< Back`   `Finish`   `Cancel`

23. On the Installation media menu, select the **Console Installation** link. Click on the **Next** button on the welcome screen to proceed with the console installation. Accept the **Citrix License Agreement** and click on the **Next** button.

24. In the **Customer Information** section, populate the **User Name** and **Organization** fields with valid data, specifying if the installation is for the entire machine's users (**Anyone who uses this computer**) or only for the current (**Only for me**). After this choice, click on the **Next** button.

25. Select a valid path in the **Destination Folder** screen and click on **Next** to continue the installation. To change the default path (`C:\Program Files\Citrix\ Provisioning Services Console\`), click on the **Change** button a browse for a valid location.

26. In the **Setup Type** screen, select the **Custom** option and click on the **Next** button.

27. In the **Custom Setup** screen, select all the proposed components, maintaining the previously chosen path and click on **Next**.

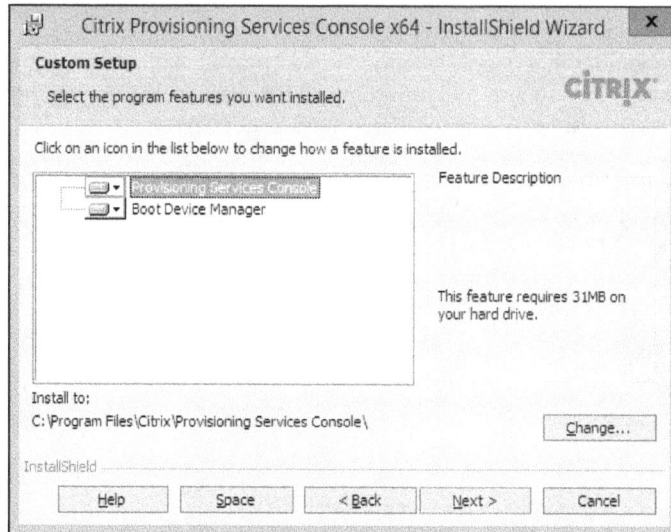

28. In the **Ready to Install the Program** screen, click on **Install** to complete the setup procedure. At the end of this setup, click on the **Finish** button

29. Click on the **Provisioning Services Console** link from the Windows Server applications list. The **Provisioning Services Console** will be executed. Right-click this link in the left-side menu and select the **Connect to Farm...** option:

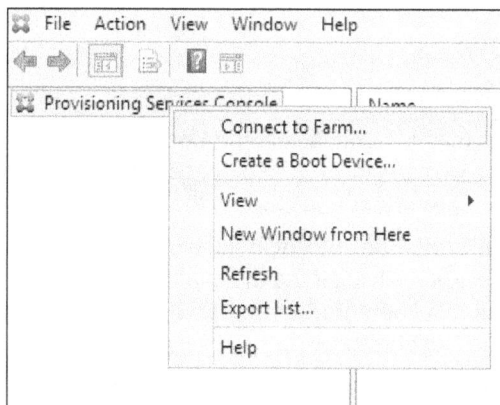

Be sure that the **Citrix PVS Soap Server** service is running, otherwise you will not be able to connect to the PVS configured farm.

30. In the **Connect to Farm** screen, populate all the fields with the correct values, specifying a valid domain username. After this, click on the **Connect** button.

Connect to Farm   **x**

Server Information

Name: vmxd7-pvs-01

(Name or IP address of a server on the farm.)

Port: 54321

(Port configured for server access.)

Credentials

○ Use my Windows credentials to login

◉ Use these credentials to login

Username: username

Domain: DOMAIN

Password: ••••••••••••••••

☐ Save password

☐ Auto-login on application start or reconnect

Connect   Cancel   Help

31. After verifying the connection parameters, you will be able to use the PVS 7.6 platform.

In the *Chapter 3, Master Image Configuration and Tuning*, we will discuss about the creation of the Target Device for the Provisioning Services in the *Configuring a target device – PVS architecture* recipe.

How it works...

PVS is one of the two deployment technologies for desktop and application deployments. Provisioning Services 7.6 is the latest release of the software used to implement this kind of architecture.

The structure is quite simple. A server component which is managed by a PVS console, delivers operating systems images to the end users' devices by creating instances of the virtual disks of an installed operating system called **Master Target Devices** and streaming them through the network from the PVS server memory every time users need them. This process permits having high-elevated network performance, dramatically reducing the impact on storage activities.

> You have to give attention to the PVS DB size. In fact, even if it starts only with 20 MB of data, its dimension has a growth of 10 MB. This means that in presence of hundreds or thousands of objects, the database size can become higher than your expectations.

There's more...

Provisioning Services use the Kerberos authentication to let its components communicate with each other, registering the components against the Active Directory through the **Service Principal Name** (**SPN**) and permitting the Domain Controller to identify the accounts, which manage the running services. In case of registration problems, your PVS service could fail. To avoid this situation, you have to use the `setSpn` command in order to give the right permissions to the account that manage the earlier described services (such as the PVS Soap Service) by applying the following syntax:

```
setSpn -a PVSSoap/PVS_Server_FQDN <username_managing_service>
```

> At the following MSDN link, you can find more information about the SPN: `http://msdn.microsoft.com/en-us/library/windows/desktop/ms677949(v=vs.85).aspx`.

See also

- ▶ The *Creating and configuring the machine catalog* recipe in *Chapter 6, Creating and Configuring the Desktop Environment*

2
Configuring and Deploying Virtual Machines for XenDesktop® 7.6

In this chapter, you will cover the following recipes:

- ▶ Configuring the XenDesktop Site
- ▶ Configuring XenDesktop 7.6 to interact with XenServer 6.2
- ▶ Configuring XenDesktop 7.6 to interact with VMWare vSphere 5.x
- ▶ Configuring XenDesktop 7.6 to interact with Microsoft Hyper-V

Introduction

The first step in implementing a fully functioning infrastructure is to configure XenDesktop's components. After this, the second, and maybe the most important, step is to deploy the virtual desktop instances.

To accomplish this task, you need to interface the **Citrix Delivery Controllers** with a **hypervisor**, a bare-metal operating system that is able to create, configure, and manage virtual machines. XenDesktop is able to communicate with three important hypervisor systems on the market: **XenServer**, **VMware vSphere**, and **Microsoft Hyper-V**, plus the Citrix Cloud platform automation known as **CloudPlatform**. The mechanism implemented is the following: after you have created a template, a virtual machine with a Microsoft desktop or server operating system on board, XenDesktop is able to deploy OS instances to the end users starting with the virtual machine image using different deployment technologies.

The main task of the Delivery Controller is to start virtual machines and assign them dynamically or statically to end users. At the end of a desktop session, the Delivery Controller can send a request to the hypervisor to restart or shutdown the virtual desktop instance.

In this chapter, we are going to configure the connection between hypervisors and Citrix servers.

Configuring the XenDesktop® Site

Before there is any interaction between components, after you have installed the Citrix Studio and Citrix Director, you need to configure a site, which will be the place where you will configure the hypervisor host.

Getting ready

In order to complete all the required steps for this recipe and perform a standard site deploy, you need to be assigned the administrator role for all the machines involved in the site configuration (the Delivery Controller and the database server).

How to do it...

In the following steps, we will describe how to create a site for a XenDesktop 7.6 infrastructure:

1. Connect to the Citrix Studio by searching for it within the Windows application list (Windows + C key combination – **Search** icon), then click on its icon.

2. In the **Welcome to Citrix Studio** screen, click on the **Deliver applications and desktops to your users** option to start the XenDesktop Site creation as shown in the following screenshot:

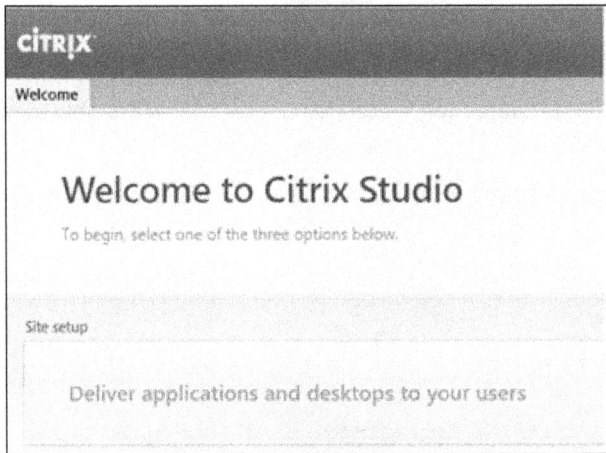

3. In the **Introduction** section, click on the second radio button option to create an empty Site, assign a name to it by populating the **Site name** field, and click on **Next** to continue.

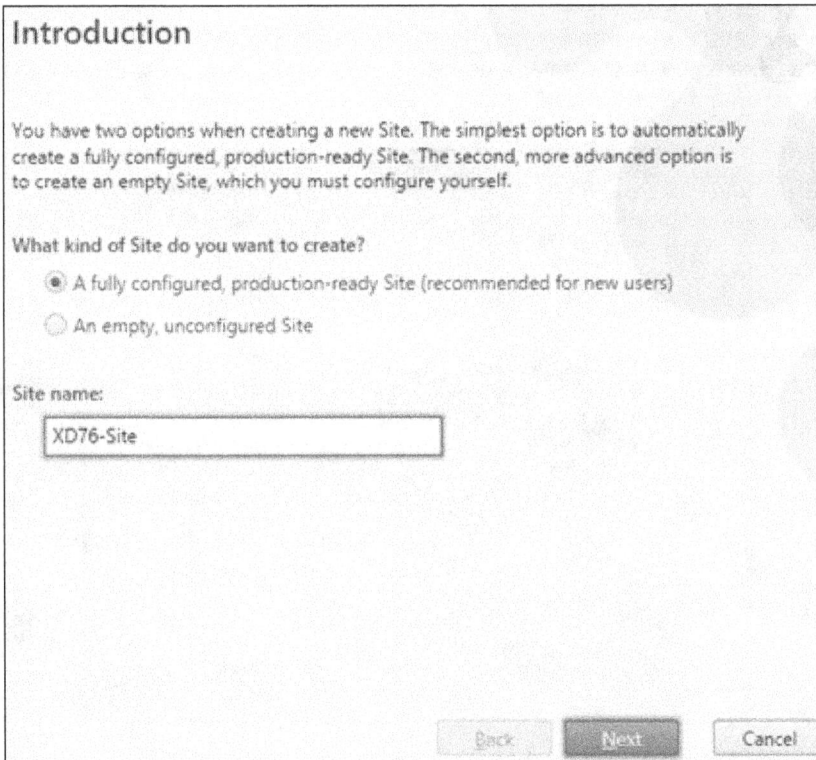

4. In the **Database** section, populate the **Database server location** field with the hostname of your database server and the XenDesktop existing instance name, in the form of `Hostname\InstanceName`, then assign a **Database name**, and click on the **Test connection** button to check that you are able to contact the database machine.

Database

The database stores all Site configuration, logging, and monitoring data.

Database server location:

```
SqlDatabaseServer.xdseven.local\CITRIX
```

Database name:

```
CitrixXD7-Site-First
```    Test connection...

If you do not have permission to edit this database, generate a script to give to your database administrator.

Generate database script...   (Optional)

---

5. When prompted for the automatic database creation, click the **OK** button to let the Studio create the database.

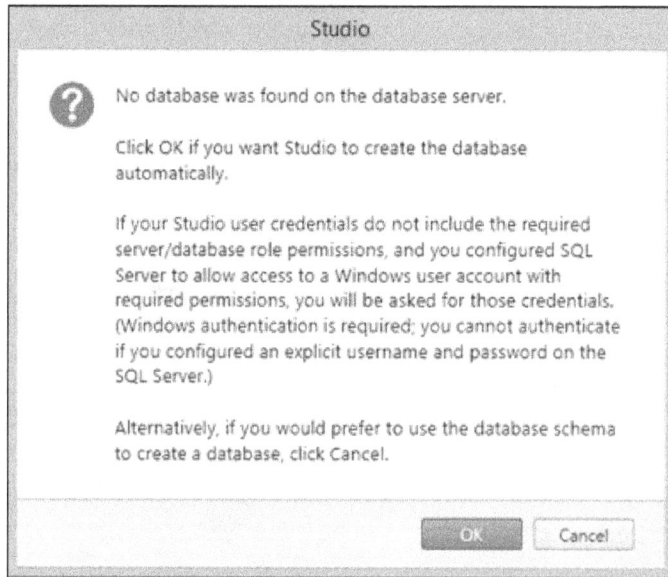

---

Studio

No database was found on the database server.

Click OK if you want Studio to create the database automatically.

If your Studio user credentials do not include the required server/database role permissions, and you configured SQL Server to allow access to a Windows user account with required permissions, you will be asked for those credentials. (Windows authentication is required; you cannot authenticate if you configured an explicit username and password on the SQL Server.)

Alternatively, if you would prefer to use the database schema to create a database, click Cancel.

OK    Cancel

---

6. As an alternative, if you want, you can create the Citrix database manually, by clicking on the **Generate database script** button; you will get back a set of instructions, in the form of two `.sql` scripts, to generate the database for standard or mirrored mode.

```
Script_For_Database_SqlDatabaseServer.xdseven.local_CITRIX,1434 - Notepad       _ □ x
File  Edit  Format  View  Help
-- To create a database schema for a Site, use this script: execute on the principal SQL Server database instance
--
-- To learn more, visit http://support.citrix.com/article/CTX127359
--
-- You can use SQLCMD from the command line to run this script, or you can use SQL Server Management Studio in SQLCMD mode.
--
-- Note that you must use a collation which ends with "_CI_AS_KS". In general, it is best to use a collation which ends with "_100_CI_AS_KS".
--
-- To do so, use this command when creating the database:
--
--     create database [CitrixXD7-Site-First] collate Latin1_General_100_CI_AS_KS
--     go
--
-- protect against generating tables in the wrong place, if database hasn't been created
use [tempdb];
go

if db_id(N'CitrixXD7-Site-First') is null
begin
  RAISERROR('Database does not exist', 10, 127);
end
go

-- Ensure the database is using a read committed snapshot
declare @groupId uniqueidentifier = null;

if (serverproperty('IsHadrEnabled') = 1)
begin
```

> You can find the two generated scripts at the following default path:
> `C:\Users\<username>\AppData\Local\Temp\1\Create Site-<date>`

7. After the database configuration, in the **Licensing** section, enter your license server name plus the port number, in the form of `hostname:port`, and click on the **Connect** button. If you already have a configured license file, click on the **Use an existing license** radio button, otherwise, you have to click on the **Use the free 30-day trial** option, inserting a correct license file later. At the end of these configurations, click on **Next**.

Licensing

License server address: `LicenseServer.xdseven.local:27000`   🔒 Connect

Connected to trusted server
View Certificate

Select a license:

○ Use the free 30-day trial
You can add a license later.

◉ Use an existing license
The product list below is generated by the license server.

> You can verify the validity of your License Server certificate by clicking on the **View Certificate** link – **Connected to trusted server** area.

8. On the **Summary** screen, after you have verified all the configured options, click on the **Finish** button to complete the procedure.

After the configuration has been completed, in the Citrix Studio main menu, you will find information about the created Site. If you want, you can check your current implementation by clicking on the **Test Site** button.

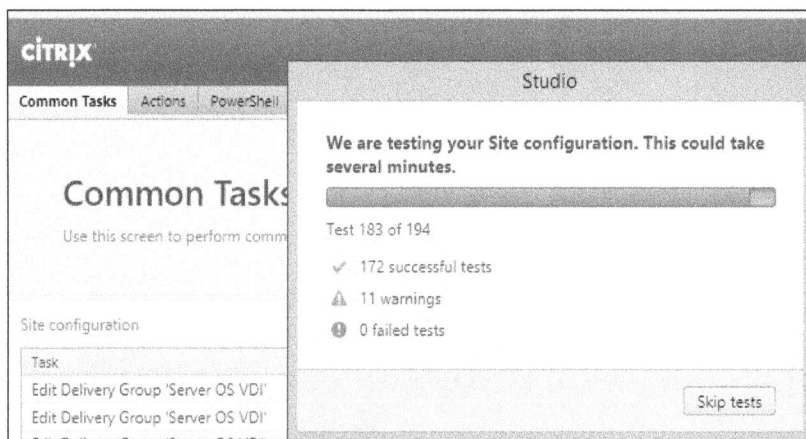

How it works...

Configuring a site lets you assemble all the components previously configured. The main operations to complete during the generic Site configuration procedure are:

- The connection to the SQL Server instance, based on which creating the XenDesktop database is created. This task can be accomplished in two ways, the first by using the Site configuration wizard (automated operation), and the second by generating two database creation scripts and running them within the SQL Server database environment.

- The connection to the License Server: by using the configuration Site wizard, you can connect to a specified License Server address and port, deciding whether to use a trial (30 days) license, or already configured license.

- In the presence of available resources, you can consider configuring multiple sites with multiple databases, one for each main company location.

If you want, at the end of the procedure, you can check the validity of your configuration using the **Test Site** button, in the **Studio Host** main menu section.

There's more...

In case you decide to use a database port other than the default SQL Server port value (`1433`), you have to insert the connection string in the following form:

- `DBSERVER\INSTANCE,SQL_PORT_NUMBER`

For example, in case you configured the `CITRIX` instance to listen to the port `1435`, the connection string will be the following:

- `SqlDatabaseServer\CITRIX,1435`

See also

- The *Administering hosts and machines – Host and MachineCreation cmdlets* recipe in *Chapter 9, Working with PowerShell.*

Configuring XenDesktop® 7.6 to interact with XenServer® 6.2

The first and the most common configuration for a XenDesktop site is interfacing it with the Citrix hypervisor, XenServer. Related to XenDesktop 7.6 is the XenServer 6.2 release.

> At the time of writing, Citrix has released the XenServer 6.5 version. The features that interact with XenDesktop are quite the same, an import update is given by the 64-bits dom0 platform. More information can be found at http://support.citrix.com/proddocs/topic/xenserver/xs-wrapper-65.html

Getting ready

The preliminary work required to perform all the operations of this recipe involves installing one or more XenServer host(s). To accomplish this task, you need to download the XenServer iso image file from http://www.citrix.com/downloads.html or from http://www.xenserver.org/. XenServer is a bare-metal hypervisor, a kind of virtualizator, which directly manages the hardware; for this reason, you have to install it as a normal operating system (you need no other operating system installed on the server).

> Please refer to the Citrix document to install the XenServer hypervisor at http://support.citrix.com/article/CTX137829

How to do it...

In this section, we will perform the operations required to configure XenDesktop 7.6 to use the XenServer hypervisor:

1. Connect to the Citrix Studio by searching for it within the Windows application list (Windows + *C* key combination – Search icon), and then click on its icon.

2. On the left-side menu, expand the **Configuration** section and select the **Hosting** link, then click on the **Add Connection and Resources** link on the right-side menu:

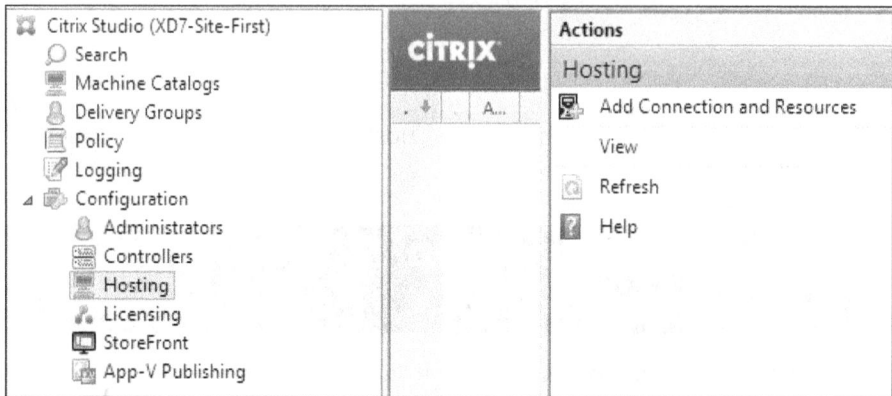

3. In the **Connection type** section, select **Citrix XenServer** from the **Host type** drop-down menu. In the **Connection address** field, input the **Full Qualified Domain Name (FQDN)** of the XenServer host (in the form of `http://FQDN`), then insert **User name** and **Password** in the respective fields, and give a name to the connection (**Connection name** input text). In the **Create virtual machine using:** subsection, select the **Studio tools (Machine Creation Services)** radio button option and after completion, click on **Next** to continue.

> You should always add the FQDN and the IP address within your DNS infrastructure; as an alternative, you could also put them in the host file of your Desktop Controller machine to avoid unexpected resolution name problems.

4. In the **Network** section, choose a configured network (depending on your XenServer host configuration, you could have one or more available networks), on which you are assigning the generated virtual desktop instances, then click on the **Next** button.

5. In the **Storage** section, flag available storage on which to create the virtual machines and select the desired radio button for personal vDisk location (use the same storage for virtual machines and personal vDisk or use different storage for personal vDisk); these are options that only refer to desktop OS instances. Select whether you're enabling the IntelliCache feature by flagging the relative option (**Use IntelliCache to reduce load on the shared storage device**). To continue, click on the **Next** button.

> Please refer to the following link to obtain information about IntelliCache:
> http://blogs.citrix.com/2011/06/22/xendesktop-and-local-storage-intellicache/

Storage

Select one or more storage devices for the new virtual machines:

Shared ▼		IntelliCache
Local		
Shared		Supported
DSNFS_02		Supported
DSiSCSI_01		Not supported

☐ Use IntelliCache to reduce load on the shared storage device.

Learn more about IntelliCache

Personal vDisk storage (Desktop OS only):   Learn more

○ Use same storage for virtual machines and Personal vDisks

◉ Use different storage for Personal vDisks

[Select storage...]   (None selected)

> In the presence of available storage, you should consider separating the operating system disk area from personal vDisk storage. Separating these areas can make it easier to locate user disk zones, especially for backup operations or troubleshooting activities.

6. On the **Summary** screen, after you have verified all the information, assign a name to the XenServer connection—**Resource Name** field—and click on **Finish** to complete the procedure.

7. In the main menu of the **Hosting** section, we can now find the configured connection to the XenServer host.

Name	Type	Address	⬇	State
XenServer-Host	Citrix XenServer®	http://xenserver.xdseven.local		Enabled
XS-602-Host				

8. In case of necessity, we have the possibility to change the connection parameters, by selecting the **Edit Connection** link on the right-side menu.

9. In the **Connection Properties** section, we can modify the credentials to access the XenServer host (**Host address**, **Username**, and **Password** fields) by clicking on the **Edit settings** button, or we can also add one or more HA hosts by clicking on the **Edit HA servers...** button.

10. Selecting the **Advanced** section, administrators have the capability to configure the following options: **Simultaneous actions (all types)**, **Simultaneous Personal vDisk inventory updates**, and **Maximum new actions per minute**. After completion, click on **OK** to complete the configuration.

> To perform any modification activity on host and connection, you must put them in **Maintenance mode**.

How it works...

XenServer is the hypervisor included in the Citrix Virtualization platform. XenServer is again an open source virtualization platform, with the alternative to pay for technical and commercial support to be followed up by the Citrix professional team.

XenServer is the best integrated hypervisor with the Citrix VDI platform, also, thanks to the co-operation between the XenDesktop Broker(s) and the XenServer pools, the way in which XenDesktop interfaces with XenServer is simpler than other hypervisors. In fact, the Desktop Controller directly contacts the XenServer pool master, without the need for an intermediate management console. One of the advantages of using this hypervisor is the capability to use the XenServer information caching feature, also known as **IntelliCache**; this technique drastically reduces the read and write activities for your storage. Another important advantage of this hypervisor is that it is the only one capable of providing the GPU pass-through for multiple VMs using NVIDIA GRID technology.

> The XenServer IntelliCache feature has to be enabled during the installation procedure of this hypervisor.

There's more...

In the presence of many tens or hundreds of virtual machines, the XenServer hypervisor can have performance issues, in terms of lack of physical resources for the Dom0 domain, the most privileged domain in a XenServer installation, which is the only domain able to directly interface with the hardware or start non-privileged domains, for instance. To solve this problem, it should be necessary to assign more physical resources to the Dom0 domain. This operation can be performed by connecting to the desired XenServer machine, using the XenCenter console or through the SSH connection, then editing the /boot/extlinux.conf file and modifying every dom0_mem parameter occurrence, assigning it the desired value in MB. You should consider using the advised value from Citrix, setting the parameter in the following way: dom0_mem=2940M. The default memory value assigned to the Dom0 is 752 MB.

> To apply the memory changes, you have to restart the XenServer node.

After the reboot operations, run the following commands from the XenServer CLI in order to let XenServer understand how to use all the new assigned memory size:

```
. /etc/xensource-inventory
```

```
staticmax=`xe vm-param-get uuid=$CONTROL_DOMAIN_UUID param-name=memory-static-max`
```

```
echo staticmax=$staticmax
```

```
xe vm-param-set uuid=$CONTROL_DOMAIN_UUID memory-dynamic-max=$staticmax
```

```
xe vm-memory-target-set uuid=$CONTROL_DOMAIN_UUID target=$staticmax
```

See also

- ▸ The *Configuring the CloudBridge™ 7.3 platform* recipe in *Chapter 8, XenDesktop® Component Integration*.

Configuring XenDesktop® 7.6 to interact with VMware vSphere 5.x

XenDesktop offers compatibility not only for Citrix proprietary platforms, but it also supports the most important virtualization architectures on the market. VMware is currently the virtualization solution that better permits you to manage the resource commitment and assignment for your virtual environments.

Getting ready

To ensure that all the activities in this chapter will be fully executed, it is required that you have an already functioning VMware vSphere environment, made up of at least two ESXi servers and a Windows server, on which to install the VMware Virtual Center software.

> As an alternative, you can download the Virtual Center Virtual Appliance OVF template, directly from the VMware website.

After this, the step you have to perform is to import the VMware Virtual Center certificate on to the XenDesktop server, to allow Desktop Studio to connect with the SSL connection to the Virtual Center SDK.

How to do it...

Following the procedures that you have to execute in order to activate the communication between the XenDesktop Controller machine and the VMware vSphere infrastructure:

1. Launch your chosen Web browser and then insert the hostname of the Virtual Center server in the address bar, using the https connection. When prompted for security risk, accept to continue with the site navigation.

2. On the certificate status bar, click on **Status error** and select the `View certificates` link (the VMware Virtual Center certificate is currently untrusted for XenDesktop):

3. After the certificate presentation, click on the **Install Certificate...** button to proceed.

> Be sure that the hostname cabled with the certificate matches the assigned name to the Virtual Center Server. In case of mismatching, in fact, XenDesktop will not be able to connect with the VMware. To avoid this, you can consider adding a record to the local file hosts of the XenDesktop server to match the IP address and hostname on the certificate.

4. In **Welcome to the Certificate Import Wizard**, select the **Local Machine** radio button option as **Store Location**, and then click on **Next**.

5. In the **Certificate Store** section, select the **Place all certificates in the following store** option, then click the **Browse** button to specify the location on which you will be installing the certificate.

6. Enable the **Show physical stores** option by flagging it, and then select **Trusted People – Registry** subsection. After completion, click the **OK** button, and then click on **Next** to continue.

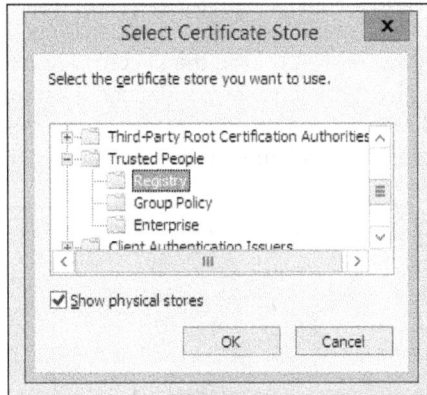

7. To complete the certificate import activities, click on **Finish**:

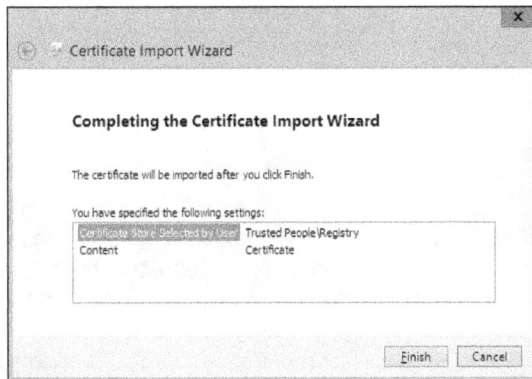

8. To verify that the certificate import was successful, you must reconnect to the SSL Virtual Center address (https://FQDN). If you don't receive anymore prompts about unsecure connections (as previously seen), the import has been successfully completed.

> This procedure must be performed for the Delivery Controller and Provisioning Services server, depending on what kind of architecture you implemented.

9. Connect to Citrix Studio console, then expand the **Configuration** section in the left-side menu, select the **Hosting** link, and click on the **Add Connection and Resources** link on the right-side menu.

10. In the **Connection** section, select **VMware vSphere** from the **Host type** drop-down menu. In the **Address** field, input the SSL address of the **VMware SDK**, in the form of `https://VirtualCenterFQDN/sdk`, then insert **Username** and **Password** in the respective fields and give a name to the connection (**Connection name** input text). In the **Create Virtual machine using:** subsection, select the **Studio tools (Machine Creation Services)** radio button option and after completion click on **Next** to continue:

Connection type:	VMware vSphere® ▾
Connection address:	https://vcenter.xdseven.local/sdk
User name:	XDSEVEN\administrator
Password:	••••••••••••••••••••
Connection name:	VMware

The Connection name appears in Studio; it helps administrators identify the Connection.

Create virtual machines using:
- ⦿ Studio tools (Machine Creation Services)
- ◯ Other tools

> The specified username and password for the connection must be valid domain credentials, with elevated privileges within the Virtual Center. Please refer to the following Citrix document to configure the right user permissions: `http://support.citrix.com/proddocs/topic/xenapp-xendesktop-76/xad-install-prep-host-vmware.html`.

11. On the **Cluster** screen, click on the **Browse** button to select a vSphere **Cluster** on which to deploy the virtual machines. After this operation, select a **Network** from the presented list on which you are deploying the virtual machine instances. Click on **Next** to continue with the Wizard.

12. In the **Storage** section, select the storage (**VMware datastore**—local or shared) for your virtual machine's system disks, and then decide whether to select a separate datastore for personal vDisks (recommended). After this, click on **Next** to continue.

13. On the **Summary** screen, after you have checked all the listed configured options, assign a name to the VMware connection and click on the **Finish** button:

Summary

Connection name:	XD7-VMware-01
Connection type:	VMware vSphere®
Connection address:	https://vmxd7-vc-01.xdseven.local/sdk
Create Virtual Machines with:	Studio tools (Machine Creation Services)
Network:	VM-LAN
Virtual Machine storage:	datastore1
Personal vDisk storage:	datastore1
Scopes:	All

Resources Name:

VMware-XD-Connection

Back   Finish   Cancel

How it works...

XenDesktop and VMWare Virtual Center communication can be realized through two kinds of channels: **http** and **https**. The second is obviously more secure, and this communication is also what is advised by Citrix, so, to be able to communicate in HTTP over SSL, you need to import your Virtual Center certificate. For these components, VMware best practice says that you should create your own certificate from a personal certification authority. Anyway, communication can be established using and importing the default self-signed VMware certificate. Once this import has been completed, the only thing remaining is to connect to the VMware API by its published SDK. The use of the VMware Virtual Center is not only necessary, but it also is a way to implement an architecture centrally managed and tuned by a controlling platform such as the VMware vSphere Virtual Center platform.

There's more...

The use of VMware vSphere as a hypervisor platform gives you the ability to reserve a set of particular resources on the deployed machine instances; by right-clicking on the desired machine and selecting the **Edit Settings** option, you can then reserve vCPU and virtual RAM on the edited virtual machine:

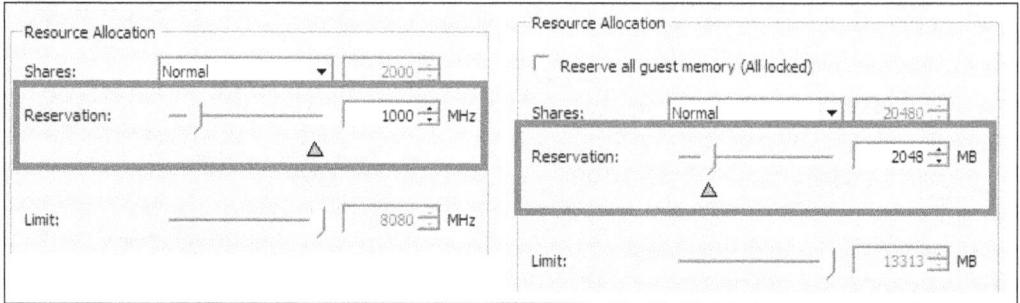

Resource Allocation		
Shares:	Normal	2000
Reservation:		1000 MHz
Limit:		8080 MHz

Resource Allocation		
Reserve all guest memory (All locked)		
Shares:	Normal	20480
Reservation:		2048 MB
Limit:		13313 MB

> You should apply these parameters to the Master Image template, replicating in this way the configurations to the deployed desktops.

In the case of equal access priority to the hypervisor resources, you can use another parameter that permits giving the XenDesktop deployed instances a higher priority in the resource queue:

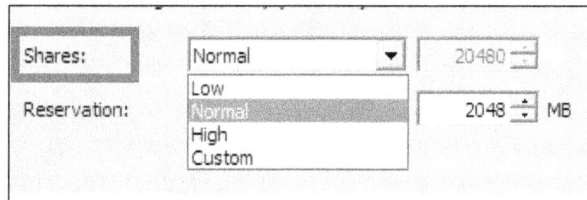

Shares:	Normal ▼	20480
	Low	
	Normal	
Reservation:	High	2048 MB
	Custom	

This is the **Shares** section under the **Resources** tab, which is configurable as **Low**, **Normal**, **High**, and **Custom**. A higher number gives priority access to the resources.

See also

▸ The *Creating and configuring the machine catalog* recipe in *Chapter 5, Creating and Configuring a Desktop Environment.*

Configuring XenDesktop® 7.6 to interact with Microsoft Hyper-V

In the last few years, collaboration between Citrix and Microsoft has grown so much that they now share the application virtualization and deployment market. Respecting this partnership, it is possible to deploy virtual desktops for Citrix with **Hyper-V**, the Microsoft hypervisor.

Getting ready

To be able to use virtual machines with Windows Server 2012, first, we need to install and configure the hypervisor server role. After this, in order to allow the Desktop Controller to interact with the Hyper-V server, it is necessary to install the Microsoft **System Center Virtual Machine Manager**, also known as **SCVMM**, release **2012 SP1**.

How to do it...

In this section, we will configure the Microsoft Hyper-V 3.0 system and the XenDesktop 7.6 installation to be able to communicate with each other:

1. On a clean Windows Server 2012 R2 installation, with no other roles installed on the **Server Manager Dashboard**, click on the **Add roles and features** link.

> A clean installation is required to install the Hyper-V hypervisor role.

2. After clicking on **Next** in the **Before You Begin** section, select the **Role-based or feature-based installation** option, then click on the **Next** button.

    ⦿ Role-based or feature-based installation
       Configure a single server by adding roles, role services, and features.

    ◯ Remote Desktop Services installation
       Install required role services for Virtual Desktop Infrastructure (VDI) to create a virtual machine-based or session-based desktop deployment.

3. On the **Server Selection** screen, choose the **Select a server from the server pool** option, highlight the server name on which you are currently installing the Hyper-V role, and click the **Next** button:

    Select a server or a virtual hard disk on which to install roles and features.

    ⦿ Select a server from the server pool
    ◯ Select a virtual hard disk

    Server Pool

Filter:		

Name	IP Address	Operating System
WIN-37FKPD58HPV	192.168.198.128	Microsoft Windows Server 2012 Datacenter

4. Select the **Hyper-V** role in the **Server Roles** section, and when prompted to install the additional features, click on the **Add Features** button to accept. After completion, click on the **Next** button three times to continue.

    ☐ DNS Server
    ☐ Fax Server
    ▷ ☐ File And Storage Services (Installed)
    ☑ Hyper-V
    ☐ Network Policy and Access Services
    ☐ Print and Document Services
    ☐ Remote Access
    ☐ Remote Desktop Services

5. In the **Virtual Switches** section, select a network card to be used by Hyper-V to create the virtual switch for the virtual machine connections, and then click on the **Next** button:

Network adapters:

Name	Description
☑ Ethernet	Intel(R) PRO/1000 MT Network Connection

6. In the **Migration** section, flag the live migration feature option and select one of the available authentication methods (**CredSSP** or **Kerberos**). After completion, click on **Next**.

Hyper-V can be configured to send and receive live migrations of virtual machines on this server. Configuring Hyper-V now enables any available network on this server to be used for live migrations. If you want to dedicate specific networks for live migration, use Hyper-V settings after you install the role.

☑ Allow this server to send and receive live migrations of virtual machines

Authentication protocol

Select the protocol you want to use to authenticate live migrations.

⦿ Use Credential Security Support Provider (CredSSP)
This protocol is less secure than Kerberos, but does not require you to set up constrained delegation. To perform a live migration, you must be logged on to the source server.

◯ Use Kerberos
This protocol is more secure but requires you to set up constrained delegation in your environment to perform tasks such as live migration when managing this server remotely.

> If your Hyper-V server will be part of a Microsoft clustered environment, you do not have to enable the live migration option. This will be performed after the cluster configuration.

7. In the **Default Stores** section, select the two available paths on which the virtual machine disks and the virtual machine configuration files are allocated, respectively. After completion, click on the **Next** button.

> Hyper-V uses default locations to store virtual hard disk files and virtual machine configuration files, unless you specify different locations when you create the files. You can change these default locations now, or you can change them later by modifying Hyper-V settings.
>
> Default location for virtual hard disk files:
>
> C:\Users\Public\Documents\Hyper-V\Virtual Hard Disks   Browse...
>
> Default location for virtual machine configuration files:
>
> C:\ProgramData\Microsoft\Windows\Hyper-V   Browse...

8. If the information in the **Confirmation** section is correct, flag the **Restart the destination server automatically if required** option and click on **Install** to complete the role installation.

> To install the following roles, role services, or features on selected server, click Install.
>
> ☑ Restart the destination server automatically if required
>
> Optional features (such as administration tools) might be displayed on this page because they have been selected automatically. If you do not want to install these optional features, click Previous to clear their check boxes.
>
> Hyper-V
> Remote Server Administration Tools
>   Role Administration Tools
>   Hyper-V Management Tools
>   Hyper-V Module for Windows PowerShell
>   Hyper-V GUI Management Tools

9. After completion of the Windows Server Hyper-V role configuration, download the SCVMM 2012 SP1 software from the Microsoft portal, at `http://technet.microsoft.com/en-us/systemcenter/cc137824.aspx`

> For performance reasons, you have to install the SCVMM server on a machine other than the XenDesktop Controller. Furthermore, SCVMM console must be installed on any configured Delivery Controller.

10. On a server other than the Delivery Controller, run the SCVMM setup by extracting the download archive or mounting the related ISO, then launch `setup.exe` from destination folder.

11. On the main screen, click on the **Install** link in the **Virtual Machine Manager** section.

> Before the SCVMM installation, be sure you have installed and configured the IIS Web Server and Windows Assessment and Deployment Kit (ADK) for Windows 8 (available at `http://www.microsoft.com/en-us/download/confirmation.aspx?id=30652`) and the update for Windows 8.1 (available at `http://www.microsoft.com/en-us/download/details.aspx?id=39982`).

12. In the **Select features to install** list, select **VMM Management Server**, and then click on **Next**. The **VMM Console** component will be automatically selected, as you can see here:

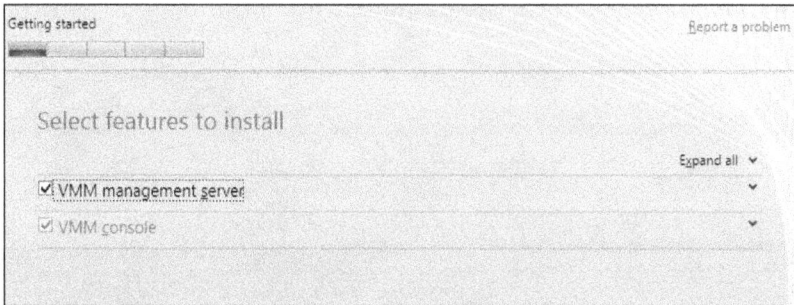

13. Populate the **Name, Organization**, and **Product Key** fields, and then click on **Next**.

> You can also insert your license number after the installation procedure.

14. Accept the license agreement (flag **I've read, understood and agree with the terms of license agreement**) and click on **Next**.

15. Check the appropriate radio button depending on whether you want to participate in the Microsoft collaboration program or not, and click on **Next** to continue.

16. In the Microsoft Update section, select the desired radio button option (**On (recommended)** or **Off**), and then click on **Next** to continue.

17. Select **Installation location** by typing it in the **Location** field and proceed by clicking on **Next**.

Getting started

Report a problem

Installation location

The recommended location for program files is displayed.

Location: C:\Program Files\Microsoft System Center 2012\Virtual Machine Manager   Browse...

Free space 43,56 GB

18. After passing the prerequisites check, you must specify the database location (**Server name** and **Port**), Windows administrative credentials (check the **Use the following credentials** checkbox), **Instance name and Database name**, choosing between **New database** creation or **Existing database** utilization.

Microsoft System Center 2012 Virtual Machine Manager Setup Wizard   X

Configuration

Report a problem

Database configuration

Provide information about the database that you would like to use for your VMM management server.

Server name: VMXD7-SCVMM-01   Browse

Port: 1433

☐ Use the following credentials

User name and domain:

Format: Domain\UserName

Password:

Instance name: |

Select an existing database or create a new database.

● New database: VirtualManagerDB

○ Existing database:

> SCVMM 2012 SP1 does not support SQL Server Express edition!

19. Select whether you are using a **Local System account** or a **Domain account** (service type) and decide if you want to save the encryption keys in the Active Directory by flagging the specific option; in this case, you also have to specify on which Active Directory machine object archiving is the keys. To proceed, click on the **Next** button.

Configuration   Report a problem

Configure service account and distributed key management

Virtual Machine Manager Service Account

Select the account to be used by the VMM service. Highly available VMM installations require the use of a domain account.
Which type of account should I use?

○ Local System account
● Domain account

User name and domain: Password:

[   ]   [   ] Select...

Distributed Key Management

Select whether to store encryption keys in Active Directory instead of on the local machine. Highly available VMM installations require the keys be stored in Active Directory.

☐ Store my keys in Active Directory

Provide the location in Active Directory. For example, CN=DKM,DC=contoso,DC=com.

How do I configure distributed key management?

> When possible, always consider using Domain accounts, in order to have a centralized profile instead of a local and replicated account.

20. Configure the ports for server communication as done in the following screenshot, then click on **Next**:

Port configuration

Management Server

Please select the ports for various VMM features.

8100	Communication with the VMM console
5985	Communication to agents on hosts and library servers
443	File transfers to agents on hosts and library servers
8102	Communication with Windows Deployment Services
8101	Communication with Windows Preinstallation Environment (Windows PE) agents
8103	Communication with Windows PE agent for time synchronization

21. On the next screen, you can choose to create a new VMM library (**Create a new library share**, including **Share location** and **Share description**) or use an existing one (**Use an existing library share**), by selecting this second radio button. Click on the **Next** button to continue:

Library configuration

Specify a share for the Virtual Machine Manager library

⦿ Create a new library share

Share name: MSSCVMMLibrary

Share location: C:\ProgramData\Virtual Machine Manager Library Files   Select...

Share description: VMM Library Share

○ Use an existing library share

Share name: MSSCVMMLibrary

Share location:

Share description:

22. If the summary information is ok, click on the **Install** button to complete the procedure.

23. Once the server components installation has been terminated, you need to install the **Management Console** on all the Delivery Controller machines within your infrastructure. Repeat the launching setup procedure seen for Server components, and then only flag the **VMM Console** component.

24. After accepting the license agreement, click on **Next** to proceed. On the next screen, you will be advised to have automatically join the Microsoft collaboration program. Click on the **Next** button to continue.

25. Click on the **On** radio button, to activate updates, then click on **Next**.

Microsoft Update

Microsoft Update offers security and important updates for Windows and other Microsoft software, including System Center 2012 VMM. Updates are delivered using Automatic Updates, or you can visit the Microsoft Update website.

⦿ On (recommended)
   Use Microsoft Update to check for updates.

○ Off
   Do not automatically check for updates.

26. Select the **Installation location** by populating the **Location** field, as seen earlier, and click on **Next**.

Installation location

The recommended location for program files is displayed.

Location: C:\Program Files\Microsoft System Center 2012\Virtual Machine Manager   Browse...

Free space 35,93 GB

27. Select a port on which to configure the console (**Communication with the VMM management server**, default port 8100) and click on **Next** to proceed.

Port configuration

Administrator Console

8100   Communication with the VMM management server

28. If the information on **Installation summary** is correct, click on **Install** to complete this procedure.

29. After the setup has been completed, click on **Close** and leave **Open the VMM console when this wizard closes** checked.

30. On the logon screen, insert the **Server name** and port (in the form of hostname:port) for the SCVMM Server and specify credential access; you can choose **Use current Microsoft Windows session identity** or select **Specify credentials**. Click on **Connect** to proceed with the login:

Microsoft®
System Center 2012

Virtual Machine Manager

Server name: VMXD7-SCVMM-01|

Example: vmmserver.contoso.com:8100

○ Use current Microsoft Windows session identity
● Specify credentials

User name: XDSEVEN\administrator

Example: contoso\domainuser

Password: •••••••••••••••••••••

31. Once logged in, right-click on **All Hosts** on the left-side menu and select **Add Hyper-V Hosts and Clusters**.

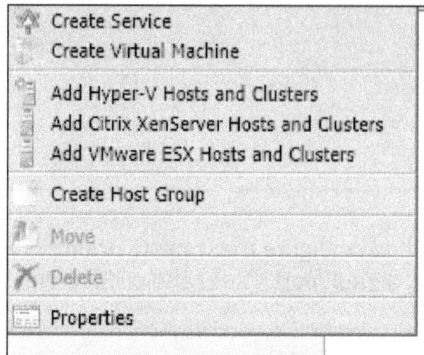

> Create Service
> Create Virtual Machine
>
> Add Hyper-V Hosts and Clusters
> Add Citrix XenServer Hosts and Clusters
> Add VMware ESX Hosts and Clusters
>
> Create Host Group
>
> Move
>
> Delete
>
> Properties

32. Select the Hyper-V host location from one of the following, and click on **Next**:

   ❑ **Windows Server computers in a trusted Active Directory domain**

   ❑ **Windows Server computer in an untrusted Active Directory domain**

   ❑ **Windows Server computers in a perimeter network**

   ❑ **Physical computer to be provisioned as virtual machine hosts**

33. Insert username and password (**Use an existing Run as account** or **Manually enter the credentials**) to run resource discovery for Hyper-V, and then click on **Next**.

> ## Specify the credentials to use for discovery
>
> The Run As account or credentials will be used to discover computers and to install the Hyper-V role and the Virtual Machine Manager agent if necessary.
>
> ○ Use an existing Run As account
>
> Run As account: [   ] Browse...
>
> ● Manually enter the credentials
>
> User name: [   ]
>
> Example: contoso\domainuser
>
> Password: [   ]

34. Specify a discovery scope (**Specify Windows Server computers by names** or **Specify an Active Directory query to search for Windows Server computer**) to reduce the range on which it performs host searches.

35. After you've received the query results, flag the desired host(s) and proceed by clicking on **Next**.

36. Select a **Host Group** on which to attach the selected Hyper-V server; if you want, you can also check the **Reassociate this host with this VMM environment** option. After this, specify a location on which to store the virtual machines and click on **Next** to proceed.

Specify a host group and virtual machine placement path settings for hosts

Assign the selected computers to the following host group:

Host group: | All Hosts | ▼ |

If any of the selected hosts are currently managed by another Virtual Machine Manager (VMM) environment, select this option to reassociate the hosts with this VMM management server.

☐ Reassociate this host with this VMM environment

VMM uses virtual machine placement paths as default locations to store virtual machines placed on a host. To add a new virtual machine placement path, specify a path and click Add.

Add the following path:

| | Add |

Selected virtual machine placement paths:

| | Remove |

37. If the configuration information is compliant with your environment parameters, click on **Finish** to complete the procedure.

38. As we did previously for XenServer and vSphere, run the Citrix Studio, and select the **Hosting** link from the **Configuration** section.

39. On the right-side menu, click on **Add Connection and Resources**.

40. In the **Connection** section, select **Microsoft System Center Virtual Machine Manager** from the **Host type** drop-down menu. In the **Address** field input the **Full Qualified Domain Name** (**FQDN**) of the Microsoft console host, then insert **Username** and **Password** in the respective fields, and give a name to the connection (**Connection name** input text). In the **Create Virtual machine using** subsection, select the **Studio tools (Machine Creation Services)** radio button option and after completion click on **Next** to continue.

41. Select your Hyper-V configured resource from the list, assign it a name by populating the **Enter a name for the Resources** field, flag the desired network virtual switch from the list, and click on **Next**.

42. In the App-V Publishing section, skip any configuration for the moment. We will discuss the App-V later in this book. Click on **Next** to continue.

43. Select the storage on which to archive the virtual machine; it is also possible to separate the VM's operating system storage from the personal vDisk storage. After completing your choice, click on **Next**.

44. On the **Summary** screen, after you have verified all the configured options, click on the **Finish** button to complete the procedure.

How it works...

XenDesktop 7.6 is able to communicate with the Microsoft Hyper-V servers only through the use of Microsoft SCVMM; in this recipe, we discussed how to install and configure the 2012 SP1 version, the release is associated with Windows Server 2012 R2 edition.

Being more specific, it uses the **SDK** platform offered by Microsoft System Center. For this reason, we previously installed the VMM console (the SDK is included in it) on the Delivery Controller. This is an interaction similar to that used for VMWare vSphere. Therefore, you can consider System Center as similar to VMWare Virtual Center. As a result, system engineers can centrally manage all configured Hyper-V hosts in a server farm.

> SCVMM is able to manage not only Hyper-V hosts, but also hypervisors from different vendors. Therefore, you can also consider using it to centrally manage XenServer and VMware vSphere machines.

See also

► The *Publishing applications using Microsoft App-V* recipe in *Chapter 6, Deploying Applications*.

3
Master Image Configuration and Tuning

In this chapter, you will cover the following recipes:

- ▸ Configuring and optimizing a Desktop OS Master Image
- ▸ Configuring and optimizing a Server OS Master Image
- ▸ Configuring a target device – the PVS architecture
- ▸ Installing and configuring the Master Image policies

Introduction

In the first two chapters, we installed and configured important infrastructural components such as database servers, XenDesktop components, and Hypervisor servers for virtual machine creation and provisioning. Now, it is time to put aside this class of elements for a while, and concentrate on our activities on the desktop client components.

End users will interact only with Windows desktops, and not with architectural components shown earlier, so you toned to take care during the configuration process of the virtual desktops, in terms of building a desktop image, optimization, and tuning.

Most of your client's activities will be based on policy usage and optimization, to obtain a high-level user experience, without losing agility, performance, and security.

Configuring and optimizing a desktop OS Master Image

The first important task will be the configuration and the optimization of the Windows desktop operating system that will be used as a Master Image, in order to deploy the desktop instances. The latest versions of the Microsoft operating systems offer many graphical enhancements, useful to better appreciate their potential and usability. In a complex VDI architecture, we need to be careful about both of these aspects. Consider that the customization process can vary depending on the configured environment. Anyway, the steps implemented in this section can generally be applied without specific issues.

Getting ready

This recipe only involves the Windows client machine. In order to be able to operate all the modifications to the services, the graphical appearance, and the system configuration, you need to use domain or local administrative credentials, for the Windows 7 and Windows 8.x OS versions.

An installed virtual machine with a Windows 7 or Windows 8.x operating system is required in order to apply the described settings.

> Please refer to the *Configuring and Deploying Virtual Machines for XenDesktop 7.6* recipe and *Chapter 2, Configuring and Deploying Virtual Machines for XenDesktop* to choose the right virtualization platform for your specific needs.

How to do it...

The desktop policies optimization only involves the Windows client machine and the domain to which it has joined. Therefore, you will need domain administrative credentials, in order to modify the necessary policies and to force their application on the involved clients. The following are the optimization processes for Windows 7 and Windows 8.x.

> Before any optimization activity, you should always run the Windows update, in order to collect the maximum number of system updates in the Master Image.

Windows 7 Master Image configuration:

1. Log in to your Windows 7 base image template with administrative credentials.

2. Click on Start and type the `services.msc` command; the Windows Services snap-in will be opened. It will look like this:

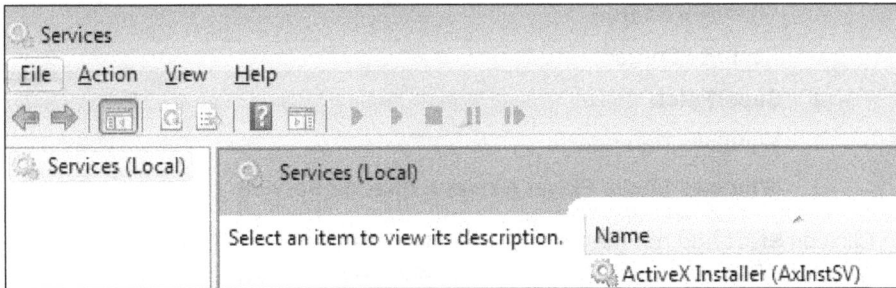

3. On the services list, search for **Background Intelligent Transfer Service**:

4. Right-click on the name service, and select **Properties** from the menu.

5. On the **Startup type** drop-down list, select **Disabled** as default state, and then click on **Stop** if the service is running. After completion, click on **OK** to exit from this area.

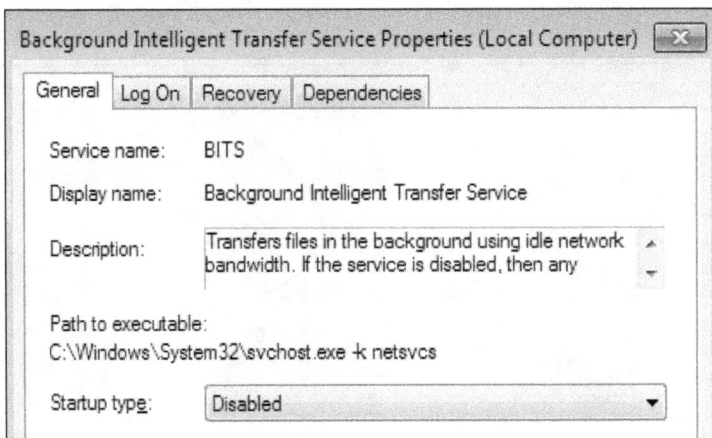

6. Repeat steps number 4 and 5 to disable the following services:

   - **Desktop Windows Manager Session Manager**
   - **HomeGroup Listener**
   - **HomeGroup Provider**
   - **Windows Search**
   - **Security Center**
   - **SuperFetch**
   - **Windows Defender**
   - **Windows Media Player Network Sharing Service**

7. Click on **Start** and run the cmd command to open a prompt shell, then run the bcdedit/setbootuxdisabled command, required to disable the Windows animation at boot time, in order to perform a faster machine startup.

8. Navigate to **Start | Control Panel** and click on the **System** icon; then, select **Advanced system settings** from the left menu.

9. Select the **Advanced** tab and click on the **Settings** button of the **Performance** area, as shown in the following screenshot:

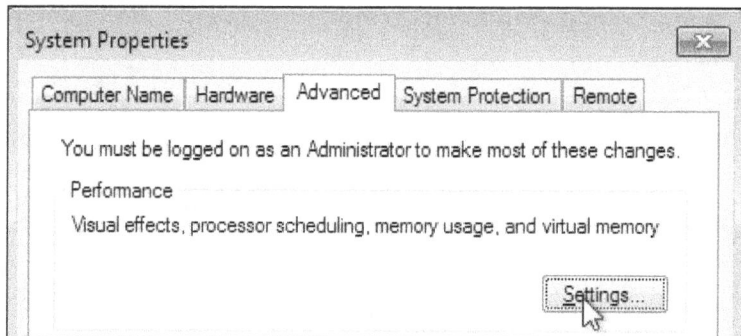

10. Select the **Advanced** tab and click on the **Change | Virtual memory** area.

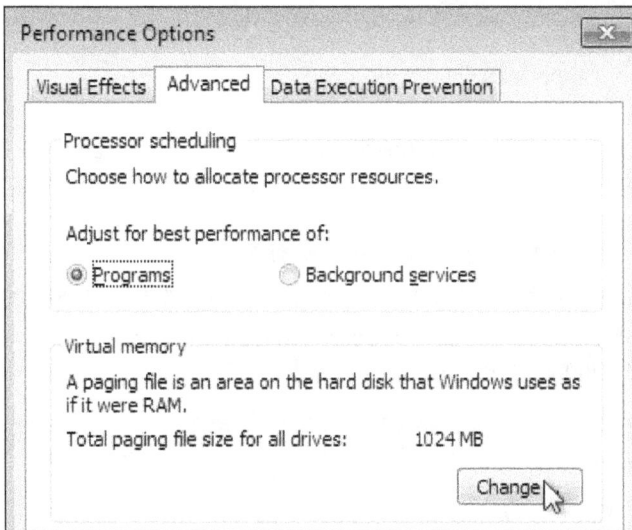

11. Remove the check from **Automatically manage paging file size for all drives**, and then select the **Custom size** radio button and enter the same value for both textboxes.

12. After this, click on **Set**, and then **OK**.

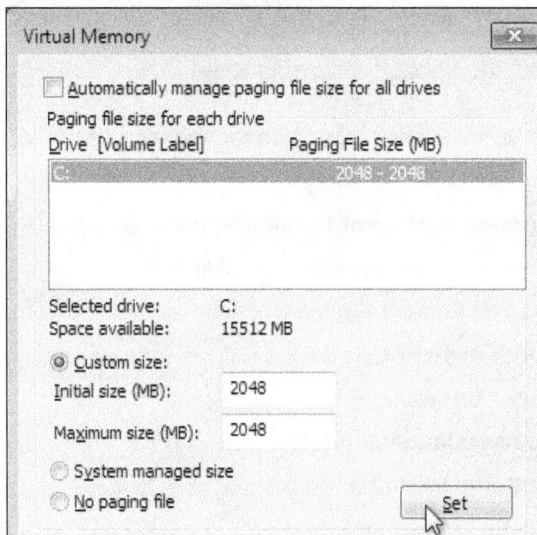

[
It is common to assign to the swap memory area a size equal to double the machine memory (for example, 1 GB of RAM = 2 GB of swap size). In the presence of a great quantity of RAM, swap sizing can have no more importance and relevance.
]

13. After the amount of swap has been modified, you need to restart your machine, in order to make the changes available.

Windows 8 Master Image configuration

1. Log in to your Windows 8 Master Image with administrative credentials.

2. Run the Windows + *R* key combination and digit the `services.msc` command. After completion, click on **OK**:

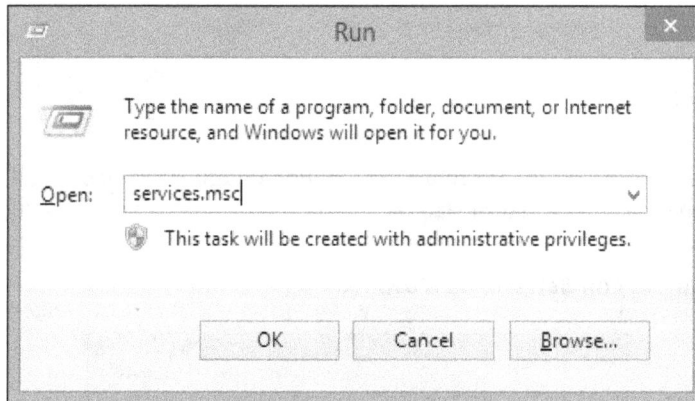

3. In the Windows Services snap-in, search for and disable the following services:
   - **Application Layer Gateway Service**
   - **Background Intelligent Transfer Service (BITS)**
   - **BitLocker Drive Encryption   Service**
   - **Block Level Backup Engine Service**
   - **Bluetooth Support Service**
   - **Computer Browser**
   - **Device Association Service**
   - **Device Setup Manager**
   - **Diagnostic Policy Service**
   - **Diagnostic Service Host**
   - **Diagnostic System Host**

- ❑ **Family Safety**
- ❑ **Function Discovery Resource Publication**
- ❑ **Internet Connection Sharing (ICS)**
- ❑ **Microsoft iSCSI Initiator Service**
- ❑ **Microsoft Software Shadow Copy Provider**
- ❑ **Optimize Drives**
- ❑ **Secure Socket Tunnelling Protocol Service**
- ❑ **SSDP Discovery**
- ❑ **Superfetch**
- ❑ **Telephony**
- ❑ **Windows Backup**
- ❑ **Windows Color System**
- ❑ **Windows Connect Now – Config Registrar**
- ❑ **Windows Error Reporting Service**
- ❑ **Windows Media Player Network Sharing Service**
- ❑ **WLAN AutConfig**
- ❑ **WWAN AutoConfig**

> If you are configuring the Master Image to use it with PVS architectures, you have to leave the Microsoft Software Shadow Copy Provider service enabled.

The setting should now look like this:

Name	Description	Status	Startup Type
ActiveX Installer (AxInstSV)	Provides User Acco...		Manual
Application Experience	Processes applicati...	Running	Manual (Trigger Start)
Application Identity	Determines and ver...		Manual (Trigger Start)
Application Information	Facilitates the runni...		Manual
Application Layer Gateway Service	Provides support fo...		Disabled
Application Management	Processes installati...		Manual
Background Intelligent Transfer Service	Transfers files in th...		Disabled
Background Tasks Infrastructure Service	Windows infrastruc...	Running	Automatic
Base Filtering Engine	The Base Filtering E...	Running	Automatic
BitLocker Drive Encryption Service	BDESVC hosts the B...		Disabled
Block Level Backup Engine Service	The WBENGINE ser...		Disabled
Bluetooth Support Service	The Bluetooth servi...		Disabled
BranchCache	This service caches ...		Disabled

> To activate the Touch features (RemoteFX Multi-Touch), you have to install the Windows 8 Enterprise edition.

4. After completing the configuration of the services components, run the Windows + *X* key combination and select the **Command Prompt (Admin)** option.

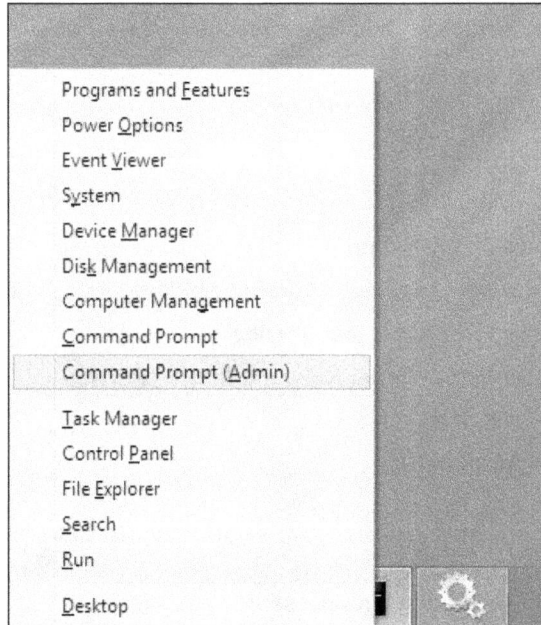

Programs and Features
Power Options
Event Viewer
System
Device Manager
Disk Management
Computer Management
Command Prompt
Command Prompt (Admin)

Task Manager
Control Panel
File Explorer
Search
Run

Desktop

5. At the shell prompt, run the commands indicated in the next lines; these will be used to customize the Windows 8 boot experience, in order to disable the Windows 8 boot screen, the Windows 8 boot logo, and the Windows 8 boot messages respectively:

```
bcdedit/set{globalsettings}custom:16000069true
bcdedit/set{globalsettings}custom:16000067true
bcdedit/set{globalsettings}custom:16000068true
```

6. To apply the boot configuration changes, you have to restart your Windows 8 machine.

7. After the reboot has been completed, execute the Windows + *X* key combination and select the **System** option. Then, click on the **Advanced system settings** link on the right hand side of the **System** screen.

8. On the **System Properties** screen, click on the **Settings** button | **Performance** subsection | **Advanced** tab:

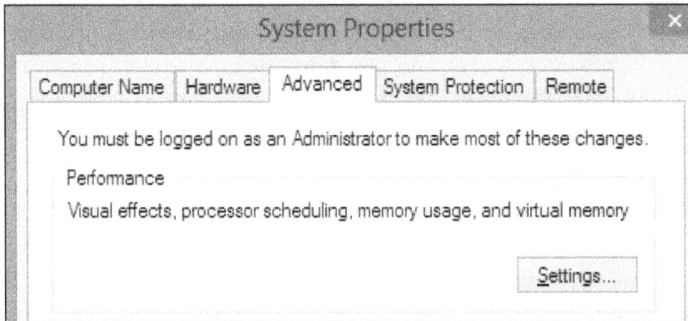

9. On the **Performance Options** screen, select the **Advanced** tab and click on the **Change** button in the **Virtual memory** subsection.

10. As seen earlier for Windows 7 we have to fix the minimum and maximum quantity of swap with a fixed and equal value. To do this, unflag the automatic paging file size management, and select the **Custom size** radio button, inserting the desired swap value (the initial and maximum sizes). Once done, click on **Set**, then click on the **OK** button. The swap size must not exceed the available space on the Master Image persistent disk.

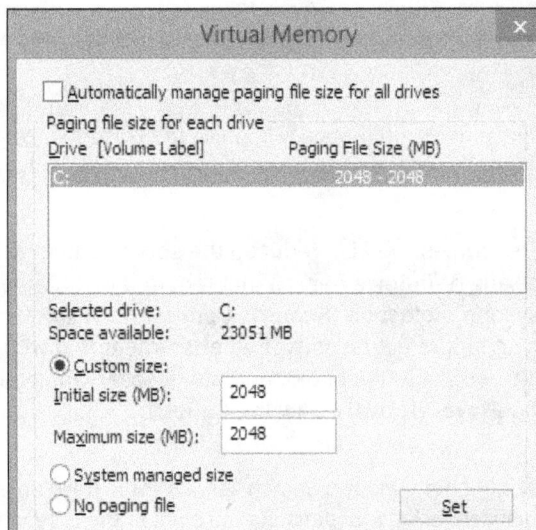

11. In order to apply the modified swap parameters, you need to reboot the Master Image.

> Even though we have talked about the Windows 7 configuration, in this book, we will only generate catalogues with the 8.x version of the operating system.

How it works...

To reduce the usual overtime needed by Windows 7 and Windows 8 machines to boot and start up all services, we disabled the parts of them that are not necessary for the regular operating system's usage in a **Virtual Desktop Infrastructure** (**VDI**) configuration.

In order to optimize the operating system, we performed the following configurations:

▸ We disabled the animation presented at boot time (with a time reduction of approximately 20 percent).

▸ We reduced the impact on the network by disabling the **BITS service** (**Background Intelligent Transfer Services**), used to automatically download programs or information with software, such as **Windows Update** or **Windows Live**.

▸ We reduced the impact on the Virtual Machine CPU and memory usage by disabling services such as Desktop Window Manager Session Manager and the **DWM** (**Desktop Windows Manager**) service, which manage, for example, the **Windows Aero** graphical user interface).

> Disabling Aero will dramatically improve the performance, but on the other hand, the user experience will be globally less rich and satisfying.

▸ For CPU / RAM resources, we also reduced the service's impact on the system by disabling indexing (**Windows Search**, not required in a nonpersistent VDI environment), system protection (**Security Center** and **Windows Defender**, substituted by system protection software better integrated with VDI that we're going to explain throughout this book), and unnecessary multimedia components (**Windows Media Player Network Sharing Center**).

> Disabling the Windows Search service could have an impact on specific indexing functions, for instance in the presence of the Microsoft Outlook mail client.

▸ The last performed operation is the assignment of a single value (for both minimum- and maximum-size parameters) for the swap area memory size.

> For both the operating systems, you can consider disabling the operating system's long-term performance optimizer (the **Superfetch** service) as discussed earlier, in case of nonpersistent machine deployments. Disabling this service is particularly useful in the presence of SSD disks, in terms of disk space and faster boot time (no more prefetch files loading during the start up phase).

For the Windows 8.x environment, we have also specified infrastructural services, which are unnecessary for a VDI deployment, such as the **Bluetooth**, **iSCSI**, and **Telephony** components initiator (you won't use them on a virtual machine), or troubleshooting components, which could cause the loss of meaning within a VDI infrastructure configured with nonpersistent machines (such as **Diagnostic Policy Service** or **Diagnostic Service / System Host**).

> Disable the Windows Search (Indexing) service only in the presence of nonpersistent Virtual Desktops; in any other case, you should keep it active to avoid general content search issues.

As a general plan, you should use desktop OS machines when your users require a particular customization of their work environment, in terms of installed software and/or personal data, with the management of the resources by the IT staff in the form of heterogeneous pools (persistent, nonpersistent, and so on).

There's more...

To improve the responsiveness of your Windows machines, you can also apply the following operating system configurations:

▸ Reduce the Event Log size and retention to the minimum, in terms of the number of days of retained events and the number and type of logged events.

▸ Remove all the unnecessary System Scheduled tasks.

▸ Install and configure an antivirus platform compatible with a VDI architecture.

> Some useful links to configure the antivirus exclusions in the correct way are:
> `http://support.citrix.com/article/CTX127030`
> `http://blogs.citrix.com/2013/09/22/citrix-consolidated-list-of-antivirus-exclusions/`

See also

▶ The *Administering hosts and machines – host and machine creation cmdlets* recipe in *Chapter 9, Working with PowerShell*.

Configuring and optimizing a server OS Master Image

Starting from the release 7, XenDesktop includes the ability to publish not only standard desktop operating systems, but also the possibility to deploy the desktop of the server edition of the Microsoft operating system. In this recipe, we will discuss the best practices, which can be applied to obtain a better user experience.

Getting ready

In order to complete all the required steps for this recipe, you need to connect to the Windows Server 2012 R2 machine with administrative credentials, to be able to install and configure all the necessary features.

How to do it...

In the following steps, we will describe how to improve the graphical and user experience for a Windows Server 2012 R2 operating system, in order to deploy the desktops of the server operating systems later in this book.

1. Connect to the selected Windows Server 2012 R2 machine with domain administrative credentials.

2. Start the **Server Manager** utility, if this has not been automatically started.

3. In the **Configure this local server** section, click on the **Add roles and features** link, as shown in the following figure:

4. On the **Add Roles and Features Wizard** screen, click on the **Next** button to continue.

5. From the **Installation Type** menu, select the **Role-based or feature-based installation** option, and click on **Next** to continue.

6. In the **Server Selection** menu, check the **Select a server from the server pool** radio button, select the machine on which you're configuring the user experience, and then click on **Next** to proceed.

7. On the **Server Roles** screen, click on the **Next** button without selecting any option to skip the roles configuration.

8. In the **Features** section, expand the **User Interfaces and Infrastructure** voice and flag the **Desktop Experience** option. When prompted for the additional required components, click on the **Add Features** button, and then click on **Next**.

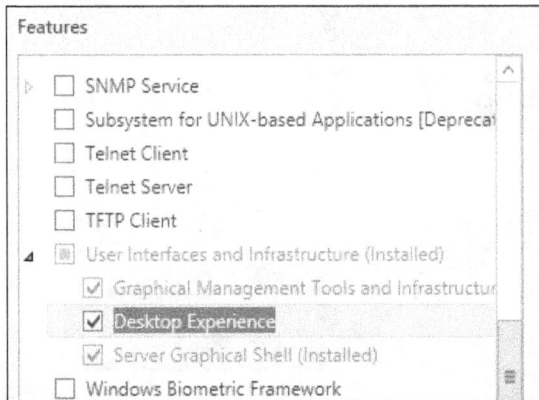

Features

▷ ☐ SNMP Service
☐ Subsystem for UNIX-based Applications [Deprecat
☐ Telnet Client
☐ Telnet Server
☐ TFTP Client
◢ ☐ User Interfaces and Infrastructure (Installed)
  ☑ Graphical Management Tools and Infrastructur
  ☑ Desktop Experience
  ☑ Server Graphical Shell (Installed)
☐ Windows Biometric Framework

9. In the **Confirmation** box, click on the **Install** button to complete the activation procedure.

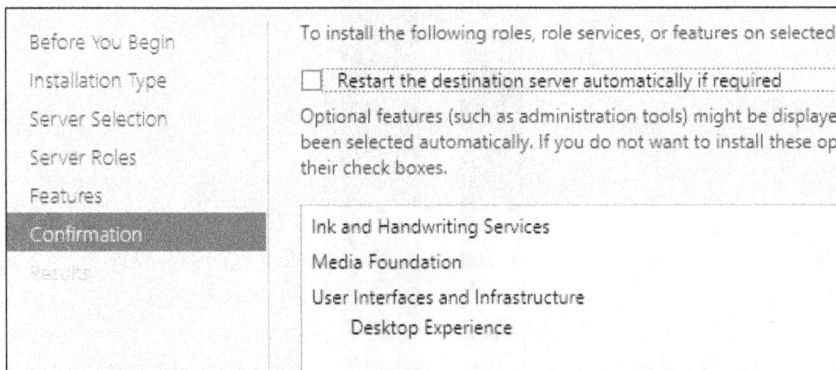

Before You Begin   To install the following roles, role services, or features on selected
Installation Type   ☐ Restart the destination server automatically if required
Server Selection   Optional features (such as administration tools) might be displaye
Server Roles   been selected automatically. If you do not want to install these op
                          their check boxes.
Features
Confirmation   Ink and Handwriting Services
Results   Media Foundation
                          User Interfaces and Infrastructure
                              Desktop Experience

10. After completion, click the **Close** button and reboot the Windows Server 2012 machine.

11. Reconnect with the same domain administrative credentials, verifying that these features have been enabled by obtaining the Windows 8 like Start menu as the first screen.

12. Using the Windows + *C* combination, it is also possible using the newly installed features.

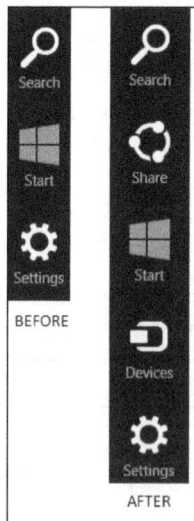

13. From the **Start** menu, click on the **Desktop** icon. Once you have been moved to the desktop view, right-click on it and select the **Personalize** option.

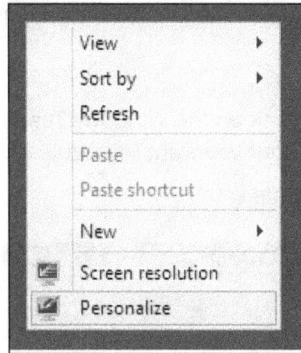

View	▶
Sort by	▶
Refresh	
Paste	
Paste shortcut	
New	▶
🖼 Screen resolution	
🖼 Personalize	

14. In the **Personalization** menu, click on **the Change desktop icons** link on the left-side menu.

15. On the **Desktop Icon Settings** screen, enable the desired icons, uncheck **Allow themes to change desktop icons**, and then click on **Apply** first, followed by the **OK** button:

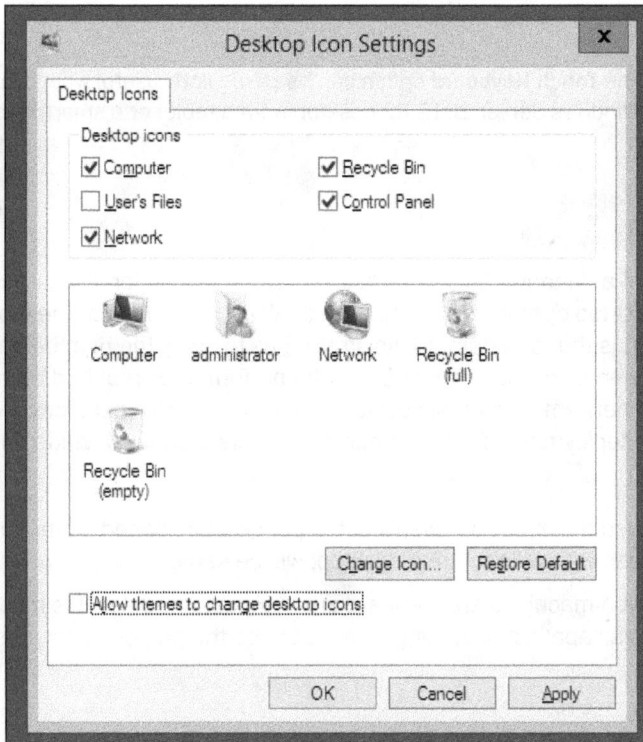

Desktop Icon Settings ☒

Desktop Icons

Desktop icons
- ☑ Computer   ☑ Recycle Bin
- ☐ User's Files   ☑ Control Panel
- ☑ Network

Computer   administrator   Network   Recycle Bin (full)

Recycle Bin (empty)

[Change Icon...] [Restore Default]

☐ Allow themes to change desktop icons

[OK] [Cancel] [Apply]

> You should avoid using desktop background images for server operating systems. The purpose of this recipe is to create the right balance between the graphical experience and the desktop performances.

16. In the desktop view, right-click on the Windows Taskbar and select the **Toolbars** voice. Click one or more options that you want to enable on the bar.

    The following image will guide you:

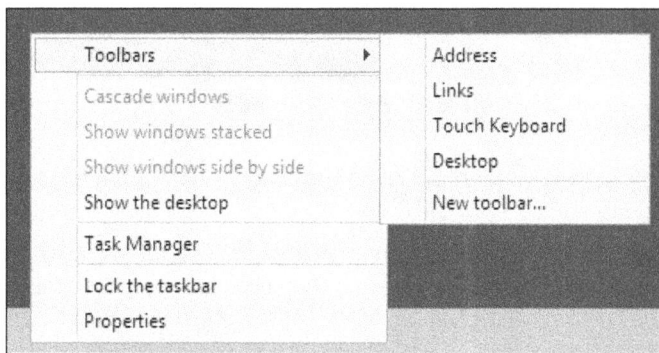

Toolbars ▶	Address
Cascade windows	Links
Show windows stacked	Touch Keyboard
Show windows side by side	Desktop
Show the desktop	New toolbar...
Task Manager	
Lock the taskbar	
Properties	

> The **Touch Keyboard** option can be particularly useful when using the Windows Server 2012 R2 desktop from a tablet or a smartphone.

How it works...

The configuration of a Windows Server operating system version for VDI purposes is slightly different than a desktop operating system, such as Windows 8; in fact, the most important thing to understand is that a system administrator has to apply the right balance between the graphical experience for the end users and the performance required by the operating system, in order to perform its normal activities. Starting with this point of view, the use case to which apply the deployment of a server operating system should include one or all of the following points:

▸ The deployed machines will be allocated per session, based on the mechanism that the first user, who will require a desktop, will be served.

▸ The deployed machines are standard and noncustomizable. This means that users cannot install applications, but only have to use the proposed environment.

> This hint can be also be applied to the previously discussed Desktop OS environments.

▸ The VDI environment has been designed to assign and maintain only the required instances, with an association of one-to-many (one server desktop, many users).

In this recipe, we performed the installation and configuration of the native Windows Server 2012 R2 feature for the user experience, Desktop Experience. By this, it's possible to add part of the Windows 8.x end user offer, such as the Windows bar seen in one of the previous pictures or system tools, such as Windows Media Player, Desktop Themes (which should be used with care, avoiding performance issues in terms of better graphics), Video for Windows, or Sound Recorder.

There's more...

If you want, you can manage and start or stop another service within your Master Image, in order to optimize the operating system's usability, without losing any required system functionality. A more detailed list of services can be found at `http://blogs.citrix.com/2014/02/06/windows-8-and-server-2012-optimization-guide`.

See also

▸ The *Configuring the XenDesktop Policies* recipe in *Chapter 7, XenDesktop Infrastructure Tuning*.

Configuring a target device – the PVS architecture

After describing the process of the basic configuration of a Master Image, desktop or server, it is time to pass from the MCS architecture configuration type to the **Provisioning Services** (**PVS**) earlier discussed in this book. In this third recipe, we will explain how to configure an operating system target device, which will be used later in this book to a deploy machine's catalogue for the PVS offer.

Getting ready

The main required step for this recipe is installing a Windows 8.x virtual machine, which will be used as the Master Image to deploy the virtual desktop instances within a XenDesktop PVS configuration.

[
![note icon] You can refer to the following Microsoft link for the Windows 8.x installation procedure: http://technet.microsoft.com/en-us/windows/hh974336.aspx.
]

How to do it...

In the following steps, we will describe how to configure a Windows 8.x machine as a target device for the PVS architecture:

1. After downloading the ISO file from your personal Citrix account, mount PVS .iso by right-clicking on it and selecting the **Mount** option. Perform this task on the machine that will be used as a target device.

2. Connect to the Windows virtual machine using domain administrative credentials.

3. Browse the mounted PVS 7.0 CD-ROM, and then double-click on the autorun.exe executable file.

4. On the **Citrix Provisioning Services** menu, select the **Target Device Installation** option by clicking on it. On the new selection menu, click on the **Target Device Installation** link again.

5. On the **Welcome** screen, click on **Next** to continue.

6. In the **License Agreement** section, accept the terms and click on the **Next** button.

7. Populate the **Customer Information** section with the required information; after completion, click on **Next** to proceed.

8. On the **Destination Folder** screen, select a valid path on which to install the agent, and then click the **Next** button.

9. In the **Ready to Install the Program** section, click on **Install** to start the installation process.

10. To prepare the image for the provisioning process, please run the following command on the command prompt:

    ❑ `ipconfig /flushdns` (DNS cache flush)

    ❑ `gpupdate /force` (forcing the Windows domain group policy application)

11. After the installation has been completed, leave the **Launch Imaging Wizard** checkbox enabled, and click on the **Finish** button.

12. After clicking on **Next** on the **Welcome** screen, populate the required fields to connect your target machine to the PVS server. Once done, click on **Next** to continue.

```
Connect to Farm
    Enter the name or address of a server in the farm to connect to.


            Server information
            Server:    |
            Port:      54321  ⬍


            Credentials
              ◉ Use my Windows credentials
              ○ Use these credentials
                User name:
                Password:
                Domain:
```

> Please refer to the *Installing and configuring Provisioning Services 7.6* recipe in *Chapter 1, XenDesktop® 7.6 – Upgrading, Installation, and Configuration* for the Citrix Provisioning Services installation steps.

13. In **Select New or Existing vDisk**, select **Create new vDisk** and click on the **Next** button.

14. On the **New vDisk** screen, assign a name to the vDisk, associate it with a configured store and select **vDisk type** (**Fixed** or **Dynamic**); in case of a Dynamic disk, you can also choose the right **vDisk block size** for your needs (**2 MB** or **16 MB**). After completing this, click on **Next**:

vDisk name:	TD-Vdisk-0
Store:	Store0000 - 31247 MB Free
	Accessible by server: VMXD7-PVS-01
vDisk type:	Dynamic
vDisk block size:	16 MB

15. Select which kind of Licenses activation mode you want to enable (**Multiple Activation Key** (**MAK**), **Key Management Services** (**KMS**), or **None**), then click on the **Next** button.

> With the latest release of the PVS, in the presence of valid KMS licenses, you should always consider using the KMS server to activate and manage your Windows licenses.

16. In the **Configure Image Volumes** section, you have to configure the dimension of the disk image size, which must be at least the minimum original disk dimension. Then click on **Next**.

Configure Image Volumes
Define the size of each volume.

	Source Volume	Used Space		Free Space		Capacity	File System
1	C: Boot	11571 MB	36 %	20845 MB	64 %	32416 MB	NTFS
2	None						
3	None						
4	None						

Destination Volume	Used Space		Free Space		Capacity	File System
C: Boot	11571 MB	38 %	18639	62 %	30210 MB	NTFS

	vDisk Store	Allocated Space		Unallocated Space		Capacity	
Summary		11579 MB	38 %	18638 MB	62 %	30217 MB	Autofit

17. In the **Add Target Device** section, configure the **Target device name**, the **MAC** network card (from the presented drop-down list), and the configured **Collection** to which the device has to be assigned. Finish this part of the setting by clicking on **Next**.

Target device name:	XD7-W8-T01
	Note: The target device name cannot be the same Active Directory name of this machine.
MAC:	Ethernet 00-0C-29-E8-0C-01
Collection:	Collection00
	In the Site00 site of server: VMXD7-PVS-01

18. On the **Summary of Farm Changes** screen, if all the information is correct, click on the **Finish** button to complete the device configuration.

The Wizard has enough information to create a new vDisk and add it to the farm.

Please review the information below and click Finish to create the vDisk.

- Create new vDisk
  - Name: TD-Vdisk-0
  - Store: Store0000
  - Type: Dynamic
  - Size: 30217
  - VHD Block Size: 16 MB
  - Microsoft Volume Licensing: Multiple Activation Key (MAK)
  - Volume: C:, 11571 MB used, 18638 MB free, 30209 MB capacity, NTFS system
- Add this machine to the farm
  - Device name: XD7-W8-T01
  - MAC: 00-0C-29-E8-0C-01
  - Collection: Collection00

Optimize for Provisioning Services

19. By clicking on the **Optimize for Provisioning Services** button, you will be able to select the checkbox to enable or disable the following features that are used to optimize the PVS device:

  - ❏ **Disable Offline Files**
  - ❏ **Disable DefragBootOptimizationFunction**
  - ❏ **Disable Last Access TimeStamp**
  - ❏ **Reduce DedivatedDumpFile DumpFileSize to 2MB**
  - ❏ **Disable Move to Recycle Bin**
  - ❏ **Reduce IE Temp File**

- ❑ **Disable Machine Account Password Changes**
- ❑ **Disable windows Defender**
- ❑ **Disable ScheduledDefrag**
- ❑ **Disable ProgramDataUpdater**
- ❑ **Disable Windows AutoUpdate**
- ❑ **Disable Backgroud Layout Service**
- ❑ **Disable Hibernate**
- ❑ **Disable Indexing Service**
- ❑ **Reduce Event Log Size to 64k**
- ❑ **Disable Clear Page File at Shutdown**
- ❑ **Disable Windows SuperFetch**
- ❑ **Disable Windows Search**
- ❑ **Disable System Restore**
- ❑ **Run NGen ExecuteQueuedItems (new Window)**

20. At the end of the vDisk creation operating, reboot the Windows target machine and configure its BIOS to perform the boot from the network or from the generated `.iso` file (BDM configuration).

> During the network boot process, the virtual machine will connect to the PVS server, so the XenConvert utility will be able to make a virtual machine copy and transfer it to the PVS server.

21. After the machine has been properly booted from the network, after the logon phase, you will find a XenConvert screen like the following:

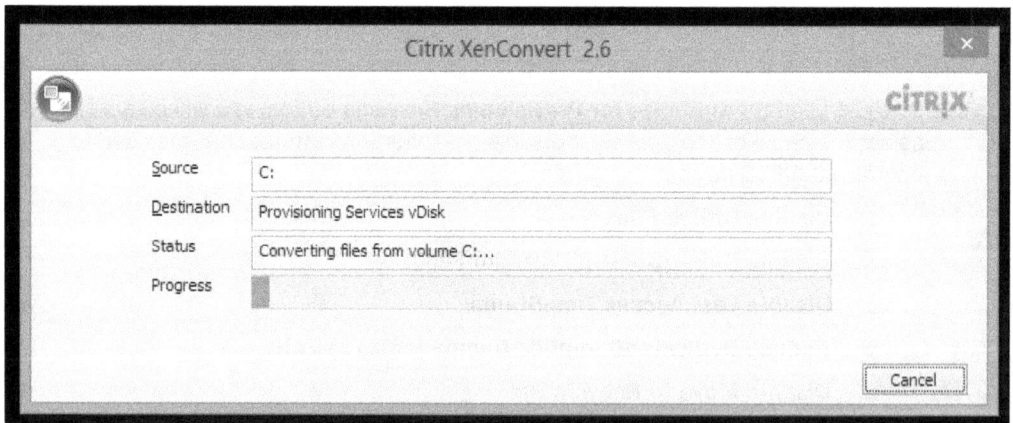

22. To check whether all the target device configurations have been properly executed, connect to the PVS Farm and check the existence of the earlier created vDisk in the **vDisk Pool** section.

Name	Store	Connections	Size	Mode
TD-Vdisk-0	Store0000	1	30.217 MB	Private

> The available **Mode** options for vDisks are **Standard** (a vDisk shared among all the involved target devices) and **Private** (a vDisk assigned and dedicated to a single specific target device).

23. After this, the conversion has been completed, and the target device will be available to be used to deploy desktop instances by the PVS Server + Desktop Studio.

> It is always possible to revert the virtual machine BIOS to boot from disk and no longer from the Provisioning Services vDisk over the network.

How it works...

The procedure seen and explained in this recipe has been about the generation of the master target device. This is the device that points to the Master Image template operating systems (in our case, Windows 8) from which the vDisk has been built. This component is the data container, which will be streamed to the configured target devices within a configured PVS farm. The device needs to be associated with a predefined PVS Store and Collection, and for this, it is necessary to specify the MAC address (for the network identification) and the vDisk type (fixed or dynamic, which will be explained in the next section). The BIOS of the configured device must also support the network boot.

There's more...

As discussed earlier in this recipe, when creating a vDisk, we have the ability to choose between two kinds of disk format: **fixed disks** and **dynamic disks**. The first type pre-allocates all assigned disk space, while dynamic allocation populates disk files during data writing activities (if you are familiar with virtualization concepts, it is the same as thick and thin disk allocation). The second type is a set of information and best practices to understand how to choose between the fixed and dynamic disks:

▸ Because of the nature of fixed disks (full space pre-allocation), using these can be a waste of storage space.

▶ PVS uses memory caching mechanisms that reduce disk I/O activities. For this reason, dynamic allocation should be the right choice, because of the huge reduction of storage reading activities. The only interface with disk component is given by write operations. In addition, in this case, after configuring the PVS vDisk image in read-only mode, we will have almost no more storage activities, except for the Write-Cache operations. To have a responsive system, on the other hand, this infrastructure needs to be supported by 64-bit systems, the right amount of memory (for a PVS server, you should have a quantity of RAM between 8 GB and 32 GB) and a block-level storage device (SAN or iSCSI and not a network share repository on NAS).

> Writecache is a cache area, on which already written data is stored, instead of being rewritten on the base vDisk. The write cache area can be a local PVS server hard disk, a specific remote server, or the PVS server's RAM cache. More information can be found at the following links:
>
> http://blogs.citrix.com/2014/04/18/turbo-charging-your-iops-with-the-new-pvs-cache-in-ram-with-disk-overflow-feature-part-one/
>
> http://blogs.citrix.com/2014/07/07/turbo-charging-your-iops-with-the-new-pvs-cache-in-ram-with-disk-overflow-feature-part-two/

See also

▶ The *Administering hosts and machines – host and machine creation cmdlets* recipe in *Chapter 9, Working with PowerShell*.

Installing and configuring the Master Image policies

Starting from this recipe, it is time to start the configurations for the policies to apply to the domain-joined machines for the MCS/PVS architectures.

Getting ready

To configure the specific domain policies for the **Virtual Desktop Infrastructure** (**VDI**) environment, you need to have domain administrative permissions and you also have to be able to propagate those to the client, which will be used as the Master Image template. You have to create a specific **organizational unit** (**OU**) containing the involved VDI resources and apply this custom configuration only to the OU containing these machines.

How to do it...

The following are the required steps to configure the policies at the domain level:

1. Log in to your Domain Controller server(s), and in order to find and use the template containing the Citrix policies to import, mount the Citrix XenDesktop 7.6 .iso image by right-clicking on it and selecting the **Mount** option.

> As an alternative, you can install the **Group Policy Management Console** on any Windows Server 2012 R2 domain machine, to manage the domain policies.

2. Run the Windows + *X* key combination, select the **Run** option, and insert the gpmc. msc command to execute the Group Policy Management Console:

3. Expand the **Forest** and **Domain** trees, then right-click on the domain name of your organization and select **New Organizational Unit** to create a container, including the MCS/PVS Windows Desktop machine.

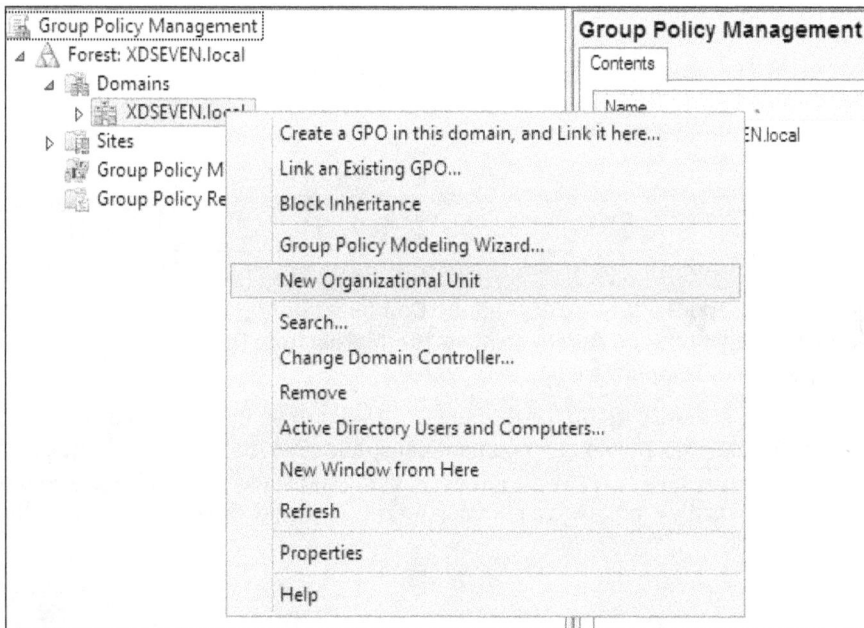

Group Policy Management	
⊿ Forest: XDSEVEN.local	**Group Policy Management**
⊿ Domains	Contents
▷ XDSEVEN.loc~	Name
▷ Sites	Create a GPO in this domain, and Link it here... ¦N.local
Group Policy M	Link an Existing GPO...
Group Policy Re	Block Inheritance
	Group Policy Modeling Wizard...
	New Organizational Unit
	Search...
	Change Domain Controller...
	Remove
	Active Directory Users and Computers...
	New Window from Here
	Refresh
	Properties
	Help

4. When prompted for the OU name, populate the required **Name** field and click on the **OK** button.

5. Right-click on the created OU, and select **Create a GPO in this domain, and Link it here**; in this way, we are starting to link Citrix policies to the Active Directory.

6. On the **New GPO** screen, assign a name to the policy and select **(none)** in the **Source Starter GPO** drop-down menu, and then click on **OK**.

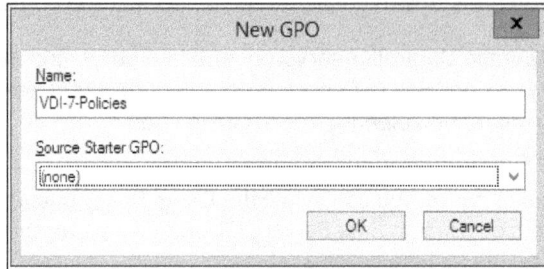

7. After the GPO is created, right-click on it and select the **Edit** option from the menu.

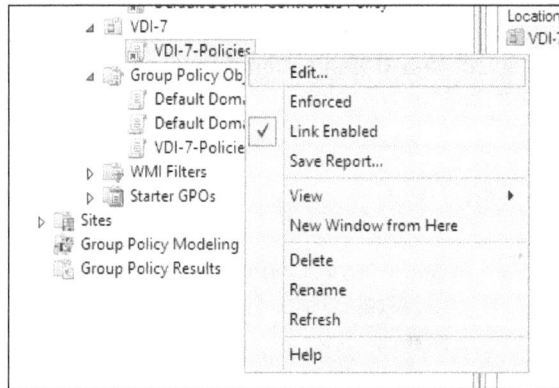

8. On the new opened screen, expand the **Computer Configuration** tree and then **Policies**. Right click on **Administrative Templates**; from the menu, select the **Add/Remove Templates** link.

9. On the new screen, click on the **Add** button, then browse the installation media for the Citrix Profile Management policy template (the `<cdrom>:\x64\ ProfileManagement\ADM_Templates` path) and select the template based on your OS installation language, searching for the `.adm` file. Once done, click on the **Close** button.

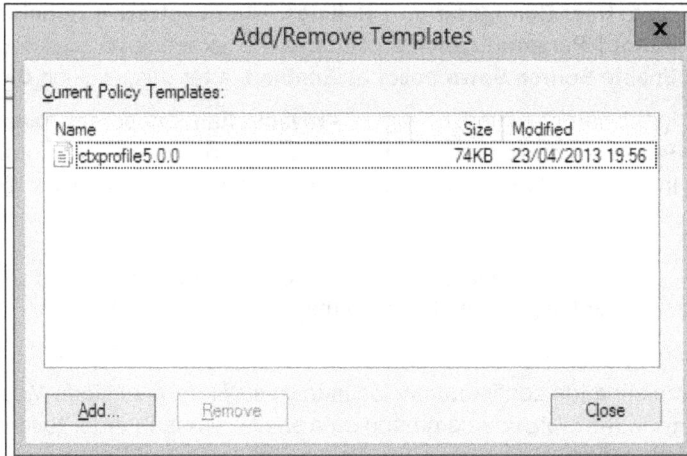

10. Expand **Computer Configuration | Administrative Templates | Classic Administrative Templates (ADM) | Citrix | Profile Management**. Within this level, you can find all the configurable options about the imported Citrix policies.

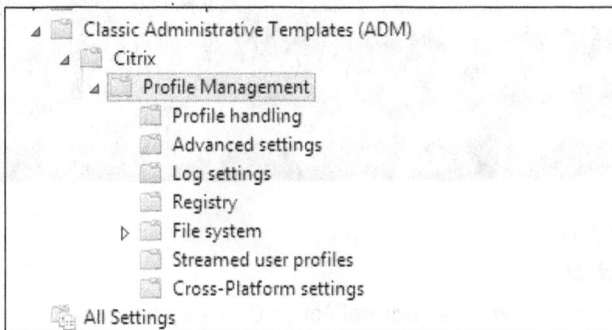

> In the next chapter, we will configure these imported policies in the *Citrix Profile Management* section.

11. Come back to the higher level of the VDI-created domain policy and configure the listed domain policies as follows:

   □ Go to **Computer Configuration | Policies | Administrative Templates | Windows Components | Windows Update** and set the **Configure Automatic Updates** policy to the **Disable** state. Then, click on **OK**.

   □ Go to **Computer Configuration | Policies | Administrative Templates | System | System Restore** and configure **Turn off System Restore** as **Enabled**. After this, click on **OK**.

- ❏ Go to **User Configuration | Policies | Administrative Templates | Control Panel | Personalization** and enable the screen saver by default configuring **Enable Screen Saver** policy as **Enabled**. After this, click on **OK** to continue.

- ❏ In the same section, configure **Prevent changing screen saver** to **Enabled**, **Password protect screen saver** to **Enabled** and assign a numeric value, in seconds, to **Screen saver timeout** policy after setting it to **Enabled**.

> These configurations have been applied in order to standardize the Master Images used to deploy the desktop instances.

12. After completing the configuration, log in to your Windows desktop Master Image and run the `gpupdate/force` command on a shell prompt, in order to force the policy update application.

```
Administrator: Command Prompt
Microsoft Windows [Version 6.2.9200]
(c) 2012 Microsoft Corporation. All rights reserved.

C:\Windows\system32>gpupdate /force
Updating policy...

Computer Policy update has completed successfully.
User Policy update has completed successfully.

C:\Windows\system32>
```

How it works...

Policies loaded in this recipe work as normal Active Directory policies. For this reason, you have to configure them, modifying their default configuration (the default state is Not Configured) to the Enabled or Disabled states. These are the Citrix Profile Management policies. In this section, we have only performed its installation process. The configuration will be executed in the next chapter, when we will discuss the Profile Management policies configuration process in detail.

The second step of the configuration process has been about the Windows Active Directory policies, due to the necessity to standardize the Windows image template as much as possible to deploy to the end users. For this reason, we disabled Windows Update on the first applied policy; the required updates will be propagated only once to the base image, and the entire set of assigned desktops will be updated every time they will be generated from the source machine. A security plus to this policy is given using a **Windows Server Update Services** (**WSUS**) server, a centralized **Server Manager**. This is the only point of contact to the public network, which covers the updates propagation task in your **Local Area Network** (**LAN**).

Moreover, we have also blocked the Screen Saver customization and system restore points. The user will be subject to a predefined configuration, in most cases, optimized for a company's requirements.

See also

▸ The *Implementing profile architecture* recipe in *Chapter 4, User Experience – Planning and Configuring*.

4
User Experience
– Planning and
Configuring

In this chapter, we will cover the following recipes:

- ▶   Implementing profile architecture
- ▶   Installing Virtual Desktop Agent – server OS and desktop OS
- ▶   Installing and configuring the HDX Monitor
- ▶   Configuring the Citrix Receiver
- ▶   Configuring Citrix Receiver for HTML5 1.5 – clientless

Introduction

In *Chapter 3, Master Image Configuration and Tuning*, we discussed how to optimize the virtual desktop component in order to standardize the operating system base image, which we are going to deploy in the future activities.

Now it is time to configure those components which are nearest to the user perspective, such as advanced profile techniques, plugin installations, and appearance configuration settings. These configurations will be more oriented toward tuning and optimization of the user experience, instead of the operations oriented to the installation and configuration of the desktop template, as explained in the previous chapter.

This was formerly known as **user experience**, the way in which an end user notices no difference between the use of a standard physical desktop and a virtual desktop deployed by **Virtual Desktop Infrastructure** (**VDI**) architecture.

Implementing profile architecture

When you decide to implement VDI architecture for your company, you need to take note of the location where you will be storing all the users' data, such as documents, projects, and mailbox file data.

Therefore, an important step is deciding what kind of profile architecture you will be implementing for your organization. With XenDesktop 7.6, you have the capability to choose among three kinds of profiles: profiles managed by the Citrix Profile Management 5.x Version, Microsoft Roaming Profiles, and Citrix solution known as **Personal vDisk**, a feature introduced in the XenDesktop 5.6 release.

Getting ready

To rightly implement any kind of profile architecture, you need to have domain administrative credentials to be able to operate on the AD user objects. Moreover, it is also necessary to have an assigned centralized storage (network share and/or SAN) to implement the roaming profile technique or Citrix Personal vDisk technology.

How to do it...

In the following steps, we will explain the ways to implement and configure the earlier described profile management technologies.

Using Citrix® Profile Management 5.x

The following steps help us to implement profile architecture using Citrix Profile Management:

1. Log in to your Windows 8 Master Image with administrative credentials.
2. Mount the Citrix XenDesktop 7 ISO by right-clicking on it and select the **Mount** option. Then, browse media support for the `Citrix Profile Management` folder (`DVDDrive:\x64\ProfileManagement`) and double-click on the `profilemgt_64.msi` setup file.
3. On the **Welcome** screen, click on the **Next** button to proceed with the installation.
4. Accept the **End-User License Agreement** by flagging the agreement option and then click on **Next**.
5. In the **Destination Folder** section, select a valid path on which you will be installing the Citrix Profile Management, and then click on the **Next** button.
6. On the **Ready to install** screen, click on the **Install** button to complete the setup.
7. Click on the **Finish** button when the setup has been completed.

[![notes] In order to complete the installation procedure, you need to restart your Windows client machine.]

8. After the machine has rebooted, run the Windows + *X* key combination, select the **Run** link, and type the `services.msc` command.

9. In the list of running Windows services, check whether Citrix Profile Management is running or not.

Certificate Propagation	Copies user ...	Running	Manual
Citrix Profile Management	Manages us...	Running	Automatic
CNG Key Isolation	The CNG ke...		Manual (Trig...

10. Connect to your Windows Domain Controller machine, then run Windows + *X* key combination, select the **Run** option, and insert the `gpmc.msc` command to execute the Group Policy Management Console.

11. Expand the Forest and Domain trees, then search for the VDI group policy created in the previous chapter, right-click on it, and select the **Edit** option from the menu.

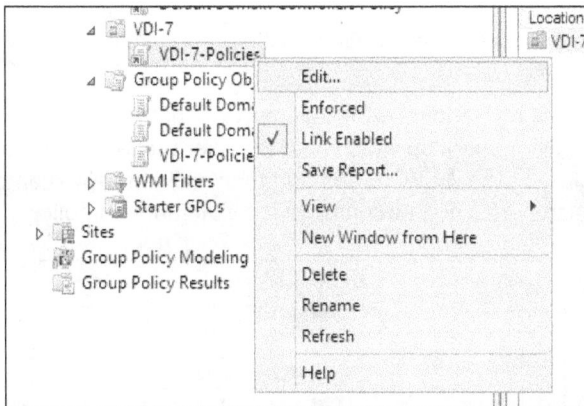

12. Navigate to **Computer Configuration | Policies | Administrative Templates | Classic Administrative Templates (ADM) | Citrix | Profile Management** and enable the following Citrix Profile Management policies:

   ❑ **Profile management** section:

   Enable profile management

   Path to user store

   Active write back

   Offline profile support

❑ **Profile handling** section:

Local profile conflict handling

❑ **Advanced settings** section:

Number of retries when accessing locked files

❑ **Log settings** section:

Log settings

❑ **Streamed user profiles** section:

Profile streaming option configured to enabled

The **Profile streaming** option should be always configured to **Enabled**, in order to speed up the logon process, by enabling the fast logons capability.

Using roaming profiles

The following steps help us to implement the profile architecture using roaming profiles:

1. Right-click on the created (or already existing) user profile, and then select the **Properties** voice.

2. Select the **Profile** tab, and insert a valid network path (for example, a network share governed by a file server), on which both the user profile and the user home folder are stored. Click on the **Apply** button and then click on **OK** to complete the procedure. This can be also performed by configuring a valid domain policy.

Remote control		Remote Desktop Services Profile		COM+
Member Of		Dial-in	Environment	Sessions
General	Address	Account	Profile	Telephones	Organization

User profile

Profile path: \\networkshare\Folder\%username%

Logon script:

Home folder

○ Local path:

⦿ Connect: Z: ∨ To: etworkshare\Home\%username%

> For both the explained profiles (Citrix Profile / Microsoft Roaming Profile), you should configure a centralized repository share for allocating the user profiles. Consider using the Microsoft Windows file server role for these purposes.

Using Personal vDisk

The profile architecture can be implemented using Personal vDisk as follows:

▶ In the Citrix Virtual Desktop Agent installation, when you arrive at step number five, you have to enable the **Personal vDisk** option, in order to be able to deploy during the book, the desired number of Virtual Desktop instances with the additional feature of having a virtual disk assigned to every user.

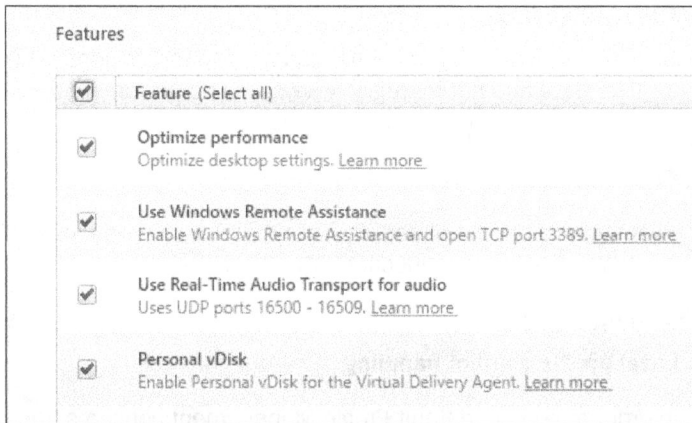

Features

- ☑ Feature (Select all)
- ☑ Optimize performance
  Optimize desktop settings. Learn more
- ☑ Use Windows Remote Assistance
  Enable Windows Remote Assistance and open TCP port 3389. Learn more
- ☑ Use Real-Time Audio Transport for audio
  Uses UDP ports 16500 - 16509. Learn more
- ☑ Personal vDisk
  Enable Personal vDisk for the Virtual Delivery Agent. Learn more

> In the next recipe, *Installing Virtual Desktop Agent – server OS and desktop OS*, we will discuss the full agent installation procedure.

How it works...

The user profile is the location where all the user data is usually stored. The first and most common profile is the local profile. With this option, you will have a copy of your user profile for every device, from which you will start a user session. This technique is usable, only when you have deployed static and persistent virtual desktops (this will be explained in detail, later in this book). In this case, you will not lose your profile data when executing a logoff (persistent deployment) session. With the static machine assignment, you can avoid the profile's duplication on different devices, because you will have a one-to-one association between the user and the assigned machine.

The second chance to deploy a profile technique is using the Citrix Profile Management. In this recipe, we configured (enabled) a set of domain policies, which will be applied to the deployed desktop instances with the profile management on board, in the following ways:

- **Profile management** section:
  - **Enable profile management**

    Enabling this policy will activate the processing of the logon and logoff phases by the Citrix Profile Manager.

  - **Path to user store**

    You must enable this policy to be able to specify the centralized folder on the file server on which you store the profiles. By enabling this policy, you have to specify the right network path.

  - **Active write back**

    By enabling this policy, synchronization between desktop and user store (only for user data and not for registry keys) will be performed during an active session, before logoff action.

  - **Offline profile support**

    Enabling this policy will permit users that are also working offline, without any kind of network connection.

- **Profile handling** section:
  - **Local profile conflict handling**

    In order to respect default Profile Management concepts (the only profiles used are domain profiles), you should configure this policy to delete a local profile, in order to substitute any non-domain resources with information stored on the Central Profile Manager.

- **Advanced settings** section:
  - **Number of retries when accessing locked files**

    This policy has a default value of five retries when accessing locked files. After being enabled, you can reuse this parameter.

- **Log settings** section:
  - **Enable logging**

    With this, only errors will be logged; if you want to activate the debug mode to log activities in a verbose mode, you can decide to enable the policy.

❑ **Log Settings**

Enable this policy and select what you want to log in, in a more detailed way, select options shown in the following screenshot:

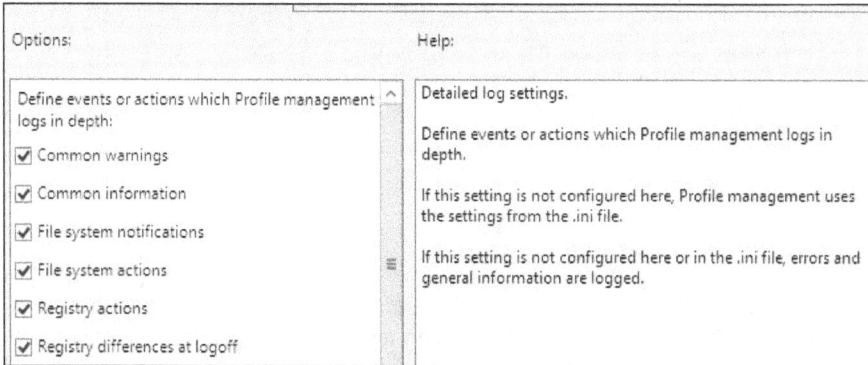

> These settings can also be applied using the `.ini` file present in the Citrix UPM destination folder.

❑ **Maximum size of the log file**

Default value for the log file size is 1 MB. Define a preferred value in bytes after which the current log will be rotated in a `.bak` file and a new active log file will be generated.

❑ **Path to log file**

Specify this location, if possible, using a centralized location as done for the user profile store.

▶ **Registry** section:

❑ **Exclusion list**: Depending on your requirements, you can specify a set of registry keys to exclude during synchronization activities. Therefore, any changes made to these values will be discarded and not sent to the user profile store.

❑ **Inclusion list**: If you specify keys in this policy, they will be synchronized during the logoff phase.

▶ **Filesystem** section:

  ❑ Exclusion list | Files

  Specify the files that must be not saved after a user performs a logoff operation.

  ❑ Exclusion list | Directories

  Specifying the folders that must be not saved after a user performs a logoff operation.

▶ **Streamed user profiles** section:

  ❑ **Profile streaming**

  With this policy enabled, profile synchronization activates caching on the local computer only when file and folders are accessed; for registry keys, sync is in real time.

The latest release of the Citrix Profile Management has been improved with the help of the following features:

▶ Instead of assigning a temporary profile to the users, in presence of multiple active sessions for the same user, the profile management now forces the user to logoff, notifying it by a system pop-up message.

▶ Citrix Profile Management is now able to automatically configure its main options, based on analysis of the configured environment.

▶ Within a configured Citrix Profile Management infrastructure, you have now the ability to integrate the use of the **Citrix ShareFile** platform.

> You can find more information on the Citrix ShareFile platform available at http://www.citrix.com/products/sharefile/overview.html.

As an alternative, we have the Windows roaming profile; this solution is similar to the Citrix User Profile Manager seen earlier, but with less features. Also, because Microsoft solution has been developed in the past, we can consider the Citrix product an evolution of this technique. It is based on a centralized store on a network share, on which you have to archive all the user data. This is the way to solve the problem of the duplicated information caused by a local profile.

At the end, we have the Citrix Personal vDisk. This is a secondary virtual disk created by the Hypervisor chosen for your infrastructure and assigned to every deployed desktop machine instance associated to only one user. Therefore, also in this case, we will have a one-to-one association between the user and its Personal vDisk. Citrix PvD is made up of two components—a hidden volume identified with the V: drive letter, which is a sort of catalog of the applications installed by the user, and a visible volume identified with the default P: drive letter, on which the users can archive their personal data. The last solution permits you to have a huge reduction of storage occupation, giving more flexibility to the users about the applications' installations and data modifications without affecting the operating system volume.

The following table is useful to compare the pros and cons of every profile method, with a set of real-world application cases:

Profile Technology	Pros	Cons	Use cases
Local profile	Faster than centralized profiles.	Data duplication with multiple desktops.	Persistent virtual desktops and physical desktops.
Citrix Profile Management	Centralized profile location, no duplicated data, efficient solution to the last write wins issue (only changed filesystem's objects are overwritten).	An alternative to the roaming profiles only in the presence of a low number of users.	Persistent virtual desktops and physical desktops.
Roaming profile	Centralized profile location, no duplicated data.	Slower than local profiles. Last write wins problems (overwrite of files or settings managed and modified by two or more applications simultaneously).	Nonpersistent (pooled) virtual desktops.
Personal vDisk	Virtualization of the user profile space, no reason to use centralized profiles to maintain the user customization.	Backup and restore of data is a little bit more difficult than other technologies, performed at the Hypervisor level.	Nonpersistent (pooled) virtual desktops.

There's more...

The Personal vDisk drive letters can be modified, but they follow two different procedures:

- ▶ For the user data visible drive (default `P:`), you can modify the assigned letter in phase of creation using the Desktop Studio.

- ▶ For the V: hidden drive, you have to modify a registry key on the template virtual machine. The key is located under the `HKLM\Software\Citrix\personal vDisk\Config` section of your Windows machine registry, and its name is **VHDMountPoint**. The only operation to perform is to edit the value of the registry voice, specifying the drive letter that you want to assign.

> Please remember that you must perform the `V:` hidden drive letter modification before creating the Personal vDisk inventory and before generating any machine catalog from the Desktop Controller.

See also

- ▶ *Creating and configuring the machine catalog* recipe in *Chapter 5, Creating and Configuring a Desktop Environment*.

Installing Virtual Desktop Agent – server OS and desktop OS

After you have chosen the way to implement the profile technology, it is time to allow your Windows Master Image to communicate with your XenDesktop infrastructure. You can accomplish this task by installing the Virtual Desktop Agent. In this latest release of the Citrix platform, the VDA has been redeployed in three different versions: desktop operating systems, server operating systems, and Remote PC, a way to link an existing physical or virtual machine to your XenDesktop infrastructure.

Getting ready

You need to install and configure the described software with domain administrative credentials within both the desktop and server operating systems.

How to do it...

In the following section, we are going to explain the way to install and configure the three different types of Citrix Virtual Desktop Agents.

Installing VDA for a server OS machine

1. Connect to the server OS Master Image with domain administrative credentials.

2. Mount the XenDesktop 7.6 ISO on the server OS machine by right-clicking on it and selecting the **Mount** option.

3. Browse the mounted XenDesktop 7.6 DVD-ROM and double-click on the `AutoSelect.exe` executable file.

4. On the **Welcome** screen, click on the **Start** button to continue.

5. On the XenDesktop 7.6 menu, click on the **Virtual Delivery Agent for Windows Server OS** link, in the **Prepare Machines and Images** section.

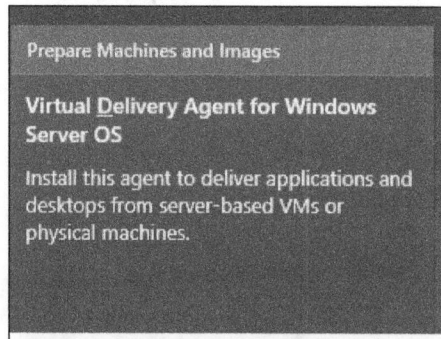

6. In the **Environment** section, select **Create a Master Image** if you want to create a Master Image for VDI architecture (**MCS/PVS**) or by enabling a direct connection to a physical or virtual server. After completing, click on **Next**.

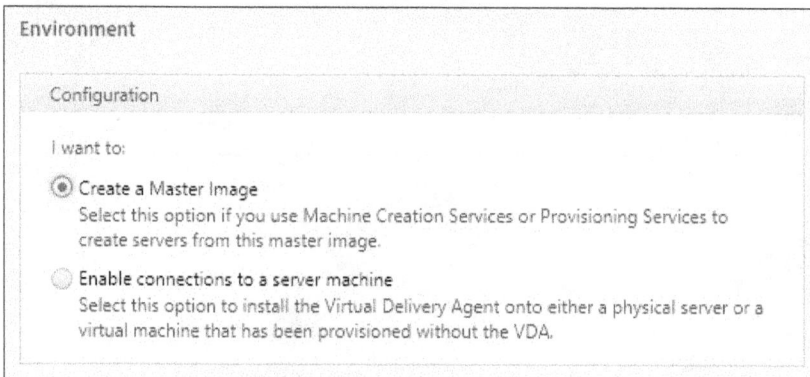

7. In the **Core Components** section, select a valid location to install the agent and click on the **Next** button.

8. In the **Delivery Controller** section, select **Do it manually** from the drop-down list. In order to manually, configure the Delivery Controller, type a valid controller address, and click on the **Add** button. To continue with the installation, click on **Next**.

Delivery Controller

Configuration

How do you want to enter the locations of your Delivery Controllers?

Do it manually

Controller address:

vmxd7-xddc-01

Test connection...   Add

To verify that you entered a valid address, click on the **Test connection...** button.

9. In the **Features** section flag, choose the optimization options that you want to enable, then click on **Next** to continue.

Features

☑   Feature (Select all)

☑   Optimize performance
      Optimize desktop settings. Learn more

☑   Use Windows Remote Assistance
      Enable Windows Remote Assistance and open TCP port 3389. Learn more

☑   Use Real-Time Audio Transport for audio
      Uses UDP ports 16500 - 16509. Learn more

10. In the **Firewall** section, select the right radio button to open the required firewall ports. In **Configure firewall rules:** choose **Automatically**, if you are using the Windows Firewall, or **Manually** if you have a firewall other than that on board. After completion, click on the **Next** button.

Firewall

The default ports are listed below.   Printable version

Controller Communications	Remote Assistance	Real Time Audio
80 TCP	3389 TCP	16500 - 16509 UDP
1494 TCP		
2598 TCP		
8008 TCP		

Configure firewall rules:

- ● Automatically
  Select this option to automatically create the rules in the Windows Firewall. The rules will be created even if the Windows Firewall is turned off.

- ○ Manually
  Select this option if you are not using Windows Firewall or if you want to create the rules yourself.

11. If the options in the **Summary** screen are correct, click on the **Install** button to complete the installation procedure.

> In order to complete the procedure, you will need to restart the server OS machine several times.

Installing VDA for a desktop OS machine

1. Connect to the desktop OS Master Image with domain administrative credentials.

2. Mount or burn the XenDesktop 7.6 ISO on the desktop OS machine.

3. Browse the mounted XenDesktop 7.6 DVD-ROM and double-click on the `AutoSelect.exe` executable file.

4. On the **Welcome** screen, click on the **Start** button to continue.

5. On the XenDesktop 7.6 menu, click on the **Virtual Delivery Agent for Windows Desktop OS** link, in the **Prepare Machines and Images** section.

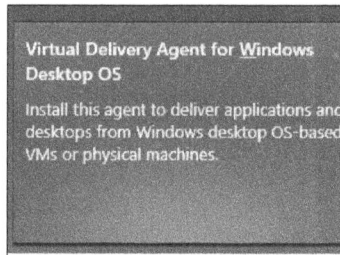

6. In the **Environment** section, select **Create a Master Image** if you want to create a Master Image for VDI architecture (MCS/PVS) or select **Enable Remote PC Access** to enable access to a physical or virtual desktop machine. After completing, click on **Next**.

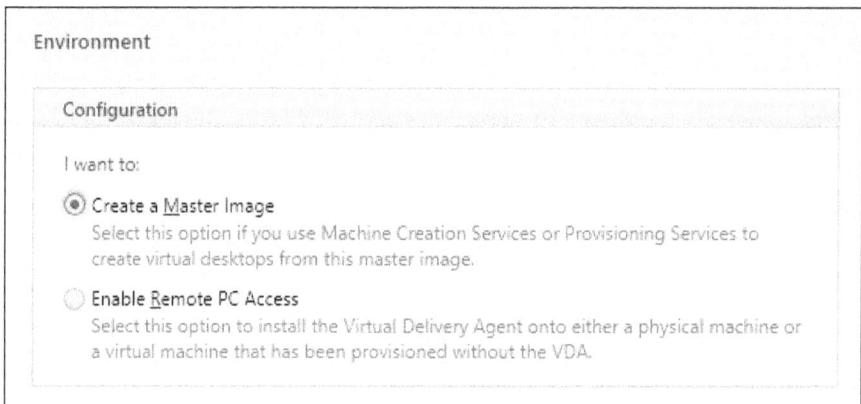

7. In the **HDX 3D Pro** section, select whether or not to install the Citrix HDX 3D-Pro plugin and click on **Next.**

HDX 3D Pro

HDX 3D Pro optimizes the performance of graphics-intensive programs and media-rich applications.

Configuration

Install the Virtual Delivery Agent (VDA) for HDX 3D Pro?

○ No, install the standard VDA
   Recommended for most desktops, including those enabled with Microsoft RemoteFX.

○ Yes, install the VDA for HDX 3D Pro
   Recommended if the machine will access a graphics processor for 3D rendering.

> In the next recipe, *Installing and configuring the HDX Monitor*, we will obtain some more information about the user experience analysis.

8. In the **Core Components** section, select a valid location to install the agent, flag the Citrix Receiver component, and click on the **Next** button.

9. In the **Delivery Controller** section, select **Do it manually** from the drop-down list in order to manually configure the delivery controller, type a valid Controller FQDN, then click on the **Add** button. Following this, click on **Next** to continue.

10. In the **Features** section, select the options you want to enable during the VDA installation. Take particular care about the Citrix Personal vDisk component activation, based on your profile management policies. After completion, click on **Next.**

Features

☑ Feature (Select all)

☑ Optimize performance
   Optimize desktop settings. Learn more

☑ Use Windows Remote Assistance
   Enable Windows Remote Assistance and open TCP port 3389. Learn more

☑ Use Real-Time Audio Transport for audio
   Uses UDP ports 16500 - 16509. Learn more

☑ Personal vDisk
   Enable Personal vDisk for the Virtual Delivery Agent. Learn more

11. In the **Firewall** section, select the right radio button to open the required firewall ports: **Automatically**, in case you're using the Windows Firewall, or **Manually**, if you've got a firewall other than that on board. After completing click on the **Next** button.

12. If the options in the **Summary** screen are correct, click on the **Install** button to complete the installation procedure.

How it works...

The Virtual Desktop Agent is the client software that connects your client machine to the XenDesktop infrastructural servers. A standard installation of the VDA will use the normal HDX protocol version, using an ICA connection to interact with the centralized controller servers.

The main difference compared to previous releases of the Virtual Desktop Agent is the ability to install it on a machine used as a **Master Image template** or a physical/virtual machine, which will be accessed directly from a remote. This is the XenDesktop feature known as Remote PC Access. This powerful option make a stronger use of the company resources from a (remote) personal device, in terms of user experience and security (any connection to the company device is encrypted and managed by the NetScaler Gateway and XenDesktop 7.6 architectures). This is a part of the FlexCast approach (access anywhere, anytime, from any device).

In presence of a configured Server OS remote machine, IT professionals have a different way to deploy desktops and applications. In fact, on the Server OS machine a Remote Desktop licensing will be activated, making the administrator able to publish resources in the XenApp style, using the new version of this Citrix software integrated in the XenDesktop architecture.

> Deploying Server OS machines for MCS architectures will let you be able to provision XenApp style servers in an easier way.

In the next step, you will be prompted to choose if installing the standard HDX suite or implementing the HDX 3D-Pro version. The 3D-Pro suite is an integrated part of VDA, configurable by the use of the Citrix policies.

> In *Chapter 7, XenDesktop Infrastructure Tuning*, we will explain how to configure HDX based on the specific platform usage (standard, 3D-Graphics, and mobile).

After this section, the installation procedure continues with the selection of the most important components for the VDA client, the Virtual Desktop Agent, and the Citrix Receiver.

Then, the next step requires inserting the Desktop Controllers server FQDN and checking its availability. This is not mandatory in this section (you can also configure it later), but in order to complete all the required steps, you should insert this information in this moment.

The last configuration step is about the firewall. You have to open the required ports for the VDA architecture, in the presence of a firewall different from the Windows Firewall platform. In the presence of this last technology, instead, the XenDesktop VDA setup will be able to automatically open the following required ports:

▸ **Controller communications**: TCP 80, TCP 1494, TCP 2598, and TCP 8008

▸ **Remote assistance**: TCP 3389

▸ **Real-time audio**: UDP 16500–16509

There's more...

Users also have the ability to run setup steps from the command line and not from the graphical interface. Citrix offers an executable file, which can substitute the previously seen installation procedure.

This file is named `XenDesktopVdaSetup.exe`, and you can find it on your XenDesktop installation media at the `x86\XenDesktop Setup` path for 32-bit installations or at `x64\XenDesktop Setup` path for 64-bit installations. Run it from the command line to perform the required installation. To see the complete options list for this executable file, run the following command:

```
XenDesktopVdaSetup.exe   /?
```

You will receive a pop-up screen with the entire list, as shown in the following screenshot:

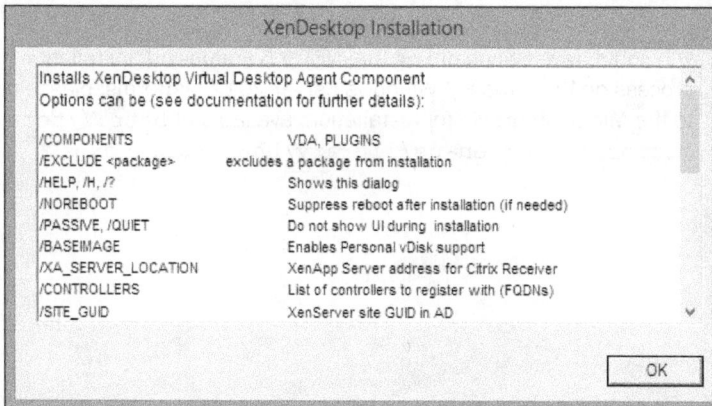

So, for example, to install the Virtual Desktop Agent with the Personal vDisk enabled, with both the VDA and receiver components and with the specified delivery controller address, you have to run from the Windows command line the following instructions:

```
XenDesktopVdaSetup.exe  /BASEIMAGE /COMPONENTS VDA,PLUGINS /CONTROLLERS
vmxd7-xddc-01.xdseven.local
```

See also

▶   *Configuring the XenDesktop policies* recipe in *Chapter 7, XenDesktop Infrastructure Tuning*.

Installing and configuring the HDX Monitor

The Citrix HDX is a collection of capabilities offered by XenDesktop, which is based on the well-known and stable ICA protocol. HDX has to be considered as a set of features oriented to the high performances without losing the resolution quality for both audio and video reproduction. The HDX Monitor is a powerful tool, which permits system administrator verifying and configuring the parameters for high-level user experience.

Getting ready

You need to download the HDX Monitor software available at `https://taas.citrix.com/AutoSupport`.

To install it, you have to connect to the related machine with domain administrative credentials, being sure to have already installed the .NET 3.5 Framework.

> You could have issues during the .NET 3.5 Framework installation process on Windows 8 / Windows Server 2012 platforms; please refer to the Microsoft article for installation, available at `http://technet.microsoft.com/en-us/library/hh831809.aspx`.

How to do it...

The following steps will explain how to install and use the Citrix HDX Monitor:

1. Connect to the Desktop OS Master Image with domain administrative credentials.

2. Locate the folder on which you downloaded the HDX Monitor software, and then double-click on the `hdx-monitor.msi` file to run it.

3. On the **Welcome** screen, click on the **Next** button to continue.

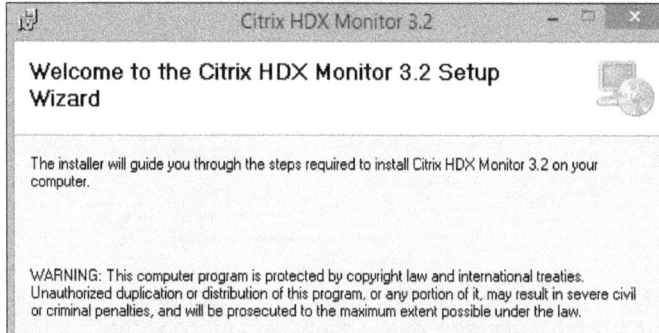

4. In the **License Agreement** section, select the **I Agree** radio button and click on **Next**.

5. In the **Select Installation folder** screen, choose a valid path on which you will install the software, and then click on **Next** to continue.

6. After completion, click on the **Next** button on the **Confirm Installation** screen to complete the software setup.

7. After completing the installation, click on the **Close** button to end the setup procedure.

8. After the end of installation, double-click on the **Citrix HDX Monitor** icon on the desktop.

9. On the main menu, insert a valid machine address for which you want to check the configuration. In this case, insert the local IP address and click on the **Open** button.

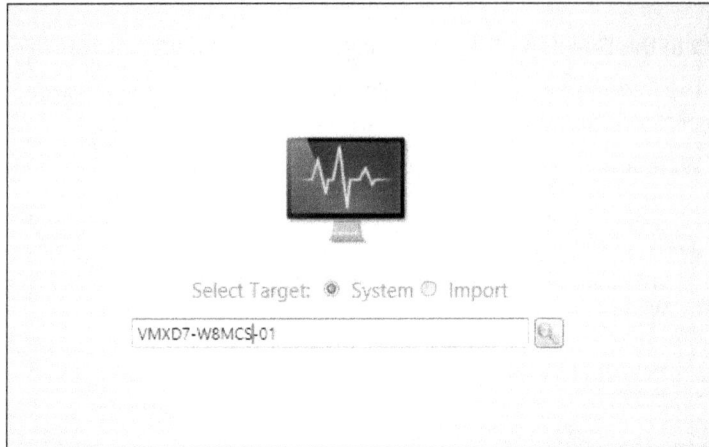

10. After connecting to the target device, you will be prompted with a summary screen with the current status of the configured components, as shown in the following screenshot:

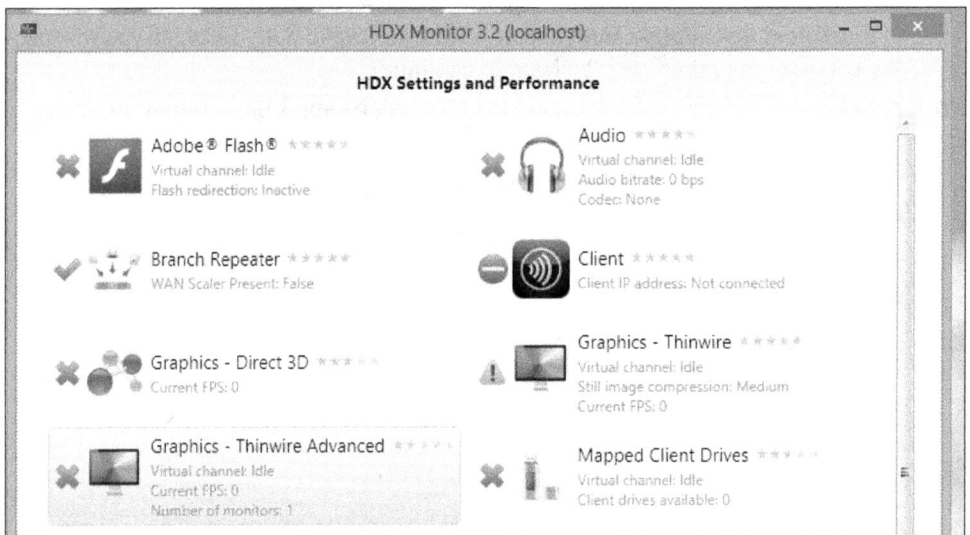

11. Click on one of the HDX settings icon to obtain further details about the selected component.

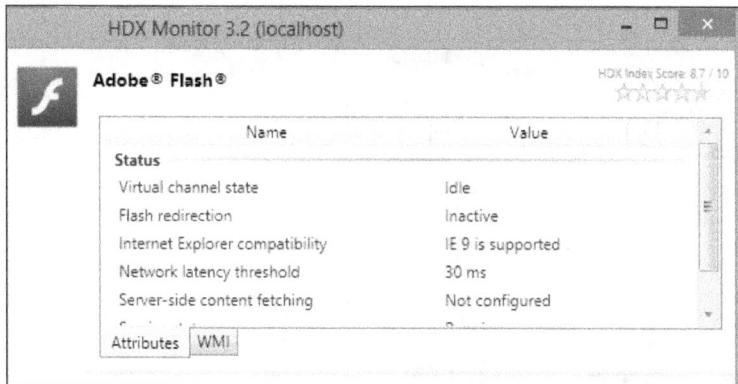

[On the right-side corner of the window, users can find the HDX score assigned to the component configuration.]

12. To change the component configuration view, click on one of the sections existing on the left-side menu.

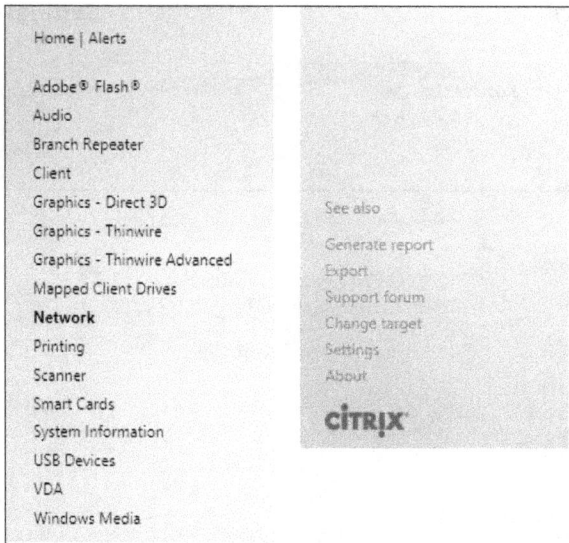

13. To see the full list of alerts presented by the HDX Monitor, click on the **Alerts** link on the top of the **Monitor menu** section. To come back to the main menu, click on the **Home** link.

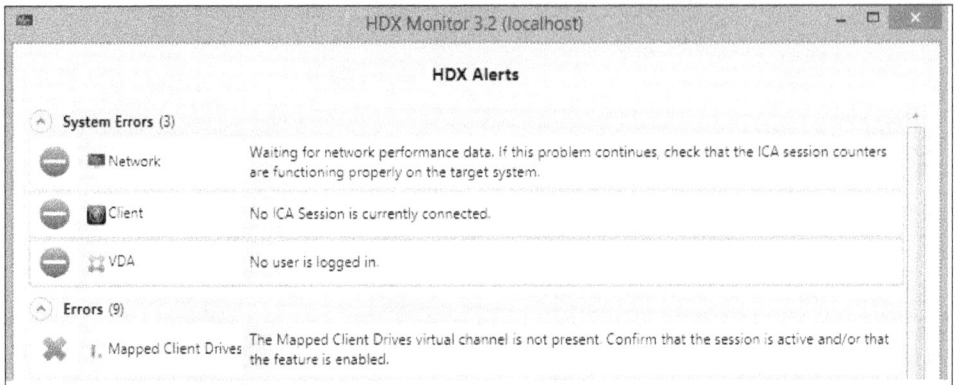

14. To configure the HDX Monitor, click on the **Settings** link in the component menu.

15. The first option tab is the **Performance Counter Update** section. Here, you can configure the time interval, in seconds, on which you will be updating the system counters.

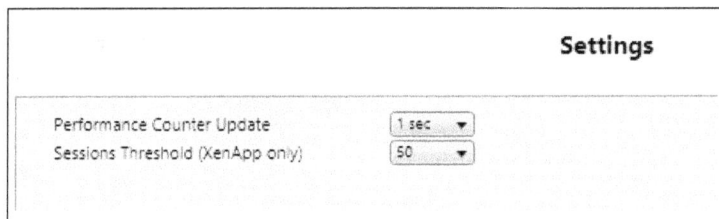

16. On the second tab, **HDX Components**, you have the updating time parameters for the system metrics to collect the statistics. You can also configure what kind of components are being showed within the monitor.

		Settings

Show components that are: ☑ Active ☑ Enabled
☑ Inactive ☑ Disabled
☑ Unknown

Provider Refresh

Component	Refresh
System Information (Required)	10 sec ▼
VDA (Required)	10 sec ▼
Sessions (Required)	5 sec ▼
Client	5 sec ▼
Network	5 sec ▼
Branch Repeater	5 sec ▼
Adobe® Flash®	5 sec ▼
Audio	5 sec ▼
Graphics - Direct 3D	5 sec ▼
Graphics - Thinwire	5 sec ▼
Graphics - Thinwire Advanced	5 sec ▼
Printing	10 sec ▼
Scanner	10 sec ▼
Smart Cards	10 sec ▼
USB Devices	10 sec ▼
Mapped Client Drives	5 sec ▼
Windows Media	5 sec ▼

17. In the **Monitor** tab, you can select an **Access Type** option from the drop-down menu list (**Auto, Winrm, COM/DCOM**). Moreover, you can also decide if it automatically reconnects the last analyzed system at startup.

Settings

Access Type: Auto ▼

☑ Automatically load last connected target system at startup
☐ On exiting, switch to a tray app (works only when connected locally to a VDA/XA-Server)

18. In the **Logging** tab, you can specify a valid path and filename on which you will be logging all the monitor activities.

19. In the last section, **Alerts**, you can enable a long available list of preconfigured alerts for your monitored machines.

Settings

Ignore	Component	Level	Message	URL	Condition
☑	Adobe® Flash®	HighWarning	The HDX Flash V1 latency threshold		HDXFlashVersion
☐	Adobe® Flash®	HighError	The version of Internet Explorer inst	http://www.microsoft.com/windows	ieVersionNumbe
☐	Adobe® Flash®	HighError	The installed Flash Player is not sup		installedVersion
☐	Adobe® Flash®	LowWarning	Adobe® Flash® redirection has bec		!isEnabled
☐	Audio	LowWarning	Audio redirection has been disablec		!isEnabled
☑	Audio	LowWarning	? redirection has been disabled with		!isEnabled
☐	Audio	HighError	The ? virtual channel is not present.		isEnabled && !is
☐	Audio	HighError	The Audio virtual channel is not pre		isEnabled && !is
☑	Audio	HighWarning	No audio devices found.		!ifAnyDeviceExis
☐	Audio	HighError	The Audio service (CtxAudioSrv) has		status == Servic
☑	Audio	HighWarning	Codec ? is not optimized to reduce		ifAnyDeviceExist
☑	Audio	HighWarning	Virtual channel priority should be se	http://support.citrix.com/search/bas	(priority != Virtu
☐	Audio	System	No user is logged in.		SessionID == nu
☑	Audio	HighWarning	Virtual channel priority should be se	http://support.citrix.com/search/bas	(priority != Virtu
☐	Audio	LowWarning	Audio over UDP could not be used		CurrentUDPProc
☐	Audio	HighWarning	Audio capture is disabled. Input fro		ifAnyDeviceExist

[
> Part of the preconfigured alerts contains a link to a related Citrix or Microsoft support links, in order to make the problem analysis easier.
]

20. After completing all the configurations, click on the **Save settings** button to make all the changes permanent, then restart the HDX Monitor to apply them.

21. The HDX Monitor permits you to export the report generated on the collected data. To perform this, you have to use the **Generate report** link in the components menu. The report will be generated in an HTML format.

How it works...

The HDX Monitor is a powerful tool developed by Citrix to check the status of a configured Master Image in a deep way. The release associated with XenDesktop 7.x is the 3.2 Version. This tool is in the form of an `.msi` package, installable on a Windows compatible machine. It is able to connect remotely to a target machine (a desktop Master Image configured to be used to deploy machine instances) to collect real-time data in order to give the status of the most important user experience components.

The Monitor collects data for the following objects:

- Adobe Flash
- Audio
- Branch Repeater
- Client
- Graphics—Direct 3D
- Graphics—Thinwire
- Graphics—Thinwire advanced
- Mapped client drives
- Network
- Printing
- Scanner
- Smart cards
- System information
- USB devices
- VDA
- Windows media

For each of these components, a **Diagnostics** section is available to retrieve the state of the Network Performance or the registered Event Logs, as shown in the following screenshot:

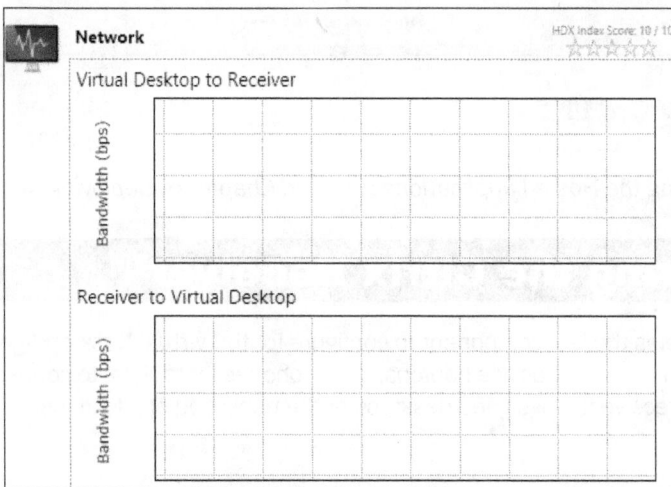

From the collected data, it is possible to generate reports, which can be used to trace the evolution or the degradation of the general system performance.

There's more...

The HDX Monitor permits you to export and reimport the saved configurations and the collected data, by exporting them in the XML format.

To accomplish this task, you have to go to the component view, click on the **Export** link, and assign a name to the XML parameters file.

This WMI data can be reimported on any other HDX Monitor installation within your infrastructure.

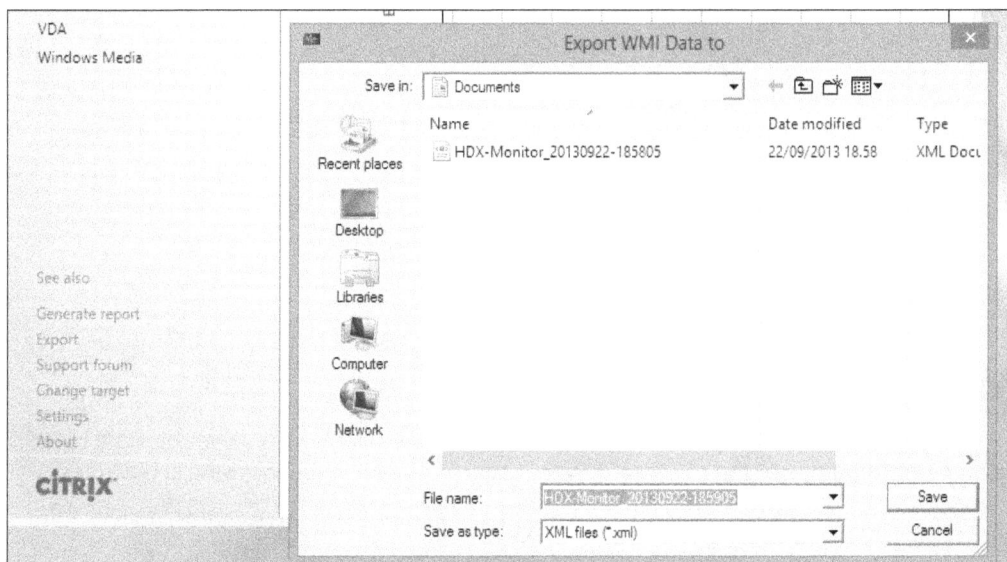

See also

▸ *Publishing the Hosted applications* recipe in *Chapter 6, Deploying Applications*.

Configuring the Citrix Receiver™

The Citrix Receiver is the last component to configure for the Virtual Desktop Agent. This plugin is the connector used by any device (laptops, smart phones, or tablets) to connect to the server's sites, in order to receive the assigned desktops or the published applications.

Getting ready

No preliminary operations are required to perform the configurations for the Citrix Receiver. In fact, you have already installed all the necessary components to use the Citrix plugin. On the other side, a XenDesktop configured server and a StoreFront store are required to use the plugin for its main purpose—the interaction with the published resources.

How to do it...

In the following steps, we will configure the Citrix Receiver component, used by user's devices to connect to the published resources:

1. Log in to the configured StoreFront server with domain administrative credentials.
2. Run the StoreFront Console by searching for it within the Windows Apps catalog (Windows + C key combination, click on the **Search** button, and search for the **Citrix StoreFront** application).

[You can also manage the StoreFront configured store using the **Citrix Studio** console.]

3. On the **StoreFront** console left-side menu, click on the **Stores** link, then select **Export Provisioning File** on the right-side menu.

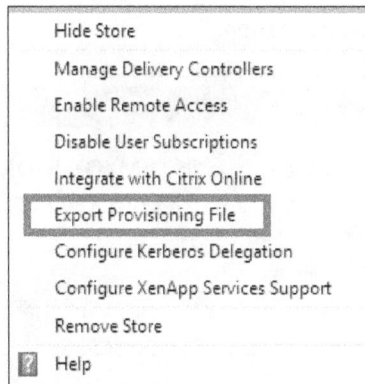

Hide Store
Manage Delivery Controllers
Enable Remote Access
Disable User Subscriptions
Integrate with Citrix Online
Export Provisioning File
Configure Kerberos Delegation
Configure XenApp Services Support
Remove Store
? Help

4. When prompted to save the provisioning file, click on the **Export** button to complete the procedure.

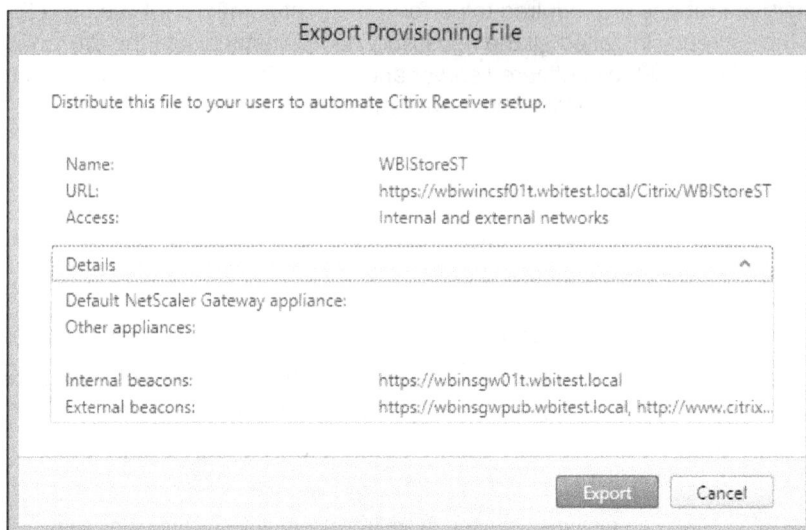

5. Select a valid path, on which you will be saving the `.cr` file, and then click on the **Save** button.

6. Copy the generated store file to the Master Image template, then double-click on it to configure the Citrix Receiver. Click on the **Add** button when prompted for the Citrix Receiver configuration confirmation.

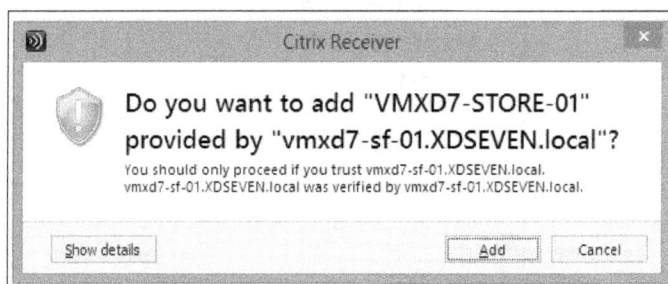

> Be sure you installed the right StoreFront SSL certificate in the Trusted Root Certification Authorities store on the destination machine, otherwise you won't be able to use the preconfigured store file.

7. When prompted for the logon, enter valid domain credentials in order to be authenticated by the StoreFront server.

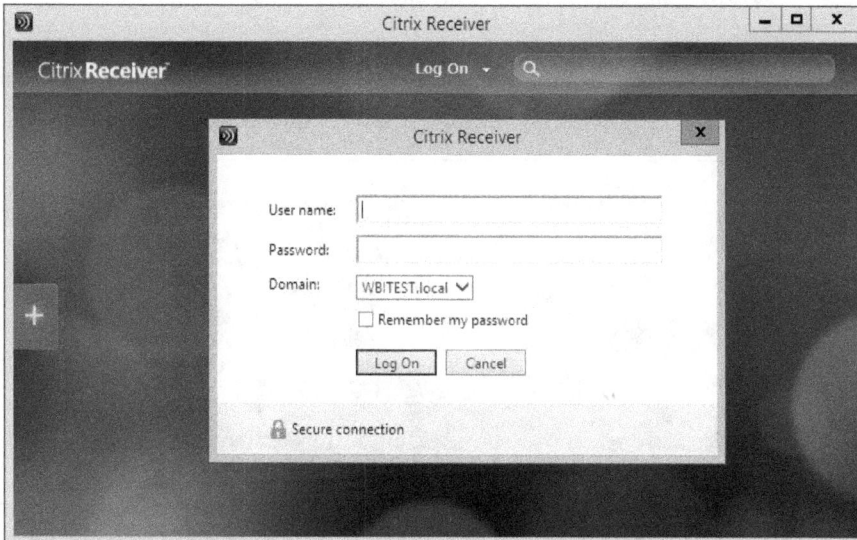

8. Click on the Plus (**+**) symbol on the left side, to show the list of the available resources (applications and desktops).

9. In the **User Settings** section, you can flag both the presented options. These are recommended parameters you should activate for your client.

[By default, you will find the Citrix Online applications (Citrix **GoToMeeting**, **GoToTraining**, and **GoToWebinar**) already available for your account.]

10. To configure additional accounts within the Citrix Receiver, click on the username link on the top of the windows, and then select the **Accounts** options from the list.

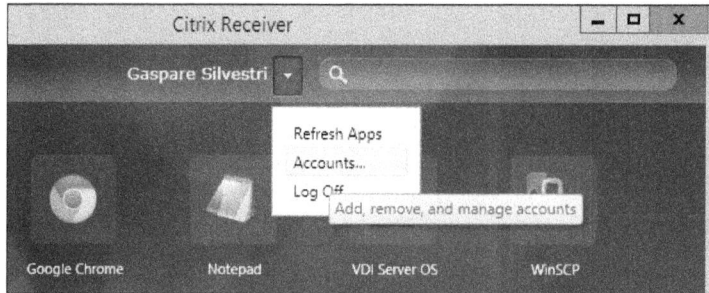

11. In the **Edit Accounts** window, click on the **Add** button, then insert a valid e-mail address linked to the account you want to add. As an alternative, you can retype a valid StoreFront address.

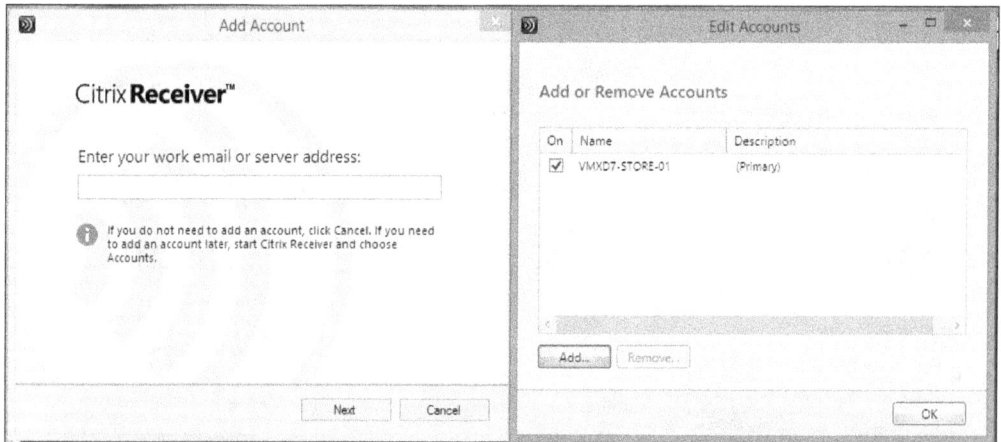

12. Now that all the configurations steps have been completed, the Citrix Receiver is ready to work with the server farm's components.

How it works...

The Citrix Receiver is a set of features used to receive the applications and the desktops installed and presented to the end users or streamed and published for them.

The XenDesktop 7.6 release presents two different versions of the Citrix Receiver. The client, discussed in this chapter in terms of implementation and configuration; the other one is the Web Client, which we will talk about in the next recipe.

After you have logged in with your domain credentials, you will see your applications published on your desktop or on your Start menu, if configured as later in this book. All the changes made to your applications, such as a new software assigned to your user or a previously existent application removed from your area, are immediately applied to your running desktop(s). Moreover, you can also customize the appearance and the quality of your applications in order to privilege the speed in some situations or decide to have a higher quality image with a probable impact on the general performance. All these features permit us to have an extremely flexible approach. You can have a Windows client machine without any installed application and populate it with a software from other clients and servers, based on the permissions assigned to a user on that specific application. This can permit you to reduce the operating system attack surface, separating the applications from the operating system area, using XenDesktop 7.6 integrated application packaging platforms, such as Microsoft App-V.

> The Citrix Receiver Store can be also configured by the use of the Domain Group Policies. In this way, it is possible to avoid updating the Master Image after you have changed the StoreFront configuration.

There's more...

While using remote applications published with XenDesktop 7, you may end up with a content redirection problem, when double-clicking on a file associated to specific software. Without any further operation on the client, you could probably receive an error for the file path locations. To avoid this problem, you have to perform the following tasks:

- Modify the registry key `NativeDriveMapping` located at either of the following two loactions:
  - `HKEY_LOCAL_MACHINE\SOFTWARE\Citrix\ICA Client\Engine\Configuration\Advanced\Modules\ClientDrive` (32 bit machines)
  - `HKEY_LOCAL_MACHINE\ SOFTWARE\Wow6432Node\Citrix\ICA Client\Engine\Configuration\Advanced\Modules\ClientDrive` (64 bit machines)

Assign **TRUE** value to this registry key.

	Name	Type	Data
▷ Ica	(Default)	REG_SZ	(value not set)
▲ ICA Client	CacheDisable	REG_SZ	FALSE
▲ Engine	CacheTimeout	REG_SZ	600
▲ Configuration	CacheTimeoutHigh	REG_SZ	0
▲ Advanced	CacheTransferSize	REG_SZ	0
▲ Canonicalization	CacheWriteAllocateDi...	REG_SZ	FALSE
ClientComm	CDMReadOnly	REG_SZ	FALSE
ClientDrive	DisableDrives	REG_SZ	
Server	DriverName	REG_SZ	VDCDM30.DDL
TCP/IP	DriverNameWin16	REG_SZ	VDCDM30W.DLL
Thinwire3.0	DriverNameWin32	REG_SZ	VDCDM30N.DLL
WFClient	HighThroughputWin...	REG_SZ	262144
▲ Modules	MaxRequestSize	REG_SZ	1440
AudioConverter	MaxRequestSize2	REG_SZ	4116
AudioConverterList	MaxWindowSize	REG_SZ	8650
AudioHardware	MaxWindowSize2	REG_SZ	62500
Baud Rates	NativeDriveMapping	REG_SZ	TRUE
Baud Rates - WIN16	SFRAllowed	REG_SZ	FALSE
Cirrus Logic 546X - ISDCorp (c) v2.00			
Cirrus Logic 546X 1.71			
Cirrus Logic 546X 1.71g			
ClientAudio			
ClientComm			
ClientDrive			

▸ Modify the `module.ini` file located in your Citrix Online Plugin installation path (usually `C:\Program Files (x86)\Citrix\ICA Client\Configuration`). Search for the **[ClientDrive]** section, and assign to the `NativeDriveMapping` key, the `TRUE` value.

```
[ClientDrive]
    DriverName                    = VDCDM30.DDL
    DriverNameWin16               = VDCDM30W.DLL
    DriverNameWin32               = VDCDM30N.DLL
    MaxWindowSize                 = 8650
    MaxWindowSize2                = 62500
    MaxRequestSize                = 1440
    MaxRequestSize2               = 4116
    CacheTimeout                  = 600
    CacheTimeoutHigh              = 0
    CacheTransferSize             = 0
    CacheDisable                  = FALSE
    CacheWriteAllocateDisable     = FALSE
    DisableDrives                 =
    CDMReadOnly                   = FALSE
    NativeDriveMapping            = TRUE
    SFRAllowed                    = FALSE
    HighThroughputWindowSize      = 262144
```

After completion, you will receive no more errors when trying to access a file type redirected to its native application.

See also

▸ The *Publishing the hosted applications* recipe in *Chapter 6, Deploying applications*.

Configuring the Citrix Receiver™ for HTML5 1.5 – clientless

As an alternative to the classic resource access performed by the use of the Citrix Receiver component earlier discussed, in this latest version of XenDesktop, a component has been developed and improved in terms of functionality—Citrix Receiver for HTML5.

In this recipe, we are going to discuss this clientless access mode.

Getting ready

Citrix Receiver for HTML5 is part of the StoreFront component, so no setup tasks or prerequisites are required to perform its configuration. You need administrative credentials to logon to and manage StoreFront.

How to do it...

In the following steps, we will configure the Citrix Receiver for the HTML5 component, used to access resources without the necessity of the Citrix Receiver client:

1. Log in to the configured StoreFront server with domain administrative credentials, and then connect to the StoreFront console by searching for it within the Windows Application list (Windows + C key combination—**Search** icon), and then click on its icon.

2. Select the **Stores** option in the left-side menu, and then click on **Create Store** in the right-side section.

3. In the **Store Name** section, give a valid name to the store as shown in the following screenshot, and then click on **Next**:

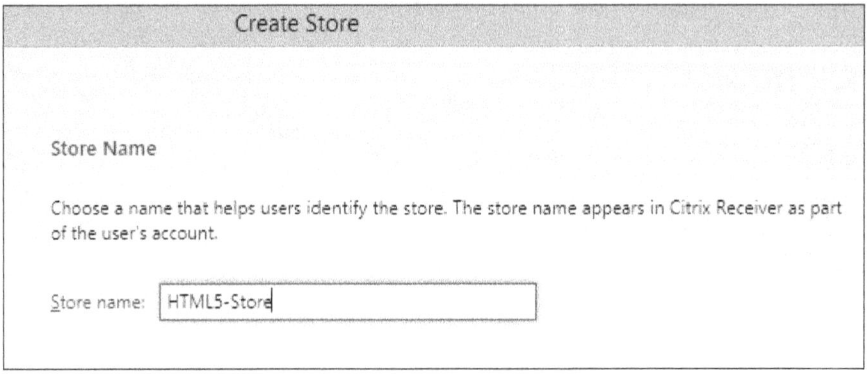

```
Create Store


Store Name

Choose a name that helps users identify the store. The store name appears in Citrix Receiver as part
of the user's account.

Store name:   HTML5-Store
```

4. In the **Delivery Controllers** screen, add a valid XenDesktop Delivery Controller by clicking on the **Add** button and selecting a configured XenDesktop Delivery Controller. Click on **OK** to proceed, and then click on **Next** to continue with the procedure:

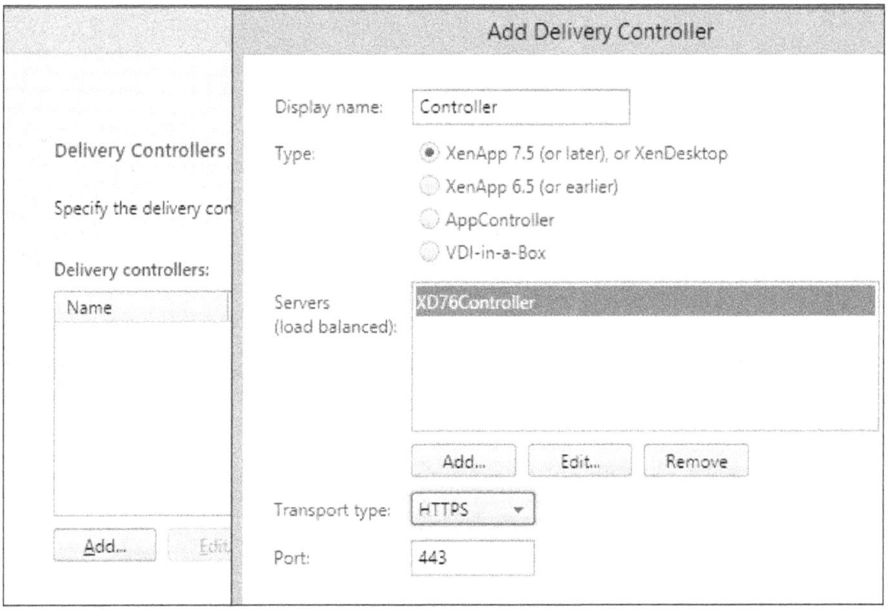

```
                                        Add Delivery Controller

                      Display name:     Controller

Delivery Controllers   Type:            ● XenApp 7.5 (or later), or XenDesktop
                                        ○ XenApp 6.5 (or earlier)
Specify the delivery con               ○ AppController
                                        ○ VDI-in-a-Box
Delivery controllers:
                      Servers           XD76Controller
  Name                (load balanced):



                                        Add...        Edit...       Remove

                      Transport type:   HTTPS   ▼
  Add...      Edit     Port:            443
```

> We already discussed this procedure in *Chapter 1,*
> *XenDesktop 7.6 – Upgrading, Installation, and Configuration.*

5. On the **Remote Access** section, leave the **None** option configured as default, and then click on **Create** to complete the Store creation procedure. After completion, click on the **Finish** button to close the Wizard.

6. Click on the **Receiver for Web** option in the left-side menu, and then select the **Deploy Citrix Receiver** option on the left-side menu:

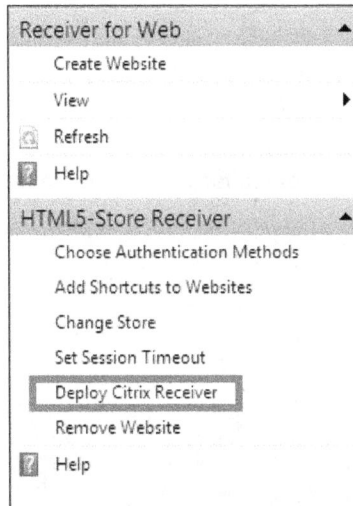

Receiver for Web	▲
Create Website	
View	▶
Refresh	
Help	
HTML5-Store Receiver	▲
Choose Authentication Methods	
Add Shortcuts to Websites	
Change Store	
Set Session Timeout	
Deploy Citrix Receiver	
Remove Website	
Help	

7. In the configuration screen, select the **Always use Receiver for HTML5** option, and then click on **OK** to continue:

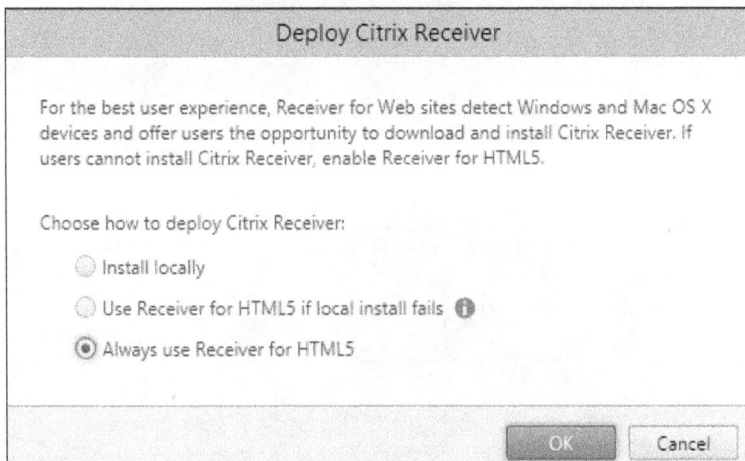

Deploy Citrix Receiver

For the best user experience, Receiver for Web sites detect Windows and Mac OS X devices and offer users the opportunity to download and install Citrix Receiver. If users cannot install Citrix Receiver, enable Receiver for HTML5.

Choose how to deploy Citrix Receiver:

○ Install locally

○ Use Receiver for HTML5 if local install fails ⓘ

◉ Always use Receiver for HTML5

OK   Cancel

8. Login to the Citrix Delivery Controller with administrative credentials, and then connect to the Citrix Studio by searching for it within the Windows Application list (Windows + *C* key combination—**Search** icon). Then, click its icon.

9. Select the **Policies** link in the left-side menu, followed by the currently configured policy (by default the **Unfiltered** policy), and then click on the **Edit Policy** link on the right side.

> We will discuss more in detail about policies in *Chapter 7, XenDesktop Infrastructure Tuning*.

10. In the policy editor screen, search for Web Socket in the search field.

Select settings

| (All Versions) ▼ | All Settings ▼ | websocket ✕ |

Settings: 3 selected ☐ View selected only

✓ ▶ **WebSockets connections**   Edit | Unselect
Computer setting - ICA\WebSockets
Allowed (Default: Prohibited)

✓ ▶ **WebSockets port number**   Edit | Unselect
Computer setting - ICA\WebSockets
(Default: 8008)

✓ ▶ **WebSockets trusted origin server list**   Edit | Unselect
Computer setting - ICA\WebSockets
(Default: *)

11. Click on **Edit** for all the three listed options and configure them as following:

   ❑ Edit the **WebSockets connections** option and set it to **Allowed**. After completion, click on the **OK** button:

   > WebSockets connections
   >
   > Applies to: Virtual Delivery Agent: 7.0 Server OS, 7.0 Desktop 7.5 Server OS, 7.5 Desktop OS, 7.6 Server OS, 7.6 Desktop OS
   >
   > ◉ Allowed
   >   This setting will be allowed.
   >
   > ○ Prohibited
   >   This setting will be prohibited.

   ❑ Edit the **WebSockets port number** option and select a valid value for your infrastructure (the default port number is 8008). Click on **OK** to continue.

   > WebSockets port number
   >
   > Applies to: Virtual Delivery Agent: 7.0 Server OS, 7.0 Desktop 7.5 Server OS, 7.5 Desktop OS, 7.6 Server OS, 7.6 Desktop OS
   >
   > Value: 8008
   >
   > ☑ Use default value: 8008

   ❑ Edit the **WebSockets trusted origin server list** option and configure one or more valid FQDN, from which XenDesktop/XenApp will accept WebSockets connections. The default value is * (all addresses). After completion, click on the **OK** button.

   > Edit Setting
   >
   > WebSockets trusted origin server list
   >
   > Applies to: Virtual Delivery Agent: 7.0 Server OS, 7.0 Desktop OS, 7.1 Server OS, 7.1 Desktop OS, 7.5 Server OS, 7.5 Desktop OS, 7.6 Server OS, 7.6 Desktop OS
   >
   > Value: https://FQDN.domain
   >
   > ☐ Use default value: *
   >
   > ▼ Details and related settings

[🔍 A valid address configuration is typically given by inserting the address
for the Citrix Receiver for Web configured store.]

12. Click on **Next** to proceed with the policy configuration, and in the **Summary** screen, click on the **Finish** button to apply the changes.

Settings configured: 3

WebSockets connections
Computer setting - ICA\WebSockets
Allowed (Default: Prohibited)

WebSockets port number
Computer setting - ICA\WebSockets
(Default: 8008)

WebSockets trusted origin server...
Computer setting - ICA\WebSockets
(Default: *)

Assigned to: user and machine objects

The settings are applied to all objects in the site.

Back   Finish   Cancel

13. Open an HTML5 compatible browser and type the address for the configured web store, in the form of `http(s)://FQDN/Citrix/(StoreName)`.

14. Type valid domain credentials to access the StoreFront web store, and then click on the **Log On** button.

Citrix **Receiver**

User name: username
Password: ••••••••
Domain: WBITEST.local
Log On

15. Click on one of the available published applications, and a new window will be opened in the browser. At this point, you will be able to use the application within the browser's session.

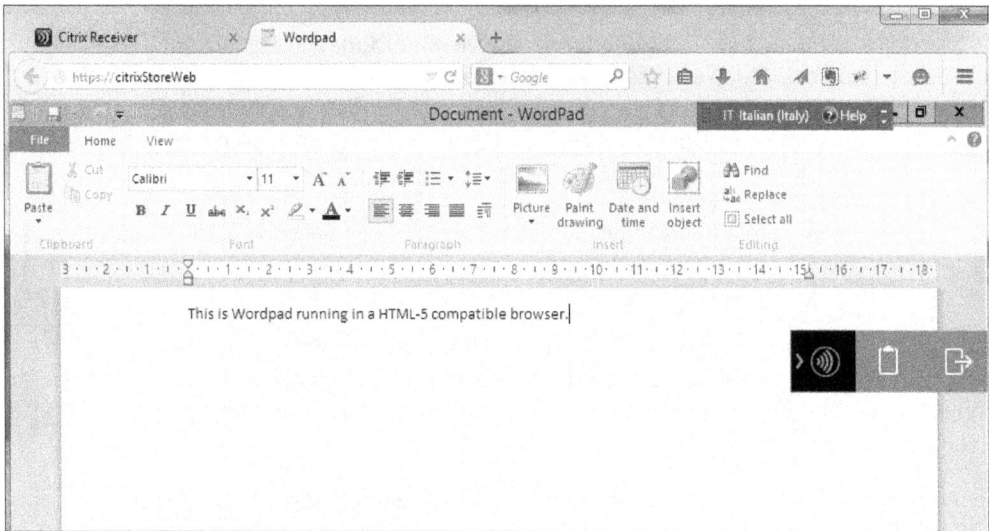

How it works...

The Citrix Receiver for HTML5 is a powerful XenDesktop feature, which permits users accessing desktops and applications without installing the classic Citrix Receiver client, accessing published resources by the use of a compatible HTML5 web browser.

To be able to use this access mode, you need to connect to the StoreFront resource using one of the following supported platforms:

- ▸ Windows 7 SP1, Windows 8, and Windows 8.1 (32 bit and 64 bit)
- ▸ Mac OS X (10.8 and 10.9)
- ▸ Internet Explorer (10 and 11 32-bit mode)
- ▸ Mozilla Firefox and Google Chrome
- ▸ Safari (6 and 7)

The configuration at the StoreFront level is performed in a standard way, as discussed in the previous chapters for the classic StoreFront store creations. The main difference is given by the fact that we have explicitly chosen to use only the HTML5 portal version, without trying the Citrix Receiver deployment.

The communication between StoreFront and XenDesktop/XenApp is established using the WebSockets protocol, which is a faster way to access web resources using a full duplex communication channel. For this reason, we edited and enabled the WebSockets protocol on the XenDesktop Delivery Controller. By default, the WebSockets protocol is disabled.

> More information about WebSocket protocol can be found at the following link: `http://en.wikipedia.org/wiki/WebSocket`.

An important option to configure in the Citrix Policies is the capability to filter the access to the WebSockets channel, by specifying only the StoreFront web store created for this specific purpose. In the previous section, we implemented this step by configuring the trusted origin server list.

The most interesting features offered by the HTML5 Receiver version are as follows:

- **PDF printer**: User have the capability to transfer documents to a PDF printer, which generates a document that users can transfer from a remote application to a local device, in order to be printed.

- **Clipboard**: Users can copy and paste data directly within the browser, from and to the local physical device. This option permits text and other objects to be transferred to the web published resources.

There's more...

With the Receiver for HTML5, you can install a component that permits you switching within the session opened in the browser among all the opened applications, in a way similar to the windows switch performed on a standard operating system.

The **AppSwitcher** can be downloaded at the following link: `http://www.citrix.it/downloads/citrix-receiver/html5/receiver-for-html5-15.html`. It must be installed on the server on which the published applications are installed (typically, the application server on which you have installed the Virtual Desktop Agent component).

The AppSwitcher will appear as shown in the following screenshot:

See also

▸   The *Configuring the XenDesktop® policies* recipe in *Chapter 7, XenDesktop® Infrastructure Tuning.*

5
Creating and Configuring a Desktop Environment

In this chapter, we will cover:

- ▶ Creating and configuring the machine catalog
- ▶ Modifying an existing machine catalog
- ▶ Using the Citrix Director 7.6 platform

Introduction

In the first four chapters of this book, we installed and configured all the main architectural components used to implement the XenDesktop 7.6 suite and to use different useful technologies.

Now, it is time to proceed with the creation of the Virtual Desktop instances. The copies of the virtual image template will be released to, and used by, the end users. In this chapter, you will learn how to perform this task to maintain and modify the desktop collections—both the server and desktop OS—and gain the ability to use existing machines (physical or virtual), collecting them in Delivery Groups.

Creating and configuring the machine catalog

All the virtual resources released to the end users are part of a group collection called a **machine catalog**. This contains information about the kind and the number of Virtual Desktop instances and/or physical remote computers, the configurations, and the assignment based on the Active Directory objects (users, groups, and computers). In this recipe, we are going to perform a full creation and configuration of all of these elements.

Getting ready

To perform the configuration tasks correctly, you need administrative credentials for the Delivery Controller server, and to be able to use the created Virtual Desktop(s), you first need to install and configure the required VDA on the client device, as shown in *Chapter 4, User Experience – Planning and Configuring*.

In the case of MCS architectures, you also have to generate a snapshot within your hypervisor environment for the Master-image virtual machine created to deploy the Virtual Desktop instances. The VM creation has been discussed in *Chapter 3, Master Image Configuration and Tuning*.

How to do it...

The following steps explain how to create and manage a XenDesktop Machine Catalog:

1. Connect to the Delivery Controller server as an administrative domain user.

2. Hit the Windows + *C* key combination, search for the Citrix Studio icon in the Citrix software section, and click on it:

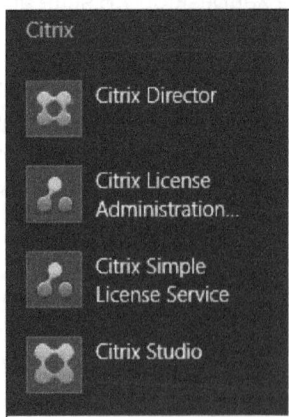

3. Based on the connection to the hypervisor explained in *Chapter 2, Configuring and Deploying Virtual Machines for XenDesktop® 7.6*, on the left-hand menu, select the **Machine Catalogs** link. After selecting the link, click on the **Create Machine Catalog** link on the right-hand panel.

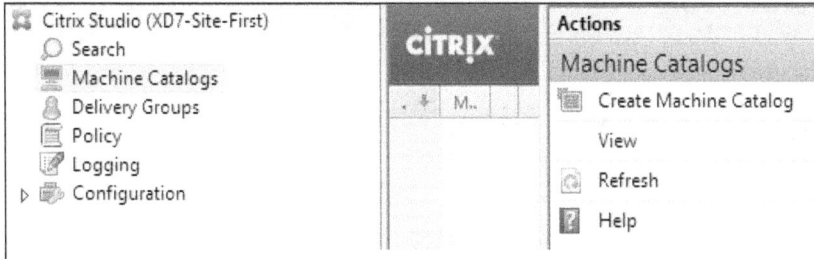

4. On the **Introduction** screen, click on the **Next** button to proceed.

Windows Desktop OS – catalog configuration

The following is the configuration procedure for the Windows Desktop OS:

1. In the **Operating System** section, select the type of desktop you want to create (**Windows Desktop OS**). After selecting the appropriate radio button, click on **Next**.

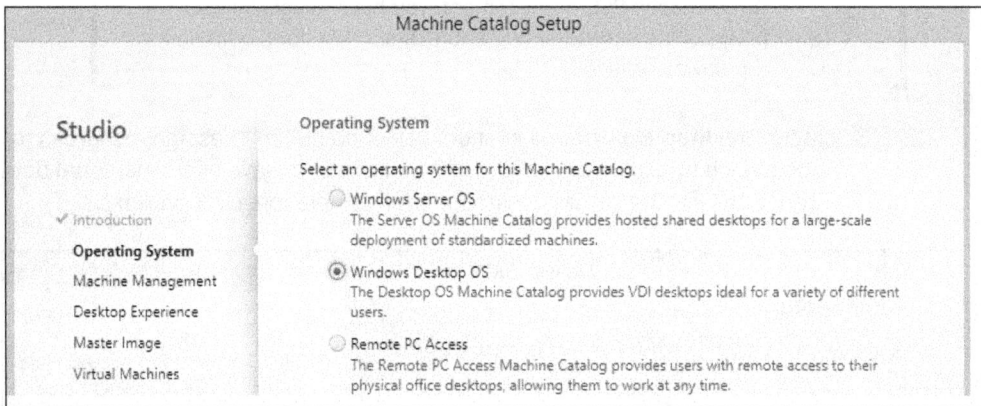

2. In the **Machine Management** section, select the kind of infrastructure to use to deploy the resources (virtual machines or physical hardware). Then choose the methodology to use to manage the catalog resources (MCS, PVS, or instances already configured). After completion, click on the **Next** button.

> Refer to the *How it works...* section, included in this recipe, to understand the differences between the listed catalogs and machine types.

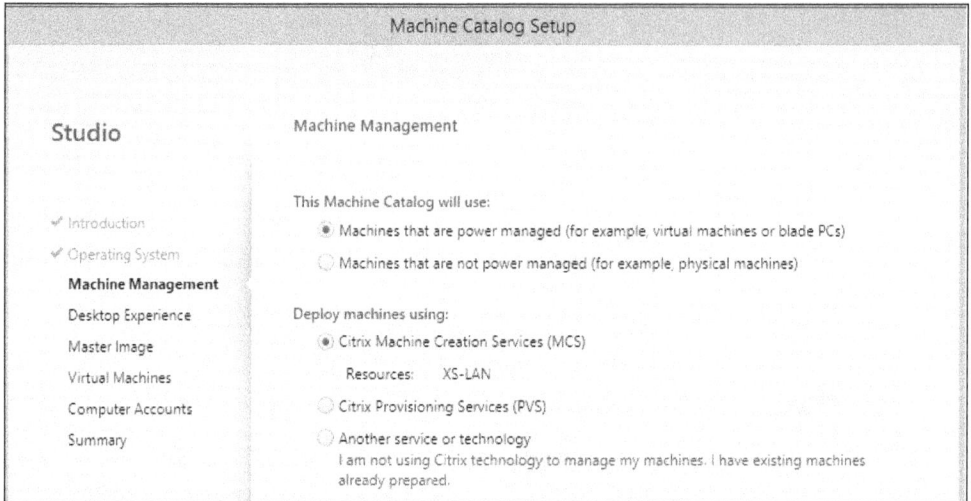

Machine Catalog Setup

Studio

Machine Management

✓ Introduction

✓ Operating System

Machine Management

Desktop Experience

Master Image

Virtual Machines

Computer Accounts

Summary

This Machine Catalog will use:

- ● Machines that are power managed (for example, virtual machines or blade PCs)
- ○ Machines that are not power managed (for example, physical machines)

Deploy machines using:

- ● Citrix Machine Creation Services (MCS)
  - Resources: XS-LAN
- ○ Citrix Provisioning Services (PVS)
- ○ Another service or technology
  I am not using Citrix technology to manage my machines. I have existing machines already prepared.

> If you choose PVS management, you have to specify a valid provisioning service server address and Windows domain for the device collection.

3. In the **Desktop Experience** section, select an option to assign resources to users each time they log on and whether or not to save users' personal data within the existing virtual desktops. After completion, click on **Next**.

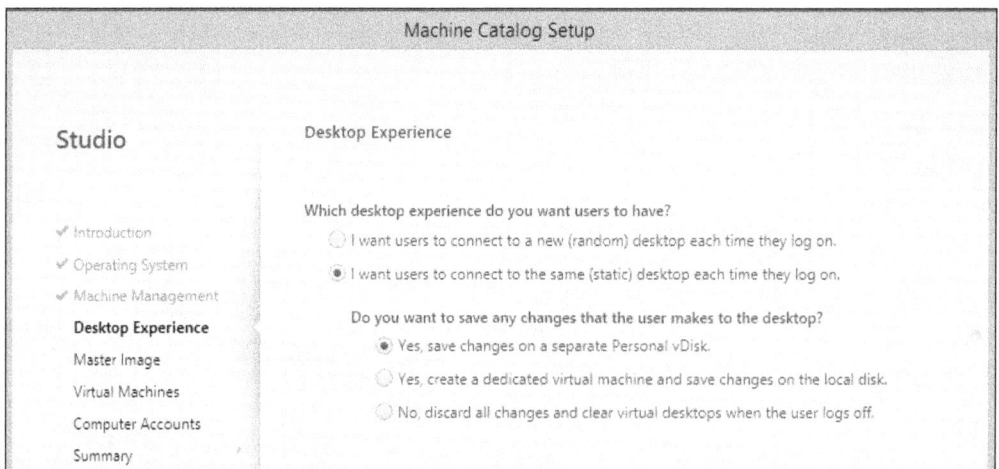

Machine Catalog Setup

Studio

Desktop Experience

✓ Introduction

✓ Operating System

✓ Machine Management

Desktop Experience

Master Image

Virtual Machines

Computer Accounts

Summary

Which desktop experience do you want users to have?

- ○ I want users to connect to a new (random) desktop each time they log on.
- ● I want users to connect to the same (static) desktop each time they log on.

  Do you want to save any changes that the user makes to the desktop?
  - ● Yes, save changes on a separate Personal vDisk.
  - ○ Yes, create a dedicated virtual machine and save changes on the local disk.
  - ○ No, discard all changes and clear virtual desktops when the user logs off.

If you select the first option, random desktop allocation, you won't be able to select the location in which the users save their profile data.

4. Select a Master Image from the list from which the desktop instances will be generated, and then select the VDA version installed on the starting point golden image. After completion, click on **Next**.

In the presence of mixed XenDesktop 5.6/7.x environments, you should always select the lowest VDA level to use in the catalog, in order to permits to the machine with a previous VDA release to work correctly.

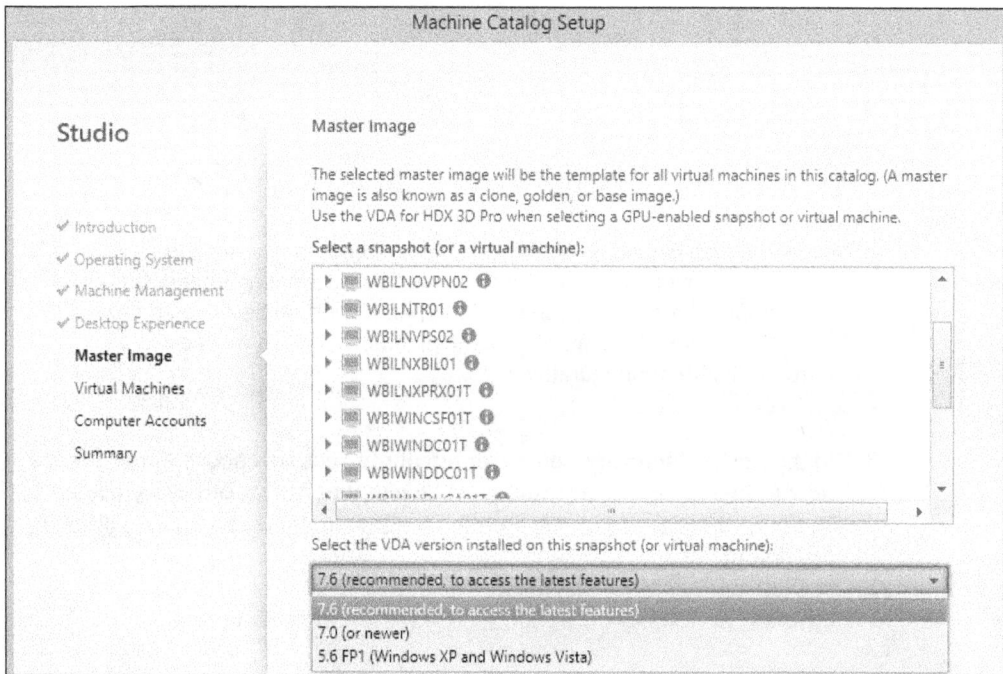

The image selected from the list is a snapshot that refers to the original virtual machine disk. In the case of snapshot absence, XenDesktop will create one by itself.

5. In the **Virtual Machines** section, select how many machines must be generated by incrementing the value of the **Number of virtual machines needed** section. After this, you need to configure the resources to assign to any instance—**Virtual CPUs** and **Memory (MB)**. Click on **Next** to proceed.

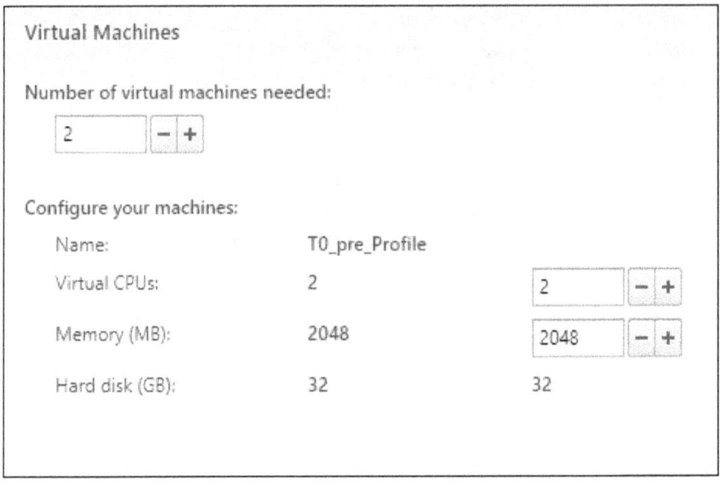

Virtual Machines

Number of virtual machines needed:

2   − +

Configure your machines:

Name:	T0_pre_Profile	
Virtual CPUs:	2	2 − +
Memory (MB):	2048	2048 − +
Hard disk (GB):	32	32

> Note that you can't modify the operating system's disk size parameter because it depends on the Master Image template configuration. On the template, make sure you have mapped the virtual disk with the ID 0 : 0 (first created disk for the machine); otherwise, you will receive an error during this configuration step.

6. In the **Active Directory Computer Accounts** section, choose either **Create new Active Directory accounts** or **Use existing Active Directory accounts**. To better understand all the creation features in this section, we will select the first option.

7. In the **Active Directory location for computer accounts** section, select the domain on which you are working from the drop-down list and choose the OU on which you want to create the computer accounts. Then, select an **Account naming scheme**, of the `MachineName##` form, where the two final characters identify a progressive code made up of letters or digits (`A-Z` or `0-9`). After completion, click on the **Next** button.

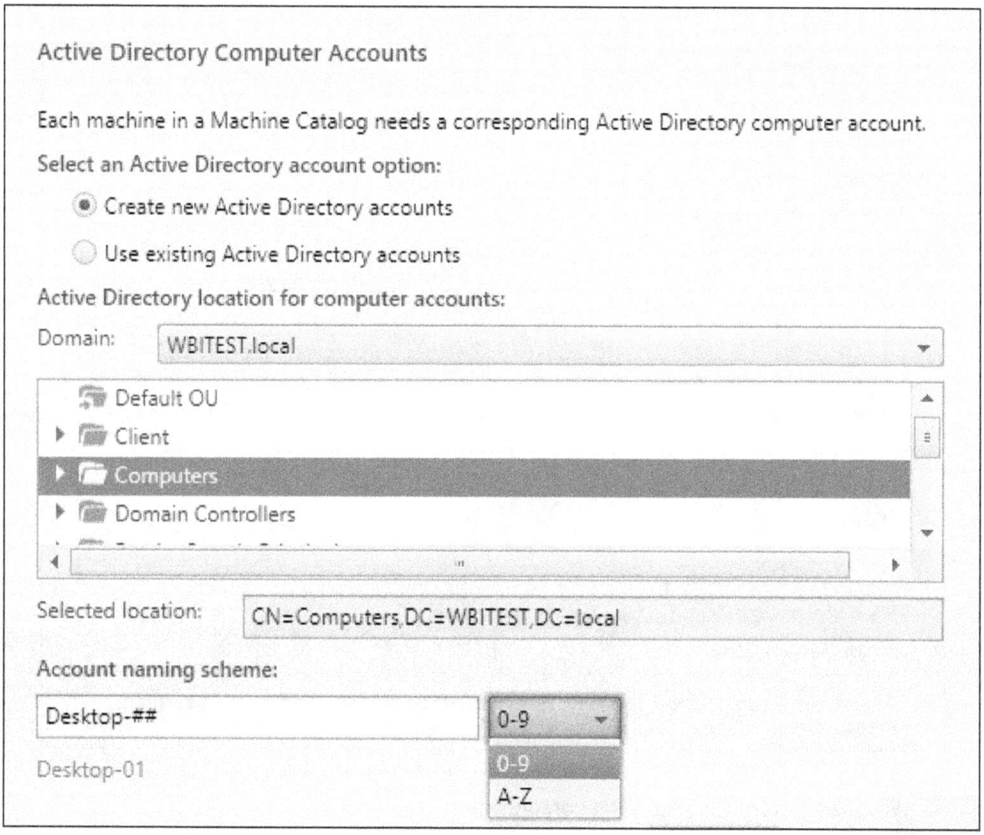

Active Directory Computer Accounts

Each machine in a Machine Catalog needs a corresponding Active Directory computer account.

Select an Active Directory account option:

- ● Create new Active Directory accounts
- ○ Use existing Active Directory accounts

Active Directory location for computer accounts:

Domain: WBITEST.local ▼

- Default OU
  - ▶ Client
  - ▶ **Computers**
  - ▶ Domain Controllers

Selected location: CN=Computers,DC=WBITEST,DC=local

Account naming scheme:

Desktop-## | 0-9 ▼

Desktop-01

| 0-9 |
| A-Z |

8. In the **Summary** section, assign a name and an optional description in the respective fields (**Machine Catalog Name** and **Machine Catalog description for administrators**), then click on the **Finish** button to complete the configuration operations.

Machine Catalog Setup

Summary

Machine type:	Windows Desktop OS
Machine management:	Virtual
Provisioning method:	Machine creation services (MCS)
Desktop experience:	Users connect to the same desktop each time they log on Discard all changes when the user logs off
Resources:	XS-LAN
Master Image name:	WBIWINXDS01T A snapshot of the Master Image VM will be created
VDA version:	7.6 (recommended, to access the latest features)

Machine Catalog name:

Desktop Catalog

Machine Catalog description for administrators: (Optional)

Desktop Catalog

To complete the deployment, assign this Machine Catalog to a Delivery Group by selecting Delivery Groups and then Create or Edit a Delivery Group.

Windows Server OS – catalog configuration

The following is the configuration procedure for the Windows Server OS:

1. In the **Operating System** section, select the type of desktop you want to create (**Windows Server OS**). After selecting the appropriate radio button, click on **Next**.

2. In the **Machine Management** section, select the kind of infrastructure to use to deploy the resources (virtual or physical machines), and then choose the methodology to use to manage the catalog resources (MCS, PVS, or Master Images already configured). After completion, click on the **Next** button.

> In this subsection, we will select the use of physical machines plus the existing Master Image option. In the case of virtual machine selection, you have to repeat the steps seen earlier in the *Windows Desktop OS* section, for both the MCS and PVS deployment options.

3. In the **Machines** section, add an existing domain-joined server to the catalog, by clicking on the **Add Computers...** button. Then, click on **Next** to continue.

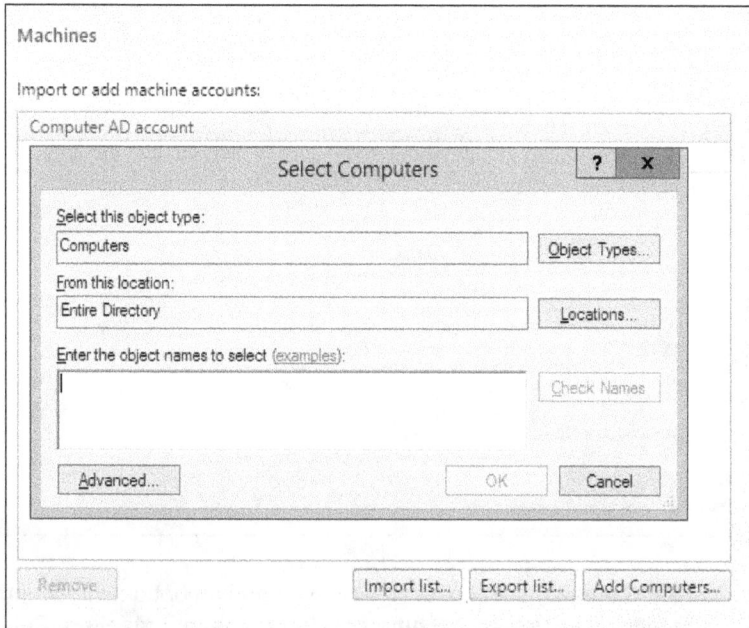

Machines

Import or add machine accounts:

Computer AD account

Select Computers   ?   X

Select this object type:

Computers   Object Types...

From this location:

Entire Directory   Locations...

Enter the object names to select (examples):

| | Check Names

Advanced...   OK   Cancel

Remove   Import list... Export list... Add Computers...

4. In the **Summary** section, enter a name and an optional description in the respective fields (**Machine Catalog Name** and **Machine Catalog description for administrators**), and then click on the **Finish** button to complete the configuration operations.

Remote PC Access – catalog configuration

The following is the configuration procedure for Remote PC Access:

1. In the **Operating System** section, select the type of desktop you want to create (**Remote PC Access**). After selecting the appropriate radio button, click on **Next**.

2. On the **Machine Accounts** screen, add an existing domain machine account or a group of them, by clicking on the **Add OUs...** button; after this, select the minimum VDA installed release, and then click on **Next** to continue.

Machine Accounts

Machines in your network domain have an associated machine account. The machine account name is usually the same name as the machine. The machine accounts you choose must match the machines that users use for remote access. To add groups of machines by Organizational Units (OUs), select Add OUs.

Select the machine accounts and/or OUs associated with your users:

To get started, add a machine account or OU.

Learn more

[Add machine accounts...] [Add OUs...] [Remove]

Select the minimum VDA version installed on machines associated with these accounts:

7.6 (recommended, to access the latest features) ▼

Machines will require the selected VDA version (or newer) in order to register in Delivery Groups that reference this machine catalog. Learn more

3. In the **Summary** section, assign a name and an optional description in the respective fields (**Machine Catalog Name** and **Machine Catalog description for administrators**), and then click on the **Finish** button to complete the configuration operations.

5. To verify that the catalog has been successfully created, click on the **Machine Catalogs** link on the left-hand menu.

6. To check that all the required objects have been generated, right-click on the catalog name in the **Machine Catalogs** section and select the **View machines** option. You will get back the full list of generated desktop instances.

Now, we will perform the creation operations for Delivery Groups:

1. On the left-side menu, click on the **Delivery Groups** link, and then select the **Create Delivery Group** option on the right-hand side of the window.

2. On the **Getting Started** screen, click on the **Next** button to continue.

3. In the **Machines** section, select an existing catalog from the list and choose how many machines need to be added to **Delivery Group** from the available machine pool(s). After completing this, click on **Next**.

4. In the **Delivery Type** section, select the purpose for the **Delivery Group** we're going to create (**Desktops**, **Desktop and applications**, or **Applications**). In our case, select the **Desktops** option, and click on **Next**.

> In *Chapter 7, Deploying Applications*, we will discuss applications Delivery Group.

5. In the **Users** section, add one or more user(s) or groups to which to assign permissions on the delivered desktops. Moreover, you can also decide to give access to unauthenticated users through StoreFront. Click on the **Next** button to continue with the configuration steps.

Users

Specify who can use the applications and desktops in this Delivery Group. You can assign users and user groups who log on with valid credentials. Alternatively or additionally, you can enable access for unauthenticated users.

Assign users:

    WBITEST\CTX_Users

[Add...] [Remove]

☑ Give access to unauthenticated (anonymous) users; no credentials are required to access StoreFront
This feature requires a StoreFront store for unauthenticated users.

6. On the **StoreFront** menu, click on the **Automatically, using the StoreFront servers selected below** radio button. Then, click on the **Add new...** button and populate the pop-up screen with the required StoreFront server information. After this, click on the **OK** button, and then click on **Next**.

StoreFront

You can configure Receiver on the machines in this Delivery Group so that users can access additional applications that aren't on the machines. Receiver can use a different StoreFront server (that you select here or in the Configuration > StoreFront node) compared with the servers (listed in the Citrix StoreFront console) used for connections to the machines themselves.

How do you want to configure Receiver on the machines in this Delivery Group?

○ Manually, using a StoreFront server address that I will provide later

⦿ Automatically, using the StoreFront servers selected below

Select the StoreFront servers for Receiver:

☑ Receiver Storefront URL
☑ http://wbiwincsf01t.wbitest.local/

Add new...

7. On the **Summary** screen, select a name for the Delivery Group, a **Display Name** for the desktops, and an optional Delivery Group description. Click on the **Finish** button to complete the creation procedure.

> Be careful with the desktop assigned to every user. You must respect both the number of generated machines and the available licenses.

8. Click again on the **Delivery Groups** link on the left-hand menu. Now, you can see the results of the last performed operations with an information area about the utilization of the assigned desktops (on the **Details** tab).

ServerDeliveryGroup	Windows Server OS	1	0
State: Enabled		Unregistered: 1	Disconnected: 0

Details - ServerDeliveryGroup

Details Machine Catalogs Usage Administrators

Delivery Group		State	
Name:	ServerDeliveryGroup	Enabled:	Yes
Display Name:	Server Delivery Group	Maintenance Mode:	Off
Description:	-	Registered Machines:	1
Type:	Random Desktops	Unregistered Machines:	1
Set to VDA version:	7.6 (recommended, to access the latest features)	Powered off Machines:	0
Users:	CTX_Users (WBITEST\CTX_Users)	Total Machines:	1
Scopes:	All	Installed VDA version:	7.6.0.5026
StoreFronts:	http://wbiwincsf01t.wbitest.local/	Operating System:	Windows 2012 R2

9. Using a configured client device, open a web browser and type the address of your StoreFront configured store. Log in with the credentials of one of the users with an assigned desktop. After the login phase, you will receive a screen with the desktop and the applications available for that user.

> The Virtual Desktop icon shown in the previous image will be gray when waiting for an available resource.

10. Click on the published resource or wait for a few minutes in order to let Citrix connect to the desktop. Once completed, the desktop instance is available to be used.

Now, we will manage the power and access management:

1. Click on the **Delivery Groups** link located on the left-hand menu, right-click on the desired Delivery Group, and select the **Edit Delivery Group** option.

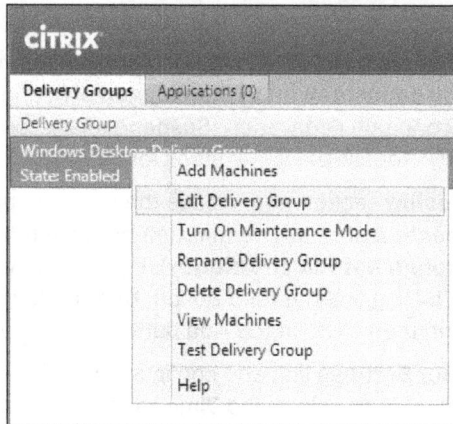

2. Select the **Power management** section, and choose from the **Power on/off** machines area. Select the week period to configure (**Weekdays** or **Weekend**). Click on the **During peak hours** bar to set the time interval to consider as the highest working activities period (in the screenshot, it's configured from 9 a.m. to 6 p.m.). After configuring all the options, click on **OK**.

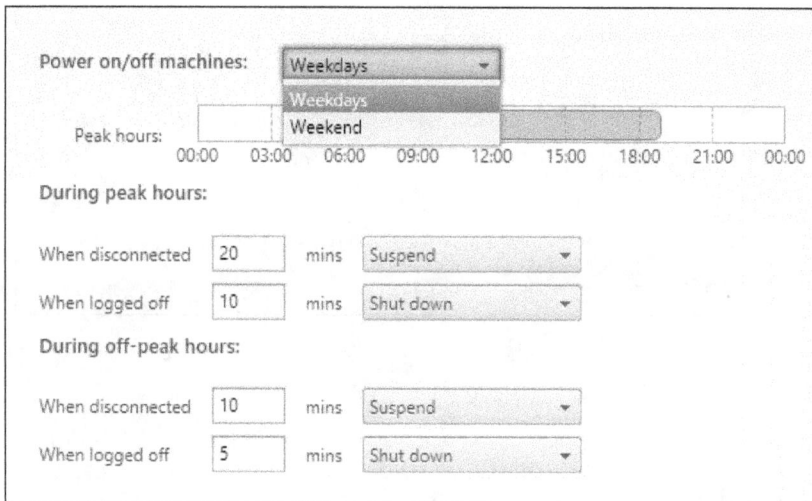

> In the presence of more than five virtual machines, if you want to start only one virtual desktop, the XenDesktop Broker will automatically power up three virtual desktops in order to prevent the possibility of the user having to wait till a virtual desktop is powered up.

3. In the **During peak hours** zone, assign a time period in minutes for the two configured conditions (**When disconnected** and **When logged off**), and select the action to execute in case of condition verification (**Suspend** for disconnection; **Suspend** or **Shutdown** for logoff). Repeat the same steps for the **During off-peak hours** section.

4. Select the **Access policy** section and choose the desired option(s) in the **Allow the following connection** area (**All connection not through NetScaler Gateway** or **Connections through NetScaler Gateway**). If you want, you can configure personalized filters by flagging the third option, **Connections meeting any of the following filters**, and then click on the **Add** button to insert the filter rule.

5. Click on the **End User Settings** link and configure the **Description**, **Color depth** (**16 or 256 colors**, **High**, or **True** color), and **Time zone** settings for the Delivery Group of the clients. Then, if you want to use an encrypted connection between the client and the XenDesktop farm, flag the **Enable Secure ICA** option. After this, click on the **OK** button to register all the modifications.

End User Settings

Description: | Windows Desktop Delivery Group

☑ Enabled

Desktops per user: | 1 | − + |

Color depth: | True Color ▼

Time zone: | (UTC+01:00) Amsterdam, Berlin, Bern, Rome, Stockholm, Vienna ▼

☑ Enable Secure ICA

How it works...

The creation of the XenDesktop catalog is a fundamental operation in order to redistribute the desktop and application resources to end user devices. The most important choice to make is what kind of machines the catalog creates, depending on specific company requirements.

In this latest release of XenDesktop, the first choice to make is about the kind of desktop you want to deploy to the end user. Starting with the fact that the XenApp platform has been integrated in this release, you have the ability to deploy both the server OS and desktop OS instances, applying your choice for existing physical and virtual machines. Another important feature for this software version is given by Remote PC Access. This substantially permits users to link their clients to existing physical or virtual PCs in order to use them as their default client(s). This solution can prevent system administrators and end users from migrating contents and applications to the VDI architecture, centrally managing the company workstation through Citrix Studio.

Desktops can be deployed in one of the following ways:

- ▸ **Random**: This choice is equal to what was called the **Pooled** catalog in previous versions. This means that every time a user logs on, a new desktop can be released, basing the assignment only on the logon priority.

- ▸ **Static**: By selecting this option, the same desktop will be assigned to the same user at every log on phase. With this option, you have got the ability to select three more options: saving the changes written to the user date area on a separate disk—the Personal vDisk (nonpersistent machines), creating a dedicated machine (persistent mode), or discarding all the changes made to the desktop, including the user data area, when users log off (non-persistent mode).

Non-persistent machines let you consume less storage space, based on the fact that a single virtual machine is used, and starting from it, all the other instances are generated as linked clones, snapshots of the original disk. This configuration applies to the MCS infrastructure. In this case, you have to take care about the way to save the user data. Centralized profiles, such as Microsoft Roaming Profile or Citrix Profile Management, or the use of the Personal vDisk technology, permit you to avoid the loss of data. Without these choices, all changes will be lost.

The Personal vDisk is a virtual disk created on the Hypervisor's data store. This file size will be equal to the quota assigned in the user disk creation procedure, but it will be generated as a thin virtual disk. In this case, the virtual disk's file size will increase only when the space is actually used by a user and will only increase up to the predefined maximum size, with a 50-50 percent split between user data and user programs in the default configuration.

Persistent machines, on the other hand, give you the assurance that user data won't be lost at the expense of the higher consumption of storage space.

> This catalog type, based on the MCS architecture, has the limitation to use only one NIC for the virtual desktops. To be able to use more network cards, you have to refer to the Streamed catalogs (PVS architecture).

Moreover, we can also generate a catalog of existing virtual or physical machines by the use of the Delivery Controller. This will make it possible to import already generated workstations, assigning them to the domain users. This method of operation is quite different from the general purpose of a VDI infrastructure. You can consider this as an additional FlexCast management type.

The last available catalog is the PVS catalog. In this case, the Delivery Controller will create machines starting from an existing desktop—physical or virtual—generated under the Citrix Provisioning Services machine, as explained in the first chapter. For this kind of deployment, you have to connect to the PVS server created in *Chapter 1, XenDesktop® 7.6 – Upgrade, Installation, and Configuration*, right-click on the configured site, and select the **XenDesktop Setup Wizard...** option from the menu.

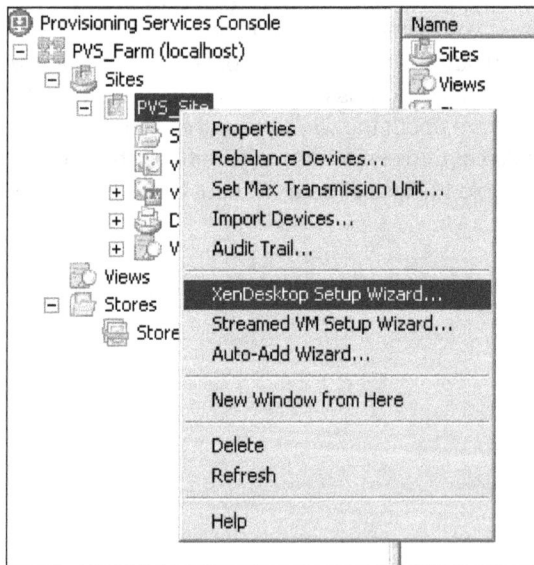

> Be sure you have configured at least one of your PVS-configured vDisks in have Standard Image access mode; otherwise, you will not be able to deploy a XenDesktop Streamed catalog.

You can also create a streamed catalog from the Citrix Studio wizard (by typing the PVS server address and specifying the Windows domain, on which to operate and the type of the existing target device (virtual or physical). This method should be used only to synchronize the Desktop Studio with an existing streamed catalog created under the PVS server.

For all the supported catalogs, except the existing and physical types, you have to specify the way in which to create computer accounts under your Active Directory domain. In this last scenario, you can reuse existing domain accounts or generate them from scratch, choosing the right naming convention for your company.

> Be sure to create the computer and user accounts within an OU included in the Citrix Policies application discussed earlier in this book.

An important component contained by the catalog is the Delivery Group. This object allows you to allocate all or part of the available machines in the catalog to the domain users. You can create more than one Delivery Group, the only required parameter is that you have available machine instances to populate the group.

There's more...

In the **Machine Creation** section previously explained, we've seen how to create desktop instances and how to configure all the related parameters. For some of these desktop's pools, however, some more options have to be discussed.

When selecting the static desktop assignment with the separate Personal vDisk option, we need to specify, in the **Number of virtual machines needed** section, values for **Specify the size and location of the Personal vDisk**.

Specify the size and location of the Personal vDisk:

Personal vDisk size (GB): 10 − +

Personal vDisk drive letter: P: ▼

[✎ We explained what the personal vDisk is and how it works in *Chapter 4, User Experience –Planning and Configuring.*]

If you decided to deploy streamed machines in a PVS configuration, you need to configure this from the **Provisioning Service** console, specifying as a **Machine Type** the Streamed with personal vDisk option, assigning a name and a description to the catalog, selecting a domain administrative account, and then choosing the vDisk parameters shown in the following screenshot:

Number of virtual machines to create:		1	
vCPUs:	1	1	
Memory:	1024 MB	1024	MB
Local write cache disk:	4096 MB	4096 MB	
Personal vDisk size:	10 GB	10	GB
Personal vDisk drive letter:	P:	P:	

See also

▸ The *Configuring the XenDesktop® policies* recipe in *Chapter 7, XenDesktop® Infrastructure Tuning.*

Modifying an existing machine catalog

Now that we have deployed and configured the machine catalog, we are able to use and work on the Citrix Desktop infrastructure. In some cases, it can be necessary to modify the configurations, for instance, when you need to add a new desktop to the catalog because of a new colleague in the company. In this recipe, we will explain how to modify the machines, their assignments, and the configured catalogs.

Getting ready

All the operations performed in this section are on objects that already exist; so, all you need is to have administrative credentials at two different levels. You have to be the administrator of the involved virtual machine's templates and the administrator of your XenDesktop architecture to be able to modify the Director configurations.

How to do it...

Let's start by updating the existing virtual desktop machines.

Updating virtual desktop machines

1. Log on to the Windows desktop template, apply all the system and configuration changes you need, and then log off.

2. Connect to your hypervisor machine(s) or management console with administrative credentials on the specific machine and generate a new snapshot for the virtual machine disk in order to register the applied modifications.

3. Connect to the Delivery Controller server, click on the **Machine Catalog** link on the left-hand menu, right-click on the desired Desktop Catalog, and select the **Update Machines** option.

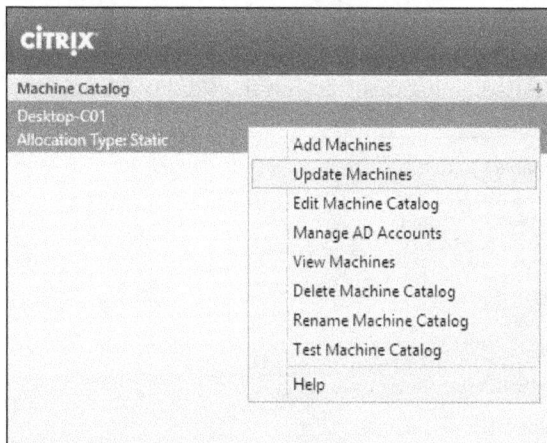

4. Select the Delivery Group you want to update in the **Overview** section, and then click on the **Next** button.

5. Select your Master Image and the last created virtual machine snapshot, then click on **Next**.

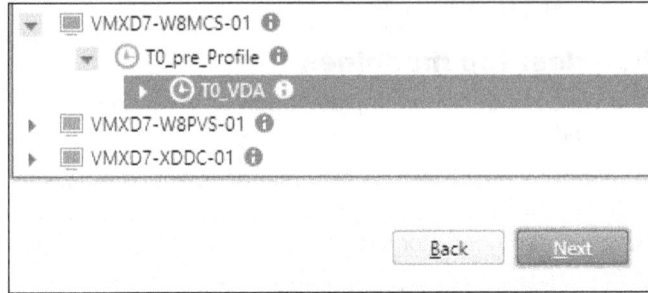

```
▼  🖳 VMXD7-W8MCS-01 ⓘ
    ▼  🕐 T0_pre_Profile ⓘ
        ▶  🕐 T0_VDA ⓘ
▶  🖳 VMXD7-W8PVS-01 ⓘ
▶  🖳 VMXD7-XDDC-01 ⓘ

                                    [ Back ]    [ Next ]
```

6. In the **Rollout Strategy** section, select a way to restart the desktops included in the update operations, deciding whether to update the images on the next reboot or to restart them immediately, whether or not to notify the users about this operation, and whether to restart all the machines at once or delay the operations within a specified time period. After selecting this, click on the **Next** button.

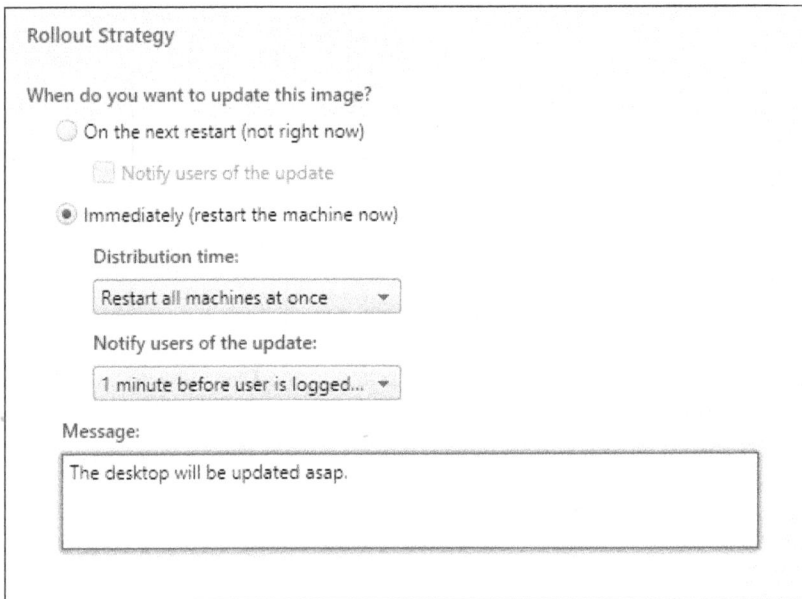

```
Rollout Strategy

When do you want to update this image?
    ○ On the next restart (not right now)
        ☐ Notify users of the update
    ⦿ Immediately (restart the machine now)
        Distribution time:
        [ Restart all machines at once      ▼ ]
        Notify users of the update:
        [ 1 minute before user is logged... ▼ ]
    Message:
    ┌─────────────────────────────────────────┐
    │ The desktop will be updated asap.        │
    │                                          │
    │                                          │
    └─────────────────────────────────────────┘
```

7. After reviewing the information in the **Summary** section, click on **Finish** to complete the machine update.

8. Click on the Citrix Studio link on the left-hand menu, and in the main panel, select the **Actions** tab. Here, you can verify the status of the updating task.

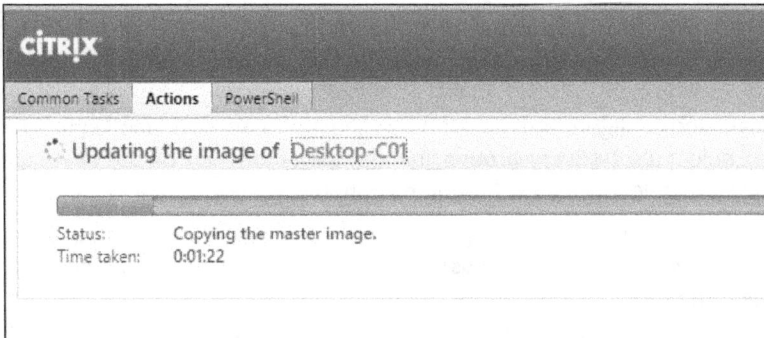

9. After all the operations have been completed, connect to a desktop instance through the StoreFront store and verify that all the updates are available.

Modifying the machine assignment

1. On the left-hand menu, select the **Delivery Groups** link; then, right-click on the group that you want to modify and run the **Edit Delivery Group** option:

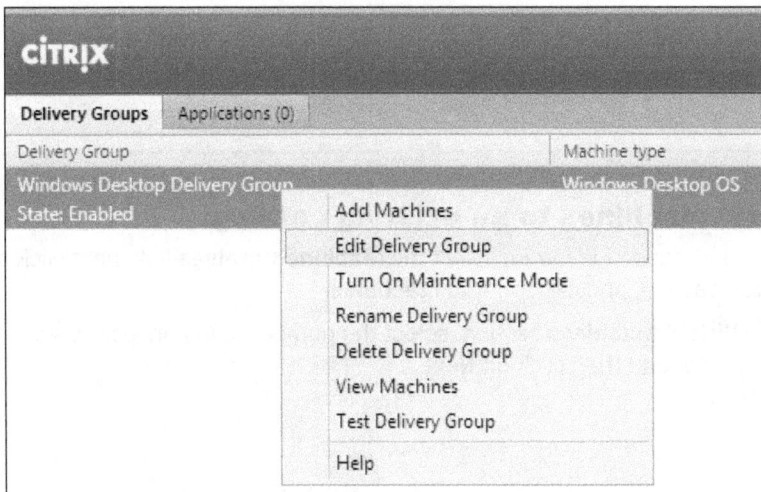

2. Select the **Machine Allocation** section, and then click on the button in the **Users** field to browse for a configured domain user to assign the virtual desktop instance.

3. To add more users to the Desktop Group, in order to let them use any available desktop instance in the pool, click on the **Users** area of the **Edit Delivery Group** option and browse for the desired domain users to add to the group. After completing all the configurations, click the **OK** button.

4. You can also configure the machine assignment in another way. On the left-hand menu, select the **Delivery Groups** link and then right-click on the desired machine catalog and select the **View Machines** option.

5. On the newly opened screen, right-click on the virtual machine instance you want to modify and select the **Change user** option. Now, you can remove the configured user and add the new virtual machine owner.

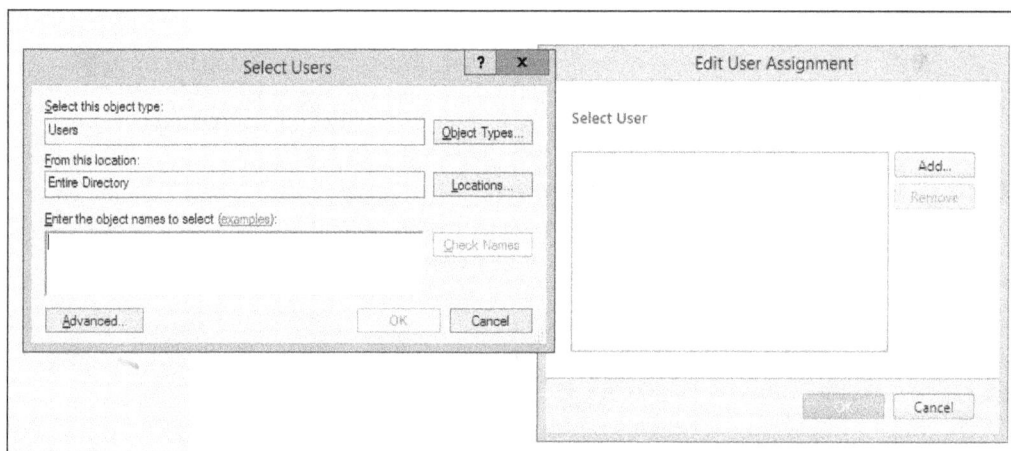

Adding new machines to an existing catalog:

1. On the left-hand side menu, select the **Machine Catalogs** link, right-click on the desired catalog, and click on **Add machines**.

2. In the **Virtual Machines** section, select the number of instances you want to add to this catalog, and then click on **Next**.

3. In the **Computer accounts** section, select **Create new Active Directory accounts** or **Use Existing Active Directory accounts**. Once done, click on the **Next** button.

4. If you've chosen to use existing accounts, you should consider maintaining the same naming convention used for the other desktop instances in the catalog, and you should also choose between resetting all the account passwords and using the same password for all the accounts. After you complete this, click on **Next**.

Active Directory Computer Accounts

Each machine in a Machine Catalog needs a corresponding Active Directory computer account.
Learn more

Select an Active Directory account option:

○ Create new Active Directory accounts

● Use existing Active Directory accounts

	Browse...
	Import...
	Remove

Required: 1   Added: 0

Computer account password management

● Reset all account passwords

○ All accounts have the same password

5. On the **Summary** screen, click on the **Finish** button to complete the procedure.

6. After the task has been completed, click on the **Delivery Groups** link on the left-hand side, right-click on the Desktop Group that you want to modify, and select the **Add Machines** option.

7. Highlight the catalog and insert the number of machines you want to add. This number must be equal to or less than the number of machines listed in the **Machines** column. After this, click on **Next**.

Machines

Select a Machine Catalog:

Catalog	Type	Machines
○ Desktop-C01 Desktop-C01	VDI MCS Static Discard	1

Choose number of machines to add: 1   − +

8. If all the information on the **Summary** screen appears to be correct, click on **Finish** to complete the process.

Removing assigned machines from an existing catalog

1. Click on the **Machine Catalogs** link on the left-hand menu, right-click on the desired catalog, and select the **View Machines** voice.

2. In the machine list, select the machine that you want to remove from the Desktop Group in the catalog, right-click on it, and select **Turn On Maintenance Mode**. Click on the **Yes** button to confirm the operation.

3. After the operation has been completed (you can verify this by checking for the presence of the **Enabled** value in the **Maintenance Mode** column), right-click on the desktop instance again and select the **Remove from Delivery Group** option. Click on **Yes** to confirm the operation.

4. After that, you will find no more information about Desktop Group assignment for the desktop machine. To completely remove the desktop, click on the **Machine Catalogs** link on the left-hand side menu, right-click on the involved catalog, and click on the **View Machines** link.

5. Select the desktop you had previously removed from the Delivery Group, right-click on it, and click on the **Delete** option.

6. In the **Deletion Options** section, select which kind of operation we need to perform. If you decide to delete the virtual machine (which will perform an instance deletion at the Hypervisor level), you have to choose whether to reuse the virtual machine instance or remove the machine from XenDesktop and leave, disable, or delete it in Active Directory. After this, click on the **Next** button.

```
Delete Options

What do you want to do with the virtual machine?

    ○ Remove the virtual machines from the Catalog but do not delete the virtual machines.
    ◉ Remove the virtual machines from the Catalog and delete the virtual machines.

        What do you want to do with the Active Directory computer accounts?

            ○ Leave the accounts in the Catalog and do not change them in Active Directory.
            ◉ Remove the accounts from the Catalog but do not remove them from Active Dir
            ○ Remove the accounts from the Catalog and disable them in Active Directory.
            ○ Remove the accounts from the Catalog and delete them from Active Directory.
```

7. If all the information on the **Summary** screen is correct, click on **Finish** to complete the task.

> To be able to complete this procedure, force the shutdown of the desired virtual desktop instances before proceeding.

Deleting a configured XenDesktop® catalog

1. Click on the **Machine Catalogs** link on the left-hand menu, right-click on the right catalog, and select the **View Machines** option.

2. Put every desktop instance in the Desktop Group in **Maintenance Mode**, and then repeat the deletion procedure as seen earlier.

3. After completing all the removal activities, return to the **Machine Catalogs** section, right-click on the catalog, and select the **Delete Machine Catalog** option.

4. In the **Summary** section of the opened window, click on the **Finish** button to complete the deletion procedure.

How it works...

The XenDesktop machine catalog is a modifiable entity, which allows you to update or rollback the configurations previously implemented.

In the presence of the MCS architecture, the machine update is perhaps the most used and most important modification task. This task is usually executed when modifications are made to the desktop base image template, for instance, software changes that must be applied to all the created desktop instances as well.

The following is a set of steps and considerations about this procedure:

- After all the required updates to the machine template have been completed, you have to regenerate a virtual machine snapshot under your hypervisor platform.

- After completing the previous step, update content for the desktop instances through the Citrix Studio console, starting with this last-created snapshot.

- Another important option is the Rollout strategy. With this option, you can choose the right way to give the less impact to the end users when updating and redeploying the desktop images.

- A desktop instance restart is required in order to apply the changes. You can choose between sending a message to the connected users about the required restart, restarting the desktops immediately, and restarting after a configured delay time.

- The rollout process can be really short for PVS configurations. For MCS architectures, in the presence of a large number of machines, the process can be very long, with a huge impact on the I/O storage performance.

> In order to avoid problems when stopping the desktops during working hours, it is better to update the machines during non-peak working hours and immediately restart the desktops.

You can also add or remove machines from the catalog. These are quite simple operations that contain all the powerful maintenance tasks of the VDI architecture. In fact, you can add instances by simply selecting the number of desired desktops. The greater part of this activity has already been performed during the creation and configuration of the desktop base image template. In the same way, you can remove single desktop instances from the catalog by right-clicking on them and selecting the appropriate deletion option. In this case, you can choose to completely delete a computer account (from both the XenDesktop architecture and Active Directory), or simply remove its assignment and preserve the desktop instance to be reused by another user.

There's more...

In case of problems for your users after updating the desktop image, the Citrix Studio allows you to roll back to a previous consistent machine state.

In the **Machine Catalogs** section already used during this chapter, you can repeat the procedure used to generate the desktop instances by selecting a snapshot generated earlier than the current machine state. This procedure is different from the rollback task used in XenDesktop Version 5.6. Instead of having a rollback point managed by Citrix Studio, you now have to maintain the snapshots at the hypervisor level.

Also, in this case, you need to select a **Rollout** strategy when stopping the desktop instances to complete the rollback activities. As previously described, you should plan a rollback strategy with a really low impact on user operation during working hours.

For the Provisioning services infrastructure, a rollback activity is managed in quite a different way. The vDisks are based on versions and categories. Every virtual disk has a version number and a category assigned to it (**Access version: Maintenance**, **Test**, and **Production**). In the case of failure after a disk update, you have the ability to revert a disk from Production to Test or Maintenance. In this way, the previously generated disk version will become the Production disk, permitting virtual machines to boot from it after they have been rebooted. This method permits you to easily manage multiple disk versions within your XenDesktop environment.

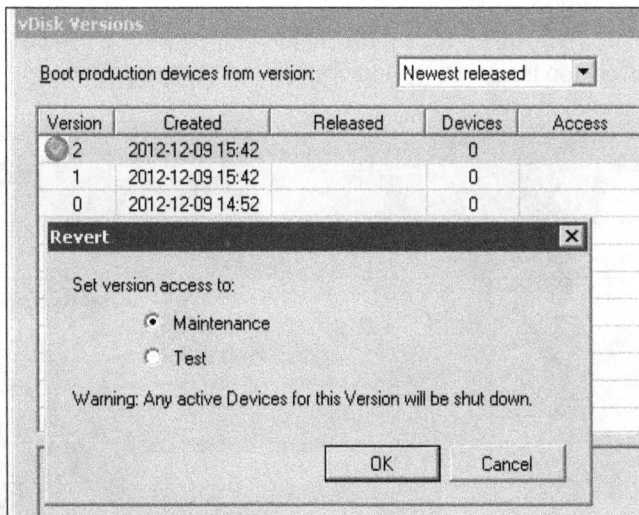

See also

▸ The *Managing the Citrix® Desktop Controller and its resources – Broker and App-V cmdlets* recipe in *Chapter 9, Working with PowerShell*

Using the Citrix® Director 7.6 platform

In the presence of huge VDI architectures, it can be hard to find standard and advanced information about the generated desktop instances, the configured users, and the relations that may occur between these two objects. Citrix Director is a useful web console that helps system administrators to easily find information about the status and the operation of a desktop infrastructure.

Getting ready

To use Desktop Director, you need an already installed and configured XenDesktop 7.6 architecture because of its necessity to interface with your Active Directory domain. You also need to configure and use a user name that is able to read your AD structure.

How to do it...

In this section, we will explain the Citrix Director platform and the way to use it:

1. Connect to the Delivery Controller machine, hit the Windows + C key combination, and search for the Citrix Director icon in the Citrix software section. Click on the icon to run the software.

2. On the login screen, insert a valid username and password, specifying the domain on which XenDesktop is operating, and click on the **Log on** button.

3. After you have logged in, you will be introduced to a dashboard, on which you can analyze and verify data about the current connected sessions, the average of the logon duration phase, and generic data about the failed desktop or server OS.

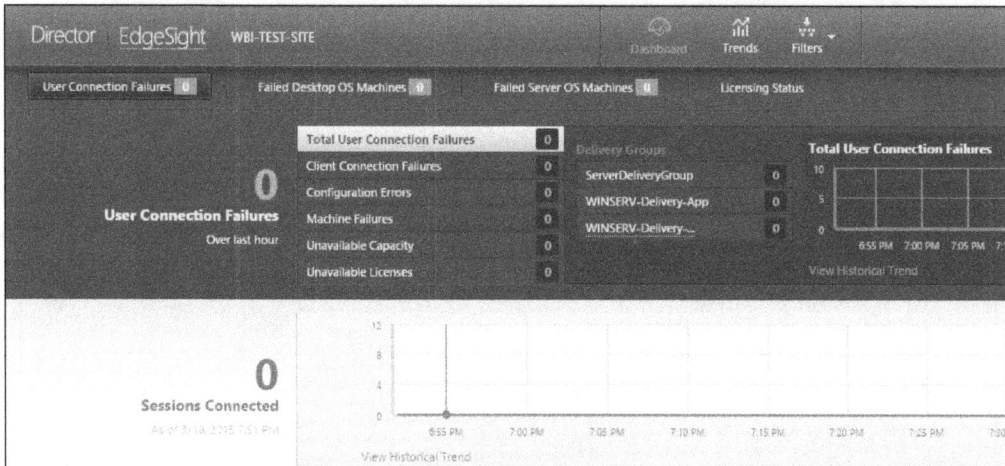

4. Click on the **Licensing Status** button to obtain information about the status of your license server and associated licenses.

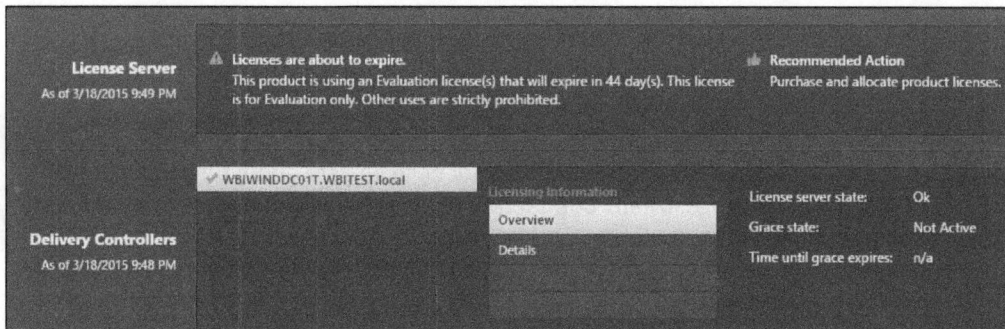

5. Click on the **Trends** icon at the top of the screen in order to analyze the data collected by the counters in the **Director** section.

6. On the first tab, **Sessions,** you will find information about the concurrent sessions that can be obtained for a specified time period (**Last 24 hours, Last 7 days, Last month, Last year,** or **Custom period**).

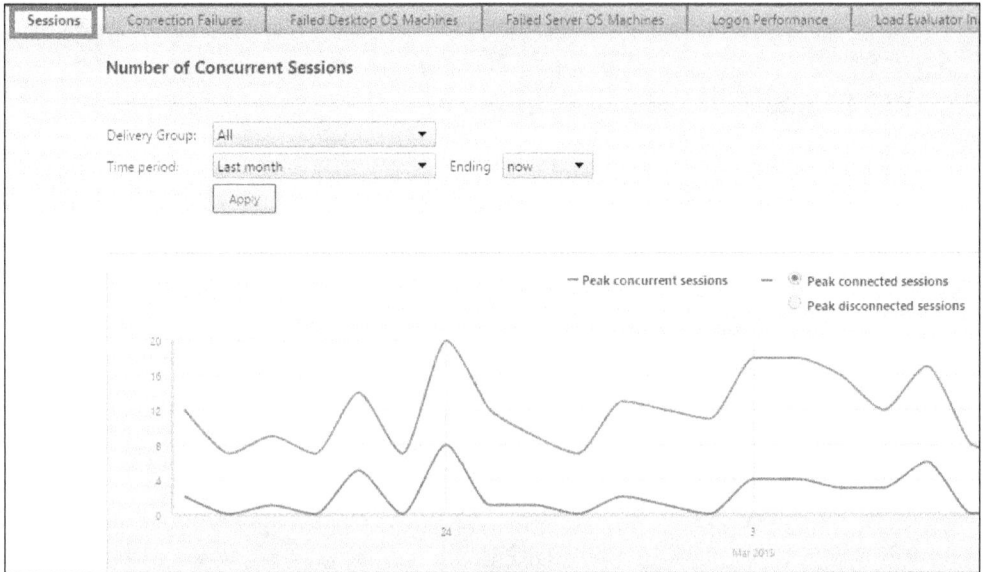

> [
> You can also filter the session data per Delivery Group.
>]

7. In the **Connection Failures** tab, the Director collects data about these problems during resource usage: **Client Connection Failures, Configuration Errors, Machine Failures, Unavailable Capacity**, and **Unavailable Licenses**. By clicking on the graphics in this section, it is also possible to obtain the details about the problems detected by the Director.

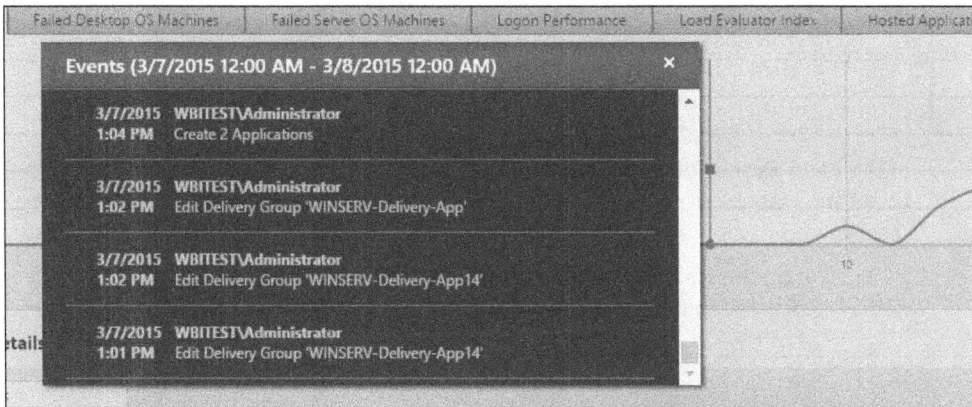

8. The same analysis can be performed by clicking on one of the other existing tabs: **Failed Desktop OS Machines** and **Failed Server OS Machines**. Also, in this case, the graph can give administrators or help desk technicians more details about the encountered problems.

9. The **Logon Performance** tab permits analysis of the time required by the user logon phase. Even in this case, you can filter the data for the desired time period:

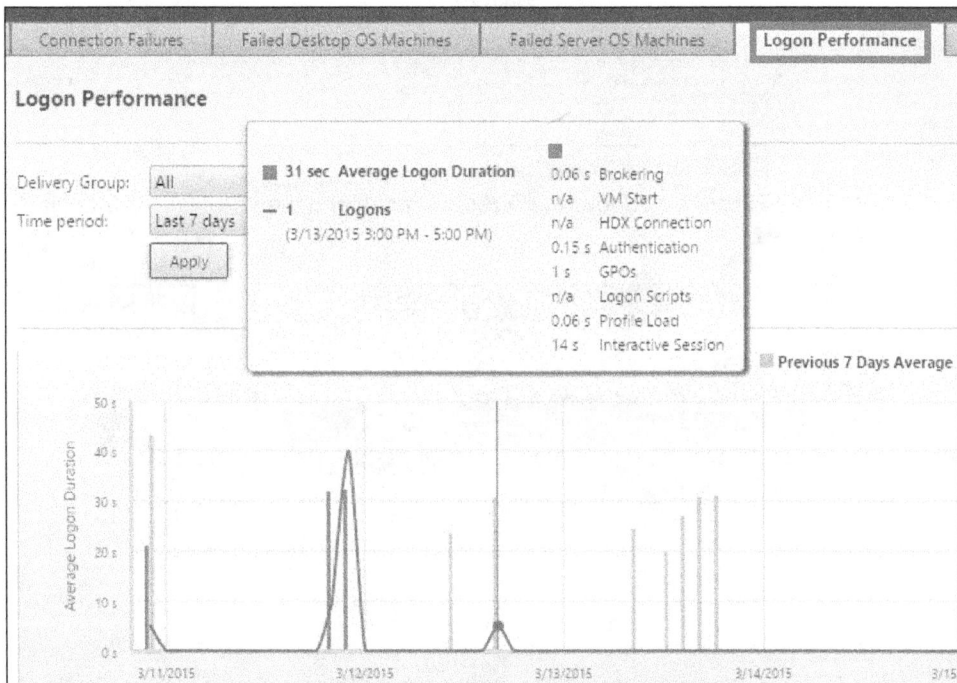

> This section is really useful when it comes to understanding and finding the bottlenecks during user attempts to log on to their virtual desktops.

10. In the **Load Evaluator Index** and **Network** tabs, you can collect useful information about the load average for resource usage (such as **CPU**, **Memory**, or **Disk**) or retrieve information about the global usage of the network resources, respectively.

11. By clicking on the **Hosted Application Usage** tab, it is possible to list and monitor details about the configured applications within your Citrix infrastructure.

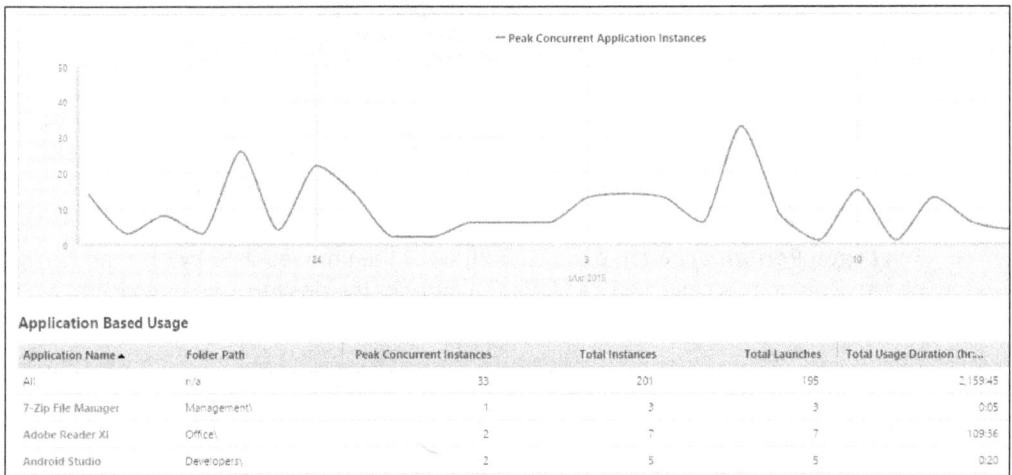

Application Based Usage

Application Name ▲	Folder Path	Peak Concurrent Instances	Total Instances	Total Launches	Total Usage Duration (hr...
All	n/a	33	201	195	2,159:45
7-Zip File Manager	Management\	1	3	3	0:05
Adobe Reader XI	Office\	2	7	7	1:09:56
Android Studio	Developers\	2	5	5	0:20

12. Click on the **Filters** icon above the **Director** menu, and then navigate to **Machines | All Machines**.

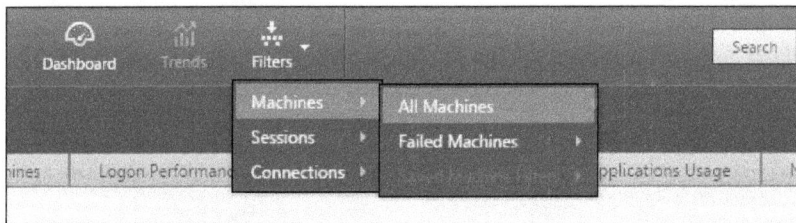

13. In the **View** section, click on the **Machines** radio button, and then click on one of the desired tabs (**Desktop OS Machines** or **Server OS Machines**), and select one or more desktops you want to manage. After that, you can use the **Power Control** button (the power management of the virtual desktop), the **Maintenance Mode** button (turning on or off the mode for the desired machine), and also sending a message to the user that is currently using the desktop.

Machine Name ▲	IP Address	Delivery Group	Power State	Sessions
WBITEST\WBIWINXAS01T	192.168.200.13	WINSERV-Delivery-App	On	2
	192.168.200.14	WINSERV-Delivery-App14	On	
WBITEST\WBIWINXDS01T	192.168.200.19	ServerDeliveryGroup	On	4

14. In presence of an elevated number of machines within your infrastructure, you can filter the information based on the **Filter by** section, filtering data for **DNS Name**, **Delivery Group**, **IP Address**, **OS version**, and so on.

Filters - All Machines*

View: ◉ Machines ○ Sessions ○ Connections

Filter by:

- Allocation Type
- DNS Name
- Delivery Controller
- Delivery Group
- Failure Reason
- Failure Time
- Failure Type
- Hosted Machine Name
- Hosting Server Name
- Hypervisor Connection Name
- IP Address
- Is Assigned
- Is Physical
- Is Preparing

15. Click on one of the listed machines in order to obtain details about its configuration (OS type, hypervisor, usage statistics, applied hotfixes, and so on).

16. In the **View** section, click on the **Sessions** radio button, flag one of the active user sessions, and choose whether to disconnect or log the user off (the **Session Control** button) or whether to send them a message on a specific resource. Also, in this case, you can filter the results based on the predefined filtering categories.

Filters - All Sessions

View: ○ Machines ● Sessions ○ Connections

Filter by:

Associated User
Associated User Display Name
Associated User UPN
DNS Name
Delivery Group
Endpoint IP
Endpoint Name
IP Address
Machine Catalog
Machine Name
OS
Receiver Version
Session Change Time
Session Start Time

1 Session

Session Control ▾

	Associated Us		Session Start Time	Session Change Time
☑	Administrator		10/16/2013 2:49 PM	10/16/2013 2:49 PM

> An alternative to **Sessions** is the **Connections** radio button. In this category, you can manage the connection status plus the active sessions.

How it works...

Citrix Director is a web application that allows system administrators to verify and analyze the status of their Citrix infrastructure, checking the utilization statistics for the entire XenDesktop infrastructure.

The main changes users will notice are in the system dashboard. Here, it is possible to verify the status of the infrastructure and the delivery controller and monitor, in real time, the number of concurrent connections, the time needed by the end users to log on to their resources, and moreover, the information about the Desktop or Server OS faults. This last feature gives the ability to understand more quickly the existing problems of the VDI architecture. Moreover, in this Director release, you have the ability to monitor the licensing status of your infrastructure, obtaining information about the exceeded licenses, unavailable license service, over drafted licenses or normal status of the platform.

The Citrix Director portal is composed of a website configured under the IIS web server installed on the Windows machine that hosts the Citrix Director installation.

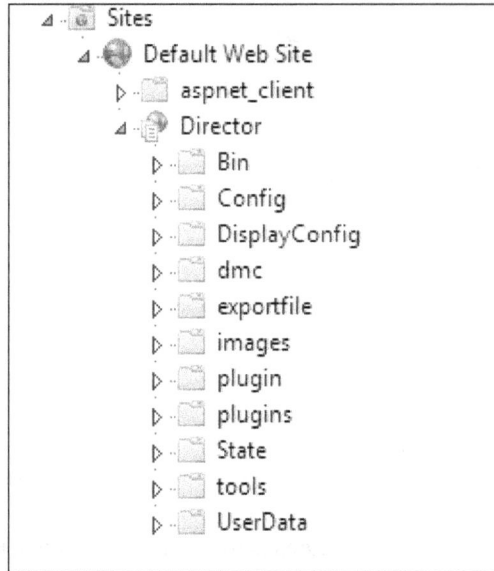

```
⊿ 🔵 Sites
    ⊿ 🌐 Default Web Site
        ▷ ⬜ aspnet_client
        ⊿ 📄 Director
            ▷ 📁 Bin
            ▷ 📁 Config
            ▷ 📁 DisplayConfig
            ▷ 📁 dmc
            ▷ 📁 exportfile
            ▷ 📁 images
            ▷ 📁 plugin
            ▷ 📁 plugins
            ▷ 📁 State
            ▷ 📁 tools
            ▷ 📁 UserData
```

Going deeper into the details, you can obtain a lot of information about the configured desktop instances. Use the filters to find the specific resources on which they are operating, and apply the information fields you want to get back on the results. Some of these are about the **Machine** identification data (**Name**, **Desktop Group**, **Machine Type**, and **OS**), the **Power State** for the machines, or the **Connection** status (**Last connection** and **Endpoint** from which the connection has been established).

The most interesting part is composed of the set of active operations that you can execute on desktop machines. It's possible, in fact, to manage the power state of the machines; for instance, you have the ability to restart or power on a desktop when necessary. Moreover, you can change the desktop assignment, moving an instance among your domain users, because of the ability of the Desktop Director to interface with the Active Directory structure. This enables you to manage and retrieve information about the domain users.

> To manage the power state of the virtual machines created under a VMware hypervisor, you need to install the VMware tools on the guest machine.

All the collected metrics are exportable from the Desktop Director in a report, in the form of an XML file.

The data collection and processing are the keys that will help IT professionals reduce the time to intercept problems with the help of Citrix Director. As discussed, with the Director 7.6 release, there is also the ability to monitor the Hosted Application's usage, in terms of concurrent application instances, global launches, and usage duration.

There's more...

The Citrix Director platform can be managed by different users with different levels of permissions.

The roles and the scopes to manage the troubleshooting web platform can be configured in the Citrix Studio by navigating to the **Configuration | Administrators** section in the menu on the left.

By clicking on the **Create Administrator** link, you can select a domain user to whom we can assign permissions on XenDesktop site objects. This was formerly known as **Role**.

For instance, assigning a user the **Help Desk Administrator** permissions will enable them to manage the user sessions, applying remediation tasks by connecting to the desktop user through session shadowing or resetting the assigned personal vDisk.

> **Shadowing** is the ability to remotely control the desktop of a user in order to offer remote assistance to troubleshoot issues.

These configurations are powerful solutions to use to delegate noncritical activities to existing company departments (help desk, customer care, monitoring area, or less privileged administrators).

See also

> ▸ The *Configuring the XenDesktop® logging* recipe in *Chapter 7, XenDesktop® Infrastructure Tuning*

6
Deploying Applications

In this chapter, we will cover the following recipes:

- ▶ Publishing the hosted applications
- ▶ Publishing the Local Access Apps (LAA)
- ▶ Publishing applications using Microsoft App-V
- ▶ Using AppDNA 7.6

Introduction

When you think about the XenDesktop suite, it seems obvious to focus on its significance as a Virtual Desktop Infrastructure solution. This approach can be correct when creating a machine with the full set of applications already installed, not when we consider delivering only the specific applications for every domain user.

In this chapter, we are going to discuss this second approach, by the use of the three supported technologies to deliver applications to the user's desktops: the creation of the **hosted applications**, the **Local Access Apps** (**LAA**) with XenDesktop, and the most recent way to publish applications, the App-V platform developed by Microsoft. Moreover, at the end of this chapter, we will discuss **AppDNA** 7.6, a Citrix software that helps Citrix professionals in the application migration process between different releases of the Windows operating system.

> In XenDesktop 7.6, for the Server OS deployment, the hosted applications technique is the successor of XenApp 6.5, which has been part of XenDesktop since the 7.0 release.

Publishing the hosted applications

The hosted applications approach is the simplest and nearest to a standard pre-installed desktop instance. With this technique, anyway, you will be able to reduce the impact on the infrastructural components, because of the absence of the terminal server licenses required in other application deployment solutions, such as the old XenApp approach. On the other hand, you have to consider the necessity of having more XenDesktop licenses.

Getting ready

To be able to deploy the hosted applications, you need the right number of XenDesktop licenses within your infrastructure. Whether you publish a "full" Windows 7/8 desktop or just a single application (or a set of applications) running on that desktop, a XenDesktop license will be needed in both cases.

Moreover, you need to generate a number of desktop instances in your catalog equal to or greater than the number of users accessing the applications. A good reference for the licensing model can be found at `http://www.citrix.com/buy/licensing/product.html`.

> Please refer to the *Creating and configuring the machine catalog* recipe in *Chapter 5, Creating and Configuring a Desktop Environment*, for the machine catalog creation.

How to do it...

We will explain how to publish the hosted apps based on the XenDesktop application catalogs:

1. Connect to the Delivery Controller server with a domain user with administrative privileges.
2. Run the Windows + C key combination, search for the **Citrix Studio** icon in the Citrix software section, and click on it.
3. Click on the **Machine Catalogs** link on the left-side menu, and then select **Create Machine Catalog** on the right-side panel.
4. On the **Introduction** screen, click on the **Next** button to proceed.
5. In the **Operating System and Hardware** section, select the type of desktop you want to create (**Windows Desktop OS**). After selecting the appropriate radio button, click on **Next**.

6. In the **Machine Management** section, select the kind of infrastructure to use to deploy the resources (virtual or physical machines), then choose the **MCS** methodology to use to manage the catalog. After completion, click on the **Next** button.

7. In the **Desktop Experience** section, select which way to assign the resources to the users each time they log on based on whether they are saving the user personal data within the existing virtual desktops. After completion, click on **Next.**

8. Select a **Master Image** from the list, which generates the desktop instances. After completion, click on **Next**.

9. In the **Virtual Machines** section, select how many machines must be generated by incrementing the value of the **Number of virtual machines needed** section. After this, you need to configure the resources to assign to any instance (**Virtual CPUs** and **Memory (MB)**). Click on **Next** to proceed.

[
To differentiate the machines in a desktop group from those in an application group, you can create new machine accounts with a naming convention different to that of the machines in the desktop group.
]

10. In the **Active Directory computer accounts** section, choose **Create new Active Directory accounts** or **Use existing Active Directory accounts**. To better understand all the creation features in this section, we will select the creation of new computer accounts.

11. In the **Active Directory location for computer accounts** section, select from the drop-down list the **Domain** on which you are working, and choose an OU on which the computer accounts are created. Then, select **Account naming scheme**, in the form of `MachineName##,` where the two final characters identify a progressive code made up of letters or digits (`A-Z` or `0-9`). After completion, click on the **Next** button.

12. In the **Summary** section, assign a name and an optional description in the respective fields (**Machine Catalog Name** and **Machine Catalog description for administrators**), then click on the **Finish** button to complete the configuration operations.

Summary

Machine type:	Windows Desktop OS
Machine management:	Virtual
Provisioning method:	Machine creation services (MCS)
Desktop experience:	Users connect to a new desktop each time they log on
Resources:	VMware01
Master Image name:	T0_VDA
Number of VMs to create:	2
Virtual CPUs:	2
Memory (MB):	2048

Machine Catalog name:

Desktop-Apps-01

Machine Catalog description for administrators: (Optional)

Desktop-Apps-01

Note: To complete the deployment, assign this machine catalog to a Delivery Group by selecting Delivery Groups and then Create or Edit a Delivery Group.

We have already seen in the previous chapter how to create a catalog, so we will work on an existing catalog in this case. For more details, please refer to the *Creating and configuring the machine catalog* recipe in *Chapter 5, Creating and Configuring a Desktop Environment*.

13. Click on the **Delivery Groups** link on the left-hand side menu, and then select the **Create Delivery Group** on the right-hand side of the screen.

14. After clicking on **Next** in the **Introduction** section, on the **machine's** screen, select the catalog from which we take the desktop instances and select the number of machines that are to be added, which should be equal to or less than the number of available machines. Then, click on **Next**.

15. In the **Delivery Type** section, select the **Applications** radio button, and then click on **Next**.

> Delivery Type
>
> You can use the machines in the Catalog to deliver desktops and applications to your users.
> Learn more
> Use the machines to deliver:
> ○ Desktops
> ⦿ Applications

16. In the **Users** section, select the users or the groups to which the application desktop instances will be assigned, then click on the **Next** button.

17. In the **Applications** section, select one of the listed discovered software, or click on **Add applications manually** to select the application to add to the Delivery Group. In this second case, a pop-up screen will ask you for the application details you want to add, as shown in the next picture. After completion, click on **Next**.

> Add an Application Manually
>
> You can manually add applications from the virtual desktop machine or from a different network location.
> Learn more
> Path to the executable file:
> *Example: %ProgramFiles(x86)%\Internet Explorer\iexplore.exe*   Browse...
> Command line argument (optional):
> *Example: http://www.example.com*
> Working directory:
> *Example: %ProgramFiles(x86)%\Internet Explorer*   Browse...
> Application name (for user):
> *Example: Example Web Site*
> Application name (for administrator):
> *Example: Internet Explorer - Example Web Site*
>
> OK   Cancel

[✎ If you configured an administrative scope, you will have the ability to assign it to the published Delivery Group.]

18. On the **Summary** screen, assign a name and an optional description to the Delivery Group and click on **Finish** to complete the procedure.

Summary

Source Machine Catalog:	VDI
Machine type:	Windows Desktop OS
Allocation type:	Static
Number of machines added:	1 unassigned
Delivery type:	Applications
Users:	-
Applications:	1
Scopes:	All

Delivery Group name:

Application-Group

Delivery Group description for users: (Optional)

Application-Group

---

19. Right-click on the published application and select the **Properties** option.

20. In the **Identification** section, insert an **Application name** for both user and administrator use, and an optional application **Description**.

Identification

Identify this application.

Application name (for user):

Notepad

Application name (for administrator):

Notepad

Description and keywords:

This is the description that will be seen by the user. You can also use this field to enter keywords for StoreFront.
Learn More

---

21. On the **Delivery** menu, you can select the icon to associate with the application, an optional category in which to group the app, and the enabling of the Add shortcut on the user's desktop flag.

Delivery

Specify how this application will be delivered to your users.

Application icon:

Browse...

Application category (optional):

TextEditors

The category in Receiver where the application appears.

☑ Add shortcut on user's desktop

---

22. In the **Location** section, select the application path executable file, the optional command line parameters, and the working directory.

Location

Enter the location information below.

Path to the executable file:

%SystemRoot%\System32\notepad.exe   Browse...

Note: By clicking Browse, you will be able to view the file directory for the machine running Citrix Studio. If this machine does not have the application you want, you will need to enter the location of the application manually.

Command line argument (optional):

Example: https://www.Example.com

Working directory:

%SystemRoot%\System32   Browse...

23. In the **Limit Visibility** section, you can decide if you want to show the application to all the Delivery Group's members or make it only usable for specific users or groups. After completing these configurations, click on the **OK** button.

> You will find out more about the Content redirection section later in this recipe.

24. Connect to the StoreFront configured store and log in using the credentials of a user holding one or more published application(s). In the resources menu, you can now find the linked software in the application's catalog. You can click on the application link to start using it.

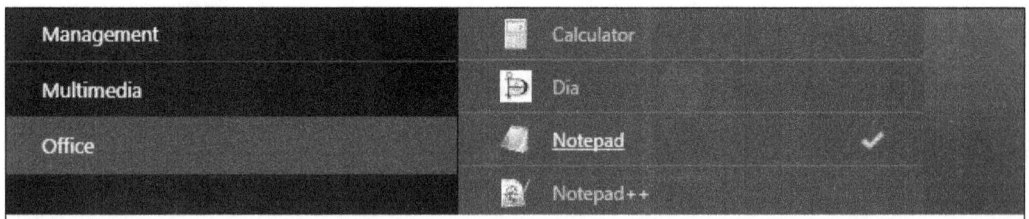

Management	Calculator
Multimedia	Dia
Office	Notepad ✔
	Notepad++

25. Come back to the Citrix Studio console, then click on the **Machine Catalogs** link on the left-hand side menu and select **Create Machine Catalog** in the right-hand side panel.

26. On the **Introduction screen**, click on the **Next** button to proceed.

27. In the **Operating System and Hardware** section, select the type of desktop you want to create (**Windows Server OS**). After selecting the appropriate radio button, click on **Next**.

Operating System

Select an operating system for this Machine Catalog.

○ Windows Server OS
The Server OS Machine Catalog provides hosted shared desktops for a large-scale deployment of standardized machines.

○ Windows Desktop OS
The Desktop OS Machine Catalog provides VDI desktops ideal for a variety of different users.

○ Remote PC Access
The Remote PC Access Machine Catalog provides users with remote access to their physical office desktops, allowing them to work at any time.

There are currently no power management connections suitable for use with Remote PC Access, but you can create one after completing this wizard. Then edit this machine catalog to specify that connection.

---

28. In the **Machine Management** section, select the kind of infrastructure to use to deploy the resources (virtual or physical machines), then choose the **MCS** methodology to use to manage the catalog. Once completed, click on the **Next** button.

29. Select **Master Image** from the list, in order to select the Master Image that will generate the desktop instances. Then, click on **Next**.

30. In the **Virtual Machines** section, select how many machines need to be generated by incrementing the value of the **Number of virtual machines needed** section. After this, you need to configure the resources to assign to any instance (**Virtual CPUs** and **Memory (MB)**). Click on **Next** to proceed.

31. In the **Active Directory computer accounts** section, choose **Create new Active Directory accounts** or **Use existing Active Directory accounts**. To better understand all the creation features in this section, we will select the creation of new computer accounts.

32. In the **Active Directory location for computer accounts** section, select from the drop-down list the **Domain** on which you are working, and choose an OU on which you are creating the computer accounts. Then, select an **Account naming scheme**, in the form of `MachineName##,` where the two final characters identify a progressive code and are made up of letters or digits (`A-Z` or `0-9`). After completion, click on the **Next** button.

33. In the **Summary** section, assign a name and an optional description to the respective fields (**Machine Catalog Name** and **Machine Catalog description for administrators**), then click on the **Finish** button to complete the configuration operations.

34. Click on the **Delivery Groups** link on the left-side menu, and then select the **Create Delivery Group** on the right-side of the screen.

35. After clicking on **Next** in the **Introduction** section, on the **Machines** screen, select the catalog from which we take the desktop instances and select how many machines to add, with a number equal to or less than the number of available machines, then click on **Next**.

36. In the **Delivery Type** section, select the **Applications** radio button, then click on **Next**.

> With the choice of a Server OS machine catalog, you will also have the ability to deploy desktops and applications on Delivery Group types.

Delivery Type

You can use the machines in the Catalog to deliver desktops and applications to your users.

Learn more

Use the machines to deliver:

- ○ Desktops
- ○ Desktops and Applications
- ● Applications

37. In the **Users** section, select the users or the groups to whom the application desktop instances will be assigned, then click on the **Next** button.

38. In the **Applications** section, click on **Next** to continue. We will deploy the required apps in the next steps.

39. On the **Summary** screen, assign a name and an optional description to the Applications Delivery Group and click on **Finish** to complete the procedure.

40. Right-click on the earlier created Delivery Group and select the **Add Applications** option.

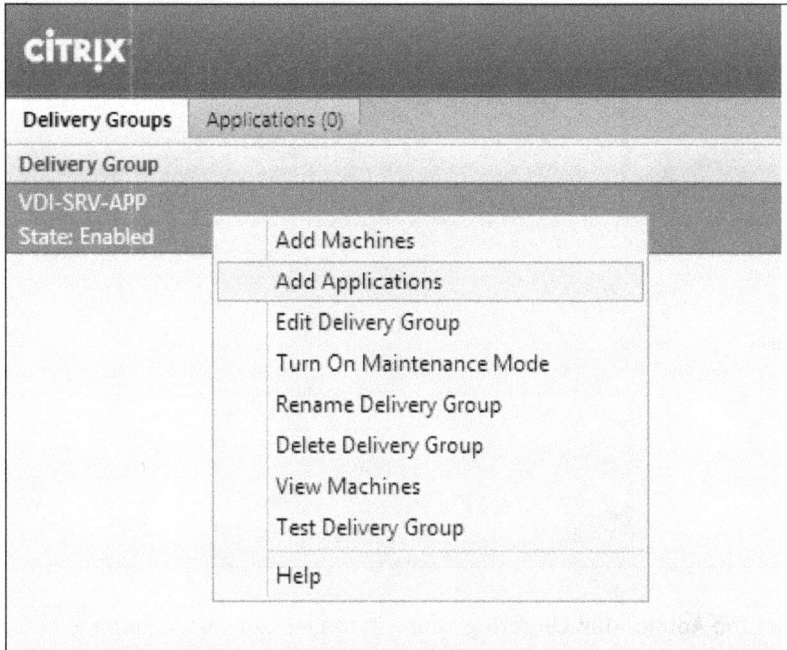

41. Click on the **Next** button on the **Introduction** screen, and then select one of the listed applications available on the Server OS instance. After selecting, click on **Next**.

42. On the **Summary** screen, click on the **Finish** button to complete the procedure.

43. Click on the Delivery Groups link on the left-side menu, select one of the existing application Delivery Groups, right-click on it, and select **Edit Delivery Group**.

44. Select the **Application Prelaunch** option, and then configure whether you want to launch applications at the user logon phase or not, and configure the time to live for the prelaunched sessions:

Studio

Prelaunch Sessions for Applications

With prelaunch, sessions launch when users log on to Receiver, so applications are available sooner.

Users

Delivery Type

Application Prelaunch

Application Lingering

Basic settings

Access Policy

Restart Schedule

When do you want sessions to launch?

○ Launch when users start an application (no prelaunch)

● Prelaunch when any user in the Delivery Group logs on to Receiver for Windows

○ Prelaunch when any of the following users log on to Receiver for Windows:

Add...   Remove

If no application is started, when do you want prelaunched sessions to end?

After a specified time: Hours ▼   2   − +

☑ When average load on all machines exceeds (%):   70   − +

☑ When load on any machine exceeds (%):   70   − +

45. Select the **Application Lingering** option in the left-side list, in order to configure if the sessions should be active even after all the applications have been closed by a user.

Studio

Lingering Sessions for Applications

With lingering, sessions remain active after all applications are closed.

Users

Delivery Type

Application Prelaunch

Application Lingering

Basic settings

Access Policy

Restart Schedule

When do you want sessions to end?

○ Immediately after all applications in the session are closed (no lingering)

● Keep sessions active until:

After a specified time:

Hours ▼   8   − +

☑ The average load on all machines exceeds (%):

70   − +

☑ The load on any machine exceeds (%):

70   − +

46. Connect to the StoreFront configured store and log in using the credentials of a user holding one or more published application(s). On the resources menu, you can now find the linked software in the application's catalog. You can click on the application link to start using it.

> Despite the execution of applications with Desktop OS machines, in this case, you will see no login phase during the published application execution.

How it works...

The hosted application's deployment is a new introduction of old techniques offered by Citrix to deploy applications to the users. Through this approach, you can deliver software to the published desktops or simply let the users run a single application.

You can deploy resources in the following ways:

▶ **Hosted applications on Windows desktop operating systems (Windows 7, Windows 8.x):** In this kind of application deployment, a single published machine is able to serve a single user at a time. For this reason, every application associated with a delivered desktop instance allows only one connection and not multiple accesses to the assigned software. This deployment approach can also be useful when you do not want to use the application streaming, offered by platforms such as Microsoft App-V that can only be installed on the desktop machines. With this configuration, you will not need the **Remote Desktop Services** (**RDS**) licenses, but any deployed application can become a consumed XenDesktop license.

- **Hosted applications on Windows Server operating systems (Windows Server 2008 R2—Windows Server 2012 and Server 2012 R2)**: In this kind of application deployment, a single machine is able to serve multiple users at a time. This deployment approach is based on the use of RDS licenses, with the consumption of XenDesktop licenses only for a number of deployed server machines. Remember that a single server machine can serve a number of users equal to the number of remote desktop installed licenses. This is one of the new features for the XenDesktop platform; in fact, it is the introduction of the well-known XenApp functionality implemented in a completely different way integrating it in the FMA-based XenDesktop infrastructure.

The user experience obtained by an application deployed with a desktop operating system can have a lower user experience. In fact, with a Server OS, you will only see the execution progress bar for the launched application, while with a Desktop OS hosted app, the entire desktop logon process will be visible, making the user experience low performance.

All the hosted apps are part of a Delivery Group quite different from the standard group used so far. It is called **Application Delivery Group,** and it is an application container on which it is possible to assign the permissions and parameters of a specific software.

You can decide to publish an application link on the user desktop, and populate the Start menu with a shortcut. In this way, the user will have the ability to run the application locally on its desktop.

With the application hosted on a server operating system, you have the ability to configure a useful feature called **Prelaunch**. To optimize and accelerate the application's execution on the user device, you can anticipate the application's execution at user logon time, reducing the amount of time required to use the software by reusing existing active sessions. This means that the Active Directory logon phase and group policy processing can be avoided by optimizing the global logon time. The application can be launched when any of the user members of a Delivery Group log on using Windows Receiver, when specific users perform the same operations, or by launching the application only at the time of the request (no application prelaunch).

In order to avoid heavy resource consumption, as well as consumed licenses, you can configure the end of the prelaunched sessions by determining a specific amount of time (hours, minutes, or days), or by specifying the load average, in a percentage, for some or all the application machines in a Delivery Group.

Another available option is the application lingering. With this, you can keep user sessions active even if all applications have been closed. Even in that case, the metrics used to free resources are a machine's load in percentage and the session time duration.

In the presence of the NetScaler Gateway, it is possible to configure the advanced access control policy. Instead of allowing any kind of connection, you can force access to resources only by using the NetScaler platform.

> We will discuss the NetScaler Gateway platform in *Chapter 8, XenDesktop® Component Integration*.

There's more...

To complete the application publishing process, it is necessary to assign the file type association with the software. To execute this task, you need to configure the Content Redirection functionality.

To be able to operate on the file extension assignment, you need to put the desktop that is offering the application in the maintenance mode (this is needed only for a desktop OS deployment). After this, select the application on which you want to operate and edit its properties. In the **Content redirection** section, click on the **Update file types** button and select the machine from which to import the file type definition. At this time, you will be able to select one or more file extension, to associate with the application (in this example, the `.txt` file types have been associated with the published Microsoft Notepad):

File Type Association

Enter the file type associations below.

By default, this application will automatically open the file extensions listed below.

⊟ Extension	File Type
✔ .txt	
☐ .compositefont	
☐ .inf	
☐ .ini	
☐ .log	
☐ .ps1	
☐ .psd1	
☐ .psm1	
☐ .scp	
☐ .sct	
☐ .wsc	
☐ .wtx	

Update file types...

This operation will allow the users to double click the associated files and open them using the associated software with the hosted app technique.

[📝 Remember to disable the Maintenance mode after completing this procedure!]

See also

▶ The *Configuring and optimizing a Desktop OS Master Image* and the *Configuring and optimizing a Server OS Master Image* recipes in *Chapter 3, Master Image Configuration and Tuning*.

Publishing the Local Access Apps (LAA)

In some cases, you should not want to migrate or reinstall applications installed on an existing working environment, because of different reasons (performance issues, installation, or compatibility problems). In which way can these necessities match with a VDI migration project?

XenDesktop 7.6 has the key. In fact, also in this latest version, you have the ability to deploy the **Local Access Apps** (**LAA**), a technique that will permit you to access the applications that are already installed on the endpoint without performing any setup or configuration procedures. In this recipe, we are going to discuss the required steps to implement it.

Getting ready

To be able to publish streamed Local Access Apps, you need a compatible source operating system (Windows Server 2012 / 2012 R2, Windows Server 2008 R2, Windows 7, and Windows 8/8.1) and at least the 4.0 version of Citrix Receiver.

[📝 The LAA deployment can **only** be applied to the Desktop Delivery Groups and not to the Applications Delivery Groups.]

How to do it...

In this recipe, we are going to explain how to use the Local Access Apps feature:

1. Connect to the Delivery Controller server with an administrative domain user.

2. Press the Windows + X key combination, select the **Run** option, and type the `regedit` command:

3. In the opened window, search for the following register location:

   `HKEY_LOCAL_MACHINE\Software\Wow6432Node\Citrix\DesktopStudio`

After you've found it, right-click on the **DesktopStudio** location, select **New | DWORD (32-bit) Value**, and insert the following reg key: `ClientHostedAppsEnabled | Value = 1`

This is necessary to enable the LAA usage.

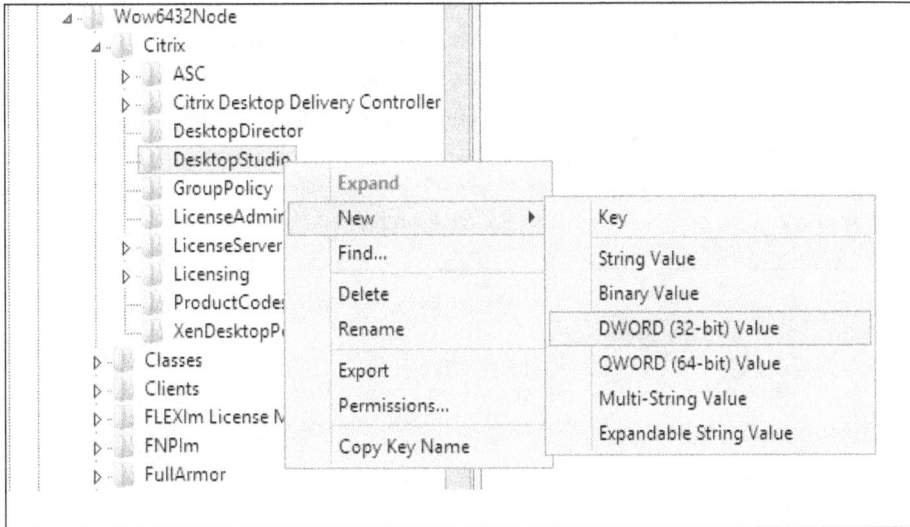

[💡 Do not forget to restart the Delivery Controller machine once this operation has been completed.]

4. After the reboot has been completed, connect again to the Delivery Controller server with an administrative domain user.

5. Press the Windows + *C* key combination, search for the **Citrix Studio** icon in the Citrix software section, and click on it.

6. Click on the **Delivery Groups** link on the left-side menu, and then select the **Applications** tab. After moving onto this section, click on the **Create Local Access Application** option on the right-side menu.

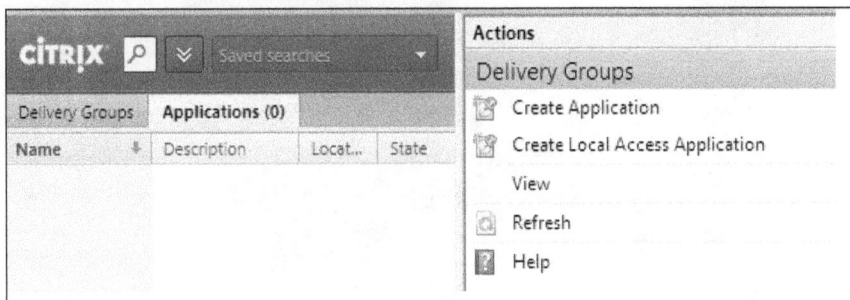

> We have already described the way to create and configure catalogs and Delivery Groups in *Chapter 5, Creating and configuring a Desktop Environment*. For this reason, we will perform the recipe's tasks on a configured infrastructure.

7. On the **Introduction** screen, click on the **Next** button to proceed.

8. In the **Delivery Group** section, select an available Desktop Group to which the application should be deployed in an LAA way, then click on **Next**.

9. In the **Location** section, select an application from the list of the local installed applications, and then assign an optional command-line argument and **Working Directory**. After completing this step, click on **Next**.

Location

Enter the location information below.

Enter path of the local application on the end users operating system:

| %SystemRoot%\System32\write.exe | Browse... |

Note: By clicking Browse, you will be able to view the file directory for the machine running Citrix Studio. If this machine does not have the application you want, you will need to enter the location of the application manually.

Command line argument (optional):

| Example: https://www.Example.com |

Working directory:

| %SystemRoot%\System32 | Browse... |

10. On the **Identification** menu, assign a name for users and administrators to the selected software, plus an optional description. Click on the **Next** button to proceed further with the configuration steps.

11. In the **Delivery** section, choose the preferred application's icon and decide on adding the software to the desktop and Start menu of the user's desktop environment. Click on **Next** to continue.

```
Delivery

Specify how this application will be delivered to your users.

Application icon:
    ● Get the icon from the user's computer at run time

    ○ Use custom icon:

       [icon]  Browse...

☑ Add shortcut to client's start menu
    Start menu location:

    Example: Folder/Subfolder

☑ Add shortcut on user's desktop
```

12. On the **Summary** screen, click on the **Finish** button to complete the configuration procedure.

13. Right-click on the published application and select the **Properties** option.

14. Select the **File Type Association** section and choose whether you are associating file type extensions at runtime from the user's computer or specifying one or more file types. Click on the **OK** button after completion.

```
○ Get the file types from the user's computer at run time

● Set the file types explicitly

   By default, this application will automatically open the file extensions listed below.

   .txt
```

15. Select the **Policy** link on the left-side menu, then edit an existing one or create a new policy.

16. In the **Search** field, search for the following policy: `Allow local app access`. Configure it as **Allowed**.

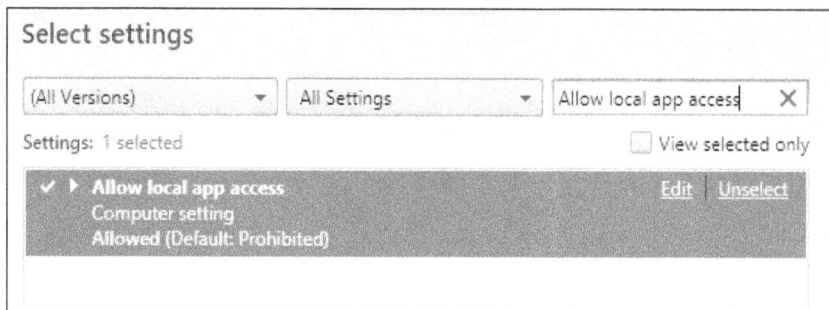

Select settings

(All Versions) ▼	All Settings ▼	Allow local app access ✕

Settings: 1 selected   ☐ View selected only

✓ ▶ **Allow local app access**	Edit Unselect
Computer setting	
Allowed (Default: Prohibited)	

17. Use the search field to filter the **URL redirection black list** policy. Within this URL list, you have to insert all the web addresses you want to execute out of the assigned VDI desktop on your personal device.

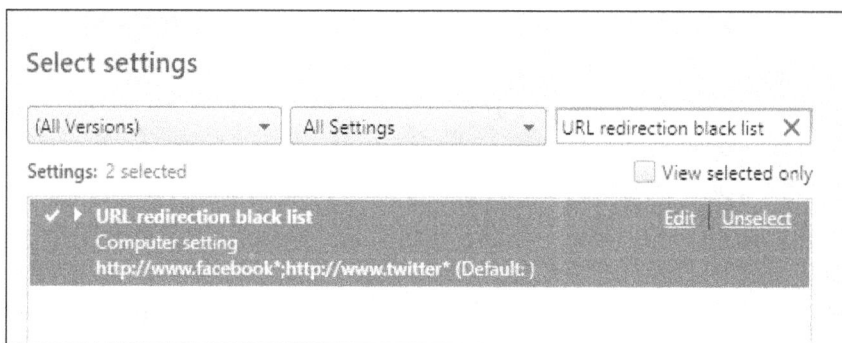

Select settings

(All Versions) ▼	All Settings ▼	URL redirection black list ✕

Settings: 2 selected   ☐ View selected only

✓ ▶ **URL redirection black list**	Edit Unselect
Computer setting	
http://www.facebook*;http://www.twitter* (Default:)	

18. Filter the Citrix policies for the **URL redirection white list** voice. In this list, you have to insert the web URLs you want to run on the company assigned virtual desktop. After completion, click on **Next**.

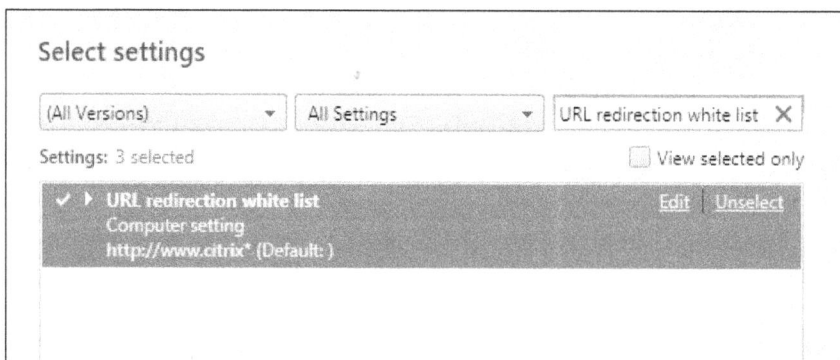

Select settings

(All Versions) ▼	All Settings ▼	URL redirection white list ✕

Settings: 3 selected   ☐ View selected only

✓ ▶ **URL redirection white list**	Edit Unselect
Computer setting	
http://www.citrix* (Default:)	

19. Connect to the personal user device involved in the LAA configuration, and execute the `gpedit.msc` command to run the Group Policy management console.

> As an alternative, you can apply the configured settings using **domain group policy objects** (**Domain GPO**). In this case, we are applying the local user device GPO.

20. Expand the **Computer Configuration** section, then right-click on the **Administrative Templates** folder and select **Add/Remove Templates**.

21. On the **Add/Remove Templates** screen, click on the **Add** button, then browse for the `icaclient.adm` template file, located at `C:\Program Files (x86)\Citrix\ICA Client\Configuration`. After you have added the file, click on the **Close** button.

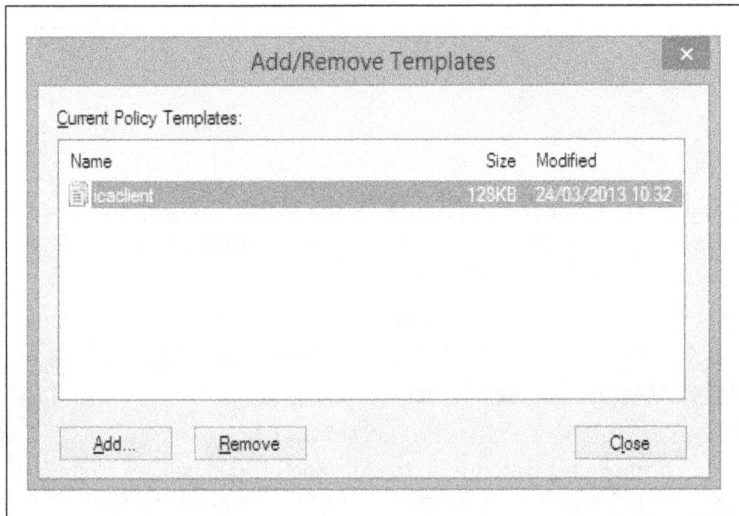

22. Expand **Computer Configuration | Administrative Templates | Classic Administrative Templates (ADM) | Citrix Components | Citrix Receiver** and select the **User Experience** folder.

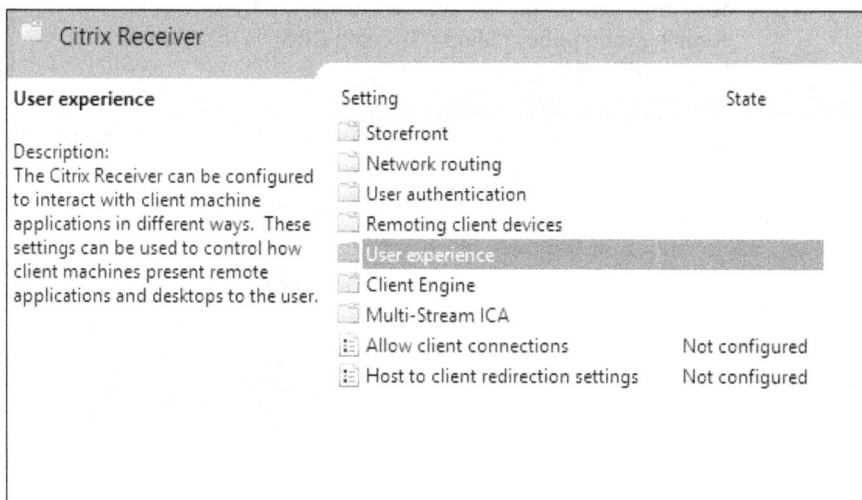

Citrix Receiver

User experience	Setting	State
Description: The Citrix Receiver can be configured to interact with client machine applications in different ways. These settings can be used to control how client machines present remote applications and desktops to the user.	Storefront	
	Network routing	
	User authentication	
	Remoting client devices	
	User experience	
	Client Engine	
	Multi-Stream ICA	
	Allow client connections	Not configured
	Host to client redirection settings	Not configured

23. Double-click on the **Local App Access settings** policy, then select the **Enabled** option, and flag the **Allow URL Redirection** voice. After completing this step, click on **Apply**, then click the **OK** button.

24. Run a shell prompt windows with administrative credentials and execute the following command to force the policy application:

    ```
    gpupdate /force /target:computer
    ```

> If you do not want to use the Microsoft Group policies to enable the LAA, you need to install, in the first instance, the Citrix Receiver, enabling the following option by the command line:
> ```
> CitrixReceiver.exe /ALLOW_CLIENTHOSTEDAPPSURL=1
> ```

25. On the same client device running the Citrix Receiver, launch a Windows command prompt shell with administrative credentials, and execute one of the following commands, required to enable the URL redirection for the configured Internet browser respectively, for Internet Explorer, Google Chrome, Mozilla Firefox of all the following listed browsers:

    ```
    C:\Program Files (x86)\Citrix\ICA Client\redirector.exe /regIE
    C:\Program Files (x86)\Citrix\ICA Client\redirector.exe /regChrome
    C:\Program Files (x86)\Citrix\ICA Client\redirector.exe /regFF
    C:\Program Files (x86)\Citrix\ICA Client\redirector.exe /regAll
    ```

26. Connect to the StoreFront portal with a domain user with published applications and desktops, then access one of the available Windows machines. You will find the published local access app on your desktop and Start menu, if configured.

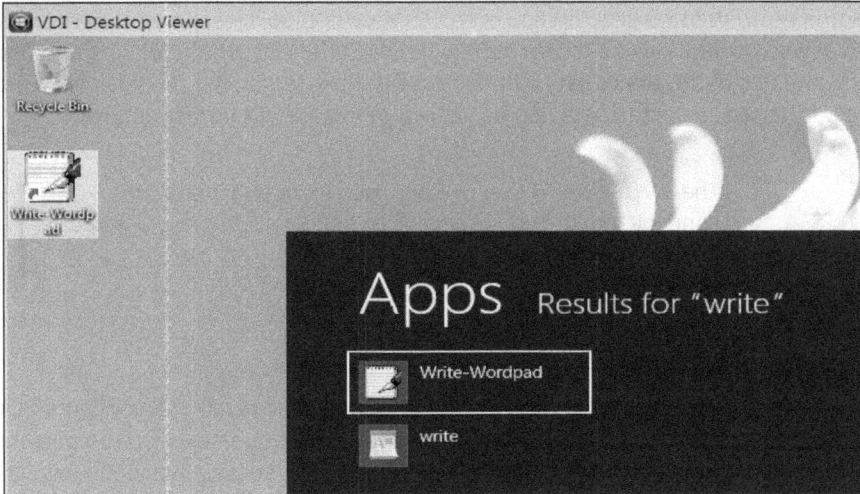

27. Execute the published LAA. The software will run out of the virtual desktop directly on to the physical personal device.

> To avoid problems and confusion during the use of a LAA, you should always run the virtual desktop in fullscreen mode. This is a necessary way to operate and obtain better user experience.

How it works...

The Local Access App functionality is a powerful option included by default with XenDesktop 7.6 version, Platinum edition, which permits user and IT professional to better improve the isolation between the personal devices and the corporate professional instruments.

By deploying it, you have the ability to decide what kind of applications directly execute on the end user's device, without affecting the security and the policy for your company's VDI architecture. The LAA resource groups can be deployed using local apps on the Citrix Delivery Controller servers. It can be also used in a more powerful way, by creating catalogs and delivered groups of Remote PC. These are domain-joined machines, physical or virtual, assigned to a specific end user and generally populated with software and platforms that do not need to be migrated.

Moreover, with this second approach, you also have the way to filter the execution of performance affecting applications on your VDI client. You can, for example, use graphical applications directly on your personal client or reproduce web and media contents out of your company virtual desktop. In the second case, the URL redirection features appear to be particularly important. In fact, by the use of the XenDesktop policies, you can differentiate what kind of web contents and sites reproduce the two different areas (working and personal profiles), by the use of the **black list** (with contents transferred on the physical device) or **white list** addresses (websites data can be viewed within the VDI infrastructure).

> The LAA feature is also typically used for special hardware connected to the end user devices that could not be redirected to a remote session.

There's more...

Once a VDI session disconnects, you can decide which way to operate the configured LAA must be applied: after a logoff phase (an application can continue to run on the personal end user device) or you can decide to stop it after a Windows user session has been logged off.

To configure your choice on which way to operate, you have to connect to the machine configured as a personal user device (out of your company), running the `regedit` command and locating the following registry key:

> ▶ HKEY_LOCAL_MACHINE\SOFTWARE\Citrix\Client Hosted Apps\Policies\ Session State

By assigning the value of 1 to this key, the LAA will continue to run after the user has logged off, instead, if you configure it with the value of 3, the applications running locally will disconnect.

See also

> ▶ The *Configuring the XenDesktop® Policies* recipe in *Chapter 7, XenDesktop® Infrastructure Tuning*.

Publishing applications using Microsoft App-V

Microsoft offers an alternative to the XenApp streaming method, a product no more supported (end of life) with its App-V platforms. This software, which is quite similar to the XenApp application profiling technique, permits you to publish the software to the end user's desktop using a specific client.

In this chapter, we will discuss the App-V components and their functionalities.

> To learn how to implement an App-V architecture you can refer to *Microsoft Application Virtualization Advanced Guide*, *Augusto Alvarez, Packt Publishing*.

Getting ready

For a full version of the App-V infrastructure, you need two or more servers to install and configure the following roles:

▸ **App-V Management System**: This component is the centralized management console for all the configured applications and the associated users:

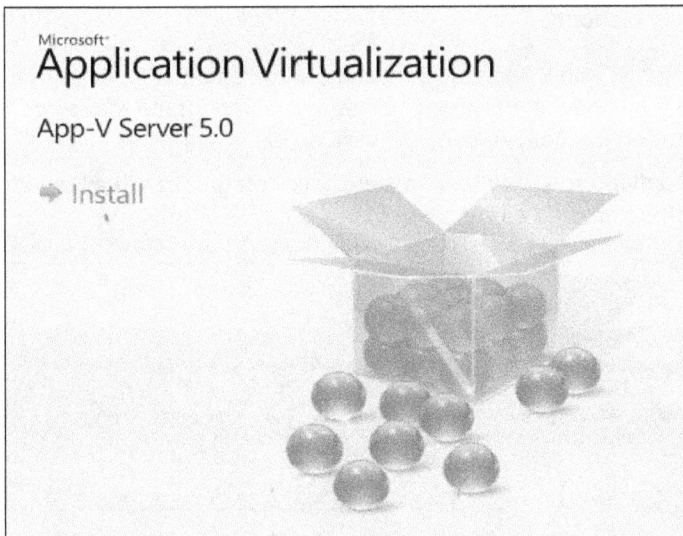

▸ **App-V Management Server**: This is the application Broker, the core of the App-V infrastructure, which delivers the software to the clients. App-V also permits you to publish the applications from a network share without using the management server directly.

> IIS 7.0, the .NET framework, and at least SQL Server 2008 R2 are required in order to implement the Management Server.

▸ **App-V Sequencer**: This is the packaging software that creates the application profiles. This must be installed on a client machine (Windows 8.x or Windows 7), on which the application's setups are located.

> ▸ **App-V Streaming Server**: This server is used to stream the published applications to the clients.

On the XenDesktop base image template, you need to install the Microsoft Application Virtualization Desktop Client component, in order to be able to contact the App-V infrastructure.

> [Remember that after the installed App-V client, you have to update the existing XenDesktop machine instances, in order to use the client on the assigned virtual desktops.]

How to do it...

Follow the necessary steps to implement the application sequencing and deployment using the Microsoft App-V platform:

1. Connect to the App-V Sequencer machine with domain administrative credentials, then run the Windows + *C* key combination, search for the **Microsoft Application Virtualization Sequencer** icon, and click on it.

2. On the **Application Virtualization** menu, click on the **Create a New Virtual Application Package option**.

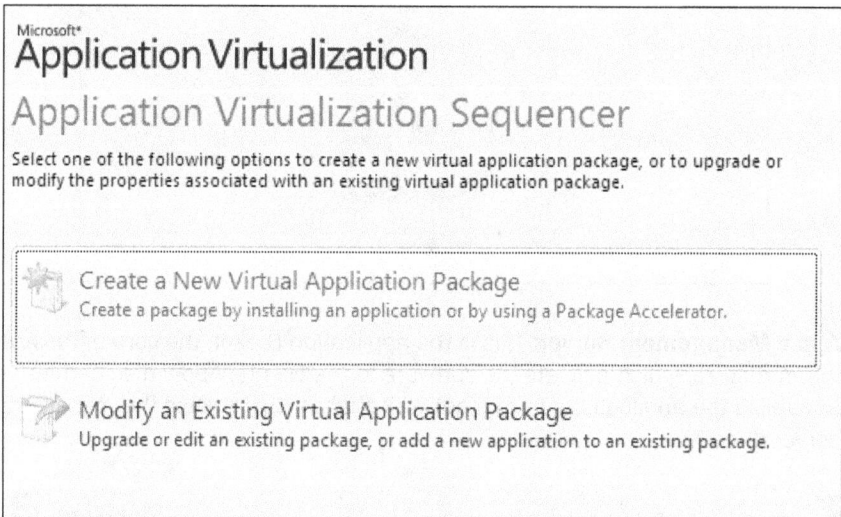

Microsoft®
Application Virtualization
Application Virtualization Sequencer

Select one of the following options to create a new virtual application package, or to upgrade or modify the properties associated with an existing virtual application package.

Create a New Virtual Application Package
Create a package by installing an application or by using a Package Accelerator.

Modify an Existing Virtual Application Package
Upgrade or edit an existing package, or add a new application to an existing package.

3. In the **Packaging Method** section, select the **Create Package (default)**, and click on **Next**.

Select the method for creating a package.

⦿ Create Package (default)

Create a package by installing an application on this computer while App-V monitors the installation.

○ Create Package Using a Package Accelerator

Create a package by applying a previously created Package Accelerator. Package Accelerator uses application setup files to create a virtual application package automatically.

4. In the **Type of Application** section, select the **Standard Application (default)** option, and then click on **Next**:

Describe the type of application you want to package.

⦿ Standard Application (default)

Create a package that contains an application or suite of applications. You should select this option for most applications.

○ Add-on or Plug-in

Create a package that extends the functionality of standard applications. For example, a plug-in for Microsoft Excel®.

○ Middleware

Create a package for middleware or framework software that is required by a standard package.

5. On the **Select Installer** menu, browse for the software setup previously copied on the Sequencer server and click on **Next**. The application chosen for this step is the Notepad++ text editor.

6. In the **Package Name** section, assign a name to the virtual application and the location on which the package will be stored (**Primary Virtual Application Directory** field). After completion, click on **Next**.

7. In the **Installation** section, perform and complete the installation procedure for the selected software. After completing this step, check **I am finished installing**, and click on **Next**.

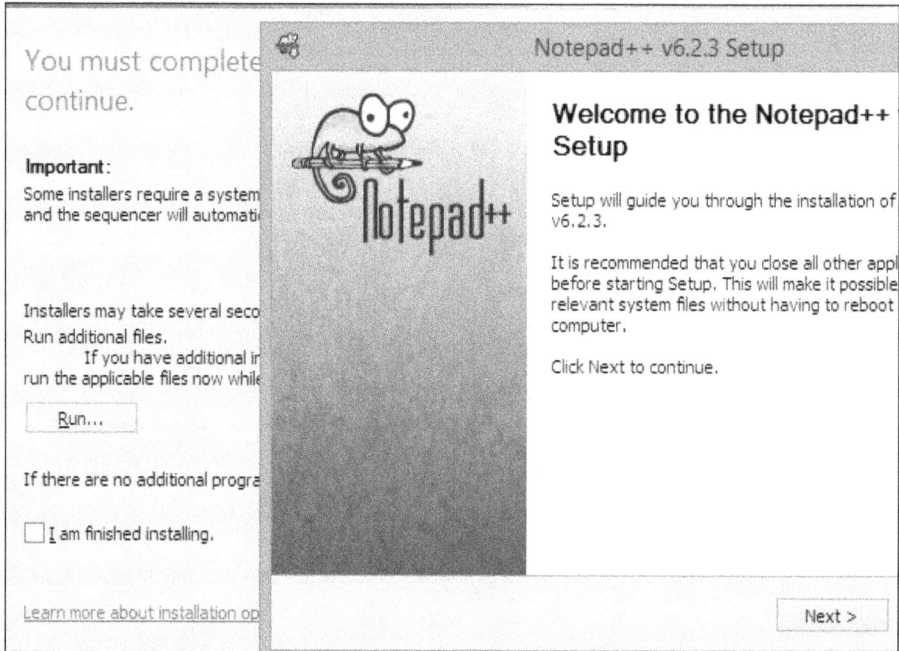

8. In the **Configure Software** section, select the earlier installed application and run it in order to complete the required configurations during the first application execution. Then, click on **Next**.

9. If the **Installation Report** section notifies you about no warnings, you can continue by clicking on the **Next** button.

10. In the **Customize** section, select the **Customize** option and click on **Next**.

11. In the **Streaming** section, highlight the software and click on the **Run Selected** button to test again its ability to be executed, and then flag the full download option, in the presence of slow network connections. Once complete, click on the **Next** button:

Run each program briefly to optimize the package over slow or unreliable networks.

To improve the initial end user experience over slow or unreliable networks, start each application and execute the most common tasks.

Name	Command Line
Notepad++	✓ "C:\Program Files (x86)\Notepad++\notepad++....

Run Selected   Run All

☑ Force application(s) to be fully downloaded before launching (recommended for slow/WAN networks). Note: if this is selected, all optimizations performed above will be lost.

12. In the **Target OS** area, you can choose to filter the target operating system versions, which allow the application to run. After selecting this, click on **Next**.

Restrict operating systems for this package.

○ Allow this package to run on any operating system.
◉ Allow this package to run only on the following operating systems.

32-bit	64-bit
☐ Windows 7 32-bit	☐ Windows 7 64-bit
☑ Windows 8 32-bit	☐ Windows Server 2008 R2 Remote Desktop Services
	☑ Windows 8 64-bit
	☑ Windows Server 2012 Remote Desktop Services

> Remember that you always sequence an application on the same operating system family. For instance, apps deployed on Windows 8 should not be deployed on Windows 7 OS versions because of compatibility and functionality problems.

13. In the **Create Package** section, choose to **Save the package now**, optionally add a **Description** to the packaged software, and select the location path previously used. To complete the entire procedure, click on the **Create** button.

14. In the **Completion** menu, click on **Close** to exit the creation wizard.

15. Connect to the App-V Management System server with domain administrative credentials, then run the Windows + C key combination, search for the **Application Virtualization Management Console** icon, and click on it.

> Microsoft Silverlight is required to run the App-V Management Console. Be sure you have installed it for the Internet Explorer browser.

16. On the left-side menu, click on the **PACKAGES** link, and then select the **ADD or UPGRADE PACKAGES** link on the right-hand side of the window.

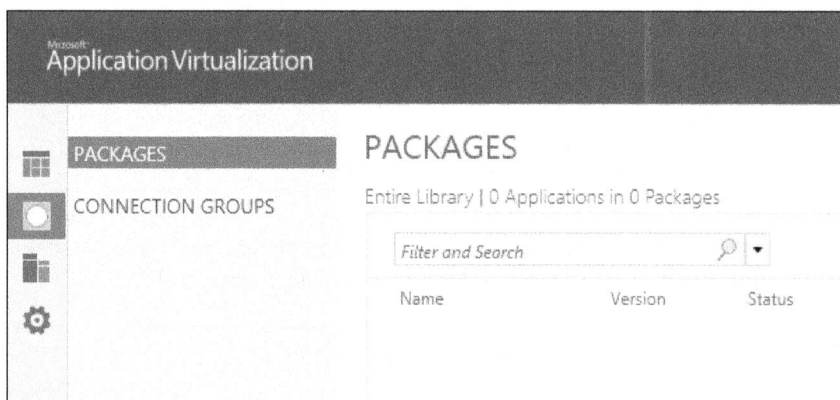

17. On the pop-up screen. insert the network path on which we previously generated the App-V sequence and locate the `.appv` sequence file. After this, click on the **Add** button to complete the procedure.

18. Wait for the package import procedure, and then click on the **Close** button on the **PACKAGE IMPORT** screen.

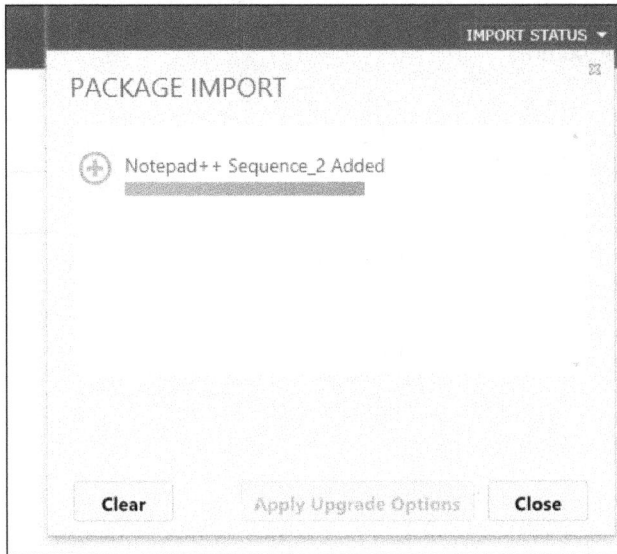

IMPORT STATUS ▼

PACKAGE IMPORT

(+) Notepad++ Sequence_2 Added

| Clear | Apply Upgrade Options | Close |

19. On the **Packages** menu, right-click on the imported sequence and select to edit one of the listed configurable options. In the following screenshot, the default configuration menu has been reported.

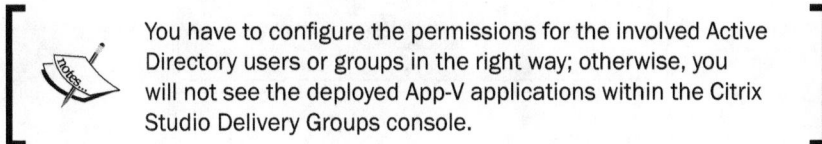

> You have to configure the permissions for the involved Active Directory users or groups in the right way; otherwise, you will not see the deployed App-V applications within the Citrix Studio Delivery Groups console.

20. If all the configurations are correct, right-click on the imported sequence and select the **Publish** link. The application status LED will become green.

21. Connect to the Delivery Controller server with an administrative domain user.

22. Run the Windows + C key combination, search for the **Citrix Studio** icon in the Citrix software section, and click on it.

23. Right-click on the **App-V Publishing** link on the left-side menu, select the **Add App-V Publishing** option, then insert two valid addresses for the App-V Management and Publishing servers, in the form of `http://fqdn:<portnumber>`. After completion, click on the **Test connection** button, to verify that you are able to connect to the App-V infrastructure:

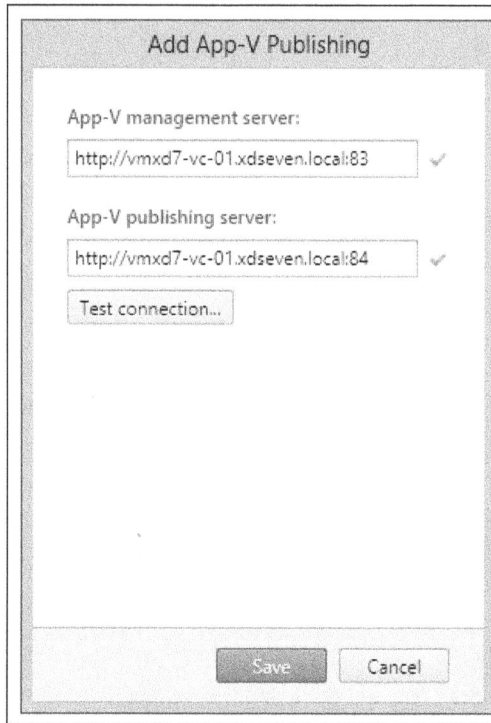

> During the application selection process from the Delivery Group application list, you will also find the associated App-V delivered packages.

24. During the Application deployment process, you will now be able to see the software delivered by the App-V infrastructure.

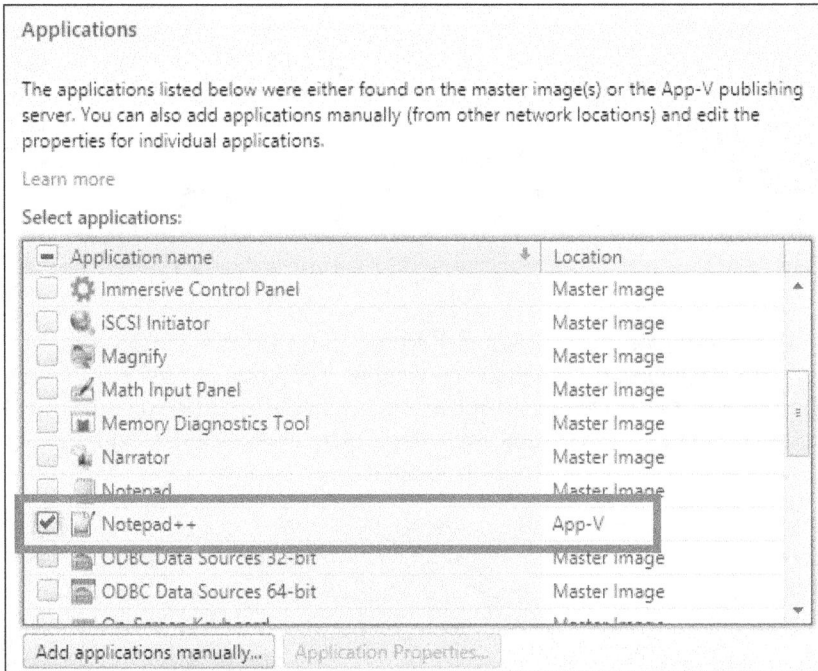

25. Connect to the StoreFront configured store and log in using the credentials of a user holding one or more published application(s). On the resources menu, you can now find the linked software in the application's catalog.

26. Connect to the Windows base image template, on which you installed the App-V Client and run it. If all the steps have been correctly executed, you will be able to see the application link on your desktop and on your Start menu.

How it works...

The Microsoft App-V platform is based on a **Central Management Console** that manages the application's profiles generated at a different location, publishing them to the clients installed on the user desktops. The process to create application profiles to redistribute to the users is called **sequencing**, the procedure earlier discussed during the application installation monitoring; the machine on which the sequencing process runs must be equal to the target clients, to whom the applications will be delivered. Through the publishing process, you have the possibility to filter the destination operating system versions. This process is now integrated into the XenDesktop 7.6 Studio console, with the possibility to associate the App-V infrastructural servers with the Citrix infrastructure, deploying applications catalog using the App-V offering, using the Citrix Delivery Controller platform.

After the application sequence is generated, it's time to use the App-V Management Server. With this platform, it is possible to load the application sequence and generate the software, which will be delivered to the users. In this section, you can also assign a particular file extension to the software, which means implementing the user experience for the application virtualization, applying it when a user needs to open a certain file.

To improve the application flow from the server to the clients, App-V permits you to use the **streaming** technology. This is particularly useful when bandwidth problems are the main issues to fight, and when isolation between the application's functionality and the user workspace is required.

There's more...

Using the Microsoft App-V technology, you can also publish particular application packages called **Package Accelerator**. These are formerly packages generated from the original installation media of complex applications, with all the setup procedure that converges at the end in a .cab archive.

Starting from this, you can create application packages to publish to the users without the necessity to repeat the installation procedure in the phase of their creation.

You can run the .cab generation procedure from the **Create Accelerator** section— the **Tools** menu on the **Sequencer** main menu. During the creation activities, you have to specify the **Installation Files** location, the Guidance for administrators (a file in the .rtf format generated from you, which should contain information about the application package use), and the destination location for the archive. Once this step is completed, you can use the .cab file to create the application package, by selecting **Create Package** using a Package Accelerator on the **Packaging Method** screen.

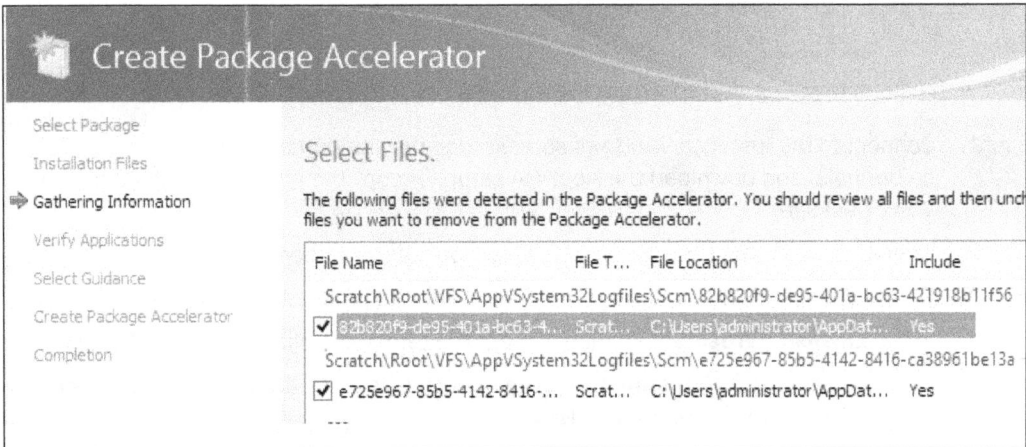

Create Package Accelerator

Select Package

Installation Files

➡ Gathering Information

Verify Applications

Select Guidance

Create Package Accelerator

Completion

Select Files.

The following files were detected in the Package Accelerator. You should review all files and then unch files you want to remove from the Package Accelerator.

File Name	File T...	File Location	Include
Scratch\Root\VFS\AppVSystem32Logfiles\Scm\82b820f9-de95-401a-bc63-421918b11f56			
☑ 82b820f9-de95-401a-bc63-4...	Scrat...	C:\Users\administrator\AppDat...	Yes
Scratch\Root\VFS\AppVSystem32Logfiles\Scm\e725e967-85b5-4142-8416-ca38961be13a			
☑ e725e967-85b5-4142-8416-...	Scrat...	C:\Users\administrator\AppDat...	Yes
---			

See also

▸ The *Configuring XenDesktop® 7.6 to interact with Microsoft Hyper-V 3.0 – SCVMM 2012 SP1* recipe in *Chapter 2, Configuring and Deploying Virtual Machines for XenDesktop® 7.6*

Using AppDNA™ 7.6

The process of migrating applications from older architectures to the newest system is not always as simple as expected. In many cases, you can have compatibility problems or unexpected application behaviors.

To mitigate application migration projects risks, Citrix offers a powerful tool called AppDNA, which performs checks and results about the possibility to move and migrate an application in a virtualized and different destination environment.

Getting ready

To install the AppDNA 7.6 software, you have to connect to the Citrix portal with a valid account, and download the software from the right section.

To install the server component, you need one of the following operating systems: Windows Server 2008 R2 SP1, Windows Server 2012, or Windows Server 2012 R2. To install only the client component, additionally, you can use the Windows 7 SP1, Windows 8, and Windows 8.1 operating systems.

To configure the database, the following Microsoft SQL Server releases can be used: SQL Server 2008 R2 SP1, SQL Server 2012 and 2012 Express, SQL Server 2014 and 2014 Express.

How to do it...

Follow the steps to set up and configure the AppDNA 7.6 software:

1. Connect to the installed Windows server machine with domain administrative credentials, and download the AppDNA setup, or copy the already downloaded `.msi` package.

2. Double click on the `Citrix-AppDNA.msi` package in order to execute it.

3. On the Welcome screen, click on the **Next** button to proceed.

4. In the **License Agreement** section, accept the terms and click on **Next** to continue.

5. On the **Citrix AppDNA Installation Type** screen, select the **Complete (server + client)** option. Once completed, click on **Next**.

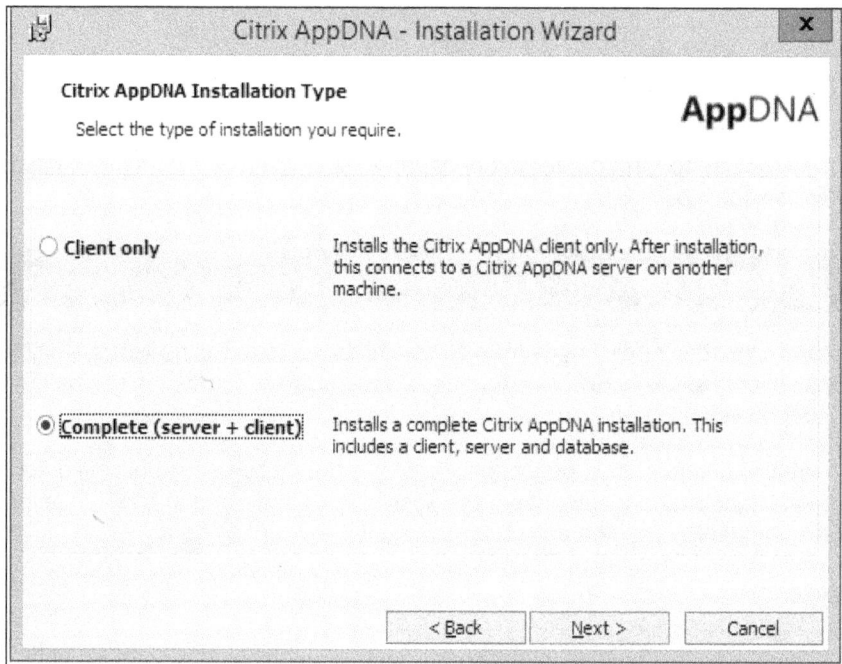

6. Select the installation paths on which the server and client components are installed, and then click on **Next**.

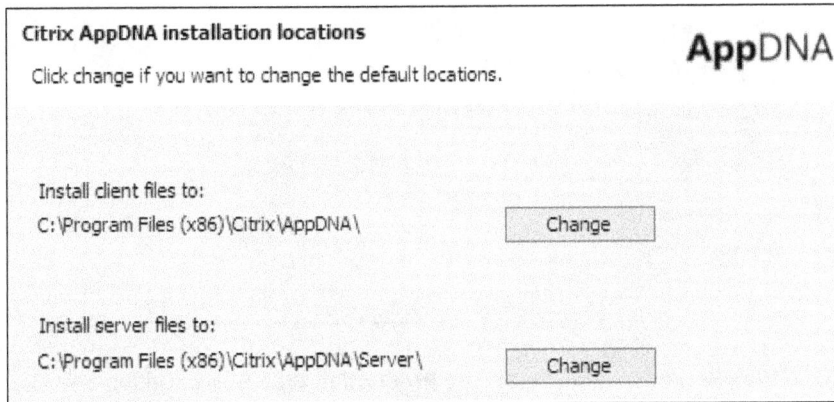

Citrix AppDNA installation locations   **App**DNA

Click change if you want to change the default locations.

Install client files to:

C:\Program Files (x86)\Citrix\AppDNA\   [Change]

Install server files to:

C:\Program Files (x86)\Citrix\AppDNA\Server\   [Change]

---

7. If all the selected options are correct, click on the **Install** button to start the setup process.

8. After the setup has been completed, leave the configuration wizard flag enabled and click on **Finish**.

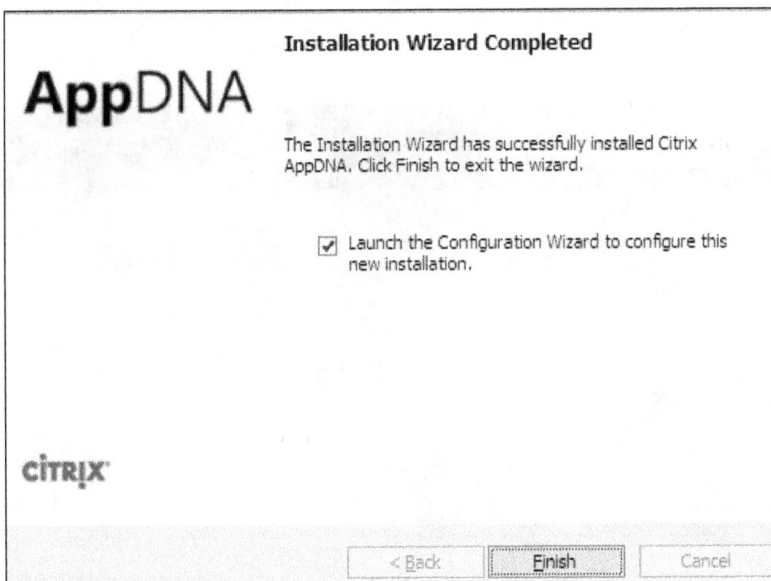

Installation Wizard Completed

AppDNA

The Installation Wizard has successfully installed Citrix AppDNA. Click Finish to exit the wizard.

☑ Launch the Configuration Wizard to configure this new installation.

CITRIX

[< Back] [**Finish**] [Cancel]

---

9. On the **Configure AppDNA** screen, select the **Configure new installation** option and click on **Next**.

```
Configure AppDNA

Web server                    ◉  Configure new installation
                                 Configure a new AppDNA installation

                              ○  Upgrade installation
                                 Upgrade an existing AppDNA installation

                              ○  Licensing
                                 Manage your AppDNA licensing
```

10. In the **Web Server** section, select the **Production Web Server** option and click on **Next**.

> You need to set up IIS to configure this option. Perform this task if it hasn't already been done.

11. On the **Create database** screen, configure the AppDNA database creation by pointing a valid server with an existing SQL Server instance. After configuring the database authentication, click on **Next**.

```
Database creation                                              CITRIX
  Enter new database details

Configure AppDNA    Server name:      DBMACHINE\INSTANCE          ∨  ...
Web server
                                      Example: MACHINE or MACHINE\INSTANCE
Create database
                    Database name:    AppDNADB


                    Database Authentication

                    ◉  Windows authentication

                    ○  SQL Server authentication
```

12. In the **Connect to database** section, select a valid domain or SQL credentials to access the selected instance, and then click on **Next**.

13. In the **License database** section, select whether activating a valid license, use the software in trial mode or activate the product by using an existing XenDesktop/XenApp Platinum license. Then, click on **Next** to continue.

○ A_c_tivate now.   Go to www.citrix.com and download your license file.

　　AppDNA

　　　License server machine: | WBIWINCSF02T | | _C_opy |

　　　　　License _f_ile: | | | _B_rowse |

○ _R_un in trial mode

○ Activate a XenDesktop or XenApp _P_latinum license

　　Platinum license server

　　　　Machine: | |

　　　　　Port: | 27000 |

| Advanced |

14. On the **System check** screen, you can proceed if all the system checks pass, by clicking the **Next** button.

15. On the Progress screen, wait for the completion of all the pending tasks, and then click on Next when finished. After completing this, click on the **Close** button.

Configure AppDNA

Web server

Create database

Connect to database

License database

System check

Progress

Step 4 of 29

15/04/2015 21:16:38: Creating Web site

Creating your database
Preparing the database
Installing the database

16. Run the Windows + *C* key combination, search for the **AppDNA** icon in the installed software section, and click on it.

17. Insert valid domain credentials in order to log in to AppDNA.

AppDNA

Username

DOMAIN\administrator

Password

••••••••••••••••••

⌄ Options

☐ Remember Me

CITRIX

Log On   Cancel

[📝 The default AppDNA credentials are administrator/apps3cur3.]

18. On the **Welcome** screen, click on the **Next** button to continue.

19. In the **Desktop** section, select which kind of desktop operating systems you have got in your environment, in terms of source and destination platforms, and then click on **Next**.

Desktop Compatibility
Select your Desktop operating systems   CITRIX

Welcome

Desktop

Server

Virtualization

Web Browser

XenApp Hosted

Progress

◉ My enterprise is working on a Windows desktop migration project

Select the operating systems you are moving from and to:

From   To

☑ Windows XP   ☐ Windows 7

☐ Windows Vista   ☑ Windows 8/8.1

☑ Windows 7

☑ We use English versions of Windows only

○ My enterprise is not working on a Windows desktop migration project at this time

20. On the **Server** screen, as done earlier for the **Desktop** section, select the source and destination operating systems involved in your migration activities. Click on **Next** to continue.

Welcome	
Desktop	◉ My enterprise is working on a Windows server migration project
Server	Select the operating systems you are moving from and to:
Virtualization	From / To
Web Browser	☐ Windows Server 2003 / ☐ Windows Server 2008 R2
XenApp Hosted	☑ Windows Server 2008 / ☑ Windows Server 2012/2012 R2
Progress	☑ Windows Server 2008 R2

21. In the **Virtualization** section, select if you have got any application virtualization platform in your environment, and click on **Next** to continue.

Welcome	
Desktop	◉ My enterprise is working on an application virtualization project
Server	Select the technologies and versions for which you want to evaluate
Virtualization	App-V
Web Browser	○ App-V 4.5 ○ App-V 4.6 SP1
XenApp Hosted	◉ App-V 5
Progress	
	○ My enterprise is not working on an application virtualization project at this time

22. In the **Web Browser** section, select which version of the main browser your company is going to adopt, and then click on **Next**.

Welcome	⦿ My enterprise is working on adopting new Web browsers
Desktop	
Server	Select the browsers for which you want to evaluate Web applications.
Virtualization	☑ Internet Explorer
Web Browser	◯ Internet Explorer 8.0 ⦿ 32-bit only
XenApp Hosted	⦿ Internet Explorer 9.0 ◯ 32-bit and 64-bit
Progress	◯ Internet Explorer 10.0
	◯ Internet Explorer 11.0
	☑ FireFox
	⦿ FireFox (all versions)
	☑ WorxWeb
	⦿ WorxWeb (all versions)
	◯ My enterprise is not working on adopting new Web browsers at this time

23. In the **XenApp Hosted** section, select whether your company has or does not have an active migration plan to XenApp. Click on the **Configure** button to complete the wizard's activities.

> For any of the aforementioned options, you can also select the option of no active migration plans for one or all specific sections.

24. In the **Progress** section, wait for the completion of the configuration activities, and then click on **Close** after the end of these tasks.

25. On the left-side menu, select the **Import & Analyze** option, and then choose which kind of application importing (**Desktop** or **Web**), in order to analyze them.

Import & Analyze ◀	AppDNA Dashboard	
Discover Applications		
Import	Applications	Desktop applications:
▪ Applications		Import desktop applications
▪ Web Applications	0	
▪ Operating Systems		Web applications: 0
▪ Managed Applications		Import web applications
Analyze		
▪ Analyze	**Report summary**	

26. Select the Desktop application, click on the **Direct Import** tab, and then select a valid .msi file or APP-V package to import and analyze:

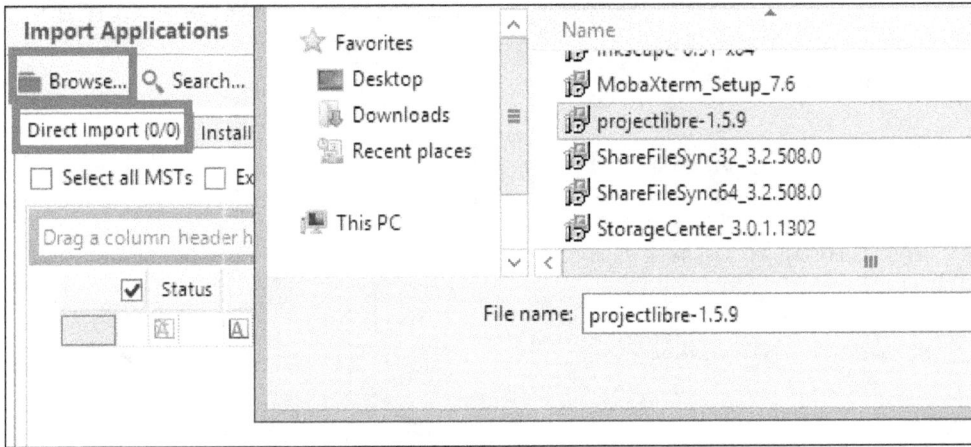

27. After you have chosen the application, flag it and click on the **Import** button; after the import has been completed, click on **Analyze** to start the application analysis.

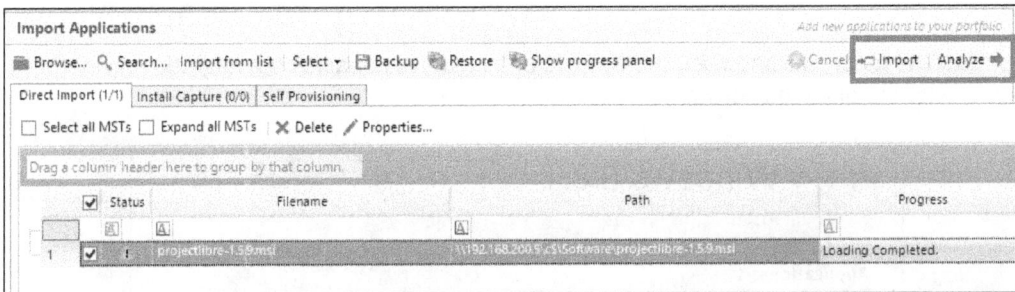

28. On the Application Analysis first screen, select the **Compatibility Manager (Desktop, Server, XenApp) environment**, then click on the **Next** button.

29. Wait for the end of the analysis, in order to receive the reports related to every analyzed environment.

30. Select which generated report you want to view, and then click on **Finish** to continue:

31. The report will show you the positive and negative impacts on a migration scenario for the analyzed software.

32. The same procedure can be performed for the Web applications, by selecting the **Import & Analyze** tab and clicking on the **Web Applications** link.

33. At this level, the checks will be performed against the browser configured within your organization, as earlier selected. Click on the **Next** button to proceed.

34. After completion, select one of the available reports as you have already done for the desktop apps, and then click on **Finish** to analyze the data:

Application Analysis

⬅ Previous

Which report would you like to view?

Overview Summary: Overview Summary ⌄
Overview Summary: Overview Summary
Forward Path: Forward Path
WebApp Compatibility Manager: Firefox
WebApp Compatibility Manager: IE

Analysis results

✓ 195 out of 195 algorithms succeeded   ⌄ 2 mins, 14 secs

Algorithm Succeeded ▽

⊟ Algorithm Succeeded : True (195 items)

Report	Algorithm Group	Algorithm	Manifestation	Time Taken	Failure Reason
Firefox	ActiveX	FF_AX_1	Detects presenc...	0:00:00,016	
Firefox	x64	FF_x64_001	AppDNA has de...	0:00:00,063	

How it works...

AppDNA is a useful utility that simplifies and accelerates the migration process of your company's applications. This is particularly useful when you have to move existing software from older operating system releases, such as Windows 2003 or Windows 2008, to the latest OS versions.

The setup phase will configure the AppDNA platform by installing the server and the client components. It also configures the link to a valid existing SQL Server instance on which the application data to be analyzed is imported and collected.

In the first configuration phase, you should only select the components, which are parts of your infrastructure, in terms of the source and destination environments. The choices can be performed on a set of predefined categories, such as the Microsoft server operating systems, Microsoft desktop operating systems, virtualization platforms (XenApp and App-V), and browsers (Internet Explorer, Mozilla Firefox and Citrix Worx).

To analyze the software that will be migrated, you need a valid installer, in the form of `.msi` or an App-V package. This will be imported and analyzed in the system by the **Direct Import** option. In absence of the listed compatible packages, you can use the **Install capture** option, but in this situation, you need a virtual machine to simulate the application installation. After this step, you will be able to analyze the application's features.

Another possible check concerns web applications. In this second case, you need to import into the system a valid web application address. The procedure will be similar to the desktop processing, adding a browser navigation simulator required to import the behavior of the web app during the navigation phase.

There's more...

Reports generated by the AppDNA system can not only be viewed within the same application, but they can also be exported in a set of different formats. After you have generated a report, based on the category listed at the end of the analysis, on the right-side report menu, you have a set of options to export the report, such as `.pdf`, `.html`, or `.csv`. Choosing one of them can be useful to archive application reports on external sources other than the AppDNA server.

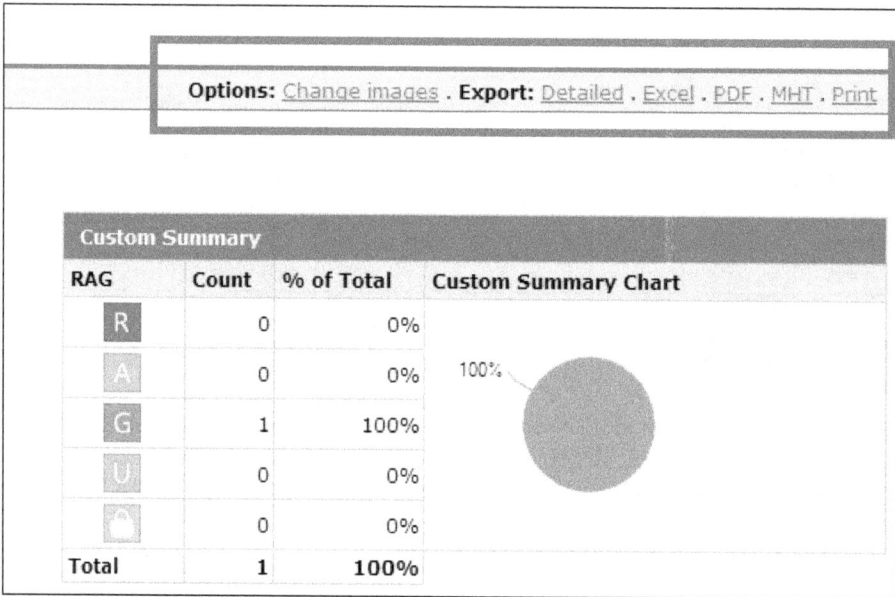

Options: Change images . **Export:** Detailed . Excel . PDF . MHT . Print			

Custom Summary

RAG	Count	% of Total	Custom Summary Chart
R	0	0%	
A	0	0%	100%
G	1	100%	
U	0	0%	
	0	0%	
Total	1	100%	

See also

▸ The *Publishing the Hosted applications* recipe in *Chapter 6, Deploying Applications.*

7

XenDesktop®
Infrastructure Tuning

In this chapter, we will cover the following recipes:

- ▸ Configuring the XenDesktop policies
- ▸ Configuring printers
- ▸ Configuring USB devices
- ▸ Configuring the XenDesktop logging

Introduction

XenDesktop offers a modular architecture in which both security and user experience are important options to consider and balance. Citrix provides best practice documents to deliver a VDI solution that the end user likes to work with. Citrix products permit you a deeper protection and avoid performance issues by enabling the right policies.

During this chapter, we will discuss the configuration of the XenDesktop infrastructural policies, the capability to regulate the use of external devices such as printers and removable storage devices, and the way to configure the logging of the activities performed on the XenDesktop infrastructure.

Configuring the XenDesktop® policies

Now that the XenDesktop infrastructure has been configured, it is time to activate and populate the Virtual Desktop Infrastructure policies. This is an extremely important part of the implementation process because, with them, you can regulate the resource use and assignment, but you will also improve the general virtual desktop performance.

Getting ready

All the policies will be applied to the deployed virtual desktop instances and the assigned users, so you need an already existent XenDesktop infrastructure on which to enable and use the configuration rules.

How to do it...

In the following steps we will explain the configuration for the user and machine policies offered by XenDesktop:

1. Connect to the Delivery Controller server with an administrative domain user.

2. Run the Windows + *C* key combination, search for the **Citrix Studio** icon in the Citrix software section and click on it.

3. Click on the **Policy** link in the left-hand menu, and then select **Create Policy** in the right-hand panel.

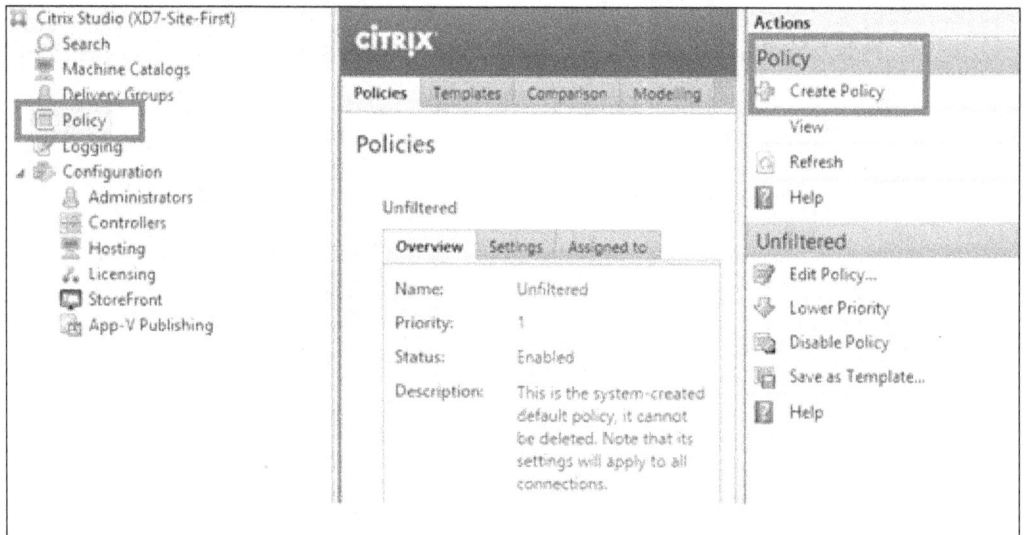

4. In the **Categories** menu, click on the following sections and configure the values for the policies that will be applied to the clients:

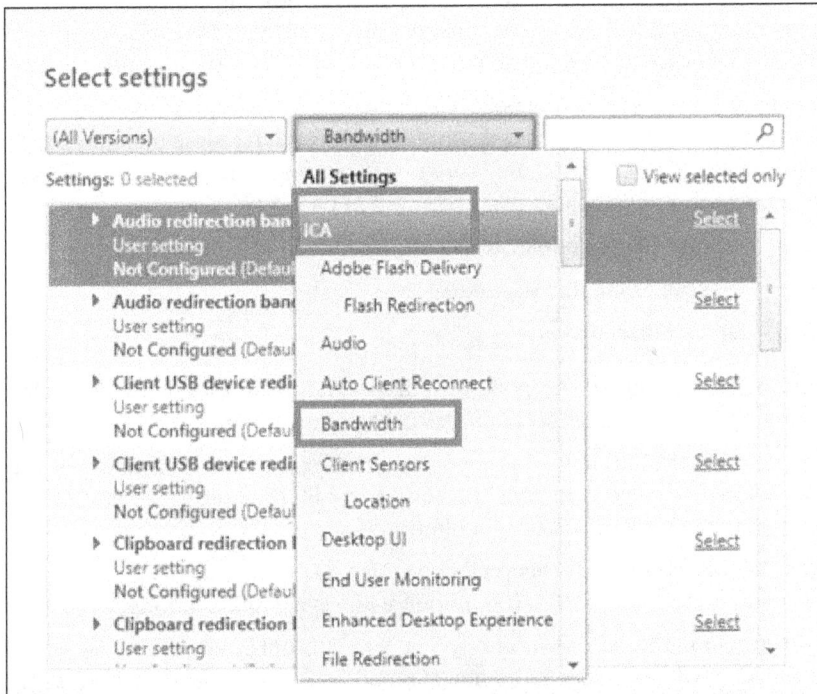

Select settings

(All Versions) ▼	Bandwidth ▼		🔎
Settings: 0 selected	**All Settings** ▲	☐ View selected only	
▶ **Audio redirection ban** User setting Not Configured (Defau	ICA	Select ▲	
▶ **Audio redirection ban** User setting Not Configured (Defaul	Adobe Flash Delivery Flash Redirection	Select	
▶ **Client USB device redi** User setting Not Configured (Defau	Audio Auto Client Reconnect	Select	
▶ **Client USB device redi** User setting Not Configured (Defau	Bandwidth	Select	
▶ **Clipboard redirection** User setting Not Configured (Defau	Client Sensors Location Desktop UI	Select	
▶ **Clipboard redirection** User setting	End User Monitoring Enhanced Desktop Experience File Redirection ▼	Select	

ICA section

▶ **ICA Listener connection timeout**: Insert a value in milliseconds—default 12000.

▶ **ICA listener port number**: The TCP/IP port number on which the ICA protocol will try to establish the connection. The default value is 1494.

Adobe Flash Delivery subsection

▶ **Flash acceleration**: In this policy, values can be either set as **Enabled** or **Disabled**. With this policy, you can decide whether to enable the rendering of the Flash contents on the client side, only in legacy mode.

> By enabling this policy, you have the ability to reduce the network usage executing the Flash web components directly on the client machine. To use this configuration, you need the latest Citrix Receiver and Adobe Flash versions. Moreover, be sure that your client supports this feature.

- **Flash background color list**: Specify a set of colors to apply to a specific URL with Flash contents. Even in this case, Flash will be rendered on the client side.

- **Flash backwards compatibility**: In this policy, values can either be set as **Enabled** or **Disabled**. With this policy you can choose to activate the compatibility of older Citrix Receiver versions with the most recent Citrix Flash policies and features.

- **Flash default behavior**: This policy regulates the use of the Adobe Flash technology, respectively enabling the most recent Citrix for Flash features (including the client-side processing), permitting only server-side processed contents, or blocking any Flash content. In this policy, values can either be set as follows:

  - ❑ **Enable Flash acceleration**

  - ❑ **Disable Flash acceleration**

  - ❑ **Block Flash player**

- **Flash event logging**: In this policy, values can be either **Enabled** or **Disabled**. Decide whether to create system logs for the Adobe Flash events.

- **Flash intelligent fallback**: In this policy, values can be either **Enabled** or **Disabled**. This policy, if enabled, activates the server-side Flash content processing when the client-side Flash content is not required.

- **Flash latency threshold**: This policy specifies a value, in milliseconds, to apply as a maximum latency threshold. The default value is **30 milliseconds**.

- **Flash server-side content fetching URL list**: This policy specifies a list of web URLs for which Flash contents can be downloaded to the server and then be sent to the client devices.

> Consider using this policy when the Internet connection is not present on the client devices.

- **Flash URL compatibility list**: This policy specifies a list of rules, for a specific web URL, to render Flash content on the client side, on the server side, or to block any rendering.

> The Flash Redirection feature has been strongly improved starting from the 5.5 version of XenDesktop.

Audio subsection

- **Audio over UDP real-time transport**: This policy can either be set as **Enabled** or **Disabled**. With this policy, you decide on which protocols to transmit the audio packets: RTP/UDP (policy enabled) or TCP (policy disabled). The choice depends on the kind of audio traffic to transmit. UDP should be better in terms of performance and bandwidth consumption.

▸ **Audio Plug N Play**: In this policy, values can be set as either **Allowed** or **Prohibited** to allow or prohibit the ability to use multiple audio devices.

▸ **Audio quality**: The values can be set as **Low**, **Medium** or **High**. These parameters depend on a compromise between the quality of the network connections and the audio level, and they respectively cover the **low-speed connections**, **optimized for speech**, and **high-definition audio** cases.

▸ **Client audio redirection**: The values can be set as either **Allowed** or **Prohibited**. Allowing or prohibiting this policy permits applications to use the audio device on the client machine(s).

▸ **Client microphone redirection**: In this policy, values can be either **Allowed** or **Prohibited**. This policy permits you to map client microphone devices to use within a desktop session.

> Try to reduce the network and load impact of the multimedia components and devices where the high user experience is not required.

Select settings

(All Versions) ▾	Audio ▾	🔍

Settings: 14 selected   ☐ View selected only

✓ ▸ **Audio over UDP real-time transport** User setting Enabled (Default: Enabled)	Edit | Unselect
✓ ▸ **Audio Plug N Play** User setting Allowed (Default: Allowed)	Edit | Unselect
✓ ▸ **Audio quality** User setting (Default: High - high definition audio)	Edit | Unselect
✓ ▸ **Client audio redirection** User setting Allowed (Default: Allowed)	Edit | Unselect
✓ ▸ **Client microphone redirection** User setting Allowed (Default: Allowed)	Edit | Unselect

Auto Client Reconnect subsection

▸ **Auto client reconnect**: The values **Allowed** or **Prohibited** specify whether to automatically reconnect a broken connection from a client.

▸ **Auto client reconnect authentication**: The values **Do not require authentication** or **Require authentication** decide whether the Citrix infrastructure should request your credentials every time you have to reperform a login operation.

▸ **Auto client reconnect logging**: In this policy, values can be set as either **Do Not Log auto-reconnect events** or **Log auto-reconnect events**. This policy enables or disables the logging activities in the system log for the reconnection process. In case of active auto client reconnect, you should also activate its logging.

Bandwidth subsection

▸ **Audio redirection bandwidth limit**: In this policy, insert a value in Kbps to set the maximum bandwidth assigned to playing and recording audio activities.

▸ **Audio redirection bandwidth limit percent**: In this policy, a maximum percentage value to play and record audio can be inserted.

▸ **Client USB device redirection bandwidth limit**: Insert a value in Kbps to set the maximum bandwidth assigned to the USB devices redirection.

▸ **Client USB device redirection bandwidth limit percent**: In this policy, insert a maximum percentage value for the USB devices redirection.

▸ **Clipboard redirection bandwidth limit**: In this policy, a value in Kbps can be inserted to set the maximum bandwidth assigned to the clipboard traffic from the local client to the remote session.

▸ **Clipboard redirection bandwidth limit percent**: Insert a maximum percentage value for the clipboard traffic from the local client to the remote session.

▸ **COM port redirection bandwidth limit**: Insert a value in Kbps to set the maximum bandwidth assigned to the client COM port-redirected traffic.

▸ **COM port redirection bandwidth limit percent**: In this policy, insert a maximum percentage value for the client COM port-redirected traffic.

▸ **File redirection bandwidth limit**: Insert a value in Kbps to set the maximum bandwidth assigned to the client drives redirection.

▸ **File redirection bandwidth limit percent**: Insert a maximum percentage value for the client drives redirection.

▸ **HDX MediaStream Multimedia Acceleration bandwidth limit**: Insert a value in Kbps to set the maximum bandwidth assigned to the multimedia contents redirected through the HDX MediaStream acceleration.

▸ **HDX MediaStream Multimedia Acceleration bandwidth limit percent**: Insert a maximum percentage value for the multimedia contents redirected through the HDX MediaStream acceleration.

▶ **LPT port redirection bandwidth limit**: Insert a value in Kbps to set the maximum bandwidth assigned to the client LPT port-redirected traffic.

▶ **LPT port redirection bandwidth limit percent**: Insert a maximum percentage value for the client LPT port-redirected traffic.

▶ **Overall session bandwidth limit**: Specify a value in Kbps for the total bandwidth assigned to the client sessions.

▶ **Printer redirection bandwidth limit**: Insert a value in Kbps to set the maximum bandwidth assigned to access a client printer.

▶ **Printer redirection bandwidth limit percent**: Insert a maximum percentage value to access a printer in a client device session.

▶ **TWAIN device redirection bandwidth limit**: Insert a value in Kbps to set the maximum bandwidth assigned to a TWAIN scanner device.

▶ **TWAIN device redirection bandwidth limit percent**: Insert a maximum percentage value to access TWAIN imaging.

[In the presence of both bandwidth limit and bandwidth limit percent enabled policies, the most restrictive value will be used.]

Client Sensors subsection

▶ **Allow applications to use the physical location of the client device** – Values: **Allowed** or **Prohibited**. With this policy you can permit applications to use the physical location of a client device.

Desktop UI subsection

▶ **Desktop Composition graphics quality**: In this policy, values can be set as **Lossless**, **High**, **Medium**, and **Low**. This policy lets you set the quality level for the desktop composition redirection. The default value is **Medium**.

▶ **Desktop Composition Redirection**: In this policy, values can be set as either **Enabled** or **Disabled**. This policy permits use of the Desktop Composition from the Virtual Desktop Agent to the client device.

[By enabling this policy, users will obtain a richer user experience. You cannot apply it to delivered Server OS instances.]

▶ **Desktop wallpaper**: In this policy, values can be set as either **Allowed** or **Prohibited**. Through this policy you can permit use of the desktop wallpaper in your session. Disable this policy if you want to standardize your desktop deployment.

▸ **Menu animation**: In this policy, values can be either **Allowed** or **Prohibited**. This policy permits use of the animated menu of the Microsoft operating systems. The choice depends on what kind of performances you need for your desktops.

▸ **View window contents while dragging**: In this policy, values can be set as either **Allowed** or **Prohibited**. This policy gives you the ability to see the entire window contents during the drag-and-drop activities between windows, if enabled. Otherwise, you will see only the window's border.

End User Monitoring subsection

▸ **ICA round trip calculation**: In this policy, values can be set as either **Enabled** or **Disabled**. Through this policy you can permit enabling calculation of the ICA network traffic time.

▸ **ICA round trip calculation interval**: Insert the time interval in seconds for the period of the round trip calculation.

▸ **ICA round trip calculations for idle connections**: In this policy, values can be set as **Enabled** or **Disabled**. You can decide whether to enable the round trip calculation for connections that are not performing traffic. Enable this policy only if necessary.

The Enhanced Desktop Experience subsection

▸ **Enhanced Desktop Experience**: In this policy, values can be set as **Allowed** or **Prohibited**. This policy, applicable only to the Server OS instances, enriches the machine graphical experience in a published desktop session, making the user experience near to the client device operating system.

File Redirection subsection

▸ **Auto connect client drives**: In this policy, values can be either set as **Enabled** or **Disabled**. With this policy, the local drives of your client either will or won't be automatically connected at the logon time.

▸ **Client drive redirection**: In this policy, values can be set as either **Allowed** or **Prohibited**. With the drive redirection, it is possible to permit saving files locally on the client machine drives.

▸ **Client fixed drives**: In this policy, values can be set as **Allowed** or **Prohibited**. This policy permits reading data from, and saving information to, the fixed drives of your client machine.

▸ **Client floppy drives**: In this policy, values can be set as **Allowed** or **Prohibited**. This policy permits reading data from, and saving information to, the floppy drives of your client machine. This should be allowed only in presence of an existing floppy drive, otherwise it has no value to your infrastructure.

▸ **Client network drives**: In this policy, values can be set as **Allowed** or **Prohibited**. With this policy, you have the possibility to map the remote network drives from your client.

- **Client optical drives**: In this policy, values can be set as **Allowed** or **Prohibited**. With this policy, you can enable or prevent the access to the optical client drives, such as CD-ROM or DVD-ROM.

- **Client removable drives**: In this policy, values can be set as **Allowed** or **Prohibited**. This policy allows or prohibits mapping in order to read and save removable drives from your client, such as USB keys.

- **Host to client redirection**: In this policy, values can be set as **Enabled** or **Disabled**. Enabling this policy will associate and execute media content to the client device. If you disable it, all the media will be executed on the server.

- **Preserve client drive letters**: In this policy, values can be set as **Enabled** or **Disabled**. Enabling this policy offers you the possibility to maintain the client drive letters when mapping them in the remote session, when possible.

- **Read-only client drive access**: In this policy, values can be set as **Enabled** or **Disabled**. Enabling this policy will not permit accessing in write mode, the mapped client drivers. By default, this policy is disabled, to permit full drive access. To reduce the impact on client security, you should enable it, then modify when necessary.

> These are powerful policies to regulate the access to the physical storage resources. You should configure them to be consistent with your company security policies.

- **Special folder redirection**: In this policy, values can be set as **Allowed** or **Prohibited**. Allowing the policy will point the Desktop and Documents user's folders to the client's directories. On the other case, they will point the host locations.

- **Use asynchronous writes**: In this policy, values can be set as **Enabled** or **Disabled**. Allows enabling of the asynchronous data disk writes. By default, they are disabled.

> You should enable this latest policy only in the presence of WAN connections and remote connected users.

Graphics subsection

- **Display memory limit**: In this policy, configure the maximum value in kB to assign to the video buffer for a session. This policy only applies to the deployed Server OS desktops.

- **Display mode degrade preference**: In this policy, values can be set as **Degrade color depth first** or **Degrade resolution first**. Configure a parameter to lower the resolution or the color quality in case of graphic memory overflow.

▸ **Dynamic Windows Preview**: The values are either **Enabled** or **Disabled**. With this policy, you have the ability to turn on the high-level preview of the open windows on the screen.

▸ **Image caching**: In this policy, values can be either **Enabled** or **Disabled**. With this parameter, you can cache images on the client to obtain a faster response.

▸ **Legacy graphics mode**: In this policy, values can be either **Enabled** or **Disabled**. By enabling this policy you will reduce the quality of the global user experience, improving the ability to scale-up resources, but degrading the graphic quality.

▸ **Maximum allowed color depth**: In this policy, values can be **8 bits per pixel**, **15 bits per pixel**, **16 bits per pixel**, **24 bits per pixel,** and **32 bits per pixel**. This policy permits you to specify the maximum permitted color depth for a session.

> The higher the color depth, the higher the memory usage.

▸ **Notify user when display mode is degraded**: The values are **Enabled** or **Disabled**. In case of degraded connections, you can display a pop up to send a notification to the involved users. This only applies to Server OS instances.

▸ **Persistent cache threshold**: In this policy, specify a value in Kbps to cache bitmaps on the client disk. This is used in case of frequently reused images.

▸ **Queueing and tossing**: In this policy, values are either **Enabled** or **Disabled**. By enabling this policy you can stop the processing of images being replaced by other pictures.

> In the presence of slow or WAN network connections, you should create a separate policy group, which reduces the display memory size, configures the Degrade color depth policy, activates the image caching, and removes the advanced Windows graphical features.

Keep Alive subsection

▸ **ICA keep alive timeout**: Insert a value in seconds to configure the keep alive timeout for the ICA connections.

▸ **ICA keep alives**: This policy includes the values **Do not send ICA keep alive messages** or **Send ICA keep alive messages**. Configure if you want to send keep alive signals for the running sessions.

Local App Access subsection

▶ **Allow local app access**: In this policy, values can be set as **Allowed** or **Prohibited**. This policy permits the use of the LAA within your environment.

▶ **URL redirection black list**: In this policy, specify a set of web URLs to run on the physical client device, out of your VDI resources.

▶ **URL redirection white list**: In this policy, specify a set of web URLs to run within your assigned VDI resources.

[We have already discussed the LAA in *Chapter 6, Deploying Applications*.]

Mobile Experience subsection

▶ **Automatic keyboard display**: In this policy, **Allowed** or **Prohibited** values allow you to automatically display the display keyboard on mobile devices. This policy is disabled by default.

▶ **Launch touch-optimized desktop**: In this policy, values are either **Allowed** or **Prohibited**. This policy will permit you to use or disable the execution of an optimized mobile touch-pad version.

▶ **Remote the combo box**: In this policy, values are **Allowed** or **Prohibited**. This policy will configure the type of combo boxes to use on your device: allow it to use the Windows combo box version on any device, such as iOS, or prohibit the use of the native combo box version.

Multimedia subsection

▶ **Limit video quality**: Choose the video quality level of the HDX connections from the following options:

❑ **Not Configured**

❑ **Maximum Video Quality 1080p/8.5Mbps**

❑ **Maximum Video Quality 720p/4Mbps**

❑ **Maximum Video Quality 480p/720Kbps**

❑ **Maximum Video Quality 380p/400Kbps**

❑ **Maximum Video Quality 240p/200Kbps**

[The level of the HDX quality should always be configured based on the speed of your network connection.]

▸ **Multimedia conferencing**: In this policy, values can be set as either **Allowed** or **Prohibited**. This policy permits the use of video conferencing applications, in terms of webcam device use and office communicator software support.

▸ **Optimization for Windows Media multimedia redirection over WAN**: In this policy, values are either **Allowed** or **Prohibited**. If allowed, this policy permits Windows media content compression over a WAN connection.

▸ **Use GPU for optimizing Windows Media multimedia redirection over WAN**: In this policy, values can be set as either **Allowed** or **Prohibited**. This policy permits the use of GPU to optimize media content elaboration over a WAN connection.

▸ **Windows Media client-side content fetching**: In this policy, values are either **Allowed** or **Prohibited**. When allowed, this policy permits client devices to directly stream multimedia contents from the source, bypassing the XenDesktop host server.

> In order to reduce the load on the XenDesktop server components, you should allow this last policy. The **Windows Media Redirection** policy configured to **Allowed** is a prerequisite to use the client-side content fetching policy.

▸ **Windows Media Redirection**: The values set as either **Allowed** or **Prohibited** decide whether to redirect the multimedia execution on the Citrix server(s) and then stream it to clients.

▸ **Windows Media Redirection Buffer Size**: Insert a value, in seconds, for the buffer used to deliver multimedia contents to clients.

▸ **Windows Media Redirection Buffer Size Use**: The values can be set as either **Enabled** or **Disabled**. This policy lets you use the previously configured media buffer size.

Multi-Stream Connections subsection

▸ **Audio over UDP**: The values can be set as either **Allowed** or **Prohibited**. This policy, where allowed, permits opening a UDP port on which to transfer the audio media for a client.

▸ **Audio UDP Port Range**: This policy specifies a port range for the UDP connections used to stream audio data. The default range is `16500-16509`.

▸ **Multi-Port Policy**: This policy configures the traffic shaping to implement the **QoS** (**Quality of Service**). You have to specify from two to four ports and assign them a priority level.

Edit Setting

Multi-Port Policy

Applies to: XenDesktop: 5.5, 5.6 Feature Pack 1, 7.0 Server OS, 7.0 Desktop OS

CGP default port:	CGP default port priority:
Default Port	High
CGP port1:	CGP port1 priority:
5100	Very High
CGP port2:	CGP port2 priority:
5004	Medium
CGP port3:	CGP port3 priority:
9100	Low

Use default value:

- **Multi-Stream computer setting**: The values can be set as **Enabled** or **Disabled**. Decide whether to activate the Multi-Stream ports previously configured, on the server side.

- **Multi-Stream user setting**: The value set as **Enabled** or **Disabled** decides whether to activate the Multi-Stream feature for specific users.

> To be able to use the Multi-Stream user setting, you need to activate the **Multi-Stream computer setting** policy.

Port Redirection subsection

- **Auto connect client COM ports**: The values can be set as **Enabled** or **Disabled**. If enabled, this policy automatically maps the client COM ports.

- **Auto connect client LPT ports**: The values can be either **Enabled** or **Disabled**. This policy auto connects the client LPT ports, if enabled.

- **Client COM port redirection**: The values can be set as **Allowed** or **Prohibited**. This policy configures the COM port redirection between the client and the remote session.

- **Client LPT port redirection**: The values can be set as **Allowed** or **Prohibited**. This policy configures the LPT port redirection between the client and the remote session.

> You only have to enable the necessary ports, so disable the policies for the missing COM or LPT.

Security subsection

▶ **Secure ICA minimum encryption level**: This configuration permits assigning an encryption level to data sent between the client and the server during a XenDesktop session. This policy only applies to Server OS instances. The values can be set as:

  ❑ **Basic**

  ❑ **RC5 (128 bit) log on only**

  ❑ **RC5 (40 bit)**

  ❑ **RC5 (56 bit)**

  ❑ **RC5 (128 bit)**

> You can find an explanation about the RC5 encryption algorithm at `http://en.wikipedia.org/wiki/RC5`

▶ **Server idle timer interval**: This policy specifies a value in milliseconds to set the interval on which to maintain active idle sessions (no input from users). This policy only applies to Server OS instances.

Session Limits subsection

▶ **Concurrent logon limit**: This policy specifies a numeric value to set the maximum number of connections made by a single user. This policy only applies to Server OS instances.

▶ **Disconnected session timer**: The values can be set as **Enabled** or **Disabled**. This policy enables or disables the counter used to migrate from a locked workstation to a logged-off session. For security reasons, you should enable the automatic logoff of the idle sessions.

> Based on the **Disconnected session timer** parameter we have the **Smooth Roaming** feature: this is a term for making user's sessions move from one end device to another end device. Smooth roaming is based on disconnected session time, and the time in between the movement from a device to another can only be less than the configured disconnected time.

▶ **Disconnected session timer interval**: Insert a value in minutes that will be used as a counter reference value to log off locked workstations. Base this parameter on a real inactivity time for your company employers.

▶ **Session connection timer**: The values can be set as **Enabled** or **Disabled**. This policy will permit using a timer to measure the duration of active connections from clients to the remote sessions.

▸ **Session connection timer interval**: This policy specifies the maximum duration for an uninterrupted connection between a user device and a client. The maximum value is **24 hours** (**1440** minutes).

▸ **Session idle timer**: The values can be set as **Enabled** or **Disabled**. If enabled, this policy will disconnect a client session after a certain amount of inactivity. The value is specified in the next policy.

▸ **Session idle timer interval**: This policy specifies the maximum duration for an idle connection (no input) between a user device and a client. The maximum value is **24 hours** (**1440** minutes).

Session Reliability subsection

▸ **Session reliability connections**: The values can be set as **Allowed** or **Prohibited**. By enabling this policy, you permit the sessions to remain active in case of network problems, permitting users to see the content of published desktops or applications, such as a screenshot of the last state, while the network issues are restored, keeping the session active.

▸ **Session reliability port number**: This policy specifies the port used by ICA to check the reliability of incoming connections. The default port is 2598.

▸ **Session reliability timeout**: This policy specifies a value, in seconds, used by the session reliability manager component to wait for a client reconnection.

> You cannot enable the ICA keep alives policy if the **Session Reliability** policies have been activated. They cannot be enabled together.

Time zone control subsection

▸ **Estimate local time for legacy clients**: The values can be set as **Enabled** or **Disabled**. If enabled, this policy will try to estimate the client time zone, in case of a lack of information. This can be only applied to Server OS instances.

▸ **Use local time of client**: The values can be set as **Use server time zone** or **Use client time zone**. Based on the policy configuration, the time zone for a XenDesktop session will be based on the client or server-configured time zone.

TWAIN Devices subsection

▸ **Client TWAIN device redirection**: The values can be set as **Allowed** or **Prohibited**. If enabled, this policy permits mapping existing TWAIN image devices, as scanners, for example.

▸ **TWAIN compression level**: The values can be set as **None, Low, Medium**, or **High**. With this policy, you can specify the compression level for transferred media files from client to server.

Visual Display subsection

▸ **Extra color compression**: The values can be set as **Enabled** or **Disabled**. If enabled, the global image quality level will be reduced to obtain a faster responsiveness.

▸ **Extra color compression threshold**: Insert a value in Kbps to specify a threshold for the color compression execution.

▸ **Heavyweight compression**: The values can be set as **Enabled** or **Disabled**. Based on a CPU consuming algorithm, this policy, if enabled, will apply a progressive data compression, reducing the global bandwidth. It can be only used by the Citrix Receiver.

▸ **Lossy compression level**: The values can be set as **None**, **Low**, **Medium**, or **High**. This policy should only be used when the quality level for the images is not important, because of the compression applied to the graphical data.

▸ **Lossy compression threshold value**: Insert a value in Kbps to specify a threshold for the lossy compression policy application.

▸ **Minimum image quality**: The values can be set as **Low**, **Normal**, **High**, **Very High**, or **Ultra High**. This policy specifies the quality level to apply to the images display. The higher the level, the higher the resource consumption.

▸ **Moving image compression**: **Enabled** or **Disabled**. When enabled, this policy activates the adaptive display feature – the ability to adjust automatically the quality graphics levels based on the available bandwidth.

▸ **Progressive compression level**: The values can be set as **None**, **Low**, **Medium**, **High**, **Very High**, or **Ultra High**. This policy sets a lossy compression-related quality image level, starting from a less detailed and faster display.

> The value of the progressive compression level must be higher than the lossy compression policy, as mandatory configuration.

▸ **Progressive compression threshold value**: Insert a value in Kbps to specify a threshold for the progressive compression policy application.

▸ **Target frame rate**: In this policy, specify a value, in terms of **frame per second** (**fps**), as the maximum number of frames sent to a client in a second.

▸ **Target minimum frame rate**: With this parameter, XenDesktop will try not to go under this fps parameter, in the presence of bandwidth problems.

▸ **Visual quality**: The values can be set as **Low**, **Medium**, **High**, **Build to Lossless**, or **Always Lossless**. These parameters configure the quality level for the image visualization; the higher the level, the higher the bandwidth usage. This policy only applies to Desktop OS instances.

> The **Always Lossless** option gives more importance to the image quality, and the **Build to Lossless** parameter either decreases or increases the image quality based on the network and resources usage level.

WebSockets subsection

▸ **WebSockets connections**: The values can be set as **Allowed** or **Prohibited**. If permitted, this policy activates a dual-channel communication between a web application and the XenDesktop server, based on the WebSocket protocol.

▸ **WebSockets port number**: This policy permits specifying the WebSockets protocol port number for incoming connections. The default value is **8008**.

▸ **WebSockets trusted origin server list**: In this case, it is possible to specify a list of trusted server's URLs as valid WebSockets platforms. By default, all the servers are included in this list, by the use of a wildcard (*).

WebSockets trusted origin server list

Applies to: XenDesktop: 7.0 Server OS, 7.0 Desktop OS

Value: `https://192.168.*`

☐ Use default value: *

▾ Details and related settings

Comma-separated list of trusted origin servers expressed as URLs with the option of using wildcards.

Load Management section

▸ **Concurrent logons tolerance**: The values can be set as **Enabled** or **Disabled**. When enabled, this policy permits you to specify the number of maximum concurrent log ons for a XenDesktop server site. This policy can only be applied to Server OS instances.

▸ **CPU usage**: The values can be set as **Enabled** or **Disabled**. When enabled, this policy configures the percentage CPU usage threshold considered as a maximum load for the XenDesktop server. This policy can only be applied to Server OS instances.

▸ **CPU usage excluded process priority** – Values: **Enabled** or **Disabled**. Enable or disable the consideration of the global server CPU usage for the system background processes, including, when disabled, their resource consumption in the global load calculation. This policy can only be applied to Server OS instances.

▸ **Disk usage**: The values can be set as **Enabled** or **Disabled**. When enabled, this policy lets you configure the disk queue length at which to consider the global disk usage at 75% of load. This policy can only be applied to Server OS instances.

> This policy permits an understanding of disk bottleneck situations; this usually happens when the disk queue length is greater than the number of disk spindles multiplied by two.

▸ **Maximum number of sessions**: The values can be set as **Enabled** or **Disabled**. When enabling this policy, you can specify the maximum number of sessions per single XenDesktop server. This policy can only be applied to Server OS instances.

▸ **Memory usage**: The values can be set as **Enabled** or **Disabled**. By enabling this policy, you can configure the memory usage percentage value considered as full load for the server. This policy can only be applied to Server OS instances.

▸ **Memory usage base load**: The values can be set as **Enabled** or **Disabled**. By enabling this policy, you can tune the zero load parameter in MB, to use as a threshold for the server load calculation. This policy can only be applied to Server OS instances.

Following is the explanation for the subsections included in the **Profile Management** section:

Advanced settings subsection

▸ **Disable automatic configuration**: The values can be set as **Enabled** or **Disabled**. With this policy, you can decide whether to activate the automatic configuration for the Profile Management, based on the environment configuration.

▸ **Log off user if a problem is encountered**: The values can be set as **Enabled** or **Disabled**. If enabled, in case of problems during the logon phase, the user will be prompted with an alert, then disconnected. If disabled, a temporary profile will be assigned to the user.

▸ **Number of retries when accessing locked files**: In this policy, specify a numeric value to retry accessing files that are locked.

▸ **Process Internet cookie files on log off**: The values can be set as **Enabled** or **Disabled**. This policy, when enabled, removes any unnecessary web cookies after a session logoff.

Basic settings subsection

▸ **Active write back**: The values can be set as **Enabled** or **Disabled**. By enabling this policy, all the modified files and directories will be synchronized in the middle of a session with the central profile store, before the users log off.

▸ **Enable profile management**: The values can be set as **Enabled** or **Disabled**. By enabling this policy, you can decide whether to activate the logon and logoff processes for the Citrix Profile Management.

▸ **Excluded groups**: The values can be set as **Enabled** or **Disabled**. When enabled, this policy permits you to exclude specific domain groups from the Profile Management processing.

```
                              Edit Setting

Excluded groups

Applies to:  XenDesktop: 5.0, 5.5, 5.6 Feature Pack 1, 7.0 Server OS, 7.0 Desktop OS


    ⦿ Enabled
      This setting will be enabled.
      ┌─────────────────────────────────────────────────────────────┐
      │ XDSEVEN\helpdesk                                              │
      │                                                               │
      │                                                               │
      │                                                               │
      │                                                               │
      └─────────────────────────────────────────────────────────────┘

    ○ Disabled
      This setting will be disabled.

    ☐ Use default value:
```

▸ **Offline profile support**: The values can be set as **Enabled** or **Disabled**. Enable this policy to permit using profiles even when disconnected from the network.

▸ **Path to user store**: The values can be set as **Enabled** or **Disabled**. Enable this policy and specify the network path on which profiles are located, to use the Citrix Profile Management.

> We have discussed the Citrix Profile Management and the path to user store in the *Using Citrix Profile Management 5.x recipe in Chapter 4, User Experience – Planning and Configuring*

▸ **Process logons of local administrators**: The values can be set as **Enabled** or **Disabled**. This policy processes, if respectively enabled or disabled, profile members of the local administrators' machine group.

▸ **Processed groups**: The values can be set as **Enabled** or **Disabled**. When enabled, this policy permits you to specify domain groups that must be processed by the Citrix Profile Manager.

Cross-Platform Settings subsection

▸ **Cross-platforms settings user groups**: The values can be set as **Enabled** or **Disabled**. If enabled, the cross-platform parameter of the Citrix Profile Management will only be applied to the specified domain groups.

▸ **Enable cross-platforms settings**: The values can be set as **Enabled** or **Disabled**. With this policy, you can turn on or off the cross-platform option for the Citrix Profile Management software.

▸ **Path to cross-platforms definitions**: The values can be set as **Enabled** or **Disabled**. In case of an enabled policy, you have to specify a valid network path on which to locate the cross-platform definition files.

▸ **Path to cross-platforms settings store**: The values can be set as **Enabled** or **Disabled**. In case of an enabled policy, you have to specify a valid network path on which to save the user's cross-platform settings.

File System subsection

▸ **Directories to synchronize**: The values can be set as either **Enabled** or **Disabled**. Enable this policy and specify a list of folders if you want to activate sync for specific additional directories other than user profiles.

▸ **Exclusion list – directories**: The values can be set as either **Enabled** or **Disabled**. Enable this policy and specify a list of folders to exclude during the profile synchronization activities.

▸ **Exclusion list – files**: The values can be set as either **Enabled** or **Disabled**. Enable this policy and specify a list of files to exclude during the profile synchronization activities.

▸ **Files to synchronize**: The values can be set as either **Enabled** or **Disabled**. Enable this policy and specify a list of files if you want to activate sync for specific additional files other than user profiles.

▸ **Folders to mirror**: The values can be set as either **Enabled** or **Disabled**. Enable this policy and list a set of folders to replicate in mirror mode.

> This policy is useful when critical profile data need having not only a single existing file.

Folder Redirection subsection

▸ **AppData(Roaming) path**: The values can be set as either **Enabled** or **Disabled**. If enabled, this policy will let you specify a network path on which to redirect AppData folders. If disabled, the specified folder will not be redirected. This is for **Roaming Profile** configurations.

▶ **Contacts path**: The values can be set as either **Enabled** or **Disabled**. Enable this policy and specify a network location path on which to redirect the `Contacts` directory. If disabled, the specified folder will not be redirected.

▶ **Desktop path**: The values can be set as either **Enabled** or **Disabled**. Enable this policy and specify a network location path on which to redirect the Desktop directory. If disabled, the specified folder will not be redirected.

▶ **Documents path**: The values can be set as either **Enabled** or **Disabled**. Enable this policy and specify a network location path on which to redirect the `Documents` directory. If disabled, the specified folder will not be redirected.

▶ **Download path**: The values can be set as either **Enabled** or **Disabled**. Enable this policy and specify a network location path on which to redirect the `Download` directory. If disabled, the specified folder will not be redirected.

▶ **Favorites path**: The values can be set as either **Enabled** or **Disabled**. Enable this policy and specify a network location path on which to redirect the `Favorites` directory. If disabled, the specified folder will not be redirected.

▶ **Grant administrator access**: The values can be set as either **Enabled** or **Disabled**. If enabled, you can configure the ability for administrators and users to access the redirected folder's contents. By default, only users can access their own redirected folders.

▶ **Include domain name**: The values can be set as either **Enabled** or **Disabled**. This policy permits including (when enabled) the `%userdomain%` variable in the UNC path.

▶ **Links path**: The values can be set as either **Enabled** or **Disabled**. Enable this policy and specify a network location path on which to redirect the `Links` directory. If disabled, the specified folder will not be redirected.

▶ **Music path**: The values can be set as either **Enabled** or **Disabled**. Enable this policy and specify a network location path on which to redirect the `Music` directory. If disabled, the specified folder will not be redirected.

▶ **Pictures path**: The values can be set as either **Enabled** or **Disabled**. Enable this policy and specify a network location path on which to redirect the `Pictures` directory. If disabled, the specified folder will not be redirected.

▶ **Redirection settings for AppData(Roaming)**: In this policy, you can specify the way to redirect the `AppData` folder for configured roaming profiles.

▶ **Redirection settings for Contacts**: In this policy, you can specify the way to redirect the `Contacts` folder for configured roaming profiles.

▶ **Redirection settings for Desktop**: In this policy, you can specify the way to redirect the `Desktop` folder for configured roaming profiles.

▶ **Redirection settings for Documents**: In this policy, you can specify the way to redirect the `Documents` folder for configured roaming profiles.

- **Redirection settings for Downloads**: In this policy, you can specify the way to redirect the Downloads folder for configured roaming profiles.

- **Redirection settings for Favorites**: In this policy, you can specify the way to redirect the Favorites folder for configured roaming profiles.

- **Redirection settings for Links**: In this policy, you can specify the way to redirect the Links folder for configured roaming profiles.

- **Redirection settings for Music**: In this policy, you can specify the way to redirect the Music folder for configured roaming profiles.

- **Redirection settings for Pictures**: In this policy, you can specify the way to redirect the Pictures folder for configured roaming profiles.

- **Redirection settings for Saved Games**: In this policy, you can specify the way to redirect the Saved Games folder for configured roaming profiles.

- **Redirection settings for Searches**: In this policy, you can specify the way to redirect the Searches folder for configured roaming profiles.

- **Redirection settings for Start Menu**: In this policy, you can specify the way to redirect the Start Menu folder for configured roaming profiles.

- **Redirection settings for Videos**: In this policy, you can specify the way to redirect the Videos folder for configured roaming profiles.

> All the Redirection settings policies by default are configured as **"Redirect to the following UNC path"**. You can specify a precious path on the next set of policies.

- **Saved Games path**: The values can be set as either **Enabled** or **Disabled**. Enable this policy and specify a network location path on which to redirect the Saved Games directory. If disabled, the specified folder will not be redirected.

- **Searches path**: The values can be set as either **Enabled** or **Disabled**. Enable this policy and specify a network location path on which to redirect the Searches directory. If disabled, the specified folder will not be redirected.

- **Start Menu path**: The values can be set as either **Enabled** or **Disabled**. Enable this policy and specify a network location path on which to redirect the Start Menu directory. If disabled, the specified folder will not be redirected.

- **Videos path**: The values can be set as either **Enabled** or **Disabled**. Enable this policy and specify a network location path on which to redirect the Videos directory. If disabled, the specified folder will not be redirected.

> Later in this chapter we will discuss the **Logging** policies applied to the XenDesktop infrastructure.

Profile Handling subsection

▶ **Delay before deleting cached profiles**: Configure a value, in seconds, as a delay for the cached profile deletion after a session logoff.

▶ **Delete locally cached profiles on log off**: The values can be set as **Enabled** or **Disabled.** With this policy, you can decide whether to delete the cached profile after a session has been logged off.

> The **Delay before deleting cached profiles** policy requires the activation of the **Delete locally cached profiles on logoff** policy.

▶ **Local profiles conflict handling**: This policy manages the profile management action in case of conflict between the centralized profile and the Windows local profile: you can configure to **Use local profile**, **Delete local profile** or **Rename local profile**.

> Choosing the renaming of the local profile permits you to back it up, and then use the centralized profiles. This is useful for rollback actions.

▶ **Migration of existing profiles**: In this policy, values can be set as **Local and Roaming**, **Local**, **Roaming**, or **None**. With this policy, it is possible to migrate the existing profiles (local or roaming) to the central user store, after the first user log on.

▶ **Path to the template profile**: The values can be set as either **Enabled** or **Disabled**. This policy, when enabled, allows you to specify a network path on which to save and locate a user profile template, which will be used for any profile creation operation.

▶ **Template profile overrides local profile**: In this policy, values can be either **Enabled** or **Disabled**. Enabling or disabling this policy will create new user profiles from the centralized template (first case) or from the default user profile (second case)—**local profile**—on the computer used for the first log on.

▶ **Template profile overrides roaming profile**: In this policy, the values can be set as either **Enabled** or **Disabled**. Enabling or disabling this policy will create new user profiles from the centralized template (first case) or from the default user profile (second case)—**Microsoft Roaming profile**—on the computer used for the first log on.

Registry subsection

▶ **Exclusion list**: The values can be set as either **Enabled** or **Disabled**. Enabling this policy will let you specify a set of registry keys—HKEY_CURRENT_USER section—to ignore during the logon phase.

▸ **Inclusion list**: The values can be set as **Enabled** or **Disabled**. Enabling this policy will let you specify a set of registry keys—HKEY_CURRENT_USER section—to process during the logon phase.

> You have to understand that, with this latest policy enabled, *only* the listed registry keys will be processed at the logon phase.

Streamed User Profiles subsection

▸ **Always cache**: The values can be set as either **Enabled** or **Disabled**. With this policy, you can decide whether to always cache data with streamed profiles. If enabled, the global limit of the cached files will be lower in size.

▸ **Always cache**: Assign a value to the cache area size, which will be associated to the **Always cache** policy.

▸ **Profile streaming**: In this policy, values are set as either **Enabled** or **Disabled**. By enabling this policy, the streamed user profiles will be synchronized on the local computer only when needed. Registry keys are always cached, and files and folders are only when accessed by users.

▸ **Streamed user profile groups**: The values can be set as **Enabled** or **Disabled**. If enabled, this policy will permit you to insert a list of domain groups containing users to configure as streamed profiles.

▸ **Timeout for pending area lock files (days)**: Assign a value, in days, after which user's locked pending files are rolled back to the user store, instead of being written to the destination server.

Receiver section

▸ **StoreFront account list**: Insert a list of StoreFront-configured locations with the following syntax:

```
StoreName;StoreURL;StoreState(Value=On/Off);StoreDescription
```

> A configuration example for the previous policy could be the following: MyCompany;https://companysf01.xdseven.local/Citrix/Store/discovery;On;"Company store"

Virtual Delivery Agent Settings section

▸ **Enable auto update of controllers**: This policy has values either **Enabled** or **Disabled**. If enabled, you can apply a list of XenDesktop Controllers to the initial bootstrap connection; if disabled, you will manage them manually.

▸ **Enable lossless**: In this policy, values can be set as either **Enabled** or **Disabled**. This policy either allows or prohibits the use of lossless codec.

▸ **HDX 3D-Pro quality settings**: This policy configures the minimum and maximum quality level for the 3D-Pro codec. The permitted values are between 0 and 100, and the maximum level must be greater than the minimum.

After configuring all the policies perform the following steps

1. Click the **Next** button to continue.

2. In the **Users and Machines** section, choose whether to apply the configured policies to specific users and/or computer, or assign them to all the site's objects. After completion, click the **Next** button.

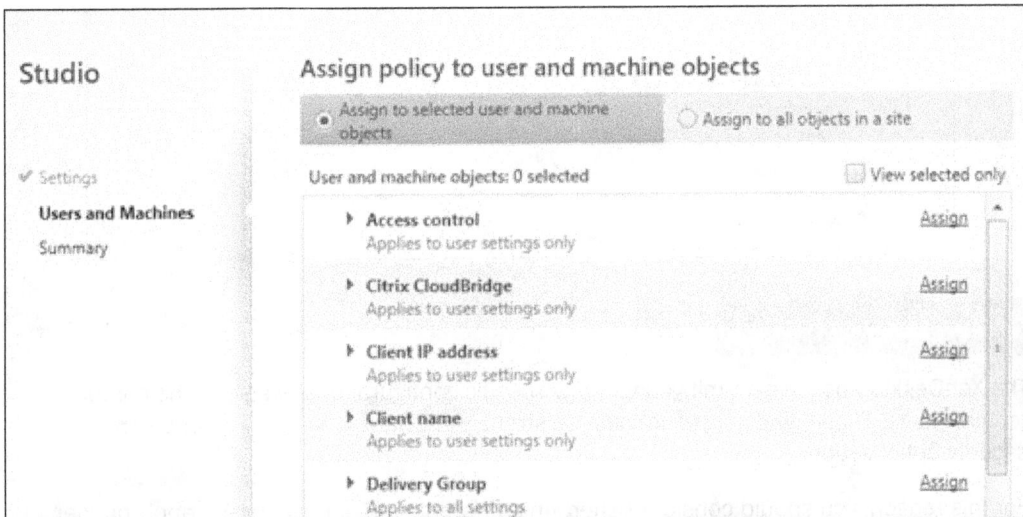

Studio	Assign policy to user and machine objects	
	● Assign to selected user and machine objects	○ Assign to all objects in a site
✔ Settings	User and machine objects: 0 selected	☐ View selected only
Users and Machines	▸ Access control	Assign
Summary	Applies to user settings only	
	▸ Citrix CloudBridge	Assign
	Applies to user settings only	
	▸ Client IP address	Assign
	Applies to user settings only	
	▸ Client name	Assign
	Applies to user settings only	
	▸ Delivery Group	Assign
	Applies to all settings	

3. In the **Summary** section, assign a name and an optional description to the configured group of policies, then flag the **Enable policy** option, and click on **Finish** to complete the procedure.

Summary

View a summary of the settings you configured and provide a name for your new policy.

Policy name: Site Configured Policies   ☑ Enable policy

Description: Site Configured Policies

Settings configured: 12   Assigned to: user and machine objects

Always cache
Computer setting
Disabled (Default: Disabled)

Always cache size
Computer setting
0 (Default: 0)

Enable auto update of controll...
Computer setting
Allowed (Default: Allowed)

Enable lossless
User setting
Allowed (Default: Allowed)

The settings are applied to all objects in the site.

How it works...

The XenDesktop policies permit you to apply specific configurations based on the corporate requirements. These configurations must be strongly oriented to the performance and security optimization.

For this reason, you should consider generating different sets of policies and applying them to different virtual desktop's configurations.

By using the **ICA settings**, you are able to configure the standard ICA port on which to listen and the relative connection timeouts. It's possible to decide whether to automatically reconnect a broken session to a client. (**Auto client reconnect** policy: enabling this policy could be the right solution in some cases, especially when you have interrupted an important working session; on the other hand, the Citrix Broker could run a new session in the presence of issues with the session cookies. So, activate it based on your priorities.)

With the **ICA round trip** policies, you can monitor the response time for the operations made by the users: this data permits you to understand the responsiveness of your Citrix infrastructure.

Moreover, you could also apply remediation to the configuration, especially for those policies that involve graphic components: you could size the display memory and the image caching area, or turn on or off specific Windows advanced graphical features, such as the **Dynamic Windows Preview** (**DWP**).

> With the queuing and tossing policy active, you could have problems with lost frames when reproducing animations.

The **Windows media redirection** policy optimizes the reproduction of multimedia objects: by applying the correct sizing to its buffer size, you should obtain evident improvements in the streaming and reproduction operations. Therefore, you should consider disabling this policy, thereby demanding the processing of audio and video to the clients, *only* when you can see no particular benefits.

Another important feature offered by this policy is the **QoS** (**Quality of Service**) implementation: you can enable the **Multi-Stream Connections** configurations and apply them to the traffic priority levels, permitting precedence and more bandwidth to traffic considered more critical than others.

> The Multi-Stream policies for the Quality of Service can be considered a less powerful alternative to the CloudBridge platform. You could also use them together, for a better, more powerful, user experience.

Other important configurations are, for instance, the **Adobe Flash** contents processing, deciding whether to activate compatibility with the oldest version of this software, and whether to elaborate the Flash multimedia objects on the user's clients or on the Citrix servers. Moreover, you can configure the **Audio** settings, such as Audio and Microphone client redirection (when using the local device resources), the **Desktop** settings (such as Desktop wallpapers and so on), or the **HDX and HDX 3D-Pro** protocol quality settings.

> Be careful when applying policies for the Desktop graphical settings: remember to be consistent with the Master Image template configurations performed in *Chapter 3, Master Image Configuration and Tuning*, and *Chapter 4, User Experience – Planning and Configuring*

To optimize the information transmission for the desktops, the **Bandwidth** policy is extremely important: by this, you can assign, in the form of maximum Kbps or percentages, the values for the following traffic types: **Audio**, **USB**, **Clipboard**, **COM**, and **LPT** ports, and **File redirection**. These configurations require a good analysis of traffic levels and their priorities within your organization.

The last great configuration is the redirection of the client drives to the remote Citrix sessions: in fact, you can activate the mount (automatic or not) and the users' rights (read only or read and write) on the client drives, removable or not, such as CD-ROM or DVD-ROM, removable USB devices and fixed drives as the client device operating system root. This option gives you the flexibility to transfer information from the local device to the XenDesktop instance, by the Virtual Desktop Agent properly configured. You should consider deactivating all the redirects that are not really needed, in order to save the bandwidth.

> This last device policy could make your infrastructure more secure, thanks to the use of the USB device redirection rules; through it, in fact, you could only permit the use of USB keys approved by your company, prohibiting any other non-policy-compliant device.

In this version of XenDesktop, the **Mobile Experience** policies are also really important: we have seen, in fact, that we are able to configure and use an optimized version of the touch interface for devices such as tablets or smartphones, enriching the user experience on this category of devices.

There's more...

Within XenDesktop 7.6, not only can you configure the policy on your own, but you have the ability to use the following existing tools, which will help you during the configuration and the optimization for the site's parameters:

Policy templates

With this feature, you can use a preconfigured group of policies, which should be applied in one of the following existing categories:

- **High Definition User Experience**: These preconfigured policies are for high-quality graphics, audio, and video application, in the presence of a high level of network and elaboration resources.

- **High Server Scalability**: This preconfigured policy fits applications on which resource usage and user experience must be balanced. The global experience level can be improved by scaling up the number of XenDesktop Controller servers.

▶ **Optimized for WAN**: This preconfigured policy is for remote workers with offices connected over WAN. The template is made to optimize bandwidth usage.

▶ **Security and Control**: This preconfigured template disables most of the remote user devices, such as USB peripherals and fixed drives, or client-side media rendering, improving the global security level, but degrading also the available bandwidth because of the high network usage.

[🔦 You can convert your own customized policies in a template to reuse for future purposes. In the **Policy** section, click the **Save as Template** link on the right-hand menu.]

Policy comparison

With this feature, you can compare two or more templates and/or policies, in order to verify the current applied options, and also check the eventual redundant configurations.

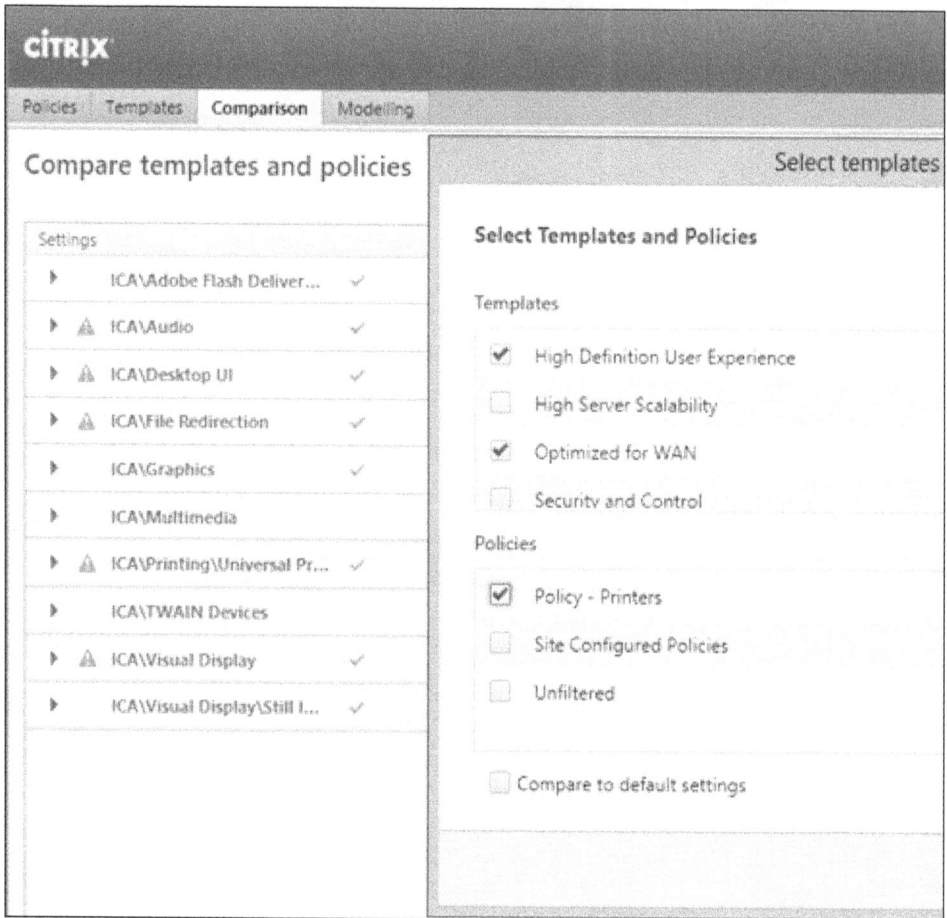

Policy modeling

To verify the effective running and applied policies to your VDI infrastructure, there is a tool inside the HDX Policy menu that performs this task—the **Citrix Group Policy Modeling Wizard**. This tool performs a simulation for the policy applications, providing you with a report with the current configuration. This is something similar to the Microsoft Windows Domain Group Policy Results.

The simulations apply to one or all of the Domain Controllers configured within your domain, being able to test the application to specific user or computer objects, including the OU containing them.

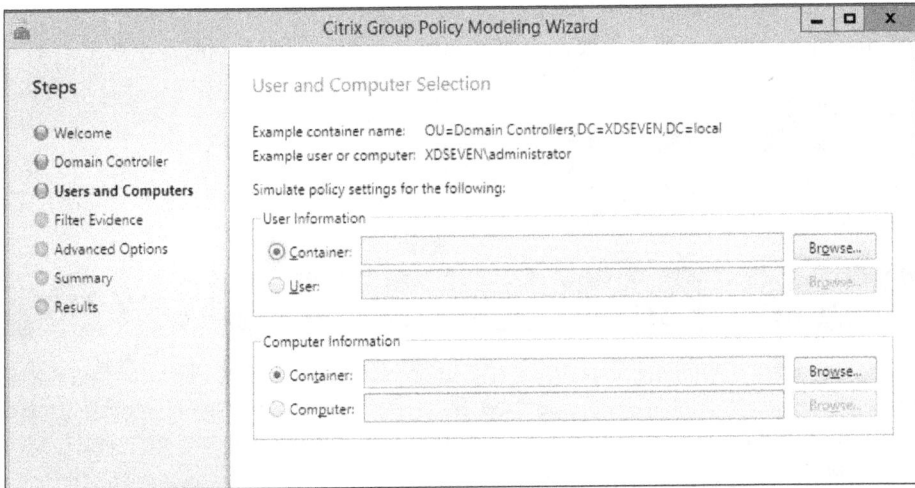

Moreover, you can apply filters based on the **Client IP address**, the **Client name**, the type of machine (**Private** or **Shared Desktop**, **Private** or **Shared Application**), or apply the simulation to a specific **Desktop group**.

In the **Advanced Options** section, you can simulate **Slow network connections** and/or **Loopback processing** (a policy application only based on the computer object locations, instead of both the user and computer object positions) for a configured XenDesktop site.

After running the policy application test, you can check the results by right-clicking on the generated report name and selecting the **View Report** option.

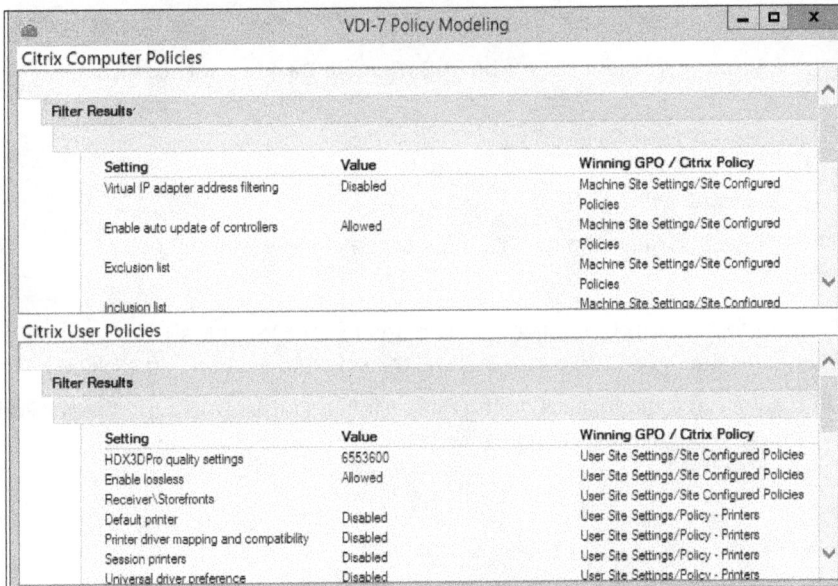

These are extremely powerful tools when you have to verify unexpected behaviors of your desktop instances or user rights, because of incorrect policy applications.

See also

▶ The *Installing and configuring the Master Image policies* recipe in *Chapter 3, Master Image Configuration and Tuning*

Configuring printers

To give users the feel of working on a virtual system, as near as possible to a standard physical workstation, you have to furnish all the peripherals available in a non-VDI architecture. One of these is given by the configuration and the use of printers. In this recipe, we are going to discuss these kinds of policies.

Getting ready

Depending on your company's requirements, you should have many different printers (network, local, multifunctional...) to configure within the virtual desktop environment. In most cases, a prerequisite (and a best practice) is configuring a **Print Server** on which we install all the devices and then deploy them using the Microsoft domain GPO.

You can install the required drivers for the printer that will be used on the Master Image; as you have already seen, in this way, you will propagate printer mapping to all the desktop instances in the pool.

[Note that printers need to be **RDS (Remote Desktop Services)** compliant.   ]

How to do it...

In this section, we will perform the configuration of the printers within the XenDesktop 7 environment:

1. Connect to the Citrix Controller machine and run the Windows + C key combination. Search for the Citrix Studio icon in the Citrix software section and click on it.

2. On the left-hand menu, click on the **Policy** link, and then select the **Create Policy** option on the right-hand menu.

Citrix Studio (XD7-Site-First)
  Search
  Machine Catalogs
  Delivery Groups
  Policy
  Logging
  Configuration
    Administrators
    Controllers
    Hosting
    Licensing
    StoreFront
    App-V Publishing

Actions

Policy

Create Policy

View

Refresh

Help

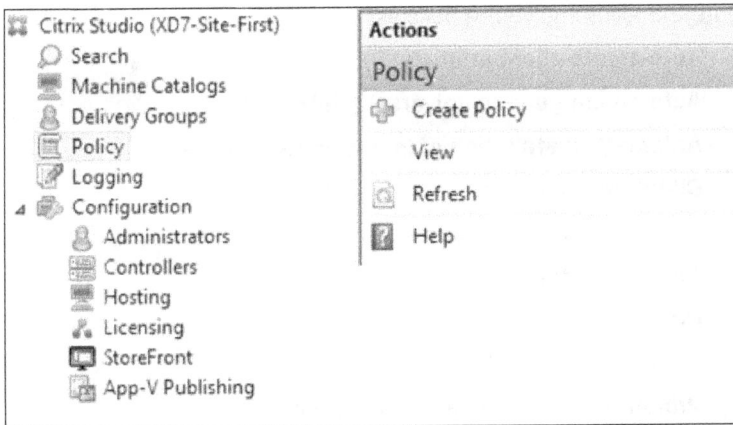

3. On the **Select settings** screen, choose the **Printing** (ICA) option in the second drop-down list.

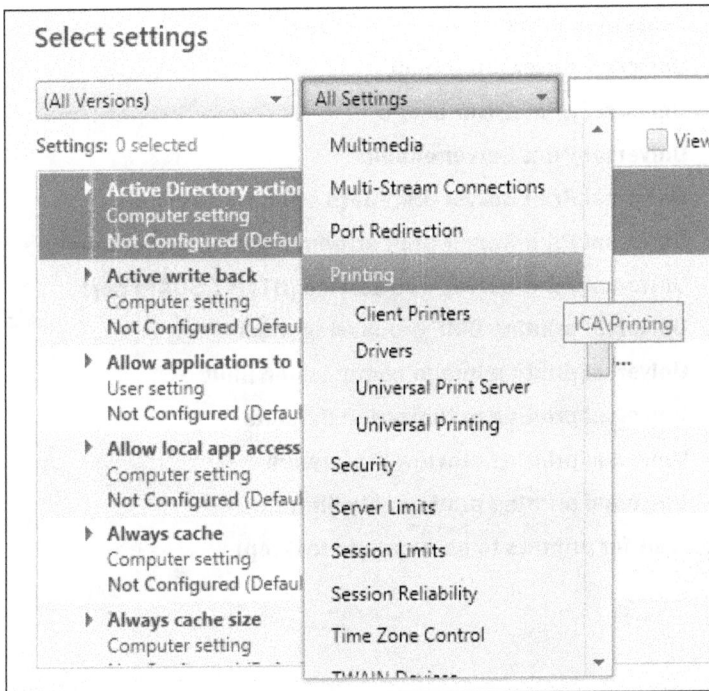

Select settings

(All Versions)   All Settings

Settings: 0 selected   View

- **Active Directory action**
  Computer setting
  Not Configured (Defau

- **Active write back**
  Computer setting
  Not Configured (Defau

- **Allow applications to u**
  User setting
  Not Configured (Defau

- **Allow local app access**
  Computer setting
  Not Configured (Defau

- **Always cache**
  Computer setting
  Not Configured (Defau

- **Always cache size**
  Computer setting

Multimedia

Multi-Stream Connections

Port Redirection

Printing   ICA\Printing

   Client Printers

   Drivers

   Universal Print Server

   Universal Printing

Security

Server Limits

Session Limits

Session Reliability

Time Zone Control

TWAIN Devices

4. Configure the following filtered policies:

- **Auto-create client printers**
- **Auto-create generic universal printer**
- **Automatic installation of in-box printer drivers**
- **Client printer names**
- **Client printer redirection**
- **Default printer**
- **Direct connections to print servers**
- **Printer assignments**
- **Printer auto-creation event log preference**
- **Printer driver mapping and compatibility**
- **Printer properties retention**
- **Retained and restored client printers**
- **Session printers**
- **Universal driver preference**
- **Universal print driver usage**
- **Universal Print Server enable**
- **Universal Print Server print data stream (CGP) port**
- **Universal Print Server print stream input bandwidth limit**
- **Universal Print Server web service (HTTP / SOAP) port**
- **Universal printing EMF processing mode**
- **Universal printing image compression limit**
- **Universal printing optimization defaults**
- **Universal printing preview preference**
- **Universal printing print quality limit**
- **Wait for printers to be created (desktop)**

The following screenshot shows the available options while configuring the printer:

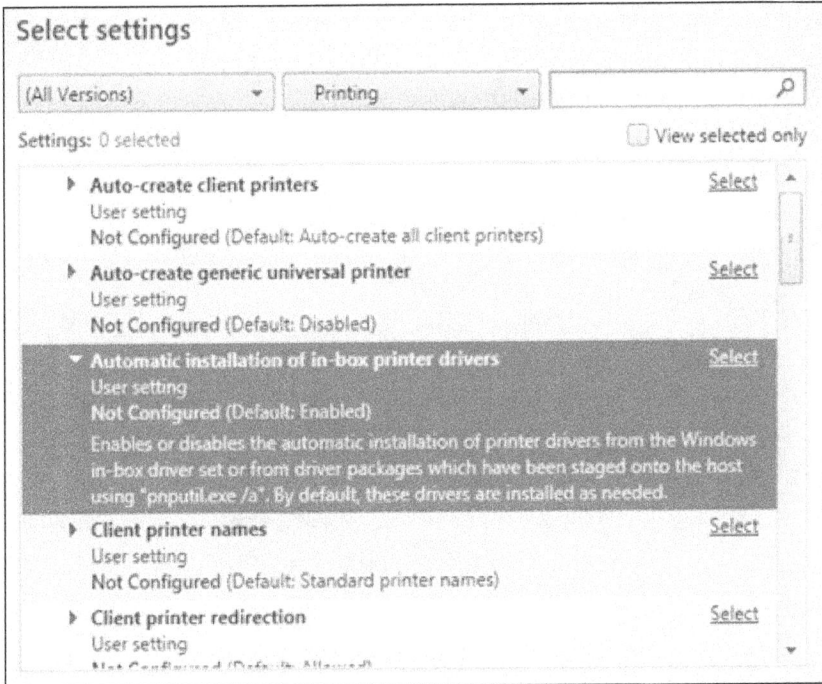

> By default, all the policies are in the **Not Configured** state.

5. After configuring the desired policies, click on the **Next** button to continue.

6. In the **User and Machines** section, you can apply the configured printing rules for a specific set of filtered objects, such as specific IP addresses or Delivery Groups, or use the policies for the entire configured XenDesktop site. After that, click on **Next**.

Assign policy to user and machine objects

○ Assign to selected user and machine objects   ○ Assign to all objects in a site

User and machine objects: 0 selected   ☐ View selected only

▶ **Access control**   Assign
Applies to user settings only

▶ **Citrix CloudBridge**   Assign
Applies to user settings only

▼ **Client IP address**   Assign
Applies to user settings only

Apply policy based on the IP address of the user device used to connect to the session.

▶ **Client name**   Assign
Applies to user settings only

▼ **Delivery Group**   Assign
Applies to all settings

Apply policy based on the delivery group membership of the desktop running the session.

7. On the **Summary** screen, assign a name to the generated policy, flag the **Enable policy** option, and click on **Finish**.

Summary

View a summary of the settings you configured and provide a name for your new policy.

Policy name: Policy - Printers   ☑ Enable policy

Description: Policy - Printers configuration

How it works...

The printer configuration process is quite a complex activity that requires you to deeply understand and study the specific needs of the users in your company.

The following are the explanation of the main configuration policies:

- **Auto-create client printers**: With this policy, you decide whether to auto-create all the listed categories by default, or one of them, including local attached printers. You can also configure to not automatically operate on the creation of the printers. The options available are:

    - **Auto-create all client printers**

    - **Auto-create local (non-network) client printers only**

    - **Auto-create the client's default printer only**

    - **Do not auto-create client printers**

- **Auto-create generic universal printer**: This policy can be set as either **Enabled** or **Disabled**. With this policy, you can decide whether to use the Citrix Universal Printer object. As explained earlier, this could be a useful option when trying to avoid printer and driver fragmentation because of the use of a single generic printing driver.

- **Automatic installation of in-box printer drivers**: This policy can be set as either **Enabled** or **Disabled**. With this policy, you can decide whether to enable the automatic installation for the in-box printer Windows drivers. The in-box drivers are those included in the operating system's distribution, tested, and optimized for better performance within that environment.

- **Client printer names**: In this policy, the options available are **Standard printer names** or **Legacy printer names**. This policy permits you to choose the naming convention to use in each phase of generic printer creation. You should always use the standard naming convention, and only use the other option when compatibility with older Citrix versions is required.

- **Client printer redirection**: In this policy, either **Allowed** or **Prohibited** option can be selected. Allowed by default, this policy permits you to redirect to a server the client printer mapping.

- **Default printer**: In this policy, we can choose either **Set default printer to the client's main printer** or **Do not adjust the user's default printer** option. With this policy, you can configure the way in which it chooses the default user printer. The first option uses the current configured printer as the default device, and the second loads the printer from the user profile instead, based on the domain policies and the loaded printer driver. This technique is usually used for the **Proximity Printing** approach, the technique of publishing the closer network printer to a user.

- **Direct connections to print servers**: In this policy, there are either **Enabled** or **Disabled** options. With this configuration, you can permit user access directly to the network printer, in order for faster printing. This is only available in LAN connections. In the case of WAN printer mappings, you have to use a non-direct connection.

- **Printer assignments**: This policy permits you to specify a list of client and default assigned printers and the session printer, by specifying one for each client machine.

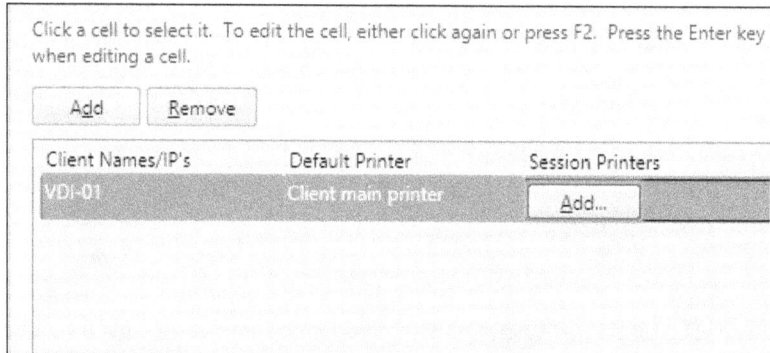

- **Printer auto-creation event log preference**: This policy gives us options to **Log errors and warnings**, **Log errors only**, and **Do not log errors or warnings**. This policy allows you to configure the level of logging for the printer autocreation activities. You can decide not to log any events, warnings or errors only, or both.

- **Printer driver mapping and compatibility**: With this policy, you can import a set of printer drivers on which to operate and define compatibility and substitutions for the client drivers. This means that you can define a rule to override customized settings, in order to standardize the printing architecture.

- **Printer properties retention**: This policy lets you decide if and where to save the configured printer settings. You should consider saving these settings in the user profile, especially in the presence of a centralized profile manager, and a non-persistent desktop machine. In this policy we have the following options:

  - ❑ **Held in profile only if not saved on the client**
  - ❑ **Retained in user profile only**
  - ❑ **Saved on the client device only**
  - ❑ **Do not retain printer properties**

- **Retained and restored client printers**: In this policy, we can choose either the **Allowed** or **Prohibited** option. In the case of customized printer configurations, you can have the ability to maintain these settings and restore them in case of configuration problems.

- **Session printers**: This policy permits you to add the list of network printers that can be autocreated with XenDesktop. You have to specify the printer UNC path when adding the network resource.

- **Universal driver preference**: By the use of this policy, you can choose the order the Universal Printer drivers are used, such as **EMF**, **PCL** in its different versions, **XPS** or **PS**.

- **Universal print driver usage**: This policy manages the situation of whether to use the universal printer driver. By default, this driver is used only when a specific driver is not available. The following options are available in this policy:

    - **Use only printer model specific drivers**

    - **Use universal printing only**

    - **Use universal printing only if requested driver is unavailable**

    - **Use printer model specific drivers only if universal printing is unavailable**

- **Universal Print Server enable**: This policy, disabled by default, configures the use of the **Universal Print Server** feature. In case of a fault or compatibility problems, you have the ability to configure the policy to roll back to the Windows native printing driver.

- **Universal Print Server print data stream (CGP) port**: This policy is particularly useful in the presence of a networked printing environment. It is possible to configure the port used by the Print Server's data stream listener. The default value is 7229.

- **Universal Print Server print stream input bandwidth limit**: With this parameter, you can specify the rate, in Kbps, for the print data transferring. The default limit is equal to 0 Kbps.

- **Universal Print Server web service (HTTP/SOAP) port**: This policy configures the port used by the Print Server SOAP service (web listener). The default value is 8080.

- **Universal printing EMF processing mode**: This policy lets us choose either **Spool directly to printer** or **Reprocess EMFs for printer** option. This policy checks the way to process the **Enhanced Metafile Format** (**EMF**) spooling queue (EMF is a device-independent format able to intercept the graphical elements in a printing task).

- **Universal printing image compression limit**: This is an important policy that allows you to configure the quality level of the printed images, deciding whether to give precedence to the quality or to the compression level. It provides us the following options:

    - **No compression**

    - **Best quality (lossless compression)**

    - **High quality**

    - **Standard quality**

    - **Reduced quality (maximum compression)**

▶ **Universal printing optimization defaults**: This policy permits you to configure the image quality and compression to apply to the Universal Printer session. It lets us choose from the following options:

- ❏ **Best quality (lossless compression)**
- ❏ **High quality**
- ❏ **Standard quality**
- ❏ **Reduced quality (maximum compression)**

The following screenshot shows the options available in compression of images:

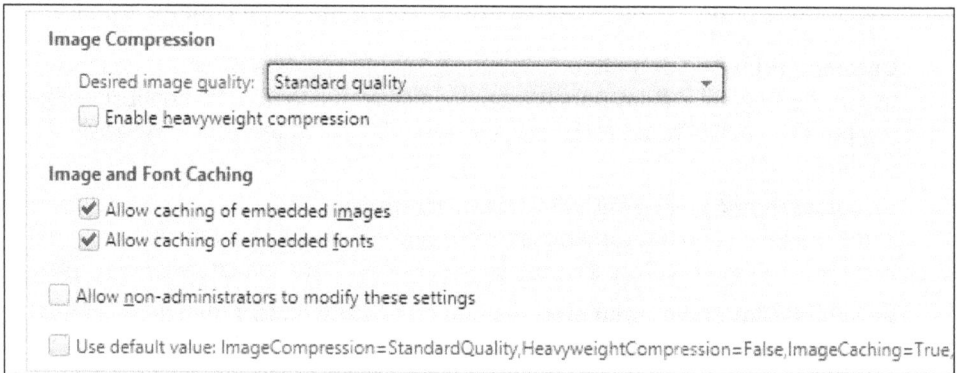

Image Compression

Desired image quality: | Standard quality ▾ |

☐ Enable heavyweight compression

Image and Font Caching

☑ Allow caching of embedded images
☑ Allow caching of embedded fonts

☐ Allow non-administrators to modify these settings

☐ Use default value: ImageCompression=StandardQuality,HeavyweightCompression=False,ImageCaching=True,

▶ **Universal printing preview preference**: With this configurable option, you can enable the preview for the documents to print, by configuring one of the options listed in the next screenshot:

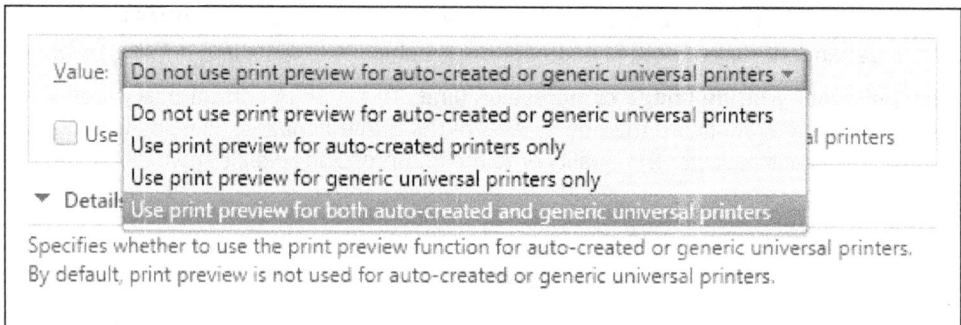

Value: | Do not use print preview for auto-created or generic universal printers ▾ |

Do not use print preview for auto-created or generic universal printers
☐ Use   al printers
Use print preview for auto-created printers only
Use print preview for generic universal printers only
▾ Detail Use print preview for both auto-created and generic universal printers

Specifies whether to use the print preview function for auto-created or generic universal printers. By default, print preview is not used for auto-created or generic universal printers.

- **Universal printing print quality limit**: This policy permits you to configure the resolution for the generated printing jobs. This policy provides the following options:
  - **No Limit, Draft (150 DPI)**
  - **Low Resolution (300 DPI)**
  - **Medium Resolution (600 DPI)**
  - **High Resolution (1200 DPI)**:

- **Wait for printers to be created (desktop)**: In this policy , the options are either **Enabled** or **Disabled**. With this parameter, you can decide whether to wait for the printer creation process when connecting with your user profile. You cannot apply this policy to a published resource.

> When possible, you should only use the generic Citrix Universal Printer driver, instead of many different printer drivers, and avoid automatically installing the printer drivers on the desktop instances, in order to reduce the troubleshooting activities in case of issues. If you do not have client printers, consider using unified printer drivers and try to consolidate the printer types in your company, if possible.

There's more...

In the wide range of free Citrix tools, you will find the Citrix Stress Printers software. It allows you to simulate multiple sessions using configured printer drivers in order to test the capability of using the driver and its response, in terms of physical and virtual resource usage.

> You can download the zip file archive at
> `http://support.citrix.com/article/CTX109374`

Run the right version for your infrastructure by double-clicking on the 32-bit or 64-bit executable file. The software will let you select the driver on which to perform the load tests, the printer name and port (for instance, LPT1 for a local printer or the configured IP address for a network device), the number of concurrent events, and how many times to repeat the tests. If you want, you can run the test in verbose mode by flagging the appropriate option checkbox. By clicking on the **Save** button, you can archive in a text file the configured tests to be loaded and later run again. To execute the tests, you have to click on the **Run** button.

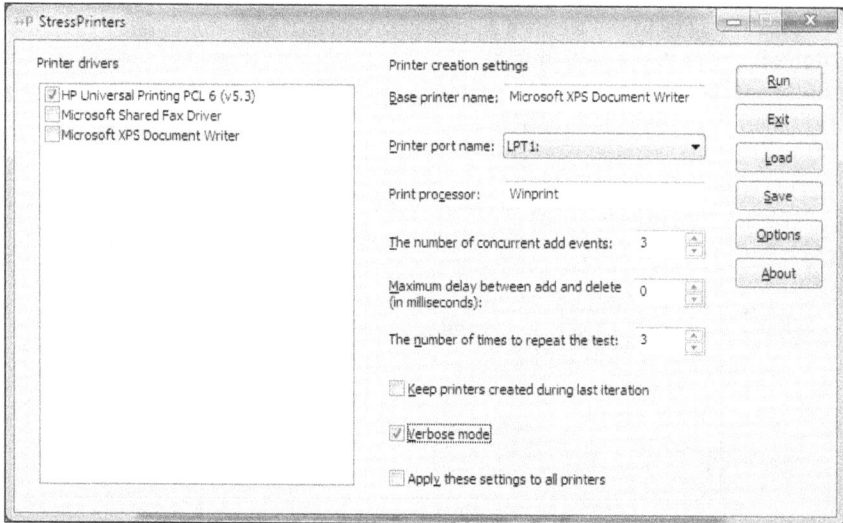

After that, you will receive a summary of the executed tests; if you want, you can save the related log file by clicking on the **Save log** button.

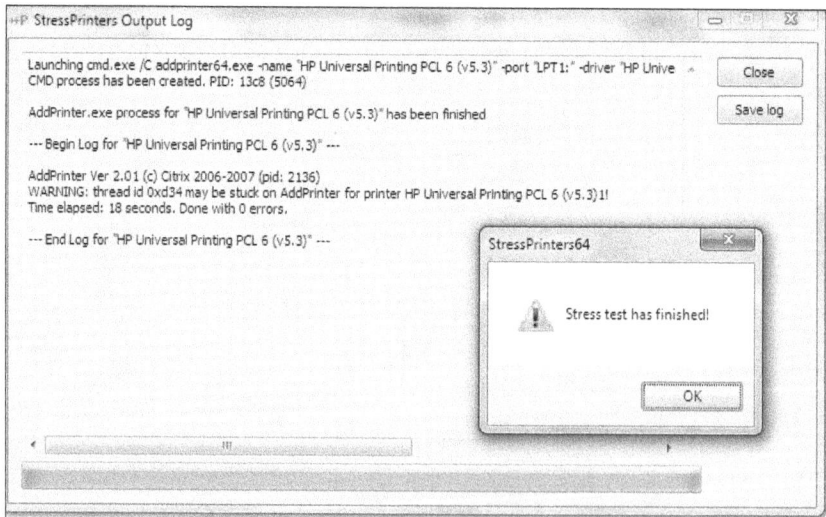

See also

▶ The *Configuring the XenDesktop® policies* recipe in *Chapter 7, XenDesktop®
    Infrastructure Tuning.*

Configuring USB devices

When making a decision about the migration from physical to virtual desktop infrastructure,
the managers and IT technicians should always consider maintaining a high operational level
for their users, such as an elevated user experience or the ability to use external devices. In
this recipe, we will discuss how to use and map the USB devices, while also looking at the
security aspects involved in this operation.

Getting ready

You need administrative access to the Citrix Controller machine, in order to configure
the required policies. The presence of a Citrix Receiver on the endpoints is, of course,
a mandatory prerequisite.

How to do it...

In this section, we will explain how to configure the use of the physical USB devices within the
XenDesktop virtual environment:

1. Connect to the Citrix Controller machine and hit the Windows + C key combination.
    Search for the Citrix Studio icon in the Citrix software section and click on it.

2. In the left-hand menu, click on the **Policy** link, and then select the **Create Policy**
    option on the right-hand menu.

3. On the **Select settings** screen, choose the **USB Devices** option in the second
    drop-down list.

4. Edit the **Client USB device redirection** policy, choosing whether to allow or prohibit
    the mappings of the USB devices. After that, click on the **OK** button.

5. Edit the **Client USB Plug** and **Play device redirection** policies, choosing whether to allow or prohibit the mapping of Plug and Play devices, such as cameras or POS. After that, click on the **OK** button.

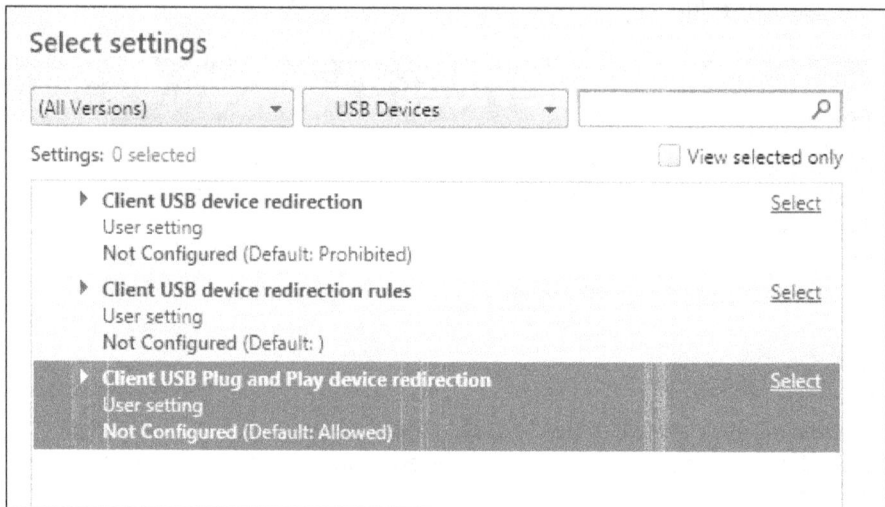

Select settings	
(All Versions) ▼ USB Devices ▼ [🔎]	
Settings: 0 selected	☐ View selected only
▶ Client USB device redirection User setting Not Configured (Default: Prohibited)	Select
▶ Client USB device redirection rules User setting Not Configured (Default:)	Select
▶ **Client USB Plug and Play device redirection** User setting Not Configured (Default: Allowed)	Select

6. Connect to one of the desktop instances, and in the **Citrix** menu bar on the top of the VDI session, click on the **Preferences** tab.

7. Select the **File Access** section, and decide which type of access to give the virtual desktop to the USB device (**No Access**, **Read only**, **Read and write**, and **Ask me each time**). After that, click on the **OK** button.

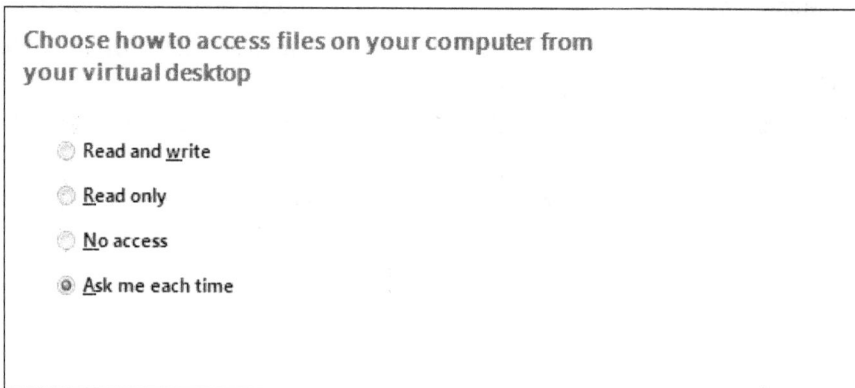

> **Choose how to access files on your computer from your virtual desktop**
>
> ○ Read and write
> ○ Read only
> ○ No access
> ◉ Ask me each time

8. Attach a USB disk to your physical client to test the ability of the Citrix Desktop instance to see and interact with it.

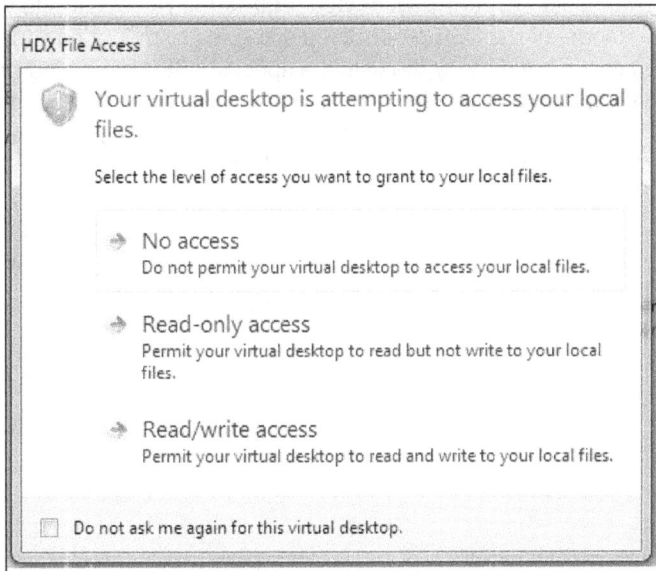

> HDX File Access
>
> Your virtual desktop is attempting to access your local files.
>
> Select the level of access you want to grant to your local files.
>
> → No access
> Do not permit your virtual desktop to access your local files.
>
> → Read-only access
> Permit your virtual desktop to read but not write to your local files.
>
> → Read/write access
> Permit your virtual desktop to read and write to your local files.
>
> ☐ Do not ask me again for this virtual desktop.

How it works...

With the USB device policies, administrators can decide whether to give the user the ability to mount and use external devices, with particular attention to USB mass storage devices. As explained later in this recipe, you can secure the resources in your infrastructure by implementing some kind of device control, limiting usage and access to only the configured USB peripherals.

After the configuration of the policies, you have to choose which way a desktop instance can access data on a mounted USB device. You could prohibit total access to the resource, allowing basic read-only access, or give full read-and-write privileges to operate on the available data.

This process applies when you connect a USB key or storage device to your physical client (thin client, notebook, and so on). The communication passes to the Citrix Receiver client, which performs a check on the applied system policies, permitting or restricting access to the content on the device.

There's more...

The second USB device policy (**Client USB device redirection rules**) permits you to implement a filter based on the model of the USB product you are going to mount on your virtual desktop. This means that you can allow or deny the use of a specific USB disk, based on hardware parameters, such as **Vendor ID (VID)**, **Product ID (PID)**, or **Release ID (REL)**.

To create a rule, edit the discussed policy and click on the **New** button, or click on **Edit** to modify an existing one.

Client USB device redirection rules

Applies to: XenDesktop: 5.0, 5.5, 5.6 Feature Pack 1, 7.0 Server OS, 7.0 Desktop OS

Values:

| New | Edit | Delete | Move Up | Move Down |

☐ Use default value:

▼ Details and related settings

Lists redirection rules for USB devices.

The filtering rule must be generated by using the following parameters:

> [Allow | Deny] : [Category] = [Category Code]

In the category section, you have to use one of the following parameters:

- **VID**: This is the Vendor ID for the USB device
- **PID**: This is the Product ID for the USB device
- **REL**: This is the Release ID for the USB device
- **Class**: This is the category to which the USB device belongs
- **SubClass**: This is the subcategory part of the class earlier described
- **Prot**: This is the communication protocol used by the device

The following is an example of a configured USB device rule:

▶ `Allow: Class=08 SubClass=03 # Mass storage devices`

> Please refer to the USB corporation (`http://www.usb.org/home`) to find all the required information about the vendor and product IDs of USB devices.

See also

▶ The *Configuring the XenDesktop® policies* recipe in *Chapter 7, XenDesktop® Infrastructure Tuning*.

Configuring the XenDesktop® logging

Any operation performed on a system, automatically or manually executed by the users, should be registered in a log file in order to troubleshoot problems and be able to reconstruct the activities for any kind of reason- for instance in case of security or legal checks. In this recipe, we will discuss the main logging activities performed by the XenDesktop machines and the way to implement them.

Getting ready

All the policies will be applied to the deployed virtual desktop instances and the assigned users, so you need an already existent XenDesktop infrastructure on which to enable and use the configuration rules.

How to do it

In this recipe, we will explain how to configure XenDesktop logging features:

1. Connect to the Delivery Controller server with an administrative domain user.
2. Run the Windows + C key combination, search for the **Citrix Studio** icon in the Citrix software section and click on it.
3. Click on the **Policy** link in the left-hand menu, then select **Create Policy** in the right-hand panel or edit an existing one.

4. In the **Categories** menu, select the **Log settings** section, and configure the following policies:

- ❑ **Active Directory actions**: This policy can be set as either **Enabled** or **Disabled**. If enabled, this policy will log all the domain-related events, in relation with the profile management activities.

- ❑ **Common information**: This policy provides option to be either **Enabled** or **Disabled**. If enabled, this policy will log all the common information-related events in a verbose manner, in relation with the profile management activities.

- ❑ **Common warnings**: This policy can be set as either **Enabled** or **Disabled**. If enabled, this policy will log all the common warnings-related events in a verbose manner, in relation with the profile management activities.

- ❑ **Enable logging**: This policy provides the option to be either **Enabled** or **Disabled**. If enabled, this policy will activate the verbose logging, also known as debug mode.

- ❑ **File system actions**: This policy can be set as either **Enabled** or **Disabled**. If enabled, this policy will log all the operations applied to the filesystem(s) in a verbose manner.

- ❑ **File system notifications**: This policy provides the option to be either **Enabled** or **Disabled**. If enabled, this policy will log all the operations applied to the filesystem(s) in a verbose manner.

- ❑ **Log off**: This policy can be set as either **Enabled** or **Disabled**. If enabled, this policy will activate verbose logging for the user logoff operations.

- ❑ **Log on**: This policy provides option to be either **Enabled** or **Disabled**. If enabled, this policy will activate verbose logging for the user logon operations.

- ❑ **Maximum size of the log file**: Insert a value in bytes as a maximum size for the log file. After the maximum size has been reached, the file is rotated in a `.bak` file, and a new log file is generated.

> If a `.bak` already exists, this will be deleted, and then the new backup log file will be generated.

- ❑ **Path to log files**: This policy provides the option to be either **Enabled** or **Disabled**. With this policy, you can specify, if enabled, a particular network path on which to create the log files; if disabled, the default path will be used (`%SystemRoot%\System32\LogFiles\UserProfileManager`)

- ❑ **Personalized user information**: This policy can be set as either **Enabled** or **Disabled**. If enabled, this policy will log all the user information customizations in a verbose manner.

- **Policy values at log on and log off**: This policy provides the option to be either **Enabled** or **Disabled**. If enabled, this policy will log all the changes applied to the policy in the time interval between the logon and logoff phase.

- **Registry actions**: This policy can be set as either **Enabled** or **Disabled**. If enabled, this policy will activate verbose logging for the operations on the registry during user sessions.

- **Registry differences at log off**: This policy provides the option to be either **Enabled** or **Disabled**. If enabled, this policy will log in a verbose manner all the changes applied to the registry during user sessions, when a user performs a log off from the assigned resource.

5. After completing the required configurations, save the policy changes, as seen earlier in this chapter.

6. By clicking on the **Logging** link in the left-hand menu, you will be prompted with a list of operations performed in the last activity times.

Administrator	Main task	Start	End	Status
Today				
XDSEVEN\Administrator	Update HDX Policies	10/11/2013 : 11.29.49	10/11/2013 : 11.29.52	Successful
Yesterday				
XDSEVEN\Administrator	Update HDX Policies	09/11/2013 : 17.41.29	09/11/2013 : 17.41.32	Successful
Three Weeks Ago				
XDSEVEN\Administrator	Create Application 'Notepad++'	27/10/2013 : 02.57.41	27/10/2013 : 02.58.20	Successful
XDSEVEN\Administrator	Remove Machine Configuration '5' from Deskt...	27/10/2013 : 02.47.53	27/10/2013 : 02.47.56	Successful
XDSEVEN\Administrator	Delete Application 'Notepad++'	27/10/2013 : 02.47.29	27/10/2013 : 02.47.59	Successful
XDSEVEN\Administrator	Update Application 'Notepad++'	27/10/2013 : 02.36.36	27/10/2013 : 02.36.52	Successful
XDSEVEN\Administrator	Update Application 'Notepad++'	27/10/2013 : 02.33.58	27/10/2013 : 02.34.19	Successful

7. Click on the **Preferences** link in the right-hand menu, then configure whether to enable or disable the logging of administrative tasks, and also whether to modify the database on which logs are stored. After completion, click the **OK** button.

Configuration Logging

○ Disable

● Enable

Logging database (where configuration logs are stored)

Database size: 0

Server location: SqlDatabaseServer.xdseven.local\CITRIX,1434

Database name: CitrixXD7-Site-First

[Change logging database...]

Security:

☑ Allow changes when the database is disconnected
Administrators can make untracked changes.

8. Click on the **Create Custom Report** link in the right-hand menu and select the date range for which to generate the required report. After selecting it, click on the **Next** button.

Date Range

Select a date range:

○ All

○ Last 24 hours

○ Last 7 days

○ Last 4 weeks

◉ Custom

　　Start date:　04/11/2013

　　End date:　10/11/2013

9. In the **Format and Location** section, specify whether to save the report in CSV format, HTML format or both, then give a valid path location on which to create the report file. After completion, click on **Next**.

Format and Location

Select a format:

○ CSV file

　　Best for exporting to a spreadsheet.

◉ HTML

　　Best for viewing or printing.

○ Both

Location where you want to save your report:

C:\Users\administrator.XDSEVEN\Downloads　　Browse...

10. In the **Summary** screen, click on the **Finish** button to complete the report-generation procedure.

How it works...

The XenDesktop logging discussed in this chapter can be divided into two different major areas: the first, configured under the XenDesktop Policies section, configures all the logging parameters for the user profile components, especially in the presence of the configured Citrix Profile Management.

These policies are particularly useful in situations where the changes to the deployed desktop also need to be logged: in fact, we have configured parameters such as the registry changes during a user session, or the performed logon and logoff actions. This means that activities on the corporate desktops could be tracked and intercepted, for instance.

The other log analysis can be performed at XenDesktop infrastructural level: within the Desktop Studio you have the ability to see all the tasks performed by administrators and delegated users for the XenDesktop 7 infrastructure. The logs can also be exported in .csv format (useful as source data to reimport on other data collections, such as external databases or spreadsheets), or in HTML format, which will give you a formatted and human-readable report. All the administrative tasks are logged in the associated site database.

> You should consider implementing a log rotation script in order to maintain the history of the operations performed on your XenDesktop infrastructure systems.

There's more...

When the XenDesktop site logs increase too much, in terms of the amount of data and number of records, you can delete and archive them by using the Desktop Studio console. In the **Logging** section, click on **Delete Logs** on the right-hand menu and, when prompted, choose a valid location on which to archive data before their cancellation.

> Before performing the log deletion, you will be prompted to log in with administrative credentials on the site database on which logs are stored.

Delete Configuration Logs

Configuration Logs will be deleted. Save a copy?
- No
- Yes

Select where to save the copy:
C:\Users\administrator.XDSEVEN\Documents\Log-Archi Browse...

[✎ Logs can be saved in `.csv` or `.txt` formats.]

This will permit you to maintain a history of all the collected data and manage the volume of the logging on the system database(s).

See also

▸ The *Installing and configuring the HDX Monitor* recipe in *Chapter 4, User Experience – Planning and Configuring*

8
XenDesktop®
Component Integration

In this chapter, we will cover the following recipes:

- ▸ Configuring the CloudBridge 7.4 platform
- ▸ Installing and configuring NetScaler Gateway 10.5
- ▸ Installing and configuring XenMobile 10

Introduction

XenDesktop 7.6 is to be considered as a suite made up of many different features, some of them acting as additional features to the core architectural software. In this chapter, we are going to discuss the important components that have the purpose to improve the quality, the performance, and the manageability of your **Virtual Desktop Infrastructure** (**VDI**) architecture: XenMobile platform (the Citrix software used to implement an application and mobile device management infrastructure), the CloudBridge Virtual Appliance (the Citrix infrastructure optimization platform for WAN connections and branch offices), and the NetScaler Gateway, the secure platform used to regulate and secure access to the Citrix applications and desktops.

> Always remember that these components are additional software, with their own licensing programs, not included by default in the XenDesktop suite.

Configuring the CloudBridge™ 7.4 platform

When we refer to a Citrix architecture, we usually mean an infrastructure located in the same area or building. In some cases, especially in the presence of very large organizations, you could have a central infrastructure used by many remote locations, also known as branch offices. In this case, the native optimization of the ICA protocol would not be sufficient for the performance needs of remote users without performance issues, because of the WAN bandwidth being constricted. In this scenario, Citrix presents CloudBridge, which is a WAN optimizer, developed for such situations. It comes in different editions: physical network devices and virtual appliances. In this chapter, we are going to discuss this second solution.

Getting ready

The CloudBridge Virtual Appliance is downloadable from your MyCitrix account as a single component, or as a part of the XenDesktop 7.6 suite Platinum version. This component is available for download in the form of a template for the XenServer, vSphere, and Hyper-V Hypervisors. After downloading, you need to import it in your infrastructure and assign a network to both the configured network cards—one connected to the LAN area and the other pointing to the WAN network. You also need to generate a license file for this platform from the license portal in your MyCitrix account: you have to assign the required number of licenses to allow all the users to work from their remote locations. Then you have to import the generated file in your License Server, as shown in the *Installing and configuring the Citrix Licensing Services (11.12.1)* recipe in *Chapter 1, XenDesktop® 7.6 – Upgrading, Installation and Configuration*.

> To generate a valid license file for the CloudBridge Virtual Appliance, you have to insert the host ID of your license server. You can find this information in the **System Information** section of the **Administration** panel.

How to do it...

In the following steps, we will perform the installation and configuration of the CloudBridge Virtual Appliance, also known as CloudBridge VPX:

1. Extract the CloudBridge archive file, select the template version for your hypervisor (VMWare vSphere, XenServer, or Microsoft Hyper-V) and import it in your virtual infrastructure.

2. Connect to your hypervisor host and open the console of the imported Virtual Appliance.

3. At the command prompt, type in the default credentials (admin/password), and then run the following command to configure the management IP address:

    ```
    set adapter apa -ip<IPADDRESS> -netmask<MASK>
    Example: set adapter apa -ip 192.168.200.97 -netmask 255.255.255.0
    ```

4. To check the configuration, type the following command:

    ```
    show adapter apa
    ```

5. After completion, run the `restart` command in order to restart the virtual appliance.

```
Use the "help" command to display help for a specific command.
Example: help show config-script

admin> show adapter apA
apA
Status:                    Enabled
IP Address:                192.168.200.152
Network Mask:              255.255.255.0
Gateway:                   192.168.200.32
IPv6 Address/PrefixLen:    0.0.0.0/0
IPv6 Gateway:              0.0.0.0
DHCP:                      Enabled
Web Management Access:     Enabled
SSH Management Access:     Enabled
VLAN:                      Disabled
VLAN Group:                0
Done
admin>
```

> Be sure you have not connected the CloudBridge interfaces on the same virtual switch configured on your Hypervisor: this could cause network loop issues.

6. Open a web browser and type the URL, `https://CloudBridge_IP_address`, in the address bar. You will see the web login interface for this Virtual Appliance as follows:

7. Insert the default credentials (username/password) and click on the **Login** button.

8. You will be prompted for the confirmation to configure CloudBridge by using the **Quick Install** configuration. Click **OK** to continue.

9. In the **Management Access** section, confirm the IP address you configured in the previous steps, then configure one or more valid DNS server(s) and a NTP server.

10. Configure the traffic settings for the WAN download/upload traffic, select a valid configured WAN adapter and then click on the **Install** button.

WAN Link Definitions

Receive (Download) Speed*   `90`   mbps ▼

Send (Upload) Speed*   `10|`   mbps ▼

WAN-Side Adapter*   `apA.2`   ▼

[Skip Initial Installation]

[Install]   [Cancel]

11. At the confirmation screen, click the **YES** button in order to restart the virtual appliance.

Restart Unit?

Installation changes were successful. You must restart your unit for these changes to take effect. Do you wish to restart now?

[YES]   [NO]

12. Reconnect to the CloudBridge Web Interface: at this point you will see the dashboard screen with the current state of the virtual appliance.

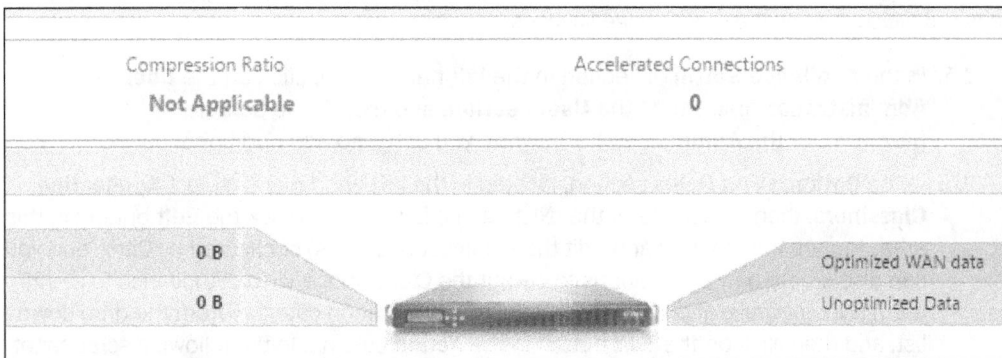

Compression Ratio   Accelerated Connections

Not Applicable   0

0 B   Optimized WAN data

0 B   Unoptimized Data

13. In the menu bar on the top of the screen, click on the **Configuration** link in order to proceed with the customization of the CloudBridge settings.

14. In the left-hand menu, expand the **Appliance Settings** section and click on the **Licensing** link. In the **Add License** section, click on the edit icon, select the **Remote** radio button and populate all the required fields with the details of your License Server. Then, click on the **Save** button and wait for the time needed to restart the appliance.

Remember that you need to pre-allocate the licenses to your License Server by generating the required file containing the CloudBridge licenses.

15. In the **Appliance Settings** section in the left-hand menu, click on the **User Administration** link, select the **User section**, and modify the default password for the **Admin** user. If you want, you can also add additional users.

16. In the **Optimization Rules** section, located in the left-hand menu, select **Application Classifiers**, then select one of the existing applications and click the **Edit** button: in this area, you are able to view and edit the application group(s) configured by Citrix, and you can also create new applications to permit the CloudBridge Virtual Appliance to identify them during acceleration activities. Select an application category from the drop-down list, and then click on the **Edit** button in the **Action** column. In the following screenshot we have selected **ICA – Citrix Protocols** as the **Application Group**:

Configure Application Classifiers

Name*

ICA

Description

XenApp and XenDeskop Traffic (ICA)

Application Group*

Available (26)	Select All		Configured (1)	Remove All
Backup and Replication	+		Citrix Protocols	—
Client-Server	+			
Content Delivery	+			
Custom	+			

Classification Type*

TCP ▼

Port*

1494

17. In the left-hand menu, in the **Appliance Settings** section, click on the **Logging** link. In the first tab, **Log Options**, select a suitable **Log Max Size** in MB (default **1024**), the **Max Export Count Default** (default value **10000**) and the log category that you want to collect (**Log System Records**, **Log Adapter Records**, **Log Flow Records**, **Log Connection Records**, **Log Open/Close Records**, **Log Text Records**, **Log Alert Records**, or **Log CIFS/SMB records**). After that, click on the **OK** button to make the changes persistent.

18. Select the **Syslog Server** tab in the **Logging** category if you have a Syslog server to which it sends the collected logs: in this case, you have to click the **Add** button, specifying the **Syslog Server IP** and **Syslog Server** port. After this is completed, click on **Create**.

19. In the **Optimization Rules** section, click on the **Links** menu and edit the traffic link shown in the **Link Definition** tab: for all of this link you can configure **Name, Link Type** (**LAN** or **WAN**), associated bandwidth (**Bandwidth In** and **Bandwidth Out**) and, if necessary, you can implement filter rules by specifying network parameters such as source and destination IP addresses or network adapters MAC. After this is completed, click on the **OK** button.

Name

> LAN Link

Link Type*

> LAN ▼

Bandwidth In*

> 1 | gbps ▼

Bandwidth Out*

> 1 | gbps ▼

Filter Rules

| Add | Edit | Delete |

Adapter	Source IP Address	Dest IP Address	VLAN
apA.1	Any	Any	Any

> The **Bandwidth** parameter is based on the CloudBridge VPX license that has been purchased: make sure you have configured the **Bandwidth** parameters in line with your license.

20. Click on the **Monitoring** link on the menu bar (at the top of the information section), then select the **Citrix (ICA/CGP)** link. In the **ICA Statistics** tab, you will find statistics about the use and the optimization of the ICA protocol. In the same section, by clicking on **Acceleration Graphs** you will obtain a real-time graphical representation of the optimized ICA traffic.

ICA Connections   ICA Statistics   Acceleration Graphs

ICA WAN Send Throughput

1 bps

0 bps
      08:05:45   08:06:00   08:06:15   08:06:30

— WAN Send Throughput

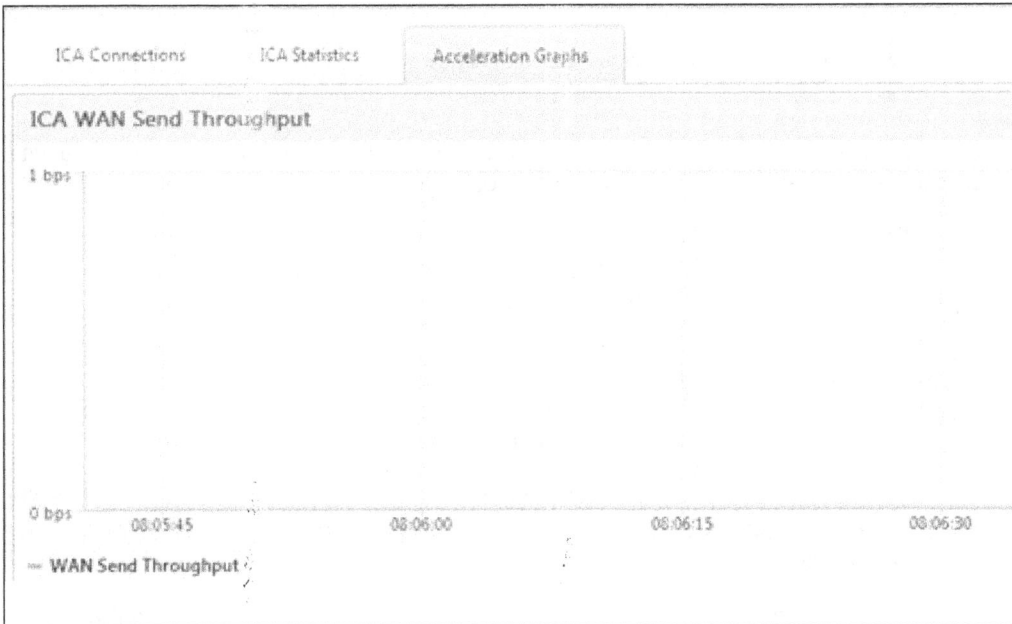

21. You can obtain similar information about network file systems or Outlook MAPI protocol use by clicking on the left-hand menu links called **Filesystem (CIFS/SMB)** and **Outlook (MAPI)**, respectively.

22. Click on the **Usage Graph** link in the left-hand menu | **Usage Graph Monitoring section** | to have general traffic information about the WAN and LAN network usage, with **Last Minute**, **Hour**, **Day**, **Week**, and **Month** views.

How it works...

The CloudBridge Virtual Appliance, also known as CloudBridge VPX, is a less expensive and more flexible solution to optimize and improve the WAN connection among remote locations; the opposite product is the complete range of CloudBridge appliances.

CloudBridge VPX has been developed to run as a virtual machine under XenServer, VMware vSphere, and Microsoft Hyper-V. Within these hypervisors, you have two possible scenarios: the first is made up of a set of CloudBridges equal to the number of the remote offices, each of them in communication with the main CloudBridge office; and the second scenario consists of single CloudBridge in the main office and the peripheral locations linked by the use of the Repeater Acceleration plug-in. With this second scenario, an SSL VPN connection and NetScaler Gateway are necessary.

[✎   We will discuss NetScaler Gateway later in this chapter.]

If you are using two or more Virtual Appliances in the common configuration, as a best practice you can choose between two different network topologies:

- **Inline mode**: With this modality, you need two network interfaces, which can be attached to two physical interfaces, to one physical interface and one virtual interface, or to two virtual interfaces. The last case is used only for test and simulation purposes.

- **One Armed mode** (**WCCP**): In this case, you also need two network adapters, but one of them must be directly attached to a router through a physical network card and the other must point through a virtual interface to the CloudBridge VPX.

With the VPX version, the only way to implement an HA configuration is by the **High Availability** (**HA**) of the hypervisor system. You cannot configure two virtual appliances in an active/passive clustered configuration.

Once you have installed the Virtual Appliance, the first operation to perform is its configuration with the use of the CLI. In this way, you will configure the virtual network adapters (identified with the `apA.x` name, where `x` is a number equal to the configured interfaces) by assigning the network parameters such as the IP address or the VLAN ID. After every critical configuration, a restart is needed in order to make the changes active. Now the web management console is available, you can log in with the same username and password used to connect to the CLI (default admin/password). Once logged in, the first action to perform is interfacing the CloudBridge with the License Server of your company. Remember that, with the non-express version of this product, you must use the standard License Server; to use the internal CloudBridge license platform, you need the express version. You have to license the right version—be careful about the final part of the product name (Vx)—as the associated number refers to the speed of the network link in Mbps for which you've bought the licenses.

[✎   Information on the available licenses can be found at
`http://www.citrix.com/products/cloudbridge/`
`features/editions.html`.]

After this step has been completed, you have to modify the default administrative password: moreover, by joining the CloudBridge to the company domain, you will be able to add users other than the default account.

The latest version of the VPX is loaded with preconfigured applications divided by category: each application has its communication ports already configured; thanks to this implementation, the CloudBridge platform is able, by default, to optimize the network use of critical applications such as Citrix Protocols, Microsoft Exchange, LDAP, or database platforms; you can also create and insert any missing application. This section is strongly linked to the **Traffic Shaping policies** and the **Service Classes** sections: for every configured application, you have the capability to specify **Acceleration Policy** (disk, memory, or flow control) and the traffic priority for the specified application. This way, you have full control and regulation of the use of the network by the application's users.

> An important configuration parameter is the available bandwidth assigned to the WAN and LAN area. Do not forget to configure these two values in the Links section!

Also, in this case, Citrix offers the logging feature, which is configurable to perform troubleshooting activities. In addition to the log size and the areas on which you are logging, you can decide to generate a message alert or an event log for every configured alert option such as **WAN or LAN loss rate**, **Out of CPU or Memory resources**, and **Compression Error detected**.

The strength of CloudBridge is its great ability in compressing and "de-duplicating" network traffic. You can monitor these activities in real time, thanks to the integrated monitoring platform offered by the CloudBridge VPX.

There's more...

The CloudBridge plugin, which is an option to allow remote users to communicate with the CloudBridge platform located in the main office, is configurable using two different approaches:

▶ **Redirector modality**: With this configuration, the plugin transfers the traffic directed to a server machine from the user client to the CloudBridge VPX. Then the accelerator transfers the request to the destination server. To enable this mode you have to select the **CloudBridge Plug-ins** link in the left-hand menu of the VPX appliance and select the **Redirector** radio button. This configuration should only be used when it is necessary to your infrastructure using the target appliance as a proxy, which redirects the traffic from the plugin to the destination server and back.

▶ **Transparent modality**: With this configuration, you have a situation similar to the connection between two appliances. So, after the plugin has successfully contacted the VPX, it performs a download of the acceleration rules, which will be seen to verify whether the established connection is regulated with the acceleration policies. To enable this mode you have to select the **CloudBridge Plug-ins** link in the left-hand menu of the VPX appliance and select the **Transparent** radio button. This option should be used in the presence of a set of preconfigured CloudBridge appliances, using a pass-through connection between the client plugin and the destination virtual appliances. Citrix recommends using this second plugin mode.

For both the options, you have to specify a private IP address, which will be available only after you have established the secure VPN connection, and a port in the **Signaling IP** and **Signaling Port** textboxes.

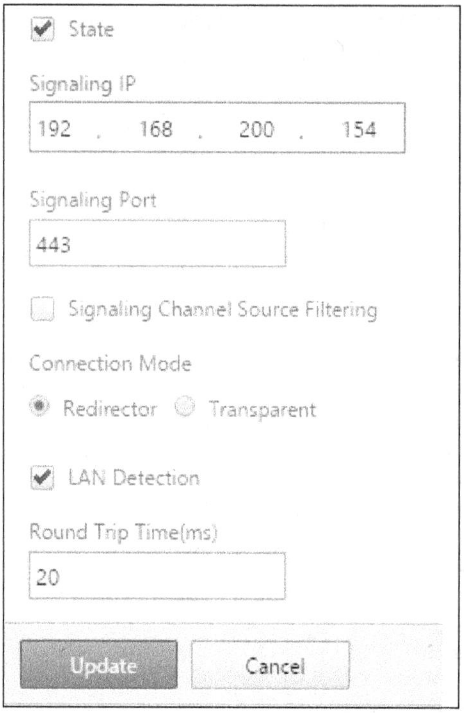

☑ State

Signaling IP

| 192 | . | 168 | . | 200 | . | 154 |

Signaling Port

| 443 |

☐ Signaling Channel Source Filtering

Connection Mode

⦿ Redirector ◯ Transparent

☑ LAN Detection

Round Trip Time(ms)

| 20 |

[Update]   [Cancel]

See also

▶ The *Installing and configuring NetScaler Gateway™ 10.5* recipe in *this chapter*

Installing and configuring NetScaler Gateway™ 10.5

Performance tuning is not the only optimization work to perform on the IT infrastructure: IT staff should also focus their attention on the security features. These concepts need particular care when it comes to infrastructures, where access is granted to users' resources. For Citrix VDI architectures, the NetScaler Gateway permits having a secure gateway in front of your connection manager, the StoreFront platform.

In this chapter, we are going to discuss how to implement the virtual appliance version of the NetScaler Gateway (VPX).

Getting ready

In order to perform the configuration operation for the NetScaler Gateway, first you need to download it from your MyCitrix account | **Download** area, selecting the **NetScaler Gateway** section | **Virtual Appliances** subsection, and then download the appropriate VPX version for your hypervisor (the supported systems are XenServer, VMware ESX/ESXi, and Microsoft Hyper-V). After the download has been completed, you have to import it within your virtual infrastructure.

> When importing the virtual appliance, during the configuration steps you should assign two different networks to the virtual appliance virtual network cards, one pointing to the private network and the other configured for the public network.

Moreover, you need to allocate a number of licenses equal to the number of your XenDesktop users: as seen in the first chapter, you have to generate a license file, associating it to the NetScaler Gateway hostname Virtual Appliance.

> You can find information about the NetScaler Gateway licensing model at http://support.citrix.com/proddocs/topic/netscaler-gateway-105/ng-license-platform-universal-con.html.

How to do it...

In this section, we will configure the NetScaler Gateway virtual appliance:

1. Connect to the console of the configured NetScaler Gateway virtual machine, and configure the following network parameters: **IPv4 address**, **Netmask**, and **Gateway IPv4 address**. After completion, select option number 4, **Save and quit**.

```
!There is no ns.conf in the /nsconfig!

Start Netscaler software
tput: no terminal type specified and no TERM environmental variable.
Enter NetScaler's IPv4 address []: 192.168.200.53
Enter Netmask []: 255.255.255.0
Enter Gateway IPv4 address []: 102.168.200.1

------------------------------------------------------------------------
Netscaler Virtual Appliance Initial Network Address Configuration.
This menu allows you to set and modify the initial IPv4 network addresses.
The current value is displayed in brackets ([]).
Selecting the listed number allows the address to be changed.

After the network changes are saved, you may either login as nsroot and
use the Netscaler command line interface, or use a web browser to
http://192.168.200.53 to complete or change the Netscaler configuration.
------------------------------------------------------------------------
    1. NetScaler's IPv4 address [192.168.200.53]
    2. Netmask [255.255.255.0]
    3. Gateway IPv4 address [102.168.200.1]
    4. Save and quit
Select item (1-4) [4]: 4
```

2. Open a compatible web browser and, in the address bar, type the address previously assigned to the virtual appliance.

3. Insert the default web portal credentials (`nsroot` / `nsroot`), and click the **Login** button to continue.

> ![note icon] Starting from the login screen, you can note the new HTML5 interface.

4. As a second configuration step, configure the NetScaler Gateway VPX with a valid **Subnet IP Address** (**SNIP**); after completion, click on **Done**. A SNIP is an address that is used by NetScaler to connect to the server-side network area.

Subnet IP Address

Specify an IP address for your NetScaler to communicate with the backend servers.

Subnet IP Address

Not configured

Subnet IP Address*

| 192 | . | 168 | . | 200 | . | 55 |

Netmask*

| 255 | . | 255 | . | 255 | . | 0 |

[Done] [Do It Later]

---

5. Click on the **Host Name** section and assign a valid hostname and, one or more DNS server(s), and configure the time zone. After completion, click the **Done** button.

Host Name, DNS IP Address, and Time Zone

Specify a host name to identify your NetScaler, an IP address for a DNS server to resolve domain names, and the time zone in which your NetScaler is located.

Host Name	DNS IP Address	Time Zone
Not configured	*Not configured*	**CoordinatedUniversalTime**

Host Name

NetscalerHostName

DNS IP Address

| 192 | . | 168 | . | 200 | . | 10 | ✕ |
| 8 | . | 8 | . | 8 | . | 8 | ✕ + |

Time Zone*

GMT+01:00-CET-Europe/Rome ▼

[Done] [Do It Later]

---

6. In the **Licenses** section, upload a valid license file for your virtual appliance, then click on **Done**, and reboot the virtual machine in order to apply the configured changes.

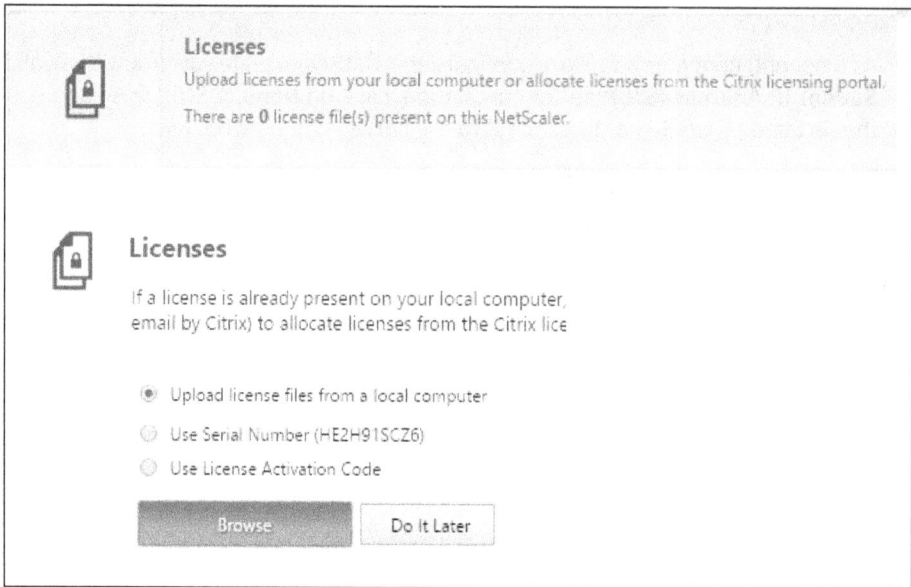

Licenses

Upload licenses from your local computer or allocate licenses from the Citrix licensing portal.

There are **0** license file(s) present on this NetScaler.

Licenses

If a license is already present on your local computer,
email by Citrix) to allocate licenses from the Citrix lice

- ● Upload license files from a local computer
- ○ Use Serial Number (HE2H91SCZ6)
- ○ Use License Activation Code

| Browse | Do It Later |

7. In the **Configuration** tab, click on the **XenApp and XenDesktop** link in the **Integrate with Citrix Products** section.

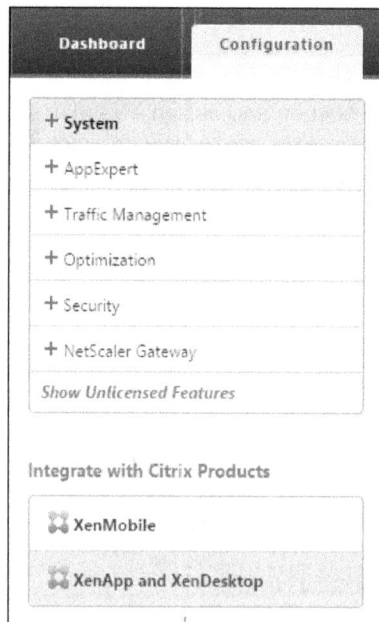

| Dashboard | Configuration |

- **+ System**
- + AppExpert
- + Traffic Management
- + Optimization
- + Security
- + NetScaler Gateway
- *Show Unlicensed Features*

Integrate with Citrix Products

- XenMobile
- **XenApp and XenDesktop**

8. Select the **XenApp/XenDesktop Setup Wizard**, and then select **StoreFront** as your Citrix Integration Point; after completion, click on **Continue**.

9. Assign a valid IP address to the configured Virtual Server, specify the port on which to configure the address (HTTP or HTTPS), and then configure a name for the virtual server. After completion, click on **Continue**.

[💡 You can select the option **Redirect requests from port 80 to secure port**, in order to force the HTTP requests to be redirected to the HTTPS.]

10. In the **Server Certificate** section, choose whether to install a valid certificate, where available, or use an already existing certificate by uploading it. Click the **Continue** button to proceed.

11. In the **Authentication Settings** section, select **Active Directory/LDAP** as the authentication method, then select the **Configure New** radio button and insert valid data for an existing configured domain. After completion, click the **Continue** button.

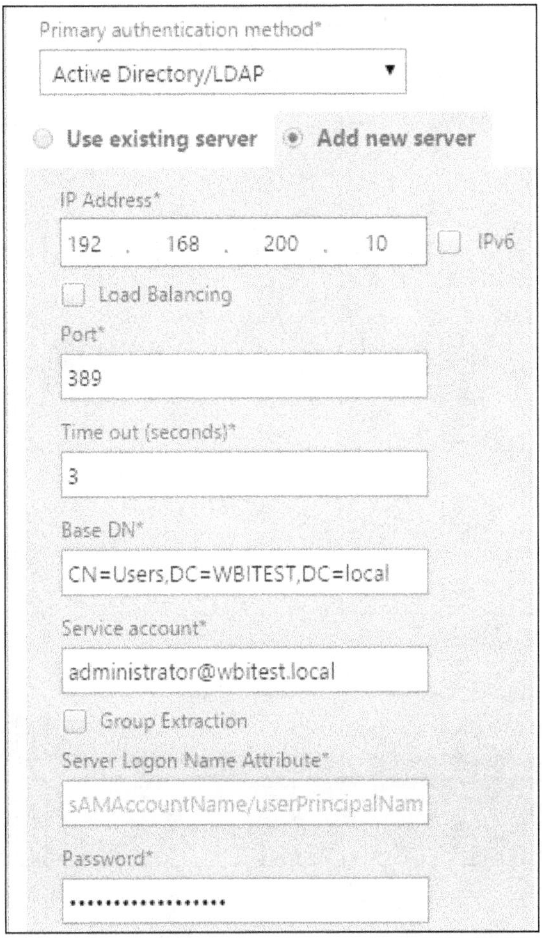

Primary authentication method*

| Active Directory/LDAP ▼ |

○ **Use existing server**   ⦿ **Add new server**

IP Address*

| 192 . 168 . 200 . 10 | ☐ IPv6

☐ Load Balancing

Port*

| 389 |

Time out (seconds)*

| 3 |

Base DN*

| CN=Users,DC=WBITEST,DC=local |

Service account*

| administrator@wbitest.local |

☐ Group Extraction

Server Logon Name Attribute*

| sAMAccountName/userPrincipalNam |

Password*

| •••••••••••••••••• |

12. In the **StoreFront** section, populate the required fields with a valid StoreFront FQDN, a site path, the logon domain, the store name, the **Secure Ticket Authority** (**STA**) address, the StoreFront server IP, and the port on which to configure the service. Click on **Continue** to proceed.

Storefront

StoreFront FQDN*

storefront.wbitest.local

Site Path*

/Citrix/StoreWeb

Single Sign-on Domain*

WBITEST.local

Store Name*

Store

Secure Ticket Authority Server*

http://xendeskbroker.wbitest.local   +

Storefront Server*

192 . 168 . 200 . 9   +

Protocol*

HTTP   ▼

| HTTP |
| SSL |
| 80 |

> The STA address is the FQDN of your Citrix XenDesktop Broker machine.

13. In the **XenFarm** section, select **XenDesktop** as the product, insert a valid combination of XenDesktop Controller IP and listening service port, and then click on **Continue**.

14. In the **Optimization** section, click the **Apply** button in order to configure the optimization profiles for caching, compression, and TCP sessions.

15. Repeat the operation for the **Security** and **Visibility** section, and then click **Done** to complete the configurations.

16. In the **System** menu, click the **Settings** link, then select the **Configure Basic Features** voice and verify that the **NetScaler Gateway** has been flagged. After pressing on **OK,** click on the save icon (in the form of a floppy disk) to register all the changes.

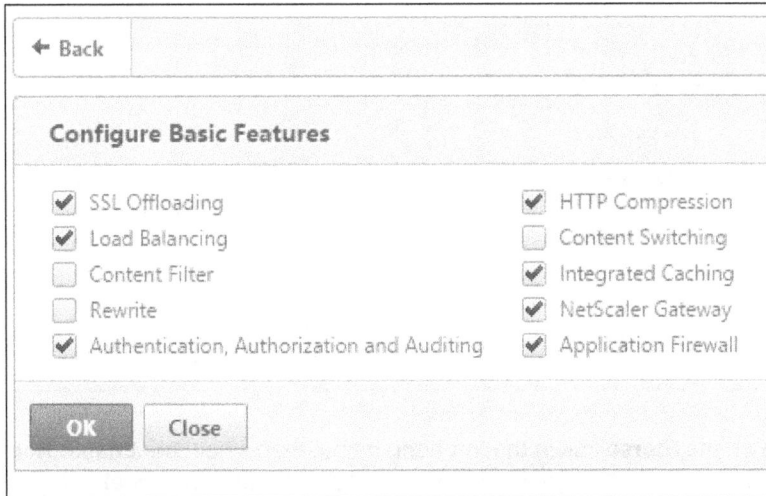

Follow the standard procedures to generate a self-signed certificate or a CA-verified certificate. In this book we will not discuss the full generation of a certificate, but remember that you need at least a Root CA certificate and a Server certificate to configure the NetScaler Gateway. For more details, you can refer to the Microsoft online article at `http://technet.microsoft.com/en-us/library/hh831740.aspx`.

17. Connect to your StoreFront machine with domain administrative credentials, then run the Windows + C key combination, search for the **StoreFront** icon in the Citrix software section, and click on it.

18. Click on the **Authentication** link in the left -hand menu, then select the **Add/Remove Methods** option in the right-hand menu, and add the **Pass-through from NetScaler Gateway** flag option. After completion, click the **OK** button.

Add/Remove Authentication Methods

Choose the authentication methods with which users can authenticate to stores on this server.

- ☑ User name and password
- ☐ Domain pass-through ⚠
- ☐ Smart card ⚠
- ☑ HTTP Basic
- ☑ Pass-through from NetScaler Gateway

OK   Cancel

---

19. Click on the **Stores** link in the left-hand menu, then select the **Enable Remote Access** option in the right-hand menu, select the **Full VPN tunnel** radio button, and click the **Add** button.

Enable Remote Access

Select NetScaler Gateway appliances to provide user access from external networks.

Remote access:
- ○ None
- ○ No VPN tunnel ❶
- ● Full VPN tunnel ❶

NetScaler Gateway appliances:

[   ]

Add...

Default appliance: [▼]

Chapter 8

Choosing the Full VPN tunnel will require you to install the Secure Access Plug-in, having full access to the entire set of published resources. To avoid installing it, consider using the **No VPN tunnel** option. This second choice will give you reduced access to the apps and desktop resources. On the other hand, you will partially reduce the security plus given by the SSL-VPN tunnel. To improve security, you should always configure NetScaler in a DMZ network configuration.

20. Click on **NetScaler Gateway** in the left-hand menu, and then click on **Add NetScaler Gateway Appliance** on the right-hand menu. In the Change **General Settings** screen, populate the required fields in order to link the previously configured NetScaler Gateway to the StoreFront store. After completion, click on **OK**.

Change General Settings

The display name is visible to users in Citrix Receiver preferences.

Display name: VGEN

NetScaler Gateway URL: https://testvo.vgen.io

Version: 10.0 (Build 69.4) or later

Subnet IP address: (optional) 192.168.200.34

Logon type: Domain

Smart card fallback: None

Callback URL: (optional) https://testvo.vgen.io /CitrixAuthService/AuthService.asmx

OK   Cancel

21. In the **Secure Ticket Authority (STA)** screen, configure a valid **STA** address, in the form of `https://DesktopControllerFQDN/scripts/ctxsta.dll`. After completion, click the **Add** button.

Secure Ticket Authority (STA)

Issues session tickets in response to application connection requests.

Secure Ticket Authority URLs:

https://vmxd7-xddc-01.xdseven.local/scripts/ctxsta.dll

Add...   Edit...   Remove

☑ Enable session reliability

☐ Request tickets from two STAs, where available

22. Click on the **Beacons** link in the left-hand menu and select the **Manage Beacons** option in the right-hand menu.

23. In the Internal beacon section, decide whether to use the service URL or a specific URL configured only for internal access. For **External beacons**, add one or more web addresses that must be resolved from external networks. After completion, click the **Add...** button.

Manage Beacons

Beacon points are used to determine whether users are connecting from internal or external networks. Two external addresses that can be resolved from the Internet are required.

Internal beacon: ⦿ Use the service URL

         ◯ Specify beacon address:

         https://mycompany.net

External beacons: https://nsgw01.xdseven.local

         http://www.citrix.com

Add...   Edit...   Remove

The Beacon configurations are used to determine whether users access resources from internal or external networks. For External beacons, you have to specify at least two Internet addresses.

24. Open a web browser and type the address of the configured FQDN VIP NetScaler gateway, in the form of `https://NetScalerGatewayAddress`. You will receive a logon screen on which to insert valid domain credentials. At this point, you will be able to connect to your published resources through the NetScaler Gateway.

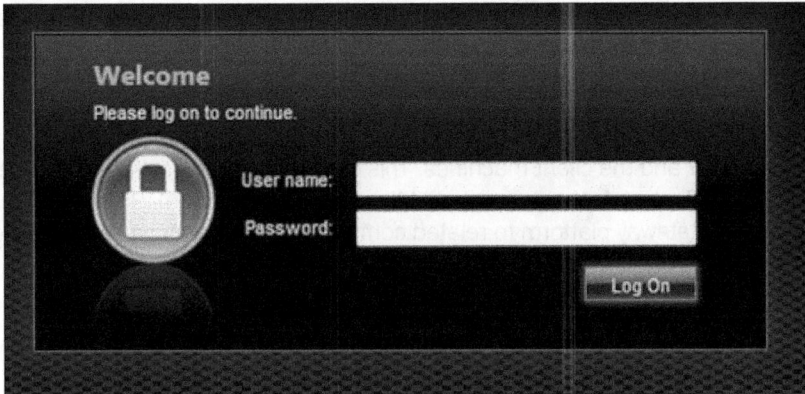

Welcome
Please log on to continue.

User name:

Password:

Log On

To avoid resolution errors for the NetScaler Gateway VIP address, you should create a DNS record for it, or insert a row in the host file of the StoreFront server.

How it works...

The NetScaler Gateway is a secure gateway that permits users to connect to an existing XenDesktop infrastructure in a secure manner.

The installation procedure for the Virtual Appliance only consists of import activities under the supported hypervisor. After this phase, you have to configure the two network interfaces assigned to the gateway: one is used to communicate with the internal area of your architecture, and the other one to connect the infrastructure with the outside world. This is not a mandatory configuration, but it is preferable to differentiate the traffic for the internal and the external worlds.

During the configuration of the network, especially when configuring the Gateway IP Address (also known as **NSIP (NetScaler IP** Address)), you will find two other kinds of network addresses: the **MIP (Mapped IP** Address) and the **SNIP (Subnet IP** Address). The first address is used to contact the back-end machines; the second allows users to access the NetScaler Access Gateway from hosts located on different networks. Another important network component is given by the **VIP (Virtual IP** Address), associated to a configured Virtual Server, which was formerly the gateway web interface contacted by users and systems to access the published virtual resources.

A fundamental operation is linking the NetScaler Gateway to the existing StoreFront installations: in this way you will establish communication between the first point of access for the users (NetScaler Gateway) and the stores configured with StoreFront, which in this configuration has been transformed into a sort of back-end authentication server.

To be able to communicate with the NetScaler Gateway it is necessary to generate a certificate to install on the server and the client machines. This certificate can be self-signed or generated from an existing Certification Authority (such as Microsoft CA, and so on). Remember that, in order to connect the gateway platform to related components such as StoreFront, the certificate must be at least 1,024 bits in size.

> You should always consider generating a certificate from a valid and existing Certification Authority. Self-signed certificates should only be used for PoC and testing environments.

An important aspect is the ability to contact a LDAP server, including Microsoft Active Directory domains: you will be able to use a single authentication method for the secure gateway, the applications, and the virtual desktop created for your infrastructure.

> In *Chapter 10, Configuring the XenDesktop® Advanced Logon*, we will discuss different strong authentication methods to implement with XenDesktop.

At this point, the critical configurations move from the NetScaler VPX to the configured StoreFront system(s): NetScaler needs to be linked to the existing store infrastructure, specifying a pass-through authentication and then linking the gateway web interface address previously configured (VIP address). Moreover, we have also registered the STA by specifying the XenDesktop controller address in the pre-populated global STA URL section. An STA server is used to release authorization tickets when a connection request has been performed, in order to access a published resource (a XenApp application or a XenDesktop virtual desktop instance).

> You should save your configuration after you have tested it: it runs in a `Running-Config` manner and, without explicitly registering the modifications, you will lose any update in the event of a virtual appliance failure or reboot!

There's more...

With the NetScaler Gateway platform it is possible to configure the **Email-Based account discovery** feature. This feature permits users to authenticate to the StoreFront platform by using their own domain-related e-mail addresses.

To perform this, you need to execute the following configuration steps:

- On your infrastructure's DNS server(s) you need to add a **Service Location (SRV)** record; this step is made up of the following tasks:
  - Right click the configured DNS **Forward Lookup Zone** and select the **Other New Records** option.
  - Select the **Service Location (SRV)** option on the **Resource Record Type** screen and click the **Create Record** button.
  - Populate the **Service** field with **_citrixreceiver**, the **Protocol** field with the **_tcp** value, the **Port number** field with **443**, and the **Host offering this service** field with your NetScaler Gateway FQDN.

► On your NetScaler Gateway Virtual Appliance, edit the configured session policy, select the **Published Applications** tab, locate the **Account Service Address** field, check the **Override global** option, and type your StoreFront address in the form of `https://StoreFront/Citrix/Roaming/Accounts`.

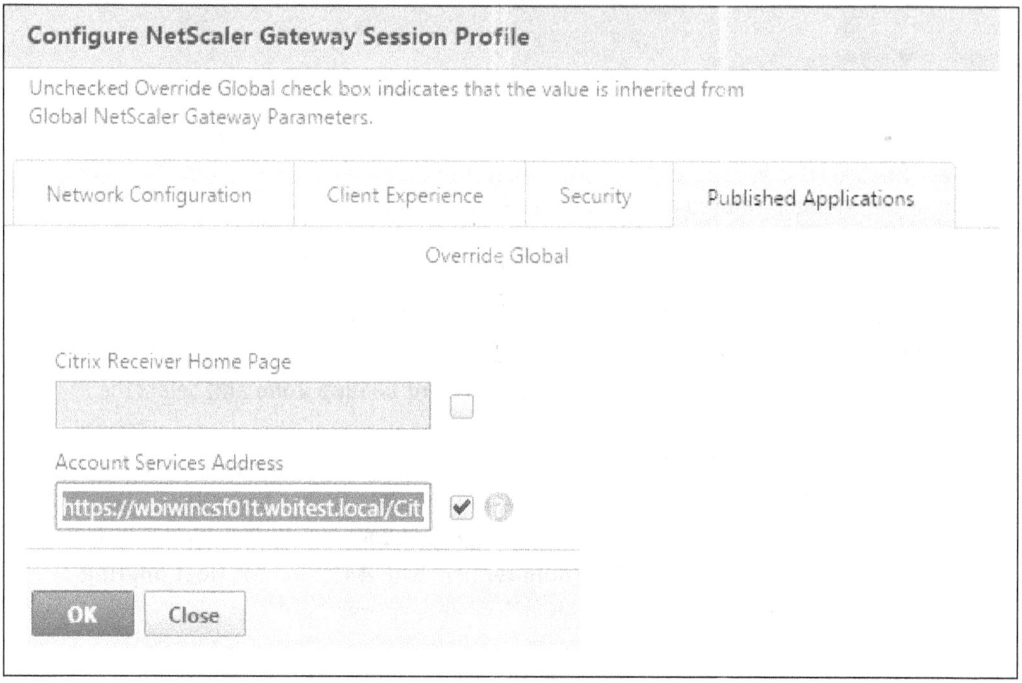

Configure NetScaler Gateway Session Profile

Unchecked Override Global check box indicates that the value is inherited from Global NetScaler Gateway Parameters.

Network Configuration	Client Experience	Security	Published Applications

Override Global

Citrix Receiver Home Page

[   ] ☐

Account Services Address

[https://wbiwincsf01t.wbitest.local/Cit] ✔ ◯

[OK]   [Close]

> ☐ Please refer to the *How it works...* section for the session profile configuration.

► In the same **Session Policy** section, select the **Client Experience** tab and enable **Clientless access** by checking the **Override Global** checkbox and selecting the **Allow** option.

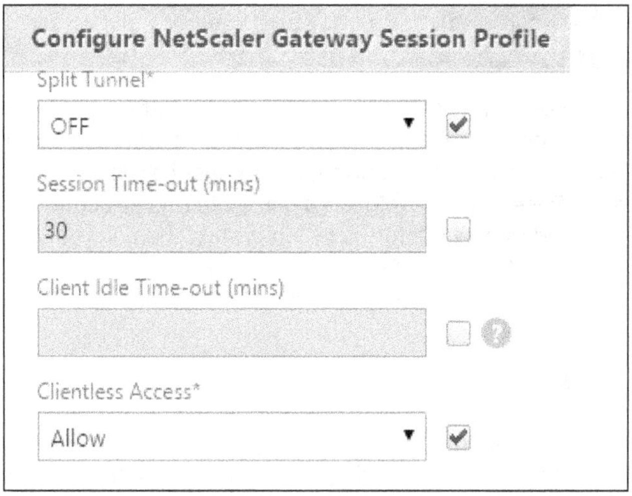

Configure NetScaler Gateway Session Profile

Split Tunnel*

OFF ▼ ☑

Session Time-out (mins)

30 ☐

Client Idle Time-out (mins)

☐ ❓

Clientless Access*

Allow ▼ ☑

▸ To complete the configuration, add to the **Expression** section the highlighted expressions indicated in the following screenshot:

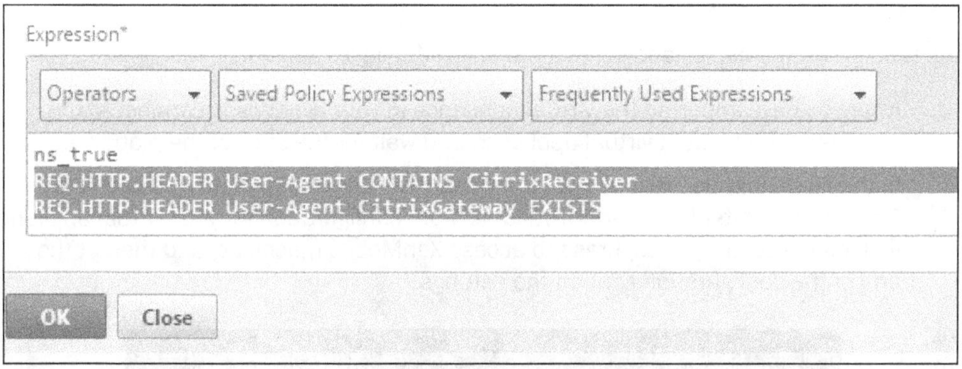

Expression*

| Operators ▼ | Saved Policy Expressions ▼ | Frequently Used Expressions ▼ |

```
ns_true
REQ.HTTP.HEADER User-Agent CONTAINS CitrixReceiver
REQ.HTTP.HEADER User-Agent CitrixGateway EXISTS
```

OK   Close

Users will be now able to authenticate to the StoreFront using their corporate e-mail address.

> You can better understand how to use the e-mail-based account discovery feature by reading the Citrix article at http://support.citrix.com/article/CTX139059.

See also

▸ The *Installing and configuring StoreFront™ 2.6* recipe in *Chapter 1, XenDesktop® 7.6 – Upgrading, Installation, and Configuration*

Installing and configuring XenMobile® 10

In the era of mobile devices being used as classic working platforms, the requirements for security and integration, and the capability to work on their own resources by using mobile devices is even greater. To meet these demands, in the last few years after the acquisition of a company called ZenPrise, Citrix developed a complete and structured platform that permits using the indicated mobile platforms by integrating them in your existing XenDesktop infrastructure: this is the XenMobile software. In this chapter we will discuss the release number 10 of this software and the interaction with XenDesktop.

Getting ready

You need to download the XenMobile template from the Citrix website by using a valid MyCitrix account. After completing its download, you have to import it within your hypervisor infrastructure. XenMobile is downloadable for the following virtualization platforms: XenServer, Hyper-V, and VMware vSphere.

How to do it...

In this section, we will deploy and configure the XenMobile 10 software:

1. After you have imported the virtual appliance in your hypervisor, connect to the console of the created virtual appliance and wait for the start of the platform.

2. In the First Time Use wizard, type in twice a new admin password and click the *Enter* button. After this, insert a valid network configuration for your virtual appliance, including a security passphrase to access XenMobile machines, and then at the end of the configuration confirm the settings.

```
Welcome to the XenMobile First Time Use wizard. This wizard
he initial configuration of XenMobile. Accept options offere
Return or type your own response and then press Enter/Return

Command prompt window administrator account:
This is the user name and password you use when logging on t
ommand prompt.
  Username: admin
  New password:
  Re-enter new password:

Network settings:
  IP address []: 192.168.200.89
  Netmask []: 255.255.255.0
  Default gateway []: 192.168.200.1
  Primary DNS server []: 192.168.200.10
  Secondary DNS server (optional) []: 192.168.200.6

  Commit settings (y/n) [y]:
```

> [Optionally, you can also enable the FIPS security standard for your XenMobile setup. More information about the FIPS standard can be found at `http://en.wikipedia.org/wiki/Federal_ Information_Processing_Standards`.]

3. Choose the kind of database connection you want to implement (local or remote), and press *Enter* to continue; if all the settings are valid, commit the configurations to proceed.

> [Local databases should be only used in POC or testing scenarios.]

4. Type in a valid FQDN for your XenMobile site, and then click the *Enter* button to continue. After completion, accept to commit the configurations.

5. In the Communication ports section, decide on which ports to configure your services for HTTP (default: 80), HTTPS with certificate authentication (default: 443), HTTPS without certificate (default: 8443), and management on HTTPS (default: 4443). After completion, commit the settings you have configured.

```
Hostname []: xenmobile.wbitest.local

Commit settings (y/n) [y]:
Applying fqdn settings...

Communication ports:
 HTTP [80]:
 HTTPS with certificate authentication [443]:
 HTTPS with no certificate authentication [8443]:
 HTTPS for management [4443]:

Commit settings (y/n) [y]: █
```

6. In the Public Key Certification (PKI) configuration, decide whether to use the same password for the generated certificates. Press the *Enter* button to apply your choice and then commit the settings.

7. Configure a valid username/password combination to access the XenMobile management console. After completion, commit the settings to apply the configurations.

```
Do you want to use the same password for all the certificates of the PKI [y]:
New password:
Re-enter new password:

Commit settings (y/n) [y]:
Generating SAML signing certificate...
Generating server and client certificates...

XenMobile console administrator account:
This is the user name and password you use when logging on to the XenMobile cons
ole through a web browser.
Username [administrator]:
Password:
Re-enter new password:

Commit settings (y/n) [y]: █
```

8. Skip the upgrade section by selecting the n option when asked for upgrading by a previous release, and then type *Enter*.

9. Open a compatible web browser, type the XenMobile address in the form of `https://<XenMobileAddress>:4443`, and then insert the configured credentials to access it. After completion, click on **Sign in**.

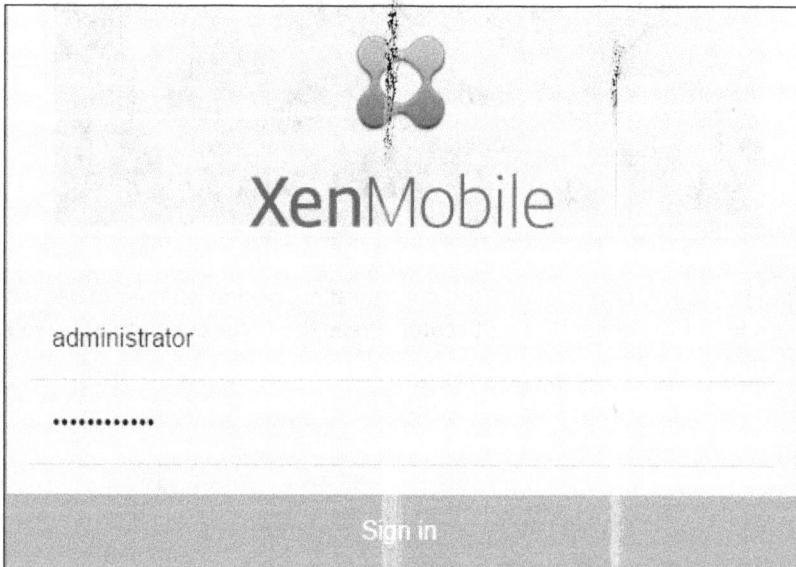

10. On the Get Started screen, click the **Start** button to continue.

11. In the **Licenses** section, configure a valid license for your product; as an alternative, you can configure a free 30-day trial license. Click the **Next** button after completion.

Initial Configuration

Default license	Evaluation license
Trial period	**30** day(s) left
Configure license	ON
License type	Local license ▾

1 Licenses

2 Certificates

   SSL Certificate (optional)

3 NetScaler Gateway (optional)

4 LDAP Configuration (optional)

5 Notification Server (optional)

6 Summary

Add

Product name	Active	Total
No results found.		

Expiration notification	ON
Notify every*	7 day(s)

12. In the **Certificates** section, configure a valid certificate used to establish the connection between the device and the XenMobile server; for testing purposes, you should consider using the default self-signed certificate that already exists. After completion, click on **Next**.

1 Licenses ✓

2 Certificates

   SSL Certificate (optional)

3 NetScaler Gateway (optional)

4 LDAP Configuration (optional)

5 Notification Server (optional)

your HTTPS connections.

While SSL Certificate is an optional setting, once data is entered into the

Import

Name	Description
XMS.example.com	Self Signed/Generated
xenmobile.wbitest.local	Self Signed/Generated
cacerts.pem	Self Signed/Generated

13. In the **NetScaler Gateway** section, you can configure the interaction between XenMobile and an existing NetScaler Gateway, inserting a valid name and an external URL for XenMobile, and using one of the available **Logon Type**(s). After completion, click on **Next**.

NetScaler Gateway

Enables secure mobile user access.

While NetScaler Gateway is an optional setting, once data is entered into the form, the required fields r page.

Name*	Appliance name
Alias	
External URL*	Publicly accessible URL
Logon Type	Domain only ▼
Password Required	Domain only
	Security token only
Set as Default	Domain and security token
	Certificate
	Certificate and domain
Callback URL* Virtual IP*	Certificate and security token

14. In the **LDAP Configuration** section, configure a valid Microsoft Active Directory infrastructure by typing in all the required parameters, then click the **Next** button.

LDAP Configuration

Provides connection to one or more LDAP-compliant directories, such as Active Directory, to import groups, user accounts.
While LDAP Configuration is an optional setting, once data is entered into the form, the required fields must be cleared or c
the page.

Directory type*	Microsoft Active Directory ▾
Primary server*	192.168.200.10
Secondary server	192.168.200.6
Port*	389
Domain name*	WBITEST.local
User base DN*	dc=WBITEST,dc=local
Group base DN*	dc=WBITEST,dc=local

15. In the **Notification Server** section, you have the ability to configure an SMTP server used to send notifications to users and administrators in case of necessity. Click the **Next** button to continue.

16. In the **Summary** section, after you have verified that all the configured options are correct, click the **Finish** button to complete the configuration process.

17. In the **Dashboard** screen you will see a summary of the current configuration of your mobile infrastructure, in terms of policies, devices, and compliance status.

▓ XenMobile	Dashboard	Manage	Configure

NOTIFICATIONS

Compliance
⊙ 0   ⊙ 0   ⊙ 0
ActiveSync blocked   Non-compliant   inactive

Decommission
⊙ 0   ⊙ 0   ⊙ 0
Last 24 hours   Last 24 hours   Pending (selective
(wipes)   (selective wipes)   wipes)

PLATFORMS   **CARRIERS**

18. Click on the **Manage** button in the top side bar menu and select one of the available methods to add a device to XenMobile: **Devices** or **Enrollment**.

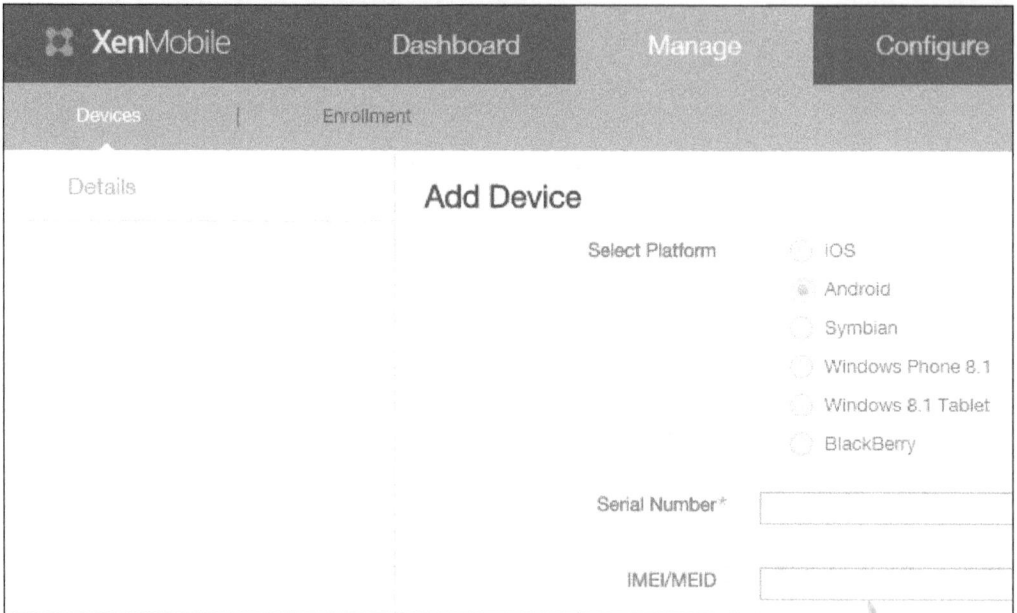

19. Click on the **Configure** button in the top side bar menu, and then click the **Add** button in the **Device Policies** subsection; here you can find a long list of configurable policies for your devices.

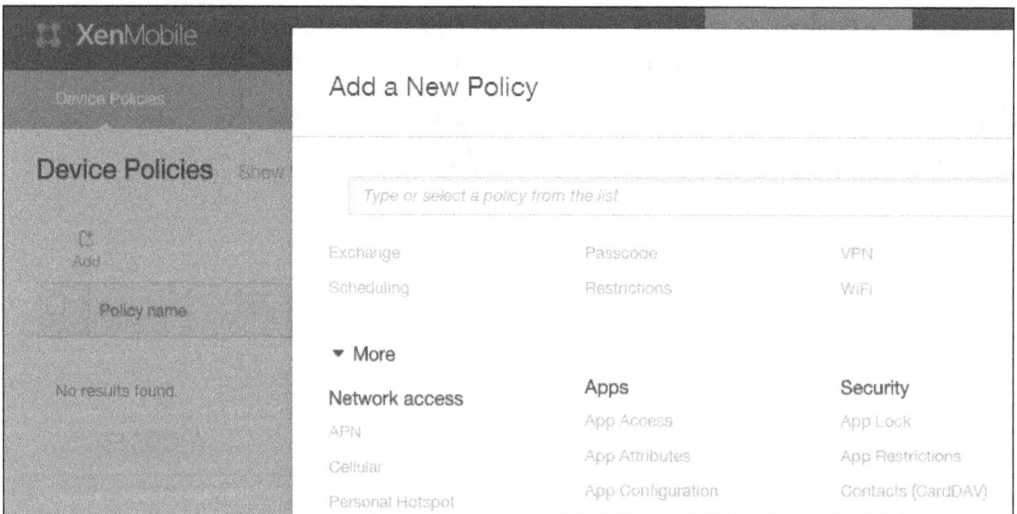

20. In the same menu, select the **Apps** section: also in this case click the **Add** button and select one or more application(s) that you want to configure for end-users' devices.

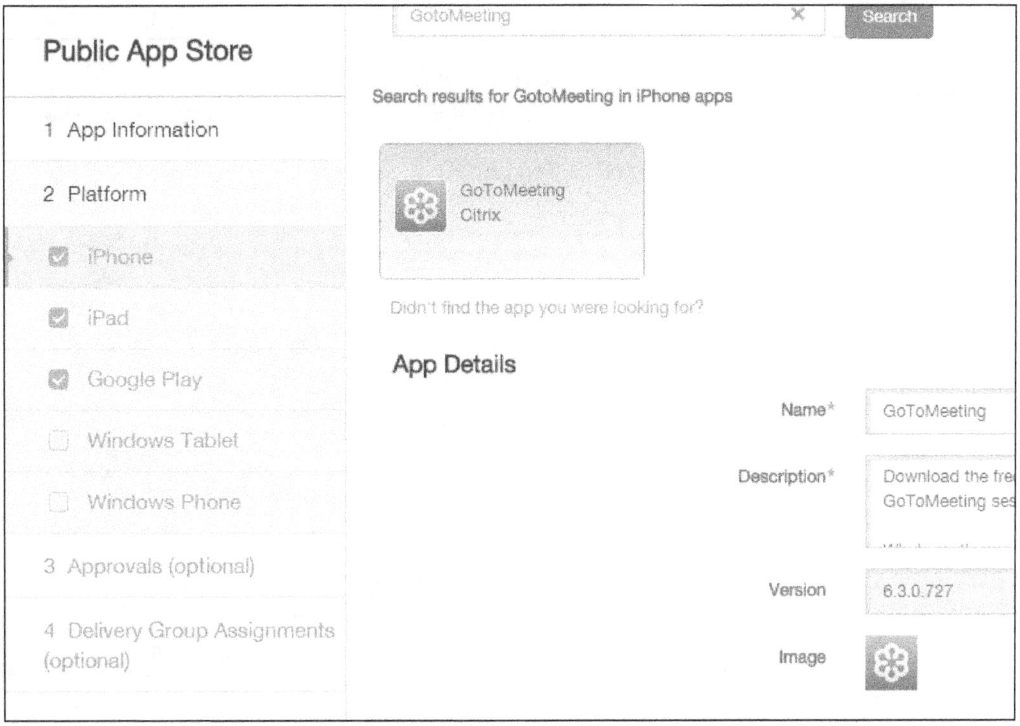

Public App Store

GotoMeeting ✕ Search

Search results for GotoMeeting in iPhone apps

1 App Information

2 Platform

☑ iPhone

☑ iPad

☑ Google Play

☐ Windows Tablet

☐ Windows Phone

3 Approvals (optional)

4 Delivery Group Assignments (optional)

GoToMeeting
Citrix

Didn't find the app you were looking for?

App Details

Name* | GoToMeeting

Description* | Download the fre GoToMeeting ses

Version | 6.3.0.727

Image

21. Click on the **Action** button in the top side menu; in this case you can configure specific actions (such as remote wipe or device revoke) when verifying a specific condition for the configured user or device.

Actions

Action details
Choose a trigger event and the associated action for that event.

1 Action Info

2 Details

3 Assignment (optional)

4 Summary

Trigger*

Device property

Select a device property

Action*

Select an action

Selectively wipe the device

Completely wipe the device

Revoke the device

Mark the device as out of compliance

Send notification

Su

If c

22. Click on the **Delivery Groups** link in the top side menu bar, and configure a valid group of domain users to which the previously configured policies, apps, and actions should be assigned.

4 Summary

Resource

Apps 0   Policies 0   Actions 1

Action

How it works...

The XenMobile 10 software is the Citrix offering for the management of mobile devices and applications, and the rules to manage both; in fact, XenMobile can be identified as an EMM (Enterprise Mobility Management. This means that XenMobile is not only a Mobile Device Management, also known as MDM, but is also for application and policy management, for the complete control of mobile devices (including BYOD) using corporate resources. This is usually called MAM, Mobile Application Management.

The setup is based on a Linux Virtual Appliance containing all the components involved with XenMobile: this is a useful change that started with release 10, because in the previous release the MDM and MAM components were split into two different virtual servers.

The setup phase permits configuration of the network settings for the virtual appliance, plus the entire certificate management process; an internal PKI is created in order to allow administrators to use self-signed certificates for their communications.

After the first-time setup has been completed, the control passes to the XenMobile Web Interface, listening by default on the 4443 SSL port. In this scenario, after configuring the main collateral infrastructural components, such as Active Directory or NetScaler systems, a XenMobile administrator can configure the main entities that this platform is able to manage: mobile devices; the Application catalog; Actions to operate on the devices when verifying specific conditions or triggers (for instance, an administrator could decide to completely wipe an iOS device that an end user has decided to jail-break); and Delivery Groups, the destination, in terms of groups made up of domain users, of the previously shown entities (apps, rules, and actions...).

At the time of writing, XenMobile 10 is able to manage the principal mobile platforms existing on the market (Apple iOS, Android, Windows Phone, and Blackberry).

There's more...

XenMobile 10 can be interfaced with the NetScaler Gateway 10.5 platform in order to secure, balance, and manage access to the platforms by using a public channel.

The latest release of the NetScaler product includes a wizard to configure the interaction between NetScaler and the mobile infrastructure, as shown in the following screenshot:

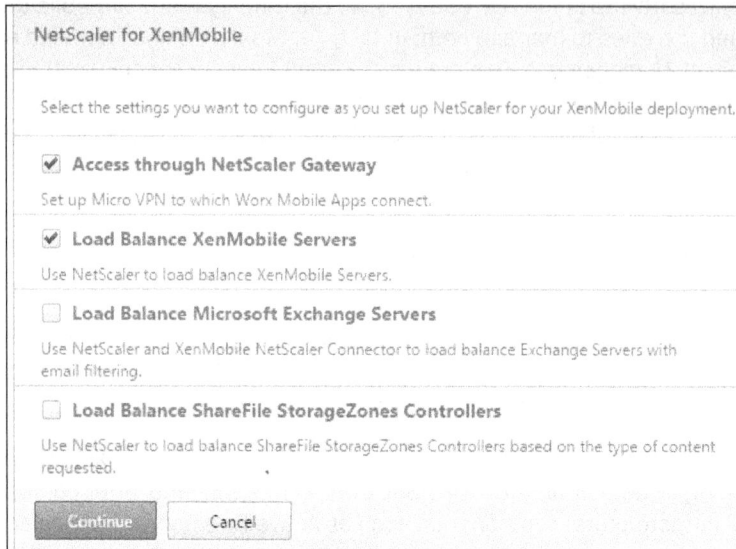

By using this wizard, you will be able to configure load balancing and the creation of virtual server IPs for load balancing the XenMobile servers, and also MAM configurations.

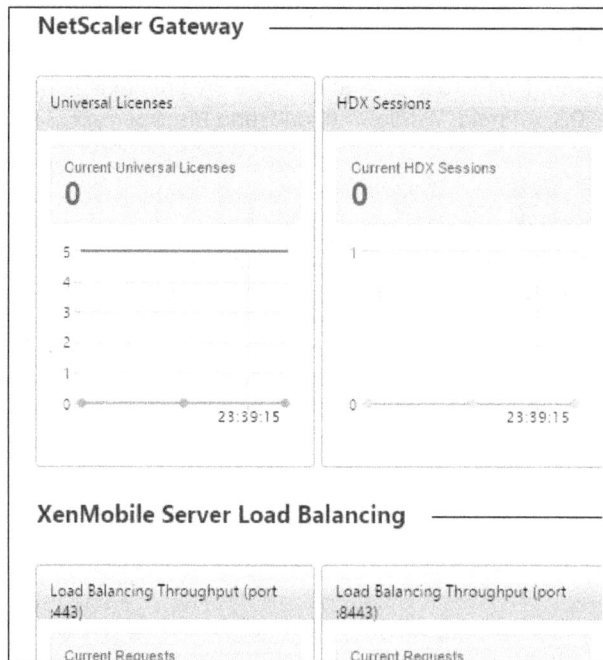

See also

▶ The *Installing and configuring NetScaler Gateway 10.5* recipe earlier in this chapter.

9
Working with PowerShell

In this chapter, you will cover:

- ▶ Retrieving system information – Configuration Service cmdlets
- ▶ Managing Active Directory accounts – ADIdentity cmdlets
- ▶ Managing the Citrix Desktop Controller and its resources – Broker and App-V cmdlets
- ▶ Administering hosts and machines – Host and MachineCreation cmdlets
- ▶ Managing additional components – StoreFront Admin and Logging cmdlets

Introduction

At this point in the book, we have implemented a fully functioning XenDesktop architecture made up of the core components, along with the additional features in terms of security and performance.

With hundreds or thousands of hosts to configure and machines to deploy, configuring all the components manually could be difficult. As for the previous XenDesktop releases, and also with the XenDesktop 7.6 version, you can find an integrated set of PowerShell modules. With its use, IT technicians are able to reduce the time required to perform management tasks by the creation of PowerShell scripts, which will be used to deploy, manage, and troubleshoot at scale the greatest part of the XenDesktop components.

Working with PowerShell instead of the XenDesktop GUI will give you more flexibility in terms of what kind of operations to execute, having a set of additional features to use during the infrastructure creation and configuration phases.

Retrieving system information – Configuration Service cmdlets

In this recipe, we will use and explain a general-purpose PowerShell cmdlet: the **Configuration Service** category. This is used to retrieve general configuration parameters, and to obtain information about the implementation of the XenDesktop Configuration Service.

Getting ready

No preliminary tasks are required. You have already installed the PowerShell SDK during the installation of the Desktop Controller role machine(s).

To be able to run a PowerShell script (.ps1 format), you have to enable the script execution from the PowerShell prompt in the following way, using its application:

```
Set-ExecutionPolicy -ExecutionPolicy RemoteSigned -Force
```

How to do it...

In this section, we will explain and execute the commands associated with the XenDesktop System and Services configuration area:

1. Connect to one of the Desktop Broker servers, by using a remote Desktop connection, for instance.

2. Right-click on the PowerShell icon installed on the Windows taskbar and select the **Run as Administrator** option.

3. Load the PowerShell modules by typing the following command and then press the *Enter* key:

   ```
   Asnp Citrix*
   ```

   > As an alternative to the `Asnp` command, you can use the `Add-PSSnapin` command.

4. Retrieve the active and configured Desktop Controller features by running the following command:

   ```
   Get-ConfigEnabledFeature
   ```

5. To retrieve the current status of the Config Service, run the following command. The output result will be **OK** in the absence of configuration issues:

   ```
   Get-ConfigServiceStatus
   ```

6. To get the connection string used by the Configuration Service and to connect to the XenDesktop database, run the following command:

```
Get-ConfigDBConnection
```

7. Starting from the previously received output, it's possible to configure the connection string to let the Configuration Service use the system DB. For this command, you have to specify the `Server`, `Initial Catalog`, and `Integrated Security` parameters:

```
Set-ConfigDBConnection -DBConnection"Server=<Servername\
InstanceName>; Initial Catalog=<DatabaseName>; Integrated
Security=<True | False>"
```

8. Starting from an existing Citrix database, you can generate a SQL procedure file to use as a backup to recreate the database. Run the following command to complete this task, specifying the `DatabaseName` and `ServiceGroupName` parameters:

```
Get-ConfigDBSchema -DatabaseName<DatabaseName> -ServiceGroupName<S
erviceGroupName>> Path:\FileName.sql
```

> You need to configure a destination database with the same name as that of the source DB, otherwise the script will fail!

9. To retrieve information about the active Configuration Service objects (Instance, Service, and Service Group), run the following three commands respectively:

```
Get-ConfigRegisteredServiceInstance
Get-ConfigService
Get-ConfigServiceGroup
```

10. To test a set of operations to check the status of the Configuration Service, run the following script:

```
#------------- Script - Configuration Service
#------------- Define Variables
$Server_Conn="SqlDatabaseServer.xdseven.local\CITRIX,1434"
$Catalog_Conn="CitrixXD7-Site-First"
#------------
write-Host "XenDesktop - Configuration Service CmdLets"
#---------- Clear the existing Configuration Service DB connection
$Clear = Set-ConfigDBConnection -DBConnection $null
Write-Host "Clearing any previous DB connection - Status: " $Clear
#---------- Set the Configuration Service DB connection string
$New_Conn = Set-ConfigDBConnection -DBConnection"Server=$Server_
Conn; Initial Catalog=$Catalog_Conn; Integrated Security=$true"
```

```
Write-Host "Configuring the DB string connection - Status: " $New_
Conn
$Configured_String = Get-configDBConnection
Write-Host "The new configured DB connection string is: "
$Configured_String
exit
```

> You have to save this script with the `.ps1` extension, in order to invoke it with PowerShell. Be sure to change the specific parameters related to your infrastructure, in order to be able to run the script.

This is shown in the following screenshot:

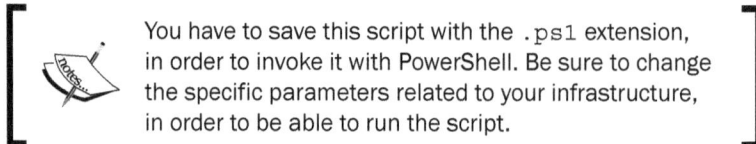

```
Administrator: Windows PowerShell
PS C:\Users\administrator.XDSEVEN\Desktop> .\c9r1s1.ps1
XenDesktop - Configuration Service CmdLets
Clearing any previous DB connection - Status:  DBUnconfigured
Configuring the DB string connection - Status:  OK
The new configured DB connection string is:  Server=SqlDatabaseServer.xdseven.local
D7-Site-First; Integrated Security=True
PS C:\Users\administrator.XDSEVEN\Desktop> _
```

How it works...

The Configuration Service cmdlets of PowerShell permit the managing of the Configuration Service and its related information: the Metadata for the entire XenDesktop infrastructure, the Service instances registered within the VDI architecture, and the collections of these services, called Service Groups.

This set of commands offers the ability to retrieve and check the DB connection string to contact the configured XenDesktop SQL Server database. These operations are permitted by the Get-ConfigDBConnection command (to retrieve the current configuration) and the Set-ConfigDBConnection command (to configure the DB connection string); both the commands use the DB Server Name with the Instance name, DB name, and Integrated Security as information fields.

In the attached script, we have regenerated a database connection string. To be sure to be able to recreate it, first of all we have cleared any existing connection, setting it to null (verify the command associated with the $Clear variable), then we have defined the $New_Conn variable, using the Set-ConfigDBConnection command; all the parameters are defined at the top of the script, in the form of variables.

> Use the `Write-Host` command to echo results on the standard output.

There's more...

In some cases, you may need to retrieve the state of the registered services, in order to verify their availability. You can use the `Test-ConfigServiceInstanceAvailability` cmdlet, retrieving whether the service is responding or not and its response time. Run the following example to test the use of this command:

```
Get-ConfigRegisteredServiceInstance | Test-ConfigServiceInstanceAvailabil
ity | more
```

> Use the `-ForceWaitForOneOfEachType` parameter to stop the check for a service category, when one of its services responds.

See also

▸ The *Preparing the SQL Server 2012 database* recipe in *Chapter 1, XenDesktop® 7.6 – Upgrading, Installation, and Configuration*

Managing Active Directory accounts – ADIdentity cmdlets

In this recipe, we will discuss the utilization of the **Active Directory Identity** cmdlets. This is a capability that permits retrieving and configuring the Active Directory objects used by XenDesktop, such as machine accounts assigned to existing desktop catalogs.

Getting ready

No preliminary tasks are required. You have already installed the PowerShell SDK during the installation of the Desktop Controller role machine(s).

To be able to run a PowerShell script (`.ps1` format), you have to enable the script execution from the PowerShell prompt in the following way:

```
Set-ExecutionPolicy -ExecutionPolicy RemoteSigned -Force
```

How to do it...

The following are the steps required to manage the XenDesktop machine identity using PowerShell:

1. Connect to one of the Desktop Broker servers, by using a Remote Desktop connection, for instance.

2. Click on the PowerShell icon installed on the Windows taskbar.

3. Load the PowerShell modules by typing the following command, and then press the Enter key:

   ```
   Asnp Citrix*
   ```

4. To generate a new Desktop Catalog, and to interface it with your company domain, run the next PowerShell command; the involved parameters are −NamingScheme and − NamingSchemeType:

   ```
   New-AcctIdentityPool -IdentityPoolName<PoolName>
   -NamingScheme<Machine-Name-Structure##> -Domain <ADDomainName>
   -NamingSchemeType<Numeric | Alphabetic>
   ```

5. To retrieve information on the currently existing machine catalogs, you have to use the following command; you can use filters such as −IdentityPoolName, −IdentityPoolUid, and −AdminAddress, which permit you to specify the address of a particular Desktop Controller:

   ```
   Get-AcctIdentityPool
   ```

   > You can sort the output results by using the −SortBy parameter, specifying the file for which you want to sort the output.

6. To rename an existing catalog / identity pool, execute the following command:

   ```
   Rename-AcctIdentityPool -IdentityPoolName<CurrentName>
   -NewIdentityPoolName<NewName>
   ```

   > To modify a catalog configuration parameter, use the Set-AcctIdentityPool command. You can retrieve information about its use by launching Get-Help Set-AcctIdentityPool -detailed | more.

7. To remove a created machine catalog from your XenDesktop architecture, use the Remove-AcctIdentityPool cmdlet in one of the following two ways:

   ```
   - Remove-AcctIdentityPool -IdentityPoolName<PoolName>
   - Remove-AcctIdentityPool -IdentityPoolUid<PoolUID>
   ```

8. To populate the created catalogs with domain machine accounts, execute the following task:

```
New-AcctADAccount -IdentityPoolName<CatalogName> -Count
<NumberofAccounts> -StartCount<Number> -AdminAddress<ControllerIPA
ddress>
```

> You can run this command only once each time. You cannot execute parallel account creations because of the serial execution nature of the command.

9. Retrieve the generated computer account data by running the next command; you can filter the information by using the -IdentityPoolName and -Lock parameters:

```
Get-AcctADAccount
```

10. The next command performs the required updates on the imported Active Directory computer accounts in a catalog; optionally you can use the -AllAccounts and -AdminAddress options:

```
Update-AcctADAccount -IdentityPoolName<PoolName>
```

11. Finally, you have the ability to remove computer accounts from an existing identity pool in the following way; you can also use the -Force option to proceed in case of system exceptions:

```
Remove-AcctADAccount -IdentityPoolName<PoolName> -ADAccountName<Co
mputerAccountName> -RemovalOption<option>
```

> You can reset the machine account password by running the Repair-AcctADAccount -ADAccountName"domain\computerName" -Force command.

12. Execute the following script to operate on the catalog and machine accounts creation:

```
#------------ Script - Configuration Service
#------------ Define Variables
$AD_Domain="ctxlab.local"
$ID_Pool="Test-Pool-01"
$Controller_Address="192.168.1.60"

#------------ Creating and Identity Pool
write-Host"XenDesktop - Creating an Identity Pool"
$ID_Pool_Create = New-AcctIdentityPool -IdentityPoolName $ID_
Pool -NamingScheme Desk-T## -Domain $AD_Domain -NamingSchemeType
Numeric
Write-Output "Pool creation activities - Status: " $ID_Pool_Create
```

```
#---------- Verify the pool creation
$Check_Pool = Get-AcctIdentityPool -IdentityPoolName $ID_Pool |
measure

if ($Check_Pool.count -gt 0)
        {Write-Host "Identity Pool correctly created."}

else
 {Write-Host "Identity pool not correctly generated. Please
verify."

exit }

#---------- Creating AD computer accounts

New-AcctADAccount -IdentityPoolName $ID_Pool -Count 3 -StartCount
10 -AdminAddress $Controller_Address

exit
```

On running the preceding commands we get the following output:

How it works...

In this recipe, we discussed the management of the XenDesktop Identity Pools and their objects, as well as the Active Directory computer accounts contained within the pools. These commands could be particularly useful in the case of the advanced management of the pools and the computer accounts within them, in terms of the changes, deletion, creation, and advanced management of the Active Directory machine accounts.

The first command collections discuss the Identity Pools and the four main operations that can be performed on them: the creation (`New-AcctIdentityPool`); the list of resources (`Get-AcctIdentityPool`); the renaming (`Rename-AcctIdentityPool`); and the deletion (`Remove-AcctIdentityPool`). The creation of an Identity Pool is based on the specification of the name of the AD objects container, on the Desktop Controller address to which the pool will refer, and on the two main configurable characteristics: the **Naming Scheme** (the naming convention assigned to the AD computer accounts generated within an Identity Pool, in the form of `MachineName##`, where the sharp symbols specify the machine progressive numbering); and the **Naming Scheme Type** (alphabetic or numeric progression). For instance, you could specify an alphabetical machine naming convention in the following way: **Desk-T-AA**.

The `Rename-AcctIdentityPool` command allows you to rename existing pools. You only have to specify the old pool name and the new name to use as its substitution. As simple as this is, with the last Identity Pool command, `Remove-AcctIdentityPool`, filtering data for the pool name or the pool UID, you can delete one or more existing pool(s).

> You can remove a pool only when it has no associated machine accounts.

The second commands group allows you to manage the Active Directory machine accounts, which can be grouped with the Identity Pools: the `New-AcctADAccount` cmdlet lets you create a computer account within your domain, based on the naming convention defined in the pool on which the machine account is linked. You can specify the starting progressive machine number (the-`StartCount` parameter) and the number of accounts to create (the-`Count` parameter). To remove created computer accounts you have to use the `Remove-AcctADAccount` command. What is particularly interesting about this cmdlet is the presence of the modality to perform the computer account deletion. With `-RemovalOption` you can remove machine accounts from XenDesktop (`None` option), removing them also from the Active Directory Domain (`Delete` option) or disabling the accounts in the AD Domain (`Disable` option).

> Additionally, use the `-Force` parameter to remove the accounts in case of warnings.

The script at the end of the recipe permits you to create an Identity Pool, referring to the related Desktop Controller, and after verifying its correct creation, the pool will be populated with a set of three computer accounts, based on the naming convention configured for the Identity Pool (Desk-T## with numeric progression). To count the number of objects, in order to verify the pool creation, the `measure` command has been used, combined with the count property of the variable containing the number of retrieved pools (`$Check_Pool.count`).

There's more...

With PowerShell, it's also possible, using existing Active Directory computer accounts, to generate machine catalog accounts, importing them into the XenDesktop infrastructure, as seen earlier in this book for the GUI component.

You can perform this operation through the command line by using the `Add-AcctADAccount` PowerShell command, using the following syntax:

```
Add-AcctADAccount -IdentityPoolName <PoolName> -ADAccountName
<ComputerName>
```

You can specify the AD computer account in all the common forms, such as the domain\computer name, `computerName@domain` or through its FQDN.

See also

> ▸ The *Creating and configuring the machine catalog* recipe in *Chapter 5, Creating and Configuring a Desktop Environment*

Managing the Citrix® Desktop Controller and its resources – Broker and App-V cmdlets

This is one of the principal PowerShell command groups for XenDesktop because of the interaction with the Desktop Broker component. This section will be about the use of the set of commands to manage the Broker, in terms of displaying configurations, setting components and parameters, including the applications published with the XenDesktop 7 infrastructure or App-V existing architectures.

Getting ready

No preliminary tasks are required. You have already installed the PowerShell SDK during the installation of the Desktop Controller role machine(s).

To be able to run a PowerShell script (`.ps1` format), you have to enable the script execution from the PowerShell prompt in this way:

```
Set-ExecutionPolicy -ExecutionPolicy RemoteSigned -Force
```

How to do it...

The following is the explanation of the commands included in the Desktop Controller's PowerShell command set:

1. Connect to one of the Desktop Broker servers.

2. Click on the PowerShell icon installed on the Windows taskbar.

3. Load the PowerShell modules by typing the following command and then press the *Enter* key:

   ```
   Asnp Citrix*
   ```

4. To retrieve the configuration of the XenDesktop Broker site, run the following command:

   ```
   Get-Brokersite
   ```

5. To modify the parameters of an existing XenDesktop Broker site, run the following command; the most important involved parameters are –BaseOU, -DnsResolutionEnabled, and –AdminAddress:

   ```
   Set-BrokerSite -BaseOU<DefaultDesktopRegistrationOU>
   -AdminAddress<BrokerAddress>
   ```

6. Run the following command in order to create a desktop catalog to your infrastructure; in the case of the Provisioning Service catalog, you have to use the –PvsAddress and -PvsDomain parameters:

   ```
   New-BrokerCatalog –Name <CatalogName> -ProvisioningType<Manual |
   MCS | PVS> -Description <CatalogDescription>
   ```

   > For the ProvisioningType parameter, the PVS option permits you to specify both physical and virtual machines.

7. After creating the desktop catalog, you can retrieve information on the existing catalogs by running the following command, filtering for information, such as the allocation type (-AllocationType parameter). Without any specific option, you can list all the infrastructure catalogs:

   ```
   Get-BrokerCatalog
   ```

8. To modify the previously configured catalog characteristics, you have to run the following command:

    ```
    Set-BrokerCatalog -Description -isRemotePC -PvsAddress -PvsDomain
    -PvsForVM
    ```

    > You cannot modify the allocation type and catalog type settings!

9. To remove an existing catalog, run the following cmdlet:

    ```
    Remove-BrokerCatalog -Name <CatalogName>
    ```

10. To list the entire set of existing desktops in your site, run the following command:

    ```
    Get-BrokerDesktop
    ```

    > Later in this recipe, we will list the most important parameters for this command.

11. To configure a Desktop Group in your Citrix Broker, execute this cmdlet:

    ```
    New-BrokerDesktopGroup -Name <DesktopGroupName> -
    DesktopKind<Private|Shared> -Enabled <True|False> -PublishedName<D
    esktopDisplayName> -SecureIcaRequired<True|False>
    ```

    > The -AutomaticPowerOnForAssigned parameter is usable only for the private desktops, -ShutdownDesktopsAfterUse can be activated only in the presence of power-managed desktops.

12. After creating a Broker Desktop Group, you can get back the information by using the Get-BrokerDesktopGroup command; you can use the same filters explained in the previous explanation.

13. To modify the configuration of an existing group, you have to use the Set-BrokerDesktopGroup cmdlet; for instance, you could put -InMaintenancemode a Desktop Group in the following way:

    ```
    Set-BrokerDesktopGroup<GroupName> -InMaintenanceMode $true
    ```

    > To display the historical usage of the Desktop Groups, run the following command:
    >
    > ```
    > Get-BrokerDesktopUsage -DesktopGroupName<Desktop
    > GroupName> -MaxRecordCount<MaxNumberofRecords>
    > ```

14. To populate the previously configured Desktop Groups, you have to use the following cmdlet:

```
Add-BrokerMachinesToDesktopGroup -Catalog <CatalogName>
-DesktopGroup<DesktopGroupName> -Count <NumberofMachines>
```

> After creating a Desktop Group machine, you can prepare it for the Personal vDisk creation by running the following command:
>
> ```
> Start-BrokerMachinePvdImagePrepare
> -InputObject<MachineName>.
> ```
> The task will be performed the next time the machine is started.

15. To retrieve any existing private Desktop Groups, run the following PowerShell commands; some useful filters are –MachineName, -DesktopGroupUid, -InMaintenanceMode, and –OSType:

```
Get-BrokerPrivateDesktop
```

> To verify the resources to which a user has access, use the Get-BrokerResource command, filtering for –User <Username> and/or –Group <GroupName> (AD group membership for the specified user).

16. After completing the machine creation and grouping, it's time to publish applications and to assign them to the existing virtual desktops. The first useful command allows you to create applications; using XenDesktop without combining it with XenApp, the only allowed application type is Hosted Applications:

```
New-BrokerApplication -CommandLineExecutable<FullApplicationPath>
-BrowserName<InternalAppName> -Enabled <True|False> -ShortcutAd
dedToDesktop<True|False> -ShortcutAddedToStartMenu<True|False> -
IconFromClient<True|False>-Description <AppDescription>
```

> You can also use resources control parameters such as -CpuPriorityLevel (Low, BelowNormal, Normal, AboveNormal, and High) and -WaitForPrinterCreation.

17. To retrieve the published applications, use the following PowerShell cmdlet, combining it with filters such as –DisplayName, -Enabled, or –BrowserName:

```
Get-BrokerApplication
```

> To rename an already published application, use the following command line:
> ```
> Rename-BrokerApplication –Name<CurrentAdministrativeName>
> -NewName<NewAdministrativeName>
> ```

18. Use the following PowerShell cmdlet to associate one or more file extension(s) to a published application:

    ```
    New-BrokerConfiguredFTA –ExtensionName<Extension>
    -ApplicationUid<ApplicationID>
    ```

19. To retrieve the association between file types and software, run the following command; you can use filters such as –Uid (a specific file type by its UID) and –ExtensionName:

    ```
    Get-BrokerConfiguredFTA
    ```

20. To remove a published application from the XenDesktop infrastructure, use the next PowerShell cmdlet:

    ```
    Remove-BrokerApplication –Name <ApplicationName>
    -DesktopGroup<DeskGroupName> -AdminAddress<BrokerAddress>
    ```

21. Once all the application configurations have been completed, you have to assign the software to an existing Desktop Group in the following way:

    ```
    Add-BrokerApplication –BrowserName<ApplicationBrowserName>
    -DesktopGroup<DeskGroupName>
    ```

22. A fundamental implementation is the access control on the XenDesktop site resources, the following command and related syntax to configure a rule:

    ```
    New-BrokerAccessPolicyRule –Name <RuleName> -IncludedUserFilterEna
    bled<True|False>  -IncludedUsers<Domain\User|Group> -IncludedDeskt
    opGroupFilterEnabled<True|False> -IncludedDesktopGroups<DesktopGro
    upName> -AllowRestart<True|False>
    ```

> You can also use excluding filters: -ExcludedClientIPs and -ExcludedUsers.

23. To retrieve the configured access rules, execute the following cmdlet, using the same filters previously explained for the rule creation process:

    ```
    Get-BrokerAccessPolicyRule
    ```

> Remove an existing access rule in this way: `Remove-BrokerAccessPolicyRule -Name <RuleName>.`

24. To create a new assignment rule, use the following syntax:

    ```
    New-BrokerAssignmentPolicyRule -Name <RuleName> -DesktopGroupUid<D
    esktopGroupUID> -IncludedUsers<Domain\User|Group> -PublishedName<D
    esktopGroupName>
    ```

> To modify and remove an assignment policy, run the `Set-BrokerAssignmentPolicyRule` cmdlet and the `Remove-BrokerAssignmentPolicyRule` command respectively.

25. After creating the new assignment rule you can retrieve the currently configured assignment rules by running the following command:

    ```
    Get-BrokerAssignmentPolicyRule -Name <RuleName>
    ```

The following are the explanations and examples for the App-V cmdlets:

1. The following command, which is part of the App-V cmdlet, will list all the applications published by using a connected App-V infrastructure:

    ```
    Get-CtxAppVApplication-AppVManagementServer<AppVServer>
    ```

2. To retrieve information about a specific application within an existing App-V package, run the following command:

    ```
    Get-CtxAppVApplicationInfo-AppVManagementServer<AppVServer>-
    AppId<ApplicationID> -PackageID<PackageID>
    ```

3. To link a new App-V infrastructure, including the management and publishing servers, execute the following command:

    ```
    New-CtxAppVServer -PublishingServer<PublishingServer>-ManagementSe
    rver<ManagementServer>
    ```

> You can also configure the following parameters:
> `-UserRefreshEnabled, -UserRefreshOnLogon,`
> `-UserRefreshInterval, -GlobalRefreshEnabled,`
> `-GlobalRefreshOnLogon,` and `-GlobalRefreshInterval.`
> They are used to enable and set the interval for the packages, refresh when a user executes a log on normally or in a specific configured interval. The `GlobalRefresh<>` applies to the machine groups.

4. The next command will give you the list of the existing App-V servers (both publishing and management) existing within your XenDesktop 7 infrastructure; you have to associate the `ByteArray` parameter with the following command:

```
Get-CtxAppVServer-ByteArray<AppVCreatedPolicy>
```

> The value for the `ByteArray` parameter can be retrieved, running the following command:
>
> `Get-BrokerMachineConfiguration -Name appv*`

5. To check a retrieved URL for an App-V Management Server you have to execute the following command:

```
Test-CtxAppVServer -AppVManagementServer<AppvManagementServer>
```

> We have discussed the App-V components in the *Publishing applications using Microsoft App-V* recipe in *Chapter 6, Deploying Applications*.

6. The following script operates on part of the discussed Broker commands:

```
#----------- Script - Hosting + MCS
#----------------------------------
#----------- Define Variables
$LicSRV="192.168.110.30"
$BrokerAddress = "192.168.110.30"
$LicPort="27000"
$CatName="SRV-APP-00"
$DeliveryGroupName="Delivery-00"
$App_Path="C:\Windows\System32\notepad.exe"

#---------- Create a XenDesktop Catalog
New-BrokerCatalog -Name $CatName -AllocationType Random
-CatalogKindPowerManaged -Description "Catalog-Book-Number-01"

#---------- Create a Desktop Group
New-BrokerDesktopGroup -Name $DeliveryGroupName -DesktopKind
Shared -Enabled $true -PublishedName"Book Desktop Group"
-SecureIcaRequired $true -ShutdownDesktopsAfterUse $true

#---------- Deploying Machines
Add-BrokerMachinesToDesktopGroup -Catalog $CatName -DesktopGroup
$DeliveryGroupName -Count 4
```

```
#---------- Publish Notepad Application
New-BrokerApplication -CommandLineExecutable $App_Path
-BrowserNameNotepadExe -DisplayName"Windows Notepad" -Enabled
$true -ShortcutAddedToDesktop $true -ShortcutAddedToStartMenu
$false -Description "Notepad Text Editor"

#---------- Associate the .txt extension
$AppID=$(Get-BrokerApplication -BrowserNameNotepadExe)
New-BrokerConfiguredFTA -ExtensionName".txt" -ApplicationUid
$AppID.Uid -HandlerName"textfile"

#---------- Retrieve published applications
Get-BrokerApplication

#---------- Filter the resources for the Help Desk team
New-BrokerAccessPolicyRule -Name HelpDeskFilter-Rule-01
-IncludedUserFilterEnabled $true -IncludedUsers"XDSEVEN\hd01"
-IncludedDesktopGroupFilterEnabled $true -IncludedDesktopGroups
$DeliveryGroupName -AllowRestart $true

exit
```

On running the preceding command we get the following output screen:

```
Administrator: Windows PowerShell

ExtensionData               : System.Runtime.Serialization.ExtensionDataObject
AllocationType              : Random
AssignedCount               : 0
AvailableAssignedCount      : 0
AvailableCount              : 0
AvailableUnassignedCount    : 0
Description                 : Catalog-Book-Number-01
HypervisorConnectionUid     :
IsRemotePC                  : False
MachinesArePhysical         : False
MetadataMap                 : {}
MinimumFunctionalLevel      : L7
Name                        : SRV-APP-00
PersistUserChanges          : OnLocal
ProvisioningSchemeId        :
ProvisioningType            : Manual
PvsAddress
```

How it works...

Using and configuring the Broker cmdlet category has allowed us to generate resource containers (catalogs and Desktop Groups) to which we can assign end-user resources (Desktops and Applications) and filtering rules (Access and Assignment); using this division, we can discuss the four main PowerShell Broker command subcategories:

- **Site and Catalog subsection**: In this area, we have configured the XenDesktop site and the contained catalogs, then we have retrieved information about them. The `New-BrokerCatalog` command performs the creation of a machines catalog: the **ThinCloned** catalogs and the **SingleImage** catalogs are part of the PVS. It's also possible to configure catalogs with the Personal vDisk technology for both the MCS and PVS infrastructures. The `New-BrokerCatalog` command lets you create random or static-assigned resource catalogs, specifying which type of catalog you want to create.

- **Desktops and Desktop Groups subsection**: In this subsection, we have created and managed Desktop Groups and the related desktops. For this second object type, the `Get-BrokerDesktop` command permits retrieving existing desktop machines by filtering the search for information such as `-MachineName` (in the form of domain\ computerName), `-ApplicationInUse`, `-CatalogName`, `-DesktopCondition` (high resource usage or latency, parameters in the form of `--CPU`, `--ICALatency`, and `--UPMLogonTime`), `-DesktopGroupName`, `-DesktopKind` (a desktop can be private or shared), `-ImageOutOfDate` (a desktop not compliant with the latest base image template updates the MCS architecture only), `-InMaintenanceMode`, `-IsAssigned` (a desktop resource already or not yet assigned to a user), `-LastConnectionTime`, `-LastConnectionUser`, `-OSType`, `-PowerState` (the current situation for the Desktop, in the form of **On | Off | TurningOn | TurningOff | Suspending | Resuming | Unmanaged | Unavailable | Unknown**), `-Protocol` (for instance, HDX or RDP), and `-LastDeregistrationReason`. This option permits you to discover why a deregistration has occurred, retrieving as result data `AgentShutdown`, `AgentSuspended`, `BrokerRegistrationLimitReached`, `AgentNotContactable`, `ContactLost`, `BrokerError`, `DesktopRemoved`, and some others. After this, we have used the `New-BrokerDesktopGroup` to generate a Desktop Group and then linked the existing machine with the related Desktop Group by using `Add-BrokerMachinesToDesktopGroup` command (the main parameters are the Desktop Group name and the number of machines to deploy).

▶ **Applications subsection**: In this subsection we have created, modified, and copied hosted applications in the XenDesktop architecture using the command line, for both the XenDesktop applications and the App-V linked architectures. The `New-BrokerApplication` command permits you to publish existing applications already installed on desktops, which are part of an Application Desktop Group, as seen earlier in this book. Also, in this case you can specify the main application option already discussed, such as the links publication for the desktop and the Start menu, and the visibility and the enabling of the app (the `-Visible` and `–Enabled` parameters). For any app you can specify the file type association (explicitly specifying it with `–ExtensionName` or importing it from the Citrix known list by using the `-ImportedFTA` parameter) with the `New-BrokerConfiguredFTA` command. After completing the software publication, you can assign them to existing desktops through the `Add-BrokerApplication` command, associating the application's `BrowserName` to the Desktop Group name to which you want to assign it. With regard to the App-V components, the `AppV.Admin` cmdlet allows you to link an existing App-V infrastructure, made up of both the Management and Publishing servers, with the ability to list the configurations applied, and the already published applications with their parameters.

> The **BrowserName** for a published application must be unique within a XenDesktop infrastructure!

▶ **Access and Assignment filtering rules subsection**: This last subsection covers covered the access and assignment rules configuration. In other words, using these two policy categories it has been possible to regulate the resource usage and access for the users. The `New-BrokerAccessPolicyRule` command creates an **accesspolicyrule** for the existing XenDesktop resources, the setting of which gives users the ability to access and use defined desktop resources; you have to enable the inclusion (`--IncludedClientIPFilterEnabled`, `-IncludedClientNameFilterEnabled`, and `-IncludedDesktopGroupFilterEnabled`) and exclusion (`-ExcludedClientIPFilterEnabled` and `-ExcludedClientNameFilterEnabled`) filters to ensure that the included (`-IncludedClientIPs`, `-IncludedClientNames`, and `-IncludedDesktopGroups`) and excluded (`-ExcludedClientIPs` and `-ExcludedClientNames`) resources are managed in the right way. For the assignment policy rule, the command to use is `New-BrokerAssignmentPolicyRule`, specifying the included and/or excluded users (in this second case you have to enable the `ExcludedUserFilterEnabled` filter) and the Desktop Group UID to which we apply the assignment task.

There's more...

With the Broker cmdlets group, it is also possible to manage the power actions to apply to the catalog machines. You can create a new power action related to an existing desktop machine (`New-BrokerHostingPowerAction –MachineName<DesktopName> -Action <TurnOn|TurnOff|ShutDown|Reset|Restart|Suspend|R esume>-ActualPriority<PriorityValue>`) and then retrieve it (`Get-BrokerHostingPowerAction`).

> The lower is the priority value, higher is its importance.

Moreover, you can also create and manage a full power time scheme for a Desktop Group, using the creation power time cmdlet (`New-BrokerPowerTimeScheme –Name <TimeSchemeName> -DaysOfWeek<SpecificDay | WeekDays | Weekend – DesktopGroupUid<GroupUID> -DisplayName<Name> -PeakHours<PeakHoursExpr ession>`) and retrieving existing configurations (`Get-BrokerPowerTimeScheme`).

The peak hours expression has the following construction: (`FromHour..ToHour | % {$_ -gt<Hour> and $_ -lt<Hour> }`), for example, on the entire day you can set the peak hour time from `10 Hour.` to `17 Hour` in the following way: (`0..23 | % {$_ -gt 10 and $_ -lt 17 }`).

See also

> ▸ The *Publishing applications using Microsoft App-V* recipe in *Chapter 6, Deploying Applications*

Administering hosts and machines – Host and MachineCreation cmdlets

In this recipe, we will describe how to create the connection between the Hypervisor and the XenDesktop servers, and the way to generate machines to assign to the end users, all by using PowerShell.

Getting ready

No preliminary tasks are required. You have already installed the PowerShell SDK during the installation of the Desktop Controller role machine(s).

To be sure to be able to run a PowerShell script (the `.ps1` format), you have to enable the script execution from the PowerShell prompt in this way:

```
Set-ExecutionPolicy -ExecutionPolicy RemoteSigned -Force
```

How to do it...

In this section, we will discuss the PowerShell commands used to connect XenDesktop with the supported hypervisors plus the creation of the machines from the command line:

1. Connect to one of the Desktop Broker servers.

2. Click on the PowerShell icon installed on the Windows taskbar.

3. Load the PowerShell modules by typing the following command, and then press the *Enter* key:

   ```
   Asnp Citrix*
   ```

4. To list the available Hypervisor types, execute this task:

   ```
   Get-HypHypervisorPlugin -AdminAddress<BrokerAddress>
   ```

5. To list the configured properties for the XenDesktop root-level location (XDHyp:\), execute the following command:

   ```
   Get-ChildItemXDHyp:\HostingUnits
   ```

> Please refer to the PSPath, Storage, and PersonalvDiskStorage output fields to retrieve information on the storage configuration.

6. Execute the following cmdlet to add a storage resource to the XenDesktop Controller host:

   ```
   Add-HypHostingUnitStorage -LiteralPath<HostPathLocation>
   -StoragePath<StoragePath> -StorageType<OSStorage|PersonalvDiskStor
   age> - AdminAddress<BrokerAddress>
   ```

7. To generate a snapshot for an existing VM, perform the following task:

   ```
   New-HypVMSnapshot -LiteralPath<HostPathLocation> -SnapshotDescript
   ion<Description>
   ```

> Use the Get-HypVMMacAddress -LiteralPath<HostPathLocation> command to list the MAC address of specified desktop VMs.

8. To provision machine instances starting from the Desktop base image template, run the following command:

```
New-ProvScheme -ProvisioningSchemeName<SchemeName> -Hosting
UnitName<HypervisorServer> -IdentityPoolName<PoolName> -Mast
erImageVM<BaseImageTemplatePath> -VMMemoryMB<MemoryAssigned>
-VMCpuCount<NumberofCPU>
```

9. To specify the creation of instances with the Personal vDisk technology, use the following option:

```
-UsePersonalVDiskStorage.
```

10. After the creation process, retrieve the provisioning scheme information by running the following command:

```
Get-ProvScheme -ProvisioningSchemeName<SchemeName>
```

> To modify the resources assigned to desktop instances in a provisioning scheme, use the `Set-ProvScheme` cmdlet. The permitted parameters are `-ProvisioningSchemeName`, `-VMCpuCount`, and `-VMMemoryMB`.

11. To update the desktop instances to the latest version of the Desktop base image template, run the following cmdlet:

```
Publish-ProvMasterVmImage -ProvisioningSchemeName<SchemeName> -Mas
terImageVM<BaseImageTemplatePath>
```

> If you do not want to maintain the pre-update instance version to use as a restore checkpoint, use the `-DoNotStoreOldImage` option.

12. To create machine instances, based on the previously configured provisioning scheme for an MCS architecture, run this command:

```
New-ProvVM -ProvisioningSchemeName<SchemeName>
-ADAccountName"Domain\MachineAccount"
```

> Use the `-FastBuild` option to make the machine creation process faster. On the other hand, you cannot start up the machines until the process has been completed.

13. Retrieve the configured desktop instances by using the next cmdlet:

```
Get-ProvVM -ProvisioningSchemeName<SchemeName>
-VMName<MachineName>
```

14. To remove an existing virtual desktop, use the following command:

```
Remove-ProvVM -ProvisioningSchemeName<SchemeName>
-VMName<MachineName> -AdminAddress<BrokerAddress>
```

15. The next script will combine the use of part of the commands listed in this recipe:

```
#------------ Script - Hosting + MCS
#----------------------------------
#------------ Define Variables
$LitPath = "XDHyp:\HostingUnits\VMware01"
$StorPath = "XDHyp:\HostingUnits\VMware01\datastore1.storage"
$Controller_Address="192.168.110.30"
$HostUnitName = "Vmware01"
$IDPool = $(Get-AcctIdentityPool -IdentityPoolName VDI-DESKTOP)
$BaseVMPath = "XDHyp:\HostingUnits\VMware01\VMXD7-W8MCS-01.vm"

#------------ Creating a storage location
Add-HypHostingUnitStorage -LiteralPath $LitPath -StoragePath
$StorPath -StorageTypeOSStorage -AdminAddress $Controller_Address

#---------- Creating a Provisioning Scheme
New-ProvScheme -ProvisioningSchemeName Deploy_01 -HostingUnitName
$HostUnitName -IdentityPoolName $IDPool.IdentityPoolName
-MasterImageVM $BaseVMPath\T0-Post.snapshot -VMMemoryMB 4096
-VMCpuCount 2 -CleanOnBoot

#---------- List the VM configured on the Hypervisor Host
dir $LitPath\*.vm

exit
```

How it works...

The Host and MachineCreation cmdlet groups manage the interfacing with the Hypervisor hosts, in terms of machines and storage resources. This allows you to create the desktop instances to assign to the end user, starting from an existing and mapped Desktop virtual machine.

The `Get-HypHypervisorPlugin` command retrieves and lists the available hypervisors to use to deploy virtual desktops and to configure the storage types. As already discussed earlier in this book, you can configure an operating system storage area or a Personal vDisk storage zone. The way to map an existing storage location from the Hypervisor to the XenDesktop controller is by running the `Add-HypHostingUnitStorage` cmdlet. In this case you have to specify the destination path on which the storage object will be created (`LiteralPath`), the source storage path on the Hypervisor machine(s) (`StoragePath`), and the `StorageType` previously discussed. The storage types are in the form of XDHyp:\ HostingUnits\<UnitName>.

> To list all the configured storage objects, execute the following command:
> `dirXDHyp:\HostingUnits\<UnitName> \*.storage`

After configuring the storage area, we have discussed the **Machine Creation Service** (**MCS**) architecture. In this cmdlets collection, we have the availability of commands to generate VM snapshots from which we can deploy desktop instances (`New-HypVMSnapshot`), and specify a name and a description for the generated disk snapshot. Starting from the available disk image, the `New-ProvScheme` command permits you to create a resource provisioning scheme, on which to specify the desktop base image, and the resources to assign to the desktop instances (in terms of CPU and RAM `-VMCpuCount` and `–VMMemoryMB`), and if generating these virtual desktops in a non-persistent mode (`-CleanOnBoot` option), with or without the use of the Personal vDisk technology (`-UsePersonalVDiskStorage`). It's possible to update the deployed instances to the latest base image update through the use of the `Publish-ProvMasterVmImage` command.

In the generated script, we have located all the main storage locations (the `LitPath` and `StorPath` variables) useful to realize a provisioning scheme, then we have implemented a provisioning procedure for a desktop based on an existing base image snapshot, with two vCPUs and 4 GB of RAM for the delivered instances, which will be cleaned every time they stop and start (by using the `-CleanOnBoot` option).

> You can navigate the local and remote storage paths configured with the XenDesktop Broker machine; to list an object category (such as VM or Snapshot) you can execute this command:
> `dirXDHyp:\HostingUnits\<UnitName>\*.<category>`

There's more...

The discussed cmdlets also offer you the technique to preserve a virtual desktop from an accidental deletion or unauthorized use. With the Machine Creation cmdlets group, you have the ability to use a particular command, which allows you to lock critical desktops: Lock-ProvVM. This cmdlet requires as parameters the name of the scheme to which they refer (`-ProvisioningSchemeName`) and the ID of the virtual desktop to lock (`-VMID`).

> You can retrieve the Virtual Machine ID by running the `Get-ProvVM` command discussed previously.

To revert the machine lock, and free the desktop instance from accidental deletion or improper use, you have to execute the `Unlock-ProvVM` cmdlet, using the same parameter showed for the lock procedure.

▶ *Chapter 2, Configuring and Deploying Virtual Machines for XenDesktop® 7.6*

Managing additional components – StoreFront™ admin and logging cmdlets

In this recipe, we will use and explain how to manage and configure the StoreFront component, by using the available PowerShell cmdlets. Moreover, we will explain how to manage and check the configurations for the system logging activities.

Getting ready

No preliminary tasks are required. You have already installed the PowerShell SDK during the installation of the Desktop Controller role machine(s).

To be able to run a PowerShell script (in the `.ps1` format), you have to enable the script execution from the PowerShell prompt in this way:

```
Set-ExecutionPolicy -ExecutionPolicy RemoteSigned -Force
```

How to do it...

In this section, we will explain and execute the commands associated with the Citrix Storefront system:

1. Connect to one of the Desktop Broker servers.

2. Click on the PowerShell icon installed on the Windows taskbar.

3. Load the PowerShell modules by typing the following command, and then press the *Enter* key:

   ```
   Asnp Citrix*
   ```

   > To execute a command, you have to press the *Enter* button after completing the right command syntax.

4. Retrieve the currently existing StoreFront service instances, by running the following command:

   ```
   Get-SfService
   ```

> To limit the number of rows as output result, you can add the `–MaxRecordCount<value>` parameter.

5. To list the detailed information about the StoreFront service(s) currently configured, execute the following command:

```
Get-SfServiceInstance –AdminAddress<ControllerAddress>
```

> The status of the currently active `StoreFront` instances can be retrieved by using the `Get-SfServiceStatus` command. The **OK** output will confirm the correct service execution.

6. To list the task history associated with the configured StoreFront instances, you have to run the following command:

```
Get-SfTask
```

> You can filter the desired information for the ID of the researched task (`-taskid`) and sort the results by the use of the `–sortby` parameter.

7. To retrieve the installed database schema versions, you can execute the following command:

```
Get-SfInstalledDBVersion
```

> By applying the `–Upgrade` and `–Downgrade` filters, you will receive respectively the schemas for which the database version can be updated or reverted to a previous compatible one.

8. To modify the StoreFront configurations to register its state on a different database, you can use the following command:

```
Set-SfDBConnection-DBConnection<DBConnectionString> -AdminAddress<ControllerAddress>
```

> Be careful when you specify the database connection string; if not specified, the existing database connections and configurations will be cleared!

9. To check that the database connection has been correctly configured, the following command is available:

```
Test-SfDBConnection-DBConnection<DBConnectionString>-AdminAddress<ControllerAddress>
```

10. The second discussed cmdlets allows the logging group to retrieve information about the current status of the logging service and run the following command:

```
Get-LogServiceStatus
```

11. To verify the language used and whether the logging service has been enabled, run the following command:

```
Get-LogSite
```

> The available configurable locales are **en**, **ja**, **zh-CN**, **de**, **es**, and **fr**. The available states are **Enabled**, **Disabled**, **NotSupported**, and **Mandatory**. The **NotSupported** state will show you an incorrect configuration for the listed parameters.

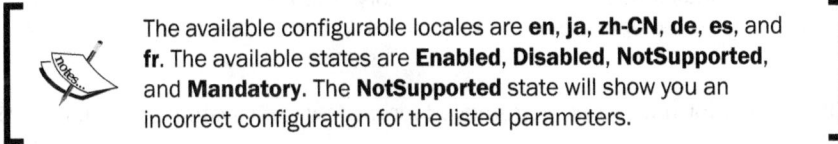

12. To retrieve detailed information about the running logging service, you have to use the following command:

```
Get-LogService
```

> As discussed earlier for the StoreFront commands, you can filter the output by applying the -MaxRecordCount<value> parameter.

13. In order to get all the operations logged within a specified time range, run the following command; this will return the global operations count:

```
Get-LogSummary -StartDateRange<StartDate>-EndDateRange<EndDate>
```

> The date format must be the following: AAAA-MM-GGHH:MM:SS.

14. To list the collected operations per day in the specified time period, run the previous command in the following way:

```
Get-LogSummary -StartDateRange<StartDate> -EndDateRange<EndDate>-
intervalSeconds 86400
```

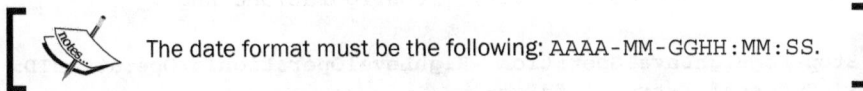

> The value 86400 is the number of seconds that are present in a day.

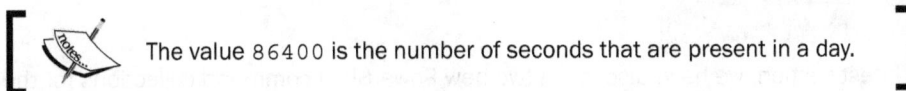

15. To retrieve the connection string information about the database on which logging data is stored, execute the following command:

```
Get-LogDataStore
```

16. To retrieve detailed information about the high level operations performed on the XenDesktop infrastructure, you have to run the following command:

```
Get-LogHighLevelOperation -Text <TextincludedintheOperation> -St
artTime<FormattedDateandTime> -EndTime<FormattedDateandTime>-
IsSuccessful<true | false>-User <DomainUserName>-
OperationType<AdminActivity | ConfigurationChange>
```

> The indicated filters are not mandatory. If you do not apply any filters, all the logged operations will be returned. This could be a very long output.

17. The same information can be retrieved for the low level system operations in the following way:

```
Get-LogLowLevelOperation-StartTime<FormattedDateandTime>
-EndTime<FormattedDateandTime> -IsSuccessful<true | false>-
User <DomainUserName> -OperationType<AdminActivity |
ConfigurationChange>
```

> In the *How it works* section we will explain the difference between the high and low level operations.

18. To log when a high level operation starts and stops respectively, use the following two commands:

```
Start-LogHighLevelOperation -Text <OperationDescriptionText>-
Source <OperationSource> -StartTime<FormattedDateandTime>
-OperationType<AdminActivity | ConfigurationChange>

Stop-LogHighLevelOperation -HighLevelOperationId<OperationID>
-IsSuccessful<true | false>
```

> The Stop-LogHighLevelOperation must be related to an existing start high level operation, because they are related tasks.

How it works...

In this latest section, we have discussed two new PowerShell command collections for the XenDesktop 7 versions: the cmdlet related to the StoreFront platform; and the activities Logging set of commands.

The first collection is quite limited in terms of operations, despite the other discussed cmdlets. In fact, the only actions permitted with the PowerShell set of commands are retrieving configurations and settings about the configured stores and the linked database. More activities can be performed regarding the modification of existing StoreFront clusters, by using the `Get-SfCluster`, `Add-SfServerToCluster`, `New-SfCluster`, and `Set-SfCluster` set of operations.

More interesting is the PowerShell Logging collection. In this case, you can retrieve all the system-logged data, putting it into two principal categories:

- **High-level operations**: These tasks group all the system configuration changes that are executed by using the Desktop Studio, the Desktop Director, or PowerShell.

- **Low-level operations**: This category is related to all the system configuration changes that are executed by a service and not by using the system software's consoles.

> With the low level operations command, you can filter for a specific high level operation to which the low level refers, by specifying the `-HighLevelOperationId` parameter.

This cmdlet category also gives you the ability to track the start and stop of a high level operation, by the use of `Start-LogHighLevelOperation` and `Stop-LogHighLevelOperation`. In this second case, you have to specify the previously started high level operation.

There's more...

In case of too much information in the log store, you have the ability to clear all of it. To refresh all the log entries, we use the following command:

```
Remove-LogOperation -UserName<DBAdministrativeCredentials> -Password
<DBUserPassword>-StartDateRange <StartDate> -EndDateRange <EndDate>
```

> The not encrypted `-Password` parameter can be substituted by `-SecurePassword`, the password indicated in secure string form.

The credentials must be database administrative credentials, with deleting permissions on the destination database.

This is a not reversible operation, so ensure that you want to delete the logs in the specified time range, or verify that you have some form of data backup.

See also

▶ The *Configuring the XenDesktop® logging* recipe in *Chapter 7, XenDesktop® Infrastructure Tuning*

10
Configuring the XenDesktop® Advanced Logon

In this chapter, you will cover the following recipes:

▶ Implementing the two-factor hardware authentication for XenDesktop 7

▶ Implementing strong authentication for XenDesktop 7 – RADIUS platform

▶ Implementing the two-factor software authentication for XenDesktop 7

Introduction

The **Infrastructure Security** is an IT area that involves a lot of different technologies and implementation techniques. The same thing can be applied to the XenDesktop architectures. As seen earlier, secure connections can be realized using a secure gateway located in front of the entire VDI architecture. The implementation of a strong authentication method is another important step to perform. In this chapter, we will discuss the use of hardware devices (such as **Smart Cards** or **PKI tokens** and **special USB keys used to authenticate users**), in order to perform the login phase through the use of a valid certificate. Then, we will discuss how to configure a two-factor authentication with software tokens. At the end of this chapter, we will discuss the implementation of the **strong authentication logon** method, a more robust and secure way to manage the user logon phase, by the use of the **Radius** platform.

Implementing the two-factor hardware authentication for XenDesktop® 7

With your personal data archived on your desktop machine, the standard authentication made up of a username and password combination can be insufficient to meet the security requirements.

A valid solution to this situation can be given by the use of devices, such as smart cards or PKI tokens, when trying to access your working resources.

XenDesktop is able to use this type of strong authentication. In this recipe, we are going to detail the implementation of this process.

Getting ready

In order to be able to utilize valid certificates, you need to perform the following configuration tasks:

1. Use an existing Enterprise CA or install an Enterprise Certification Authority machine to generate valid certificates. You can find more details at `http://technet.microsoft.com/en-us/library/hh831740.aspx`.

2. Configure an existing domain machine as the Enrollment agent station in order to configure the smart cards with your certificates. You can find more details at `http://technet.microsoft.com/en-us/library/hh831649.aspx`.

3. Install the specific CSP drivers for your authentication devices vendor on the Enrollment agent station.

4. On the StoreFront server, be sure you have installed the **Client Certificate Mapping Authentication** service for the **Internet Information Services (IIS)8** installed role.

> You have to be a member of the **Enterprise Admins** group in order to generate and release a certificate on the authentication devices.

How to do it...

In this recipe, we will explain how to authenticate users by the use of the smart cards or PKI tokens with a personal certificate on board:

1. Connect to the StoreFront machine and run the StoreFront Console by searching for it within the Windows Apps catalog (run the Windows + *C* key combination, click on the **Search** button, and search for the StoreFront application).

2. Click on the **Authentication** link on the left-hand side menu, and then select the **Add/Remove Methods** link on the right-hand side menu.

3. On the pop-up screen, flag the **Smart card** option, in order to enable it and then click on the **OK** button.

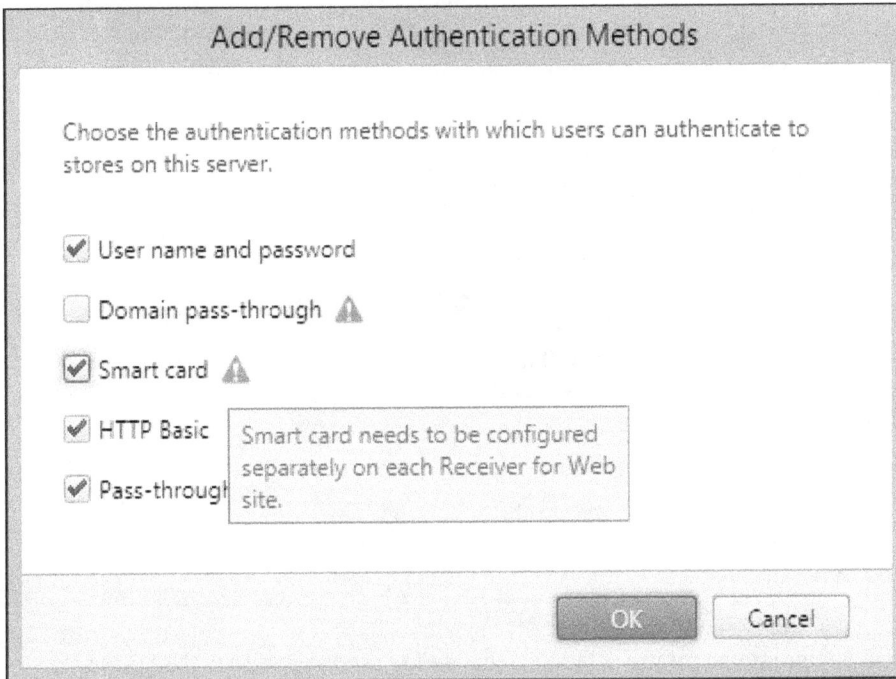

Add/Remove Authentication Methods

Choose the authentication methods with which users can authenticate to stores on this server.

- ☑ User name and password
- ☐ Domain pass-through ⚠
- ☑ Smart card ⚠
- ☑ HTTP Basic
- ☑ Pass-through

Smart card needs to be configured separately on each Receiver for Web site.

[OK] [Cancel]

> Citrix recommends having a configured store for each authentication method. Consider creating a different store for any kind of logon.

4. Connect to your Enrollment station machine, then run the Windows + X key combination, select the **Run** link, and run the mmc command.

5. Use the *Ctrl + M* key combination to open the **Snap-in** selection menu, then double-click on **Certificates** from the Snap-in list, and click the **Add** button.

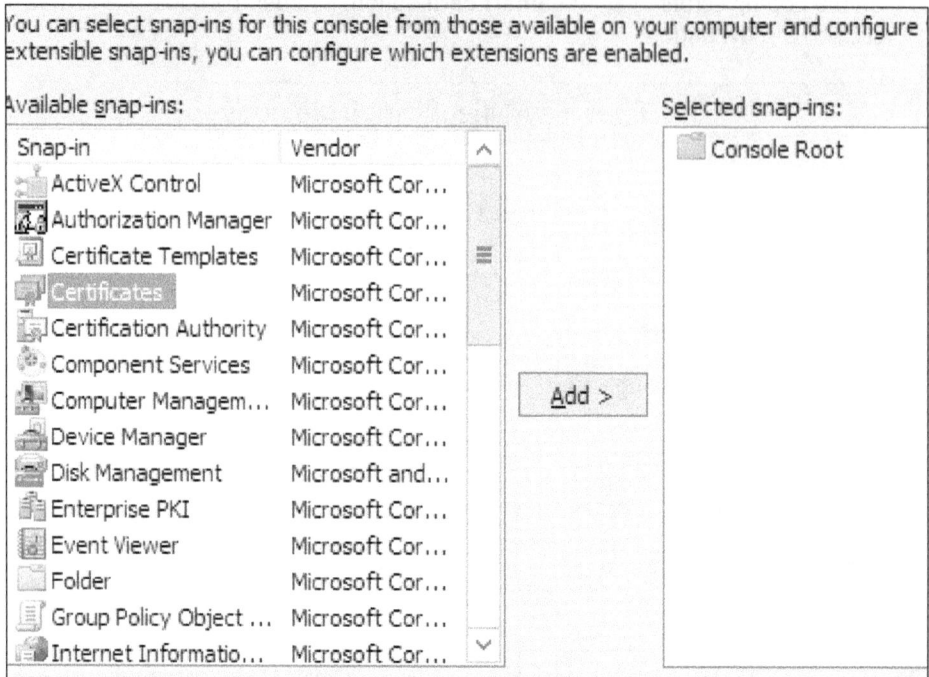

You can select snap-ins for this console from those available on your computer and configure extensible snap-ins, you can configure which extensions are enabled.

Available snap-ins: Selected snap-ins:

Snap-in	Vendor	
ActiveX Control	Microsoft Cor...	
Authorization Manager	Microsoft Cor...	
Certificate Templates	Microsoft Cor...	
Certificates	Microsoft Cor...	
Certification Authority	Microsoft Cor...	
Component Services	Microsoft Cor...	
Computer Managem...	Microsoft Cor...	
Device Manager	Microsoft Cor...	
Disk Management	Microsoft and...	
Enterprise PKI	Microsoft Cor...	
Event Viewer	Microsoft Cor...	
Folder	Microsoft Cor...	
Group Policy Object ...	Microsoft Cor...	
Internet Informatio...	Microsoft Cor...	

Console Root

Add >

6. When prompted for the selection, choose **My user account** as the certificate store, and click on **Finish**. To end the console selection, click on the **OK** button.

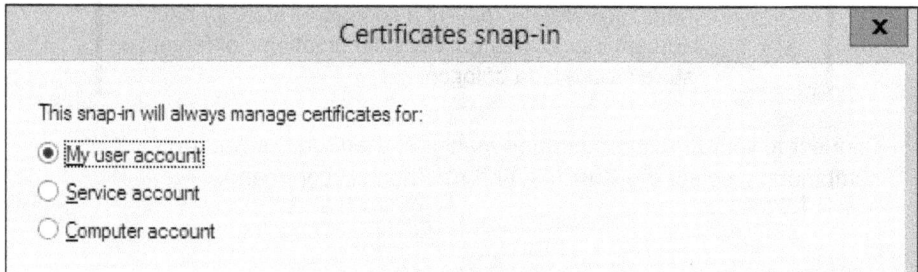

Certificates snap-in   x

This snap-in will always manage certificates for:

- ◉ My user account
- ○ Service account
- ○ Computer account

7. Expand the **Certificates - Current User** tree, right-click on the **Personal** folder, select **All Tasks**, and click on the **Request New Certificate** link.

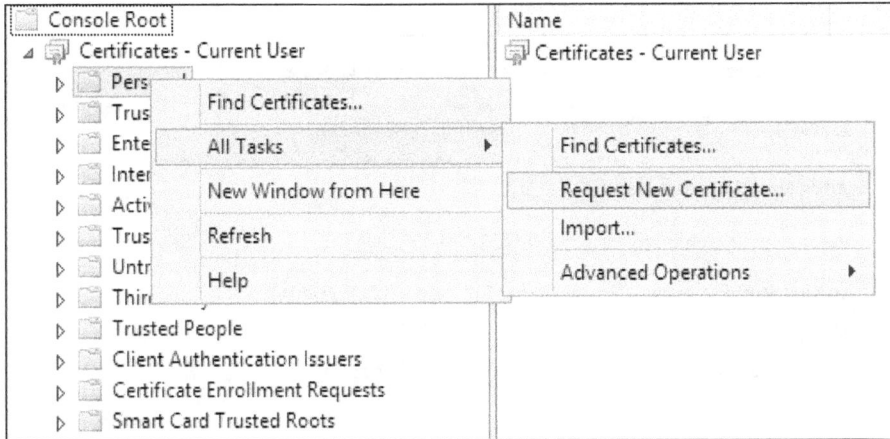

Console Root		Name
⊿ 🖳 Certificates - Current User		🖳 Certificates - Current User

▷ 📁 Pers		
▷ 📁 Trus	Find Certificates...	
▷ 📁 Ente	All Tasks ▶	Find Certificates...
▷ 📁 Inter	New Window from Here	Request New Certificate...
▷ 📁 Acti		Import...
▷ 📁 Trus	Refresh	
▷ 📁 Untr	Help	Advanced Operations ▶
▷ 📁 Thir		

▷ 📁 Trusted People
▷ 📁 Client Authentication Issuers
▷ 📁 Certificate Enrollment Requests
▷ 📁 Smart Card Trusted Roots

8. Click on **Next**, present in the **Before You Begin** section. Then, select the **Active Directory Enrollment Policy** and click on the **Next** button.

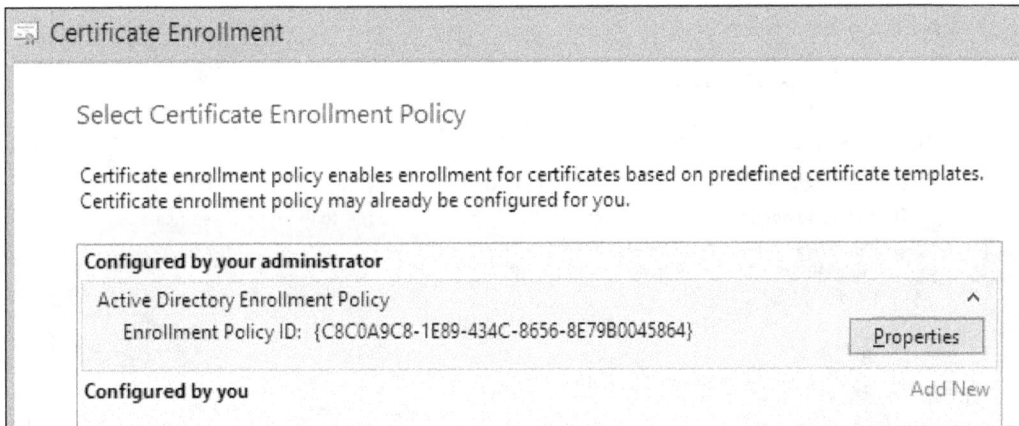

🖳 Certificate Enrollment

Select Certificate Enrollment Policy

Certificate enrollment policy enables enrollment for certificates based on predefined certificate templates. Certificate enrollment policy may already be configured for you.

Configured by your administrator

Active Directory Enrollment Policy	⌃
Enrollment Policy ID: {C8C0A9C8-1E89-434C-8656-8E79B0045864}	Properties

Configured by you Add New

9. Flag the **Enrollment Agent** option, expand it, and click on the **Properties** button.

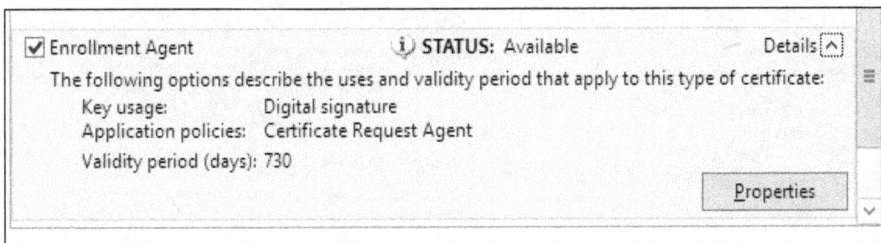

☑ Enrollment Agent ⓘ **STATUS:** Available Details ⌃
The following options describe the uses and validity period that apply to this type of certificate:
Key usage: Digital signature
Application policies: Certificate Request Agent
Validity period (days): 730

Properties

10. In the **Private Key** tab, expand the **Cryptographic Service Provider** option and verify that the **Microsoft Base Cryptographic Provider** option has been flagged. After completion, click on **OK**.

| General | Subject | Extensions | Private Key | Certification Authority |

Cryptographic Service Provider ⌃

A CSP is a program that generates a public and private key pair used in many certificate-related processes.

Select cryptographic service provider (CSP):

☑ Microsoft Enhanced Cryptographic Provider v1.0 (Signature)
☑ Microsoft Base Cryptographic Provider v1.0 (Signature)
☑ Microsoft Base DSS Cryptographic Provider (Signature)

11. On the **Certificate Enrollment** screen, click on the **Enroll** button to generate the certificate request. After completion, click on the **Finish** button.

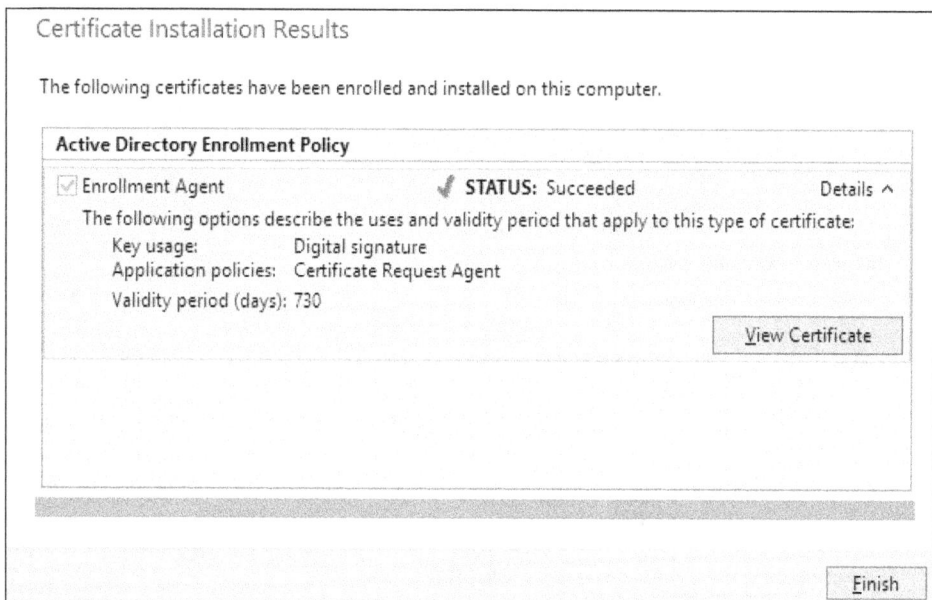

Certificate Installation Results

The following certificates have been enrolled and installed on this computer.

Active Directory Enrollment Policy

☑ Enrollment Agent   ✓ STATUS: Succeeded   Details ⌃

The following options describe the uses and validity period that apply to this type of certificate:

Key usage: Digital signature
Application policies: Certificate Request Agent
Validity period (days): 730

View Certificate

Finish

12. Expand the **Personal** folder, then right-click on **Certificates**, select **All tasks |
Advanced Operations**, and click on the **Enroll On Behalf Of...** link.

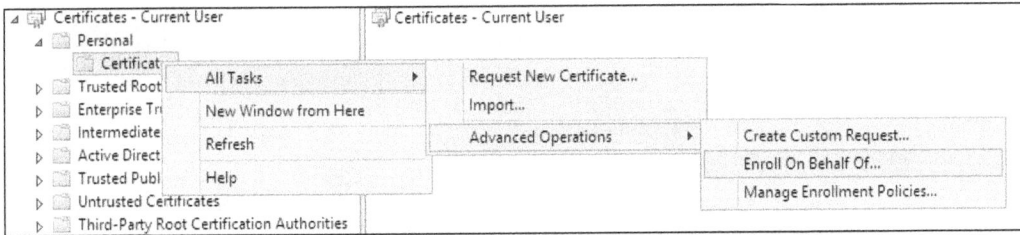

13. Click on the **Next** button, in the **Before You Begin** section, then select the **Active
Directory Enrollment Policy** option and click on the **Next** button.

14. Click on **Browse**, on the **Select Enrollment Agent Certificate** screen, choose the
certificate previously generated, and click on the **OK** button. After completion,
click on **Next** to proceed.

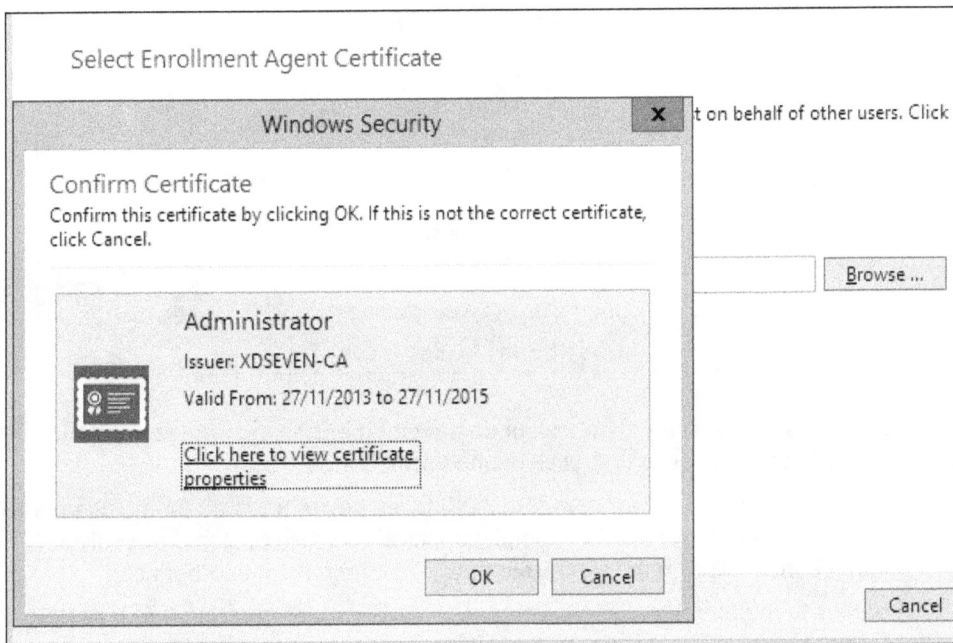

15. In the **Request Certificates** section, select the **Smartcard User** radio button, expand this section, and click on **Properties**.

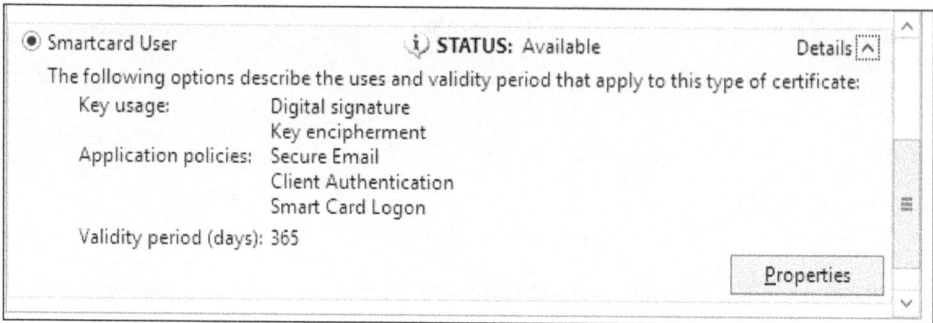

```
◉ Smartcard User                    ⓘ STATUS: Available                    Details ⌃
   The following options describe the uses and validity period that apply to this type of certificate:
       Key usage:            Digital signature
                             Key encipherment
       Application policies:  Secure Email
                             Client Authentication
                             Smart Card Logon
       Validity period (days): 365

                                                              Properties
```

16. Expand the **Cryptographic Service Provider** section, in the **Private Key** tab, and flag your vendor-specific CSP. After completion, click on **OK** to exit from the **Properties** menu, then click on **Next** to continue.

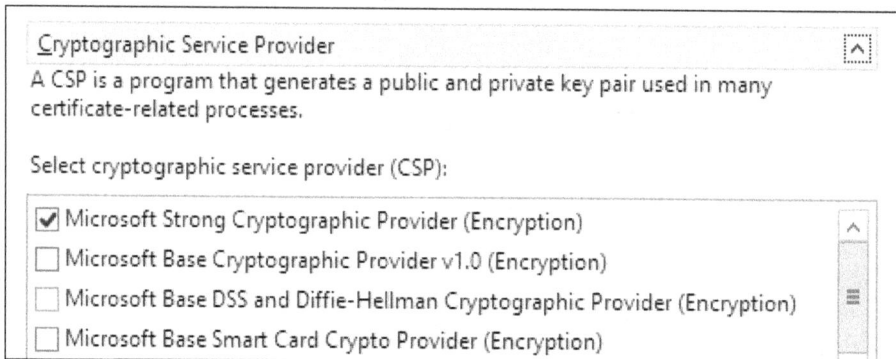

```
C̲ryptographic Service Provider                                            ⌃
A CSP is a program that generates a public and private key pair used in many
certificate-related processes.

Select cryptographic service provider (CSP):

☑ Microsoft Strong Cryptographic Provider (Encryption)                    ⌃
☐ Microsoft Base Cryptographic Provider v1.0 (Encryption)
☐ Microsoft Base DSS and Diffie-Hellman Cryptographic Provider (Encryption)  ▤
☐ Microsoft Base Smart Card Crypto Provider (Encryption)
```

17. In **Select a user screen**, browse your domain for the user you want to enrol the certificate for. After selecting, click on the **Enroll** button.

18. When required, insert the smart card / PKI token device and wait for the completion of the enrolment process. After completion, click on **Close** to stop the certificate distribution, or click on the **Next User** button to continue for another user.

19. Connect to the StoreFront server and run the **Internet Information Services (IIS) Manager** by searching for it within the Windows Apps catalog (run the Windows + C key combination, click on the **Search** button, and search for the **IIS** application).

> All the next configuration steps will be performed in relation to the **IIS 8** version.

20. In the IIS management console, select the server name on the left-hand side menu, and then on the central window zone double-click on the **Server Certificates** icon in the IIS section:

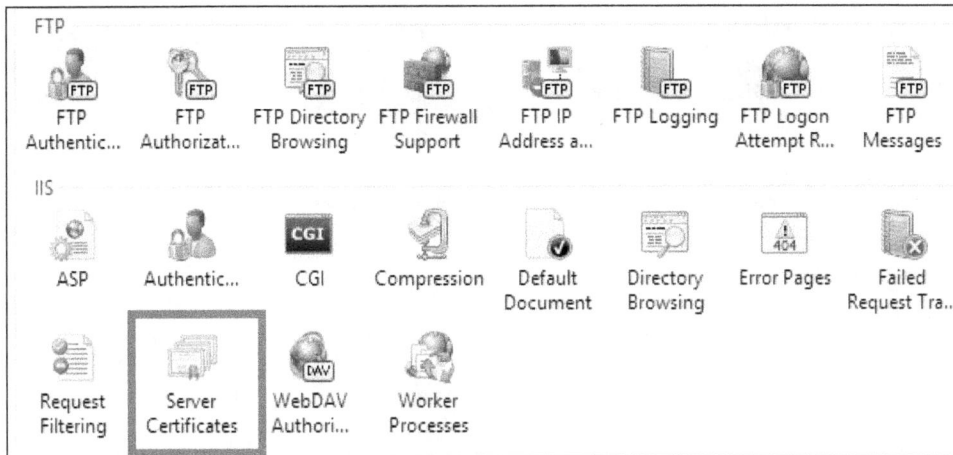

21. Click on the **Create Domain Certificate** link on the right-hand side menu, populate all the fields, and click on **Next** to continue.

In the **Common name** field, you have to insert the **Full Qualified Domain Name (FQDN)** of the StoreFront server.

22. In the **Online Certification Authority** section, click on the **Select** button and choose your configured Certification Authority, populate the **Friendly name** field with a value referring to your CA, then click on **Finish** to complete the procedure.

23. Click again on the server name on the left-hand side menu, double-click on the **Authentication** icon in the **IIS** section and enable the **Active Directory Client Certificate Authentication** option by right-clicking on it and selecting **Enable**.

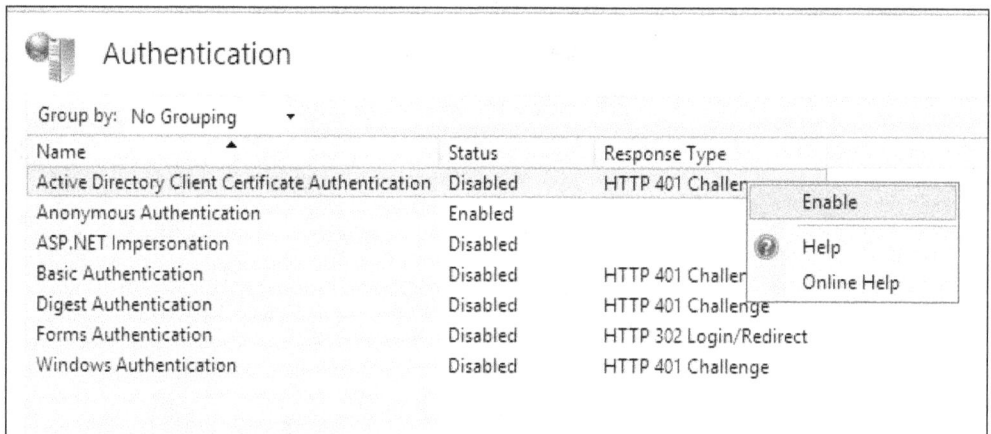

24. On the left-hand side menu, select the **Default Web Site** link, and then click the **Bindings** option on the right-hand side menu.

25. Click on the **Add** button in the **Site Bindings** screen and configure the **HTTPS** protocol type, the **IP Address**, and the Host name configured for the StoreFront store with smart card authentication and the existing **SSL Certificate** from the drop-down list. After completion, click on **OK** first and then **Close** to exit from the bindings menu.

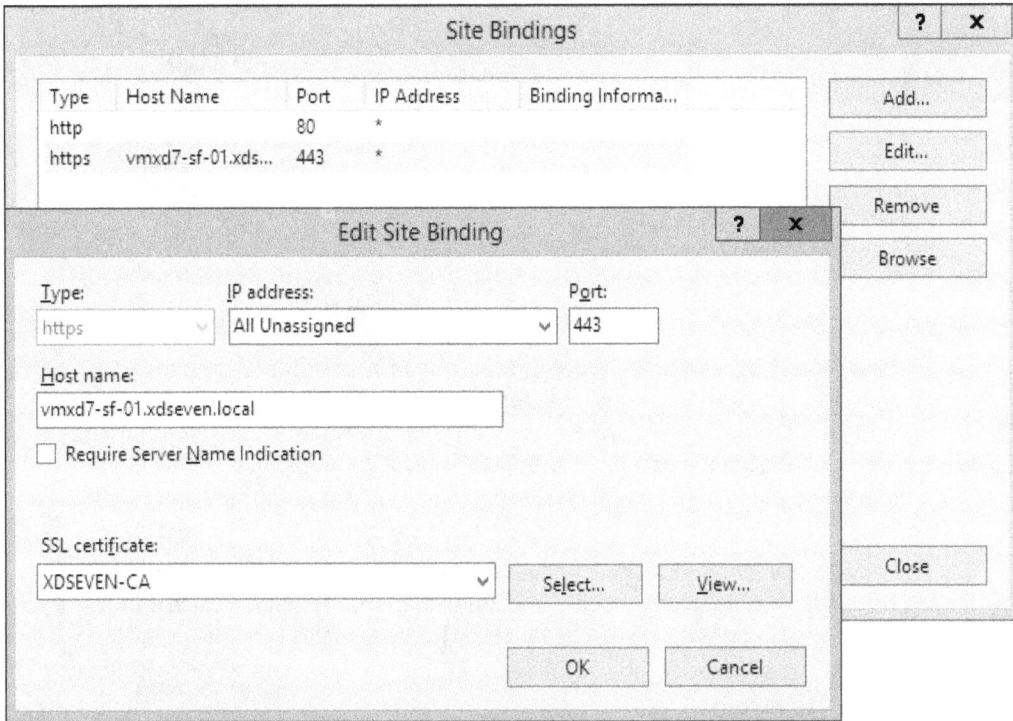

Type	Host Name	Port	IP Address	Binding Informa...
http		80	*	
https	vmxd7-sf-01.xds...	443	*	

Site Bindings   ?   X

Add...

Edit...

Remove

Browse

Close

Edit Site Binding   ?   X

Type:
https

IP address:
All Unassigned

Port:
443

Host name:
vmxd7-sf-01.xdseven.local

☐ Require Server Name Indication

SSL certificate:
XDSEVEN-CA   Select...   View...

OK   Cancel

26. On the left-hand side menu, expand the **Default Web Site** tree, select the **Citrix** folder, and double-click on the **SSL Settings** icon on the central part of the menu.

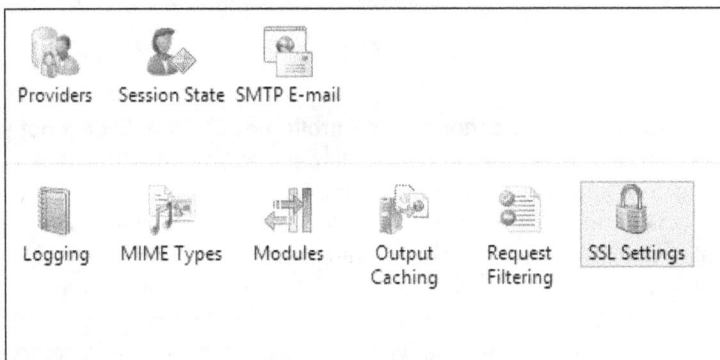

Providers   Session State   SMTP E-mail

Logging   MIME Types   Modules   Output Caching   Request Filtering   SSL Settings

27. Flag the **Require SSL** option and select the **Accept** radio button for the **Client certificates** section. Click on the **Apply** link on the right-hand side menu to confirm your choice.

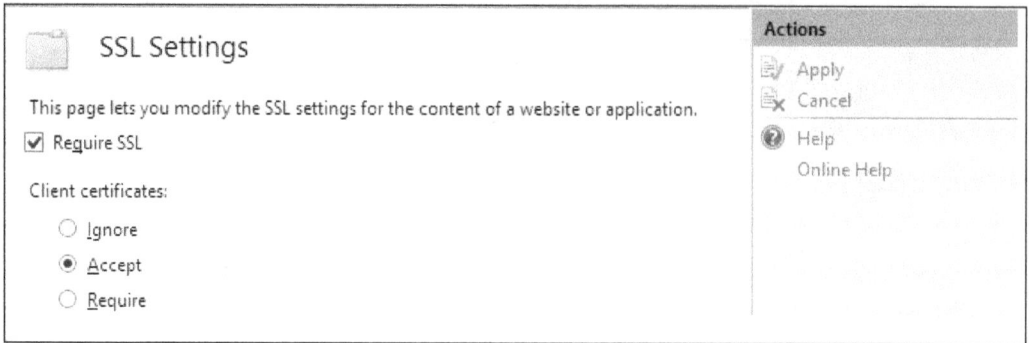

SSL Settings

This page lets you modify the SSL settings for the content of a website or application.

☑ Require SSL

Client certificates:

○ Ignore

◉ Accept

○ Require

Actions

🖹 Apply

🗙 Cancel

❓ Help

Online Help

28. Add the StoreFront site to the **Trusted Site** zone of your browser, then insert your smart card / PKI token into the appropriate device drive and connect to the configured store using the Citrix Receiver on your physical machine. If required, type the associated PIN to your authentication hardware token. It is now possible to complete the authentication phase using the smart card authentication method.

> Note that the smart card authentication is only supported using the Citrix Receiver to authenticate to StoreFront. The **Web Site** store is not able to use this kind of authentication (by default, this is not supported).

How it works...

The use of the smart cards / tokens with the StoreFront platform permits users to authenticate in a stronger and more secure way. In fact, they can access the assigned resources only through the presentation of the personal certificate installed on the physical support.

In this recipe, we implemented the XenDesktop strong authentication, passing through three different stages:

► **Enterprise Certification Authority and Enrollment Station**: Even if not explicitly discussed, the first requirement to complete the strong authentication configuration is creating an Enterprise Certification Authority, based for instance on the Microsoft CA, then configuring an Enrollment Station through which assigning the generated certificate request to the Windows domain users, and then registering this certificate on the smart card or PKI token devices. The association between the certificate and the physical device is granted by the **Cryptographic Service Provider** (**CSP**), which can be based on the Microsoft native library (using a generic and compatible smart card device), or is equipped by the vendor of the token you've decided to use.

- ▶ **Web Server – IIS 8**: At this stage, the fundamental step is implementing the SSL for the web server machine that hosts the StoreFront store site (usually the StoreFront machine itself). First, it is necessary to require a domain certificate to the previously configured Certification Authority. This certificate will then be used to bind the default IIS website configuration on the SSL port (443), in order to establish a secure connection using the HTTPS protocol. Moreover, it is also necessary to enable the SSL at the Web Server level. We have completed it navigating the SSL Settings zone, enabling the secure protocol and accepting the client certificates.

- ▶ **StoreFront**: At the StoreFront level, it is possible to use the existing website (not recommended) or to create a new one only for the strong authentication type (the recommended solution). The configurations are based on the enabling of the authentication method based on the Smart Card option.

There's more...

With StoreFront, the **Pass-Through with smart card authentication** is also possible using an alternative smart card logon technique. This method is able to reuse the user credentials from the physical machine (at the first logon step), without the necessity of retyping the logon information every time.

To correctly configure this option, you need to insert the StoreFront site in the **Local Intranet** zone of your web browser (instead of the **Trusted Site** zone previously used for the standard smart card mode), then enable the **SSL** in the **SSL Settings** zone, but this time configuring the **Client Certificates** section with the **Ignore** value.

On the smart card reader client machine, open the **Local Policy** editor in the following ways:

- ▶ For **Windows 7** physical devices:
  - ❑ Click on **Start | Run** and type the `gpedit.msc` command

- ▶ For **Windows 8.x** physical devices:
  - ❑ Execute the Windows + X key combination, select the **Run** link, and digit the `gpedit.msc` command

After you've executed the Group Policy editor, import the `icaclient.adm` template located in your Citrix Receiver installation (usually `C:\Program Files (x86)\Citrix\ICA Client\Configuration`), and enable the **Smart Card authentication** policy (located in **Computer Configuration | Administrative Templates | Classic Administrative Templates (ADM) | Citrix Components | Citrix Receiver | User authentication**) configuring it as shown in the following screenshot:

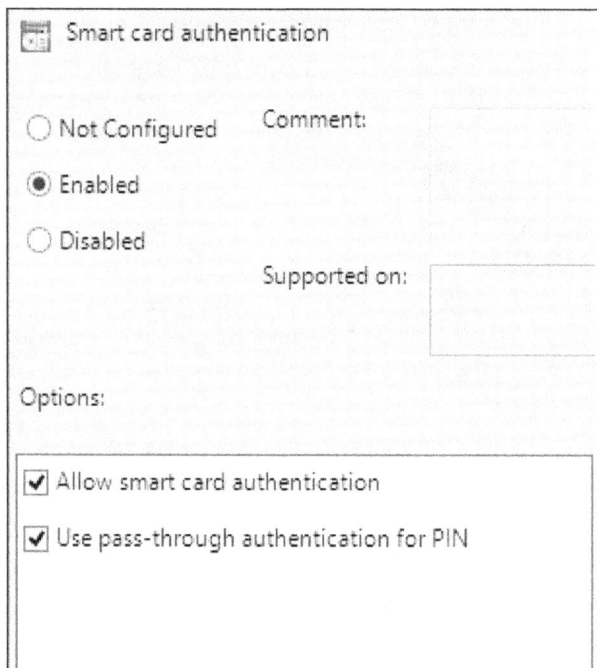

Connect to the StoreFront server and open the `default.ica` file with a text editor, located in the IIS configured store path (by default, `C:\inetpub\wwwroot\Citrix\<StoreName>\App_Data`). Once opened, add the **DisableCtrlAltDel=Off** option in the **Application** section.

> The previous configured parameter is for a connection made without a NetScaler platform. In the presence of a NetScaler Gateway, the parameter to configure in the **Application** section is **UseLocalUserAndPassword=On**

See also

▶ The *Installing and configuring NetScaler Gateway™ 10.5* recipe in *Chapter 8, XenDesktop® Component Integration*

Implementing strong authentication for XenDesktop® 7 – RADIUS platform

An alternative method to the smart card authentication is the two-factor authentication. This strong authentication type forces the user to connect to the assigned resources using the password and a second authentication key. In this recipe, we're going to discuss the configuration of the **RADIUS** (acronym of **Remote Authentication Dial In User Service**) authentication with the NetScaler Gateway, a strong authentication type based on the combination of a username, a password, and a pre-shared key, which can be delivered in the form of a static key or as a **One Time Password** (**OTP**).

Getting ready

In order to implement the earlier discussed strong authentication method, you have to install a RADIUS server. This task can be accomplished using the Microsoft RADIUS role (**NPS—Network Policy Server**) or by installing a Linux-based authentication server, such as **FreeRADIUS**.

> In this recipe, we will use the Windows version of the RADIUS server by installing the Network Policy Server role on a Windows Server 2012 machine. You can find more information about the installation procedure at `http://technet.microsoft.com/en-us/library/cc725922(v=ws.10).aspx`

How to do it...

In this section, we will explain how to configure a Windows Radius server in order to implement a multiple factor authentication through the StoreFront platform:

1. Connect to the Windows RADIUS (NPS) server with domain administrative credentials, and then run **Network Policy Server** by searching for it within the Windows Apps catalog (run the Windows + *C* key combination, click the **Search** button, and search for the **Network Policy Server** application).

2. On the left-hand side menu, expand the **RADIUS Clients and Servers** folder, then right-click on the **RADIUS Clients** link and select **New**.

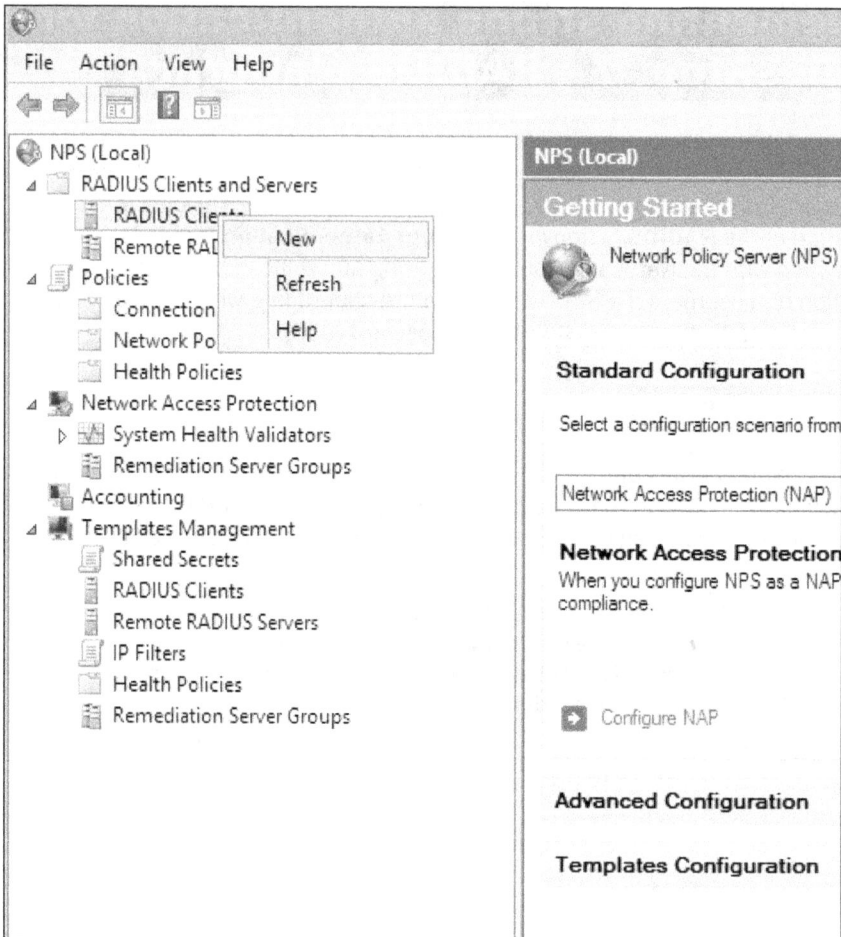

3. Assign an identification name populating the **Friendly Name** field, then insert the **IP address** or the **FQDN** of your NetScaler Gateway machine (**NSIP**, **NetScaler IP Address**), and insert a shared secret key by selecting the **Manual** radio button and typing the security code, or use a randomly-generated secret code by selecting the **Generate** radio button and clicking on the **Generate** button. After completion, click on **OK**.

Remember that the secret key is case sensitive, so you have to be careful when using it in the client configuration phase!

4. Expand the **Policies** section in the left side menu, right-click the **Network Policies** folder, and select the **New** link.

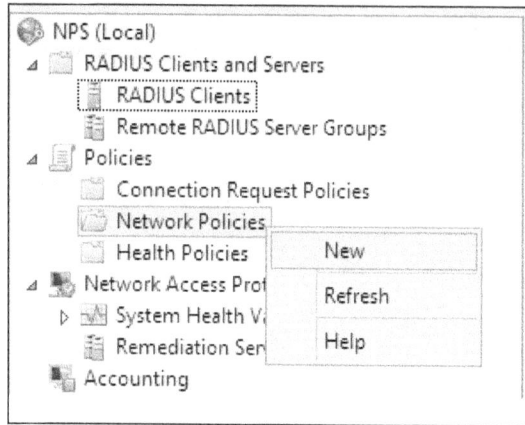

5. Assign a name to the policy in the **Policy name** field, select the **Unspecified** option for the **Type of network access server** section, and click on **Next** to continue.

6. Click on the **Add** button on the **Specify Conditions** screen, select the **User Groups** option from the list, and click on the **Add** button.

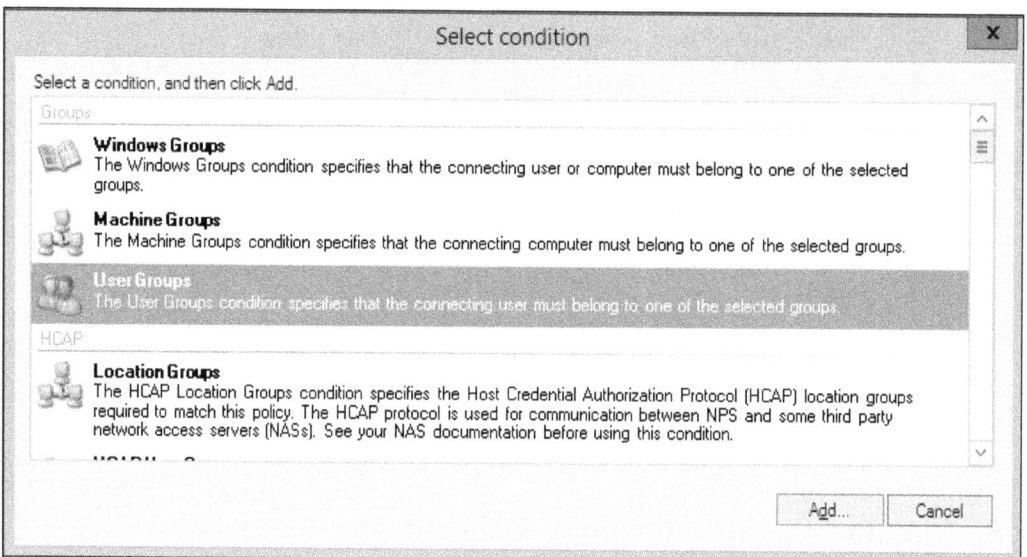

7. In the **User Groups** screen, click on the **Add Groups** button, and browse for the domain group for which you want to configure the strong authentication. After completion, click on **OK** to close the pop-up screen, then click on the **Next** button to proceed with the configuration.

8. In the **Specify Access Permission** section, select the **Access granted** radio button and click on **Next**.

New Network Policy

Specify Access Permission

Configure whether you want to grant network access or deny network access if the connection request matches this policy.

◉ Access granted
Grant access if client connection attempts match the conditions of this policy.

○ Access denied
Deny access if client connection attempts match the conditions of this policy.

☐ Access is determined by User Dial-in properties (which override NPS policy)
Grant or deny access according to user dial-in properties if client connection attempts match the conditions of this policy.

9. On the **ConfigureAuthentication Methods** screen, clear any configured option and flag one of the supported authentication methods (CHAP, MS-CHAP v1/v2, and PAP). After completion, click on **Next**.

☐ Microsoft Encrypted Authentication version 2 (MS-CHAP-v2)
   ☐ User can change password after it has expired
☐ Microsoft Encrypted Authentication (MS-CHAP)
   ☐ User can change password after it has expired
☑ Encrypted authentication (CHAP)
☑ Unencrypted authentication (PAP, SPAP)
☐ Allow clients to connect without negotiating an authentication method.
☐ Perform machine health check only

10. In the **Configure Constraints** section, you can configure specific connection options, such as the **Idle Timeout**, **Session Timeout**, or **Day and time restrictions** options. After completion, click on **Next** to proceed.

> These are collateral options, which are not fundamental in order to the correct functioning of the RADIUS server combined with the NetScaler Gateway platform.

11. On the **Configure Settings** screen, remove any configured attributes under the **Standard** category by selecting the desired attribute and clicking on the **Remove** button.

New Network Policy

Configure Settings

NPS applies settings to the connection request if all of the network policy conditions matched.

Configure the settings for this network policy.
If conditions and constraints match the connection request and the policy grants access, settings are appl

Settings:

RADIUS Attributes

- Standard
- Vendor Specific

Network Access Protection

- NAP Enforcement
- Extended State

Routing and Remote Access

- Multilink and Bandwidth Allocation Protocol (BAP)
- IP Filters
- Encryption
- IP Settings

To send additional attributes to RADIUS clients, select a RADIU then click Edit. If you do not configure an attribute, it is not sent your RADIUS client documentation for required attributes.

Attributes:

Name	Value
Framed-Protocol	PPP
Service-Type	Framed

Add...   Edit...   Remove

12. On the left-hand side menu, select the **Vendor Specific** option, click on **Add**, and choose the **Custom** option from the **Vendor** list. Then, select the **Vendor Specific** attributes. After doing this, click on the **Add** button.

Vendor:

Custom

Attributes:

Name	Vendor
Allowed-Certificate-OID	RADIUS Standard
Generate-Class-Attribute	RADIUS Standard
Generate-Session-Timeout	RADIUS Standard
Tunnel-Tag	RADIUS Standard
Vendor-Specific	RADIUS Standard

Description:

Specifies the support of proprietary NAS features.

Add...   Close

13. On the **Attribute Information** screen, click the **Add** button. Then in the **Vendor-Specific Attribute Information** menu, choose the **RADIUS standard** option from the **Select from list** section and select the **Yes. It conforms** radio button:

Vendor-Specific Attribute Information   X

Attribute name:
Vendor Specific

Specify network access server vendor.

◉ Select from list: RADIUS Standard

○ Enter Vendor Code: 0

Specify whether the attribute conforms to the RADIUS RFC specification for vendor specific attributes.

◉ Yes. It conforms

○ No. It does not conform

Configure Attribute...

14. After these selections, click twice on the **OK** button, then **Close** to complete the configuration. On the **Configure Settings** main screen, click on the **Next** button to continue.

15. In the **Completing New Network Policy** section, click on **Finish** to complete the procedure.

16. In the **Network Policies** section, be sure that the created rule has a higher priority than other configured rules.

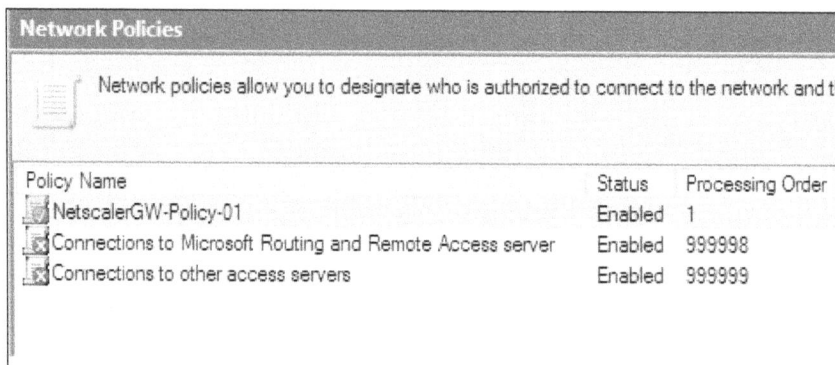

```
Network Policies

    Network policies allow you to designate who is authorized to connect to the network and th

Policy Name                                                  Status    Processing Order
NetscalerGW-Policy-01                                        Enabled   1
Connections to Microsoft Routing and Remote Access server   Enabled   999998
Connections to other access servers                         Enabled   999999
```

17. Open a compatible web browser, and in the address bar, type the address previously assigned to the virtual appliance.

18. Insert the web portal credentials (default: **nsroot / nsroot**), select **NetScaler Gateway** as the **Deployment Type** option, and click on the **Login** button to continue.

> We discuss the installation and configuration of the NetScaler Gateway platform in *Chapter 8, XenDesktop® Component Integration*.

19. After you have been logged in, click on the **Configuration** button on the main menu option bar.

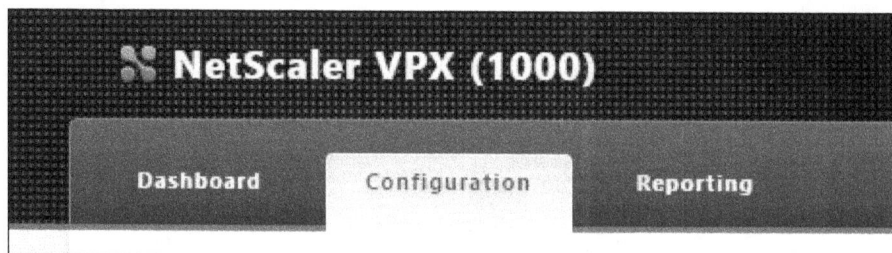

⁂ NetScaler VPX (1000)

Dashboard | Configuration | Reporting

20. In the **Configuration** section, click on the **NetScaler Gateway** link and expand the **Policies** section, followed by the **Authentication** subsection.

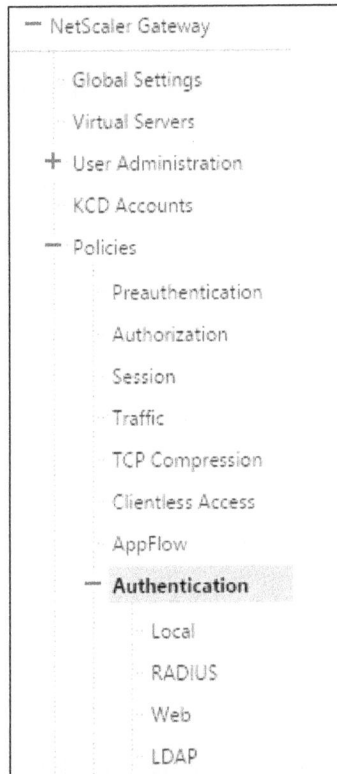

```
— NetScaler Gateway

      Global Settings
      Virtual Servers
  +  User Administration
      KCD Accounts
  —  Policies

          Preauthentication
          Authorization
          Session
          Traffic
          TCP Compression
          Clientless Access
          AppFlow
      —  Authentication

              Local
              RADIUS
              Web
              LDAP
```

21. Click on the **RADIUS** link in the **Policies** section, and then click on the **Add** button to create a new Radius authentication method.

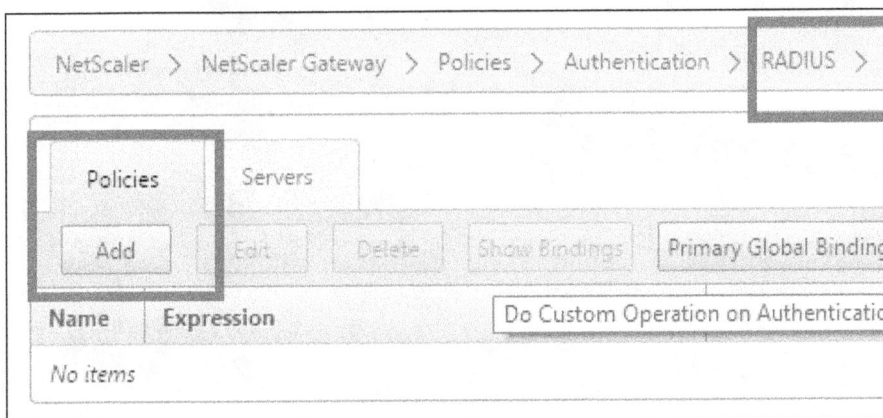

```
NetScaler  >  NetScaler Gateway  >  Policies  >  Authentication  >  RADIUS  >

  Policies      Servers

     Add         Edit      Delete     Show Bindings    Primary Global Binding

  Name   |  Expression                              Do Custom Operation on Authenticatio

  No items
```

22. In the **RADIUS Policy Name** field, populate this with a consistent name for your authentication policy. After this, click on the **+** button in the **Server** field, in order to add a valid RADIUS server.

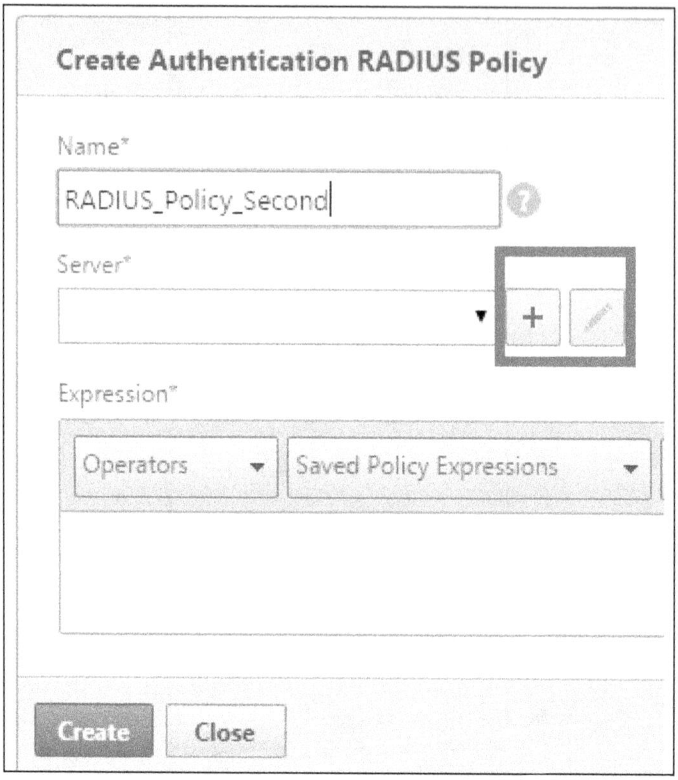

Create Authentication RADIUS Policy

Name*

| RADIUS_Policy_Second |

Server*

| | ▼ | + | ✎ |

Expression*

| Operators ▼ | Saved Policy Expressions ▼ |

| Create | Close |

23. In the **Create Authentication RADIUS Server** section, populate the required fields for your existing RADIUS server. After completion, click on the **Create** button.

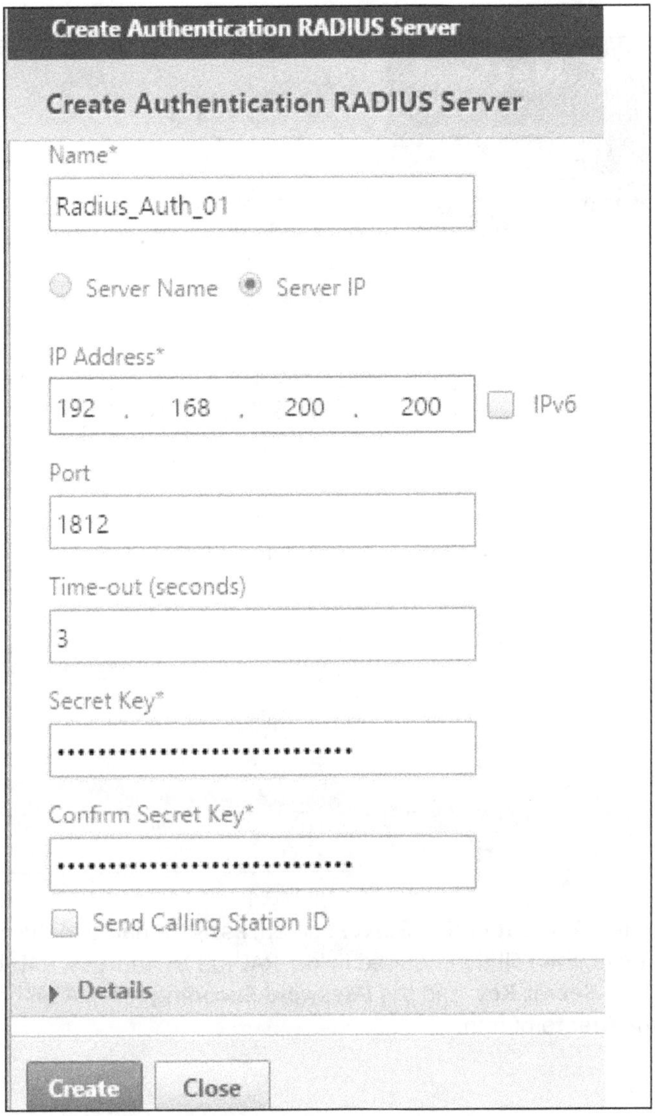

Create Authentication RADIUS Server

Create Authentication RADIUS Server

Name*

Radius_Auth_01

○ Server Name   ◉ Server IP

IP Address*

| 192 | . | 168 | . | 200 | . | 200 | ☐ IPv6 |

Port

1812

Time-out (seconds)

3

Secret Key*

•••••••••••••••••••••••••••••

Confirm Secret Key*

•••••••••••••••••••••••••••••

☐ Send Calling Station ID

▶ Details

Create   Close

24. On the **Expression** form, select the **ns_true** value from the **Saved Policy Expression** list. If all the data is correct, click on the **Create** button to save the RADIUS configuration again.

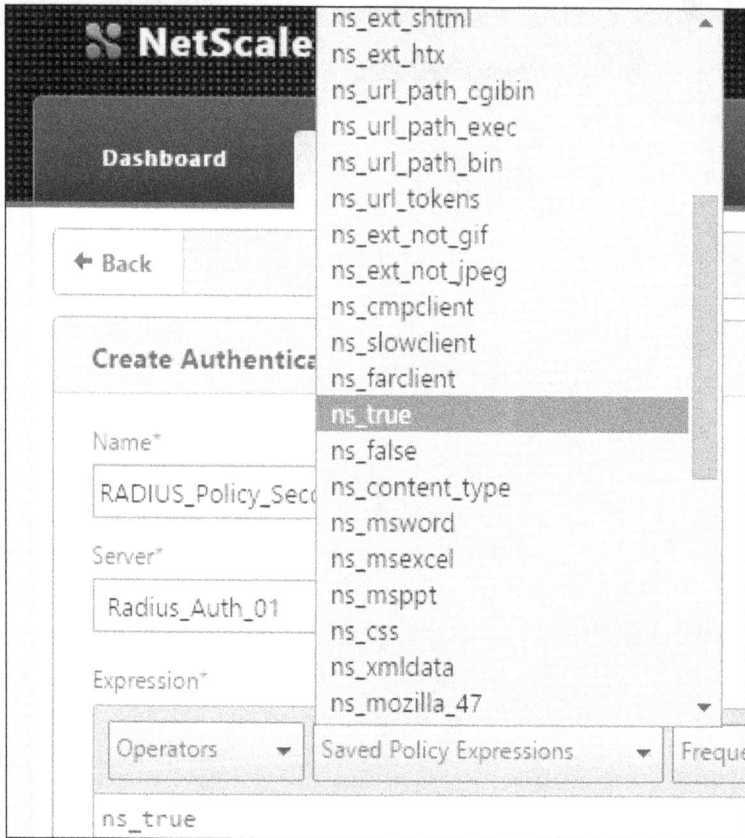

25. On the **Create Authentication Server** screen, assign a name to the configured RADIUS server, then fill the required fields (RADIUS **IP Address**, RADIUS configured **Port**, RADIUS **Secret Key**, and the **Password Encoding** type). After completing this, click on the **Create** button.

26. After completing the configuration steps, the NetScaler Gateway will be available to authenticate users by contacting the configured RADIUS platform.

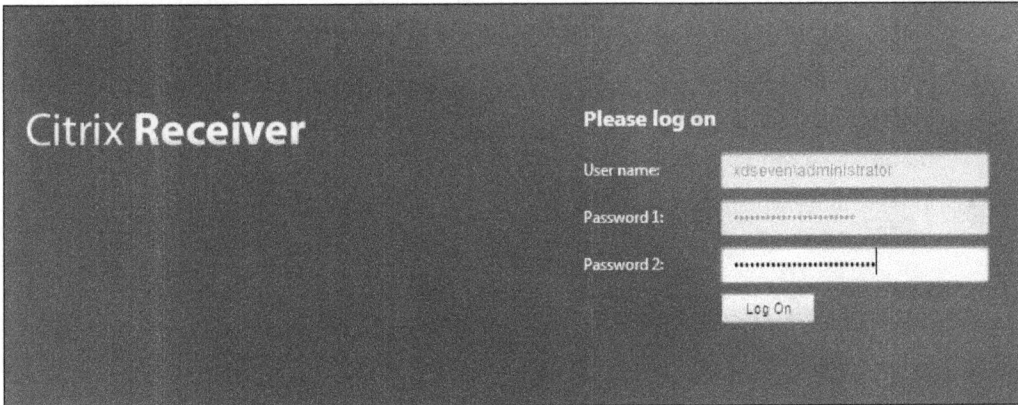

How it works...

RADIUS is a strong authentication method based on the same protocol, which is an **AAA** kind of platform (**Authentication, Authorization, and Accounting**) used as a network resource regulator in order to manage the access to the network resources.

The first operation executed in this recipe is the Microsoft RADIUS server configuration, through the use of the **Network Policy Server** (**NPS**) role configured on the Windows Server 2012 R2 machine in order to let the RADIUS communicate with the NetScaler Gateway Virtual Appliance, this second has to be configured as a client under the RADIUS server: to accomplish this task is necessary to insert the FQDN or the IP address of the NetScaler platform, then generating a secret key which will be used as a second authentication factor.

This code should be complex in order to make the ability to crack the password and reuse it harder. On the other hand, it should be not too long, because some clients will not be able to read and use it.

After this, the RADIUS configuration has been completed. This authentication method needs to be configured under the NetScaler Gateway platform. This task can be accomplished by configuring the RADIUS parameters (IP, name, secret key previously generated) within the **Policy** section. In this way, RADIUS will be considered as a secondary authentication method, permitting, filtering, and blocking users with no rights within your XenDesktop infrastructure.

> The access to the published resources is given by the configuration of the domain groups under the Windows NPS network policy category.

There's more...

It is possible to configure the NetScaler to obtain the IP addresses to assign to the users directly from the RADIUS server. This is the **IP Address Extraction** configuration.

To be able to use this configuration, you have to set the following two parameters:

> ▸ The Vendor Identifier (ID), which permits releasing local IP addresses to the users that make a request.

> ▸ The attribute type, which is a value from 1 to 255, equal to the remote IP RADIUS response.

To configure it, you have to connect to the NetScaler Gateway, then modify the configured authentication policy for RADIUS, type the required Vendor ID, and flag the **Enable NAS IP address extraction** option.

> We have already discussed the RADIUS policy creation in this recipe.

Create Authentication RADIUS Server
Create Authentication RADIUS Server
Confirm Secret Key*
••••••••••••••••••••••
☐ Send Calling Station ID
▾ Details
NAS ID
1
☑ Enable NAS IP address extraction
Group Vendor Identifier

See also

> ▸ The *Installing and configuring NetScaler Gateway™ 10.5* recipe in *Chapter 8, XenDesktop® Component Integration*

Implementing the two-factor software authentication for XenDesktop® 7

An alternative method to the smart card authentication is the **two-factor software authentication**. This strong authentication type forces the user to connect to the assigned resources through the use of the password and a second authentication key. An **OTP (One Time Password)** token is usually sent to the user's e-mail address or mobile devices. In this recipe, we're going to discuss the configuration of a specific platform, which permits using this kind of authentication, the **SMS2** software developed by the WrightCCS company.

Getting ready

For the purpose of this recipe, the following tasks and configurations are required:

▶ You need to download the SMS2 software at the following link: `http://www.wrightccs.com/get/`. Insert the required data and wait for the download link and the activation code that will be sent to the specified e-mail address.

▶ To install the software domain, administrative credentials are needed on the Windows Server 2012 machine on which you are going to install SMS2, and you also need the availability of a SQL Server machine to create the SMS2 database.

▶ An already configured RADIUS platform is needed in order to interact with it.

▶ An already configured NetScaler Gateway platform is needed in order to interact with it.

> Please refer to the previous recipe to check the NPS RADIUS and NetScaler Gateway configurations for the strong authentication.

How to do it...

Follow the required steps to install and configure the SMS2 two-factor authentication software:

1. Connect to the Windows Server 2012 R2 selected as the SMS2 server with domain administrative credentials.

2. Locate the downloaded setup (the **.x86.rg.msi** extension for the 32-bit and **x64.msi** extension for the 64-bit version) and double-click on it.

3. On the **Welcome** screen, click on the **Next** button to continue.

4. In the **Choose Setup Type** section, select the **Complete** installation option.

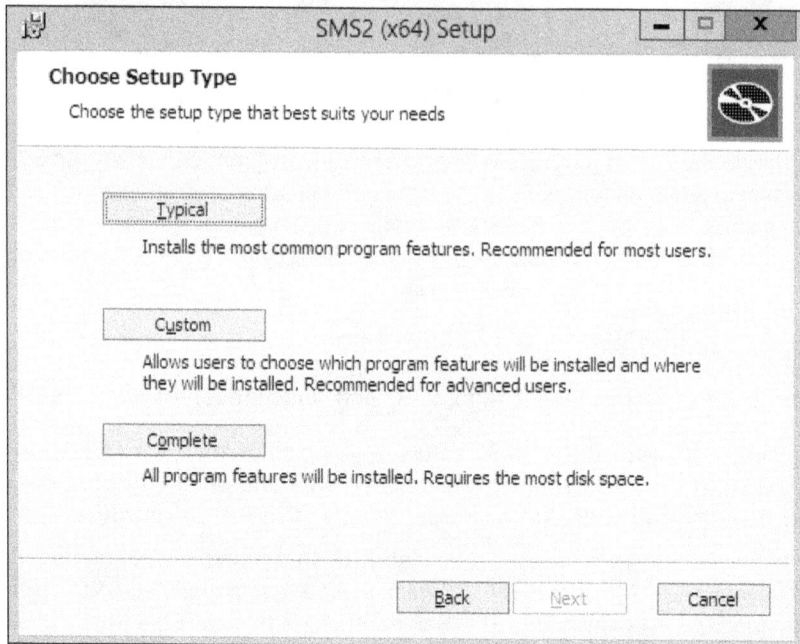

5. In the **Services configuration** screen, click on the **Configure AuthEngine** button, then insert the received license in the form of XML, and click on the **Check License** button. If the check passes, click on **Next** to continue.

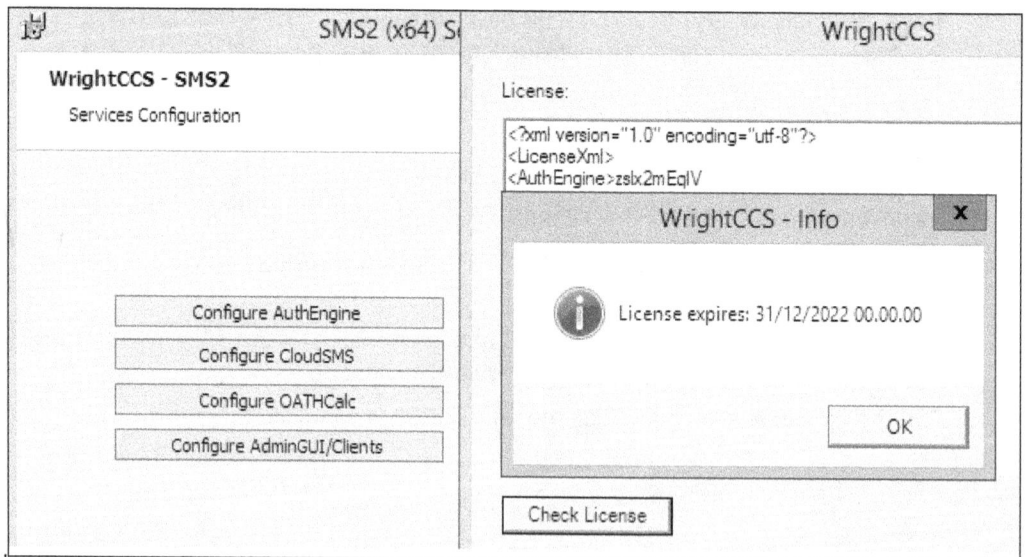

6. In the **AuthEngine Service User** section, specify a service account (**Local System, Local Service** or **Network Service**), then click on **Next** to continue.

7. Configure the network settings and the Active Directory required parameters, and then click on the **Next** button to continue.

```
Network Bindings
         AuthEngine Address  192.168.110.47        ▼
            AuthEngine Port  9060

Active Directory
            AD/LDAP Server  192.168.110.20
     AD/LDAP Query Account  Administrator
         AD/LDAP Password  ************************
          AD/LDAP BaseDN  DC=XDSEVEN,DC=local
  AD/LDAP Container (optional)
    AD/LDAP Filter (optional)  (&(objectClass=person))

                              Test AD/LDAP Config
```

> Click on the **Test AD/LDAP Config** button to ensure you have correctly configured all the parameters.

8. Insert valid information to connect to a SQL Server installed platform in order to create the SMS2 database. After completion, click on **Test Connection** to ensure the validity of the data, then click on **Next**.

```
SQL Configurations
  SQL Server Address   192.168.110.10
  SQL Server Port      1433
  SQL Username         sa
  SQL Password            WrightCCS - Info          x
  Use named pipes (local)
  Use integrated security    (i)  Test SQL connection successful
  Database Name

                                                OK
```

9. In the **E-mail Configuration** section, specify a valid e-mail server and e-mail account, to which the authentication token is sent in the form of an e-mail. Click on the **Finish** button to complete the procedure.

WrightCCS

E-Mail Configuration

(• Manual   (NHS Preset

Server: smtp.mailserver.local

Port: 465

SSL: ☑

From: user@mailserver.local

Use Auth: ☑

Username: user@mailserver.local

Password: ·····················

Test destination: user_dest@mailserver.local   Send test e-mail

Type a valid destination e-mail address and click on **Send test e-mail** to check the functionality of the mail server.

10. On the **Services Configuration** main menu, click on the **Configure CloudSMS** button. Then in the **CloudSMS Service User** section, configure a service account, as seen earlier for the e-mail service. Click on **Next** to continue.

11. In the **CloudSMS Module Parameters** section, select an SMS provider from the drop-down list, and then click on the **Load** button and select a valid module from the relative section. If necessary, modify the configured parameters in order to be able to send an SMS to the destination user's devices. Click on **Finish** to complete the procedure.

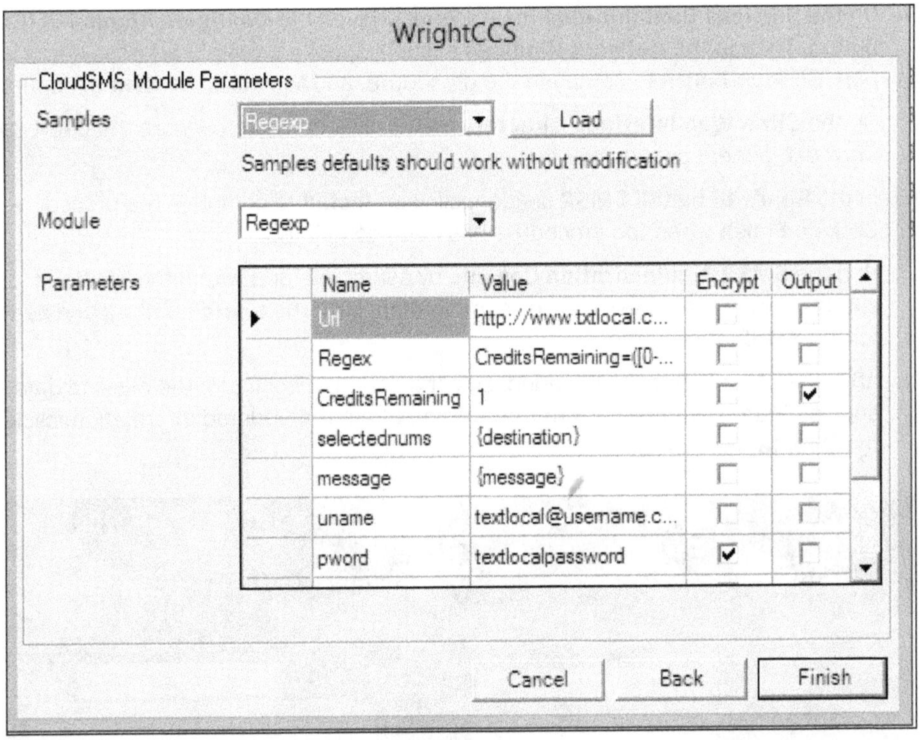

WrightCCS

CloudSMS Module Parameters

Samples | Regexp | Load

Samples defaults should work without modification

Module | Regexp

Parameters

	Name	Value	Encrypt	Output
▶	Url	http://www.txtlocal.c...	☐	☐
	Regex	CreditsRemaining=([0-...	☐	☐
	CreditsRemaining	1	☐	☑
	selectednums	{destination}	☐	☐
	message	{message}	☐	☐
	uname	textlocal@username.c...	☐	☐
	pword	textlocalpassword	☑	☐

Cancel | Back | Finish

12. On the **Services Configuration** main menu, click on the **Configure OATHCalc** button. Then in the **CloudSMS Service User** section, configure a service account, as seen earlier for the e-mail service. Click on **Next** to continue.

13. On the **OATHCalc Configuration** screen, configure the time settings and the number of tokens managed by the SMS2 Windows platform. Click on the **Finish** button to complete the configuration.

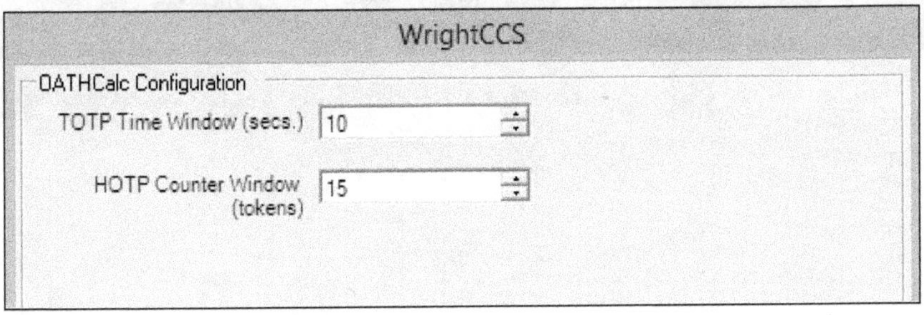

WrightCCS

OATHCalc Configuration

TOTP Time Window (secs.) | 10

HOTP Counter Window (tokens) | 15

14. On the **Services Configuration** main menu, click on the **Configure AdminGUI/Clients** button. Then in the **Network Bindings** section, specify a valid IP address and a valid port. Click on **Finish** to complete the procedure, and then click on **Next** to continue.

15. On the **Citrix Web Interface Directory** menu, click on **Next** to ignore the deprecated Citrix component configuration.

16. In the **Ready to install SMS2** section, click on **Install** to complete the procedure. Click on **Finish** when the procedure has been completed.

17. Run the **SMS2 Administration Console** by searching for it within the Windows Apps catalog (run the Windows + C key combination, click the **Search** button, and search for the **SMS2** application).

18. After the console has been loaded, select a user and configure the missing data, such as **Mobile Number** or **Pin Code**. To maintain the updated information, click on the **Update Account** button.

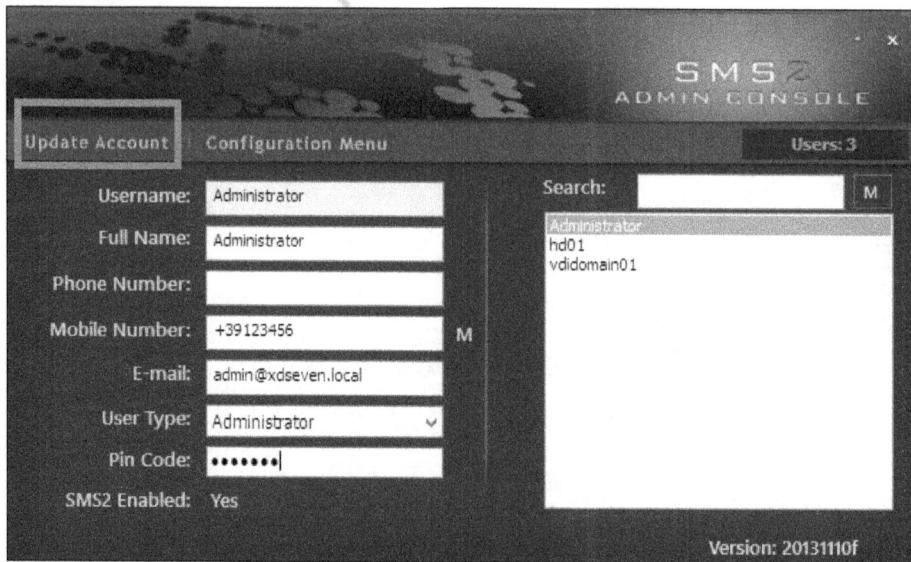

19. Click on the **Configuration Menu** link, and then on the **SMS** tab to configure the body message that will be sent to the user. Click on **Save** to update the modified information.

20. On the **Passcode** tab, configure the length of the software token sent to the users. Click on the **Save** button to update the modified parameter.

21. Open a compatible web browser, and in the address bar, type the address previously assigned to the virtual NetScaler appliance.

22. Insert the web portal credentials (default: `nsroot/nsroot`), select the **NetScaler Gateway** as a **Deployment Type** option, and click on the **Login** button to continue.

23. Edit the configured NetScaler Gateway appliance by clicking on the edit icon on the right-hand side menu.

24. Click on the **Edit** button in the **Authentication Settings** section.

25. In the **Secondary Authentication** section, select the **RADIUS** option from the drop-down list, then select the RADIUS server configured in the previous recipe, or add a new one by selecting the **Configure New** option. After completion, click on the **Continue** button.

26. Log in to the user access address of your NetScaler platform. You will find the second authentication factor added to the login web portal.

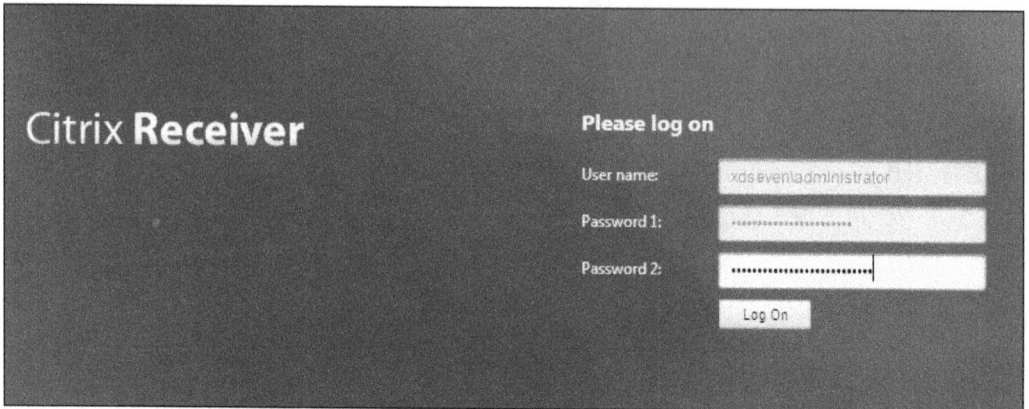

27. The same multiple-factor authentication will be possible by the use of the Citrix Receiver, as indicated in the next screenshot.

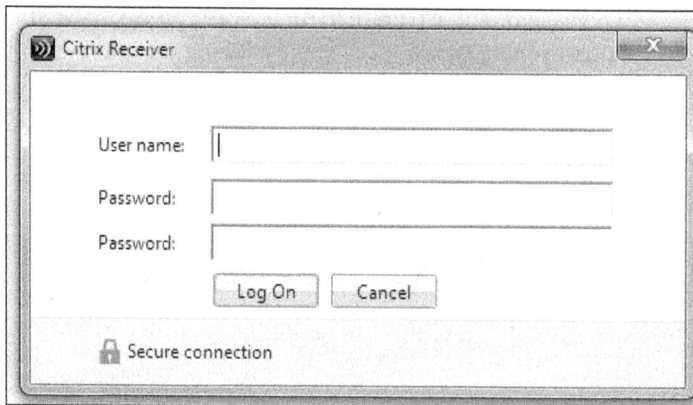

> By the fact that we are using the SMS2 platform, the second password is the PIN assigned to the user by the SMS2 administration console.

How it works...

The SMS2 platform is a free two-factor authentication platform, which permits users authenticating in a secure way to configure the XenDesktop infrastructure.

The process on which multifactor authentication platforms are based is quite simple. Together with the standard credentials (username/password) assigned to a specific user, a second authentication factor is added in order to make the success for malicious activities difficult. This is similar to the smart cards / PKI tokens authentication, with the fact that the second authentication factor is in the form of software code and not the hardware device.

The SMS2 software is based on this kind of architecture. The software, interacting with the required architectural components (an LDAP directory, such as Microsoft Active Directory, a RADIUS platform, a SQL Server database, and an optional secure access gateway such as NetScaler), is able to associate generated PIN codes to specific domain users. This code must be used as a second password to be able to authenticate and use the published corporate resources, such as desktops and/or applications.

Additionally, it is also possible configuring a third authentication factor, OTP. This is a temporary code, which must be combined with the user's PIN plus the password, and it can be in the form of an e-mail, proprietary token device, or SMS on your mobile phone.

> Proprietary—not free—alternatives to the SMS2 platform can be the following:
>
> ▸ **Safenet OTP**: http://www.safenet-inc.com/data-protection/authentication/otp-authentication/
> ▸ **Symantec OTP**: https://www.symantec.com/verisign/vip-authentication-service
> ▸ **RSA OTP**: http://www.emc.com/security/rsa-securid.htm

Together with the operations performed by the two-factor authentication platforms, there is the NetScaler Gateway, on which is necessary configuring the existing RADIUS platform(s) to use as second factor authentication.

There's more...

With the SMS2 platform, it's possible to add a third authentication factor to the logon, permitting users receiving an e-mail or an SMS directly to their personal accounts or mobile devices, being prompted for the required code after the first logon phase, on which the standard credentials plus the associated PIN have been inserted.

To enable this configuration, edit the `Configuration.xml` file located at `C:\Program Files\WrightCCS2\Settings` by default, and set the following XML parameters:

▶ `<AuthEngineChallengeResponse>True</AuthEngineChallengeResponse>`

▶ `<AuthEnginePinCodeTokenSeparated>True</AuthEnginePinCodeTokenSeparated>`

> In order to apply the modified parameters, you have to restart the **Wright AuthEngine** service.

In this way, users will be prompted to type the third factor authentication, and with the second specified parameters, in the case of wrong credentials in the first login step, the logon process will be stopped, instead of proceeding anyway with the request of the OTP.

See also

▶ The *Installing and configuring NetScaler Gateway™ 10.5* recipe in *Chapter 8, XenDesktop® Component Integration*

Index

R

RADIUS
about 377
working 389
RC5 encryption algorithm
URL 252
Release ID (REL) 284
Remote Authentication Dial In User Service.
See **RADIUS**
Remote Desktop Services (RDS) 205, 270
Rename-AcctIdentityPool command 341
resources
deploying, ways 205, 206
roaming profile
cons 119
pros 119
use cases 119
used, for implementing profile
architecture 114, 115
Role 191
RSA OTP
URL 399

S

Safenet OTP
URL 399
SCVMM 2012 SP1
URL, for downloading 72
Secure Ticket Authority (STA) 310
Security Center 90
sequencing 226
Server Manager 108
server OS machine
VDA, installing for 121-123
server OS Master Image
configuring 92-97
optimizing 92-97
Service Location (SRV) 317
Service Principal Name (SPN)
about 50
URL 50
shadowing 192
SingleImage catalogs 350
Smart Cards 363

SMS2
about 391, 399
URL, for downloading 391
SNIP (Subnet IP Address) 316
SQL Server 2012 Database
preparing 13-16
SQL Server installation
URL 16
Storage Area Network (SAN) 4
StoreFront™ 3
StoreFront™ 2.6
configuring 28-39
installing 28-39
StoreFront™ admin cmdlets 357-360
streaming 226
strong authentication
implementing, for XenDesktop® 7 377-389
strong authentication logon method 363
Subnet IP Address (SNIP) 305
Superfetch service 91
Symantec OTP
URL 399
**System Center Virtual Machine Manager
(SCVMM) 69**
system information
retrieving 334-336

T

target device
configuring 97-103
Telephony components initiator 91
**Test-ConfigServiceInstanceAvailability
cmdlet 337**
ThinCloned catalogs 350
two-factor hardware authentication
implementing, for XenDesktop® 7 364-376
two-factor software authentication
implementing, for XenDesktop® 7 391-399

U

USB corporation
URL 285
USB devices
configuring 281-283
user profile 115

[PACKT] PUBLISHING enterprise
professional expertise distilled

Thank you for buying
Citrix XenDesktop® Cookbook
Third Edition

About Packt Publishing

Packt, pronounced 'packed', published its first book, *Mastering phpMyAdmin for Effective MySQL Management*, in April 2004, and subsequently continued to specialize in publishing highly focused books on specific technologies and solutions.

Our books and publications share the experiences of your fellow IT professionals in adapting and customizing today's systems, applications, and frameworks. Our solution-based books give you the knowledge and power to customize the software and technologies you're using to get the job done. Packt books are more specific and less general than the IT books you have seen in the past. Our unique business model allows us to bring you more focused information, giving you more of what you need to know, and less of what you don't.

Packt is a modern yet unique publishing company that focuses on producing quality, cutting-edge books for communities of developers, administrators, and newbies alike. For more information, please visit our website at www.PacktPub.com.

About Packt Enterprise

In 2010, Packt launched two new brands, Packt Enterprise and Packt Open Source, in order to continue its focus on specialization. This book is part of the Packt Enterprise brand, home to books published on enterprise software – software created by major vendors, including (but not limited to) IBM, Microsoft, and Oracle, often for use in other corporations. Its titles will offer information relevant to a range of users of this software, including administrators, developers, architects, and end users.

Writing for Packt

We welcome all inquiries from people who are interested in authoring. Book proposals should be sent to author@packtpub.com. If your book idea is still at an early stage and you would like to discuss it first before writing a formal book proposal, then please contact us; one of our commissioning editors will get in touch with you.

We're not just looking for published authors; if you have strong technical skills but no writing experience, our experienced editors can help you develop a writing career, or simply get some additional reward for your expertise.

Citrix® XenDesktop® 7 Cookbook

ISBN: 978-1-78217-746-3   Paperback: 410 pages

Over 35 recipes to help you implement a fully featured XenDesktop® 7 architecture with a rich and powerful VDI experience

1. Implement the XenDesktop 7 architecture and its satellite components.

2. Learn how to publish desktops and applications to the end-user devices, optimizing their performance and increasing the general security.

3. Designed in a manner which will allow you to progress gradually from one chapter to another or to implement a single component only referring to the specific topic.

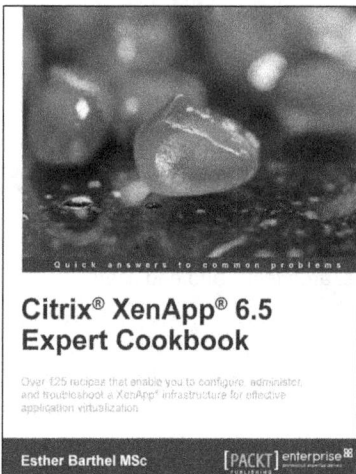

Citrix® XenDesktop® 7 Cookbook

Over 35 recipes to help you implement a fully featured XenDesktop® 7 architecture with a rich and powerful VDI experience

Gaspare A. Silvestri   [PACKT] enterprise

Citrix® XenApp® 6.5 Expert Cookbook

ISBN: 978-1-84968-522-1   Paperback: 420 pages

Over 125 recipes that enable you to configure, administer, and troubleshoot a XenApp® infrastructure for effective application virtualization

1. Create installation scripts for Citrix XenApp, License Servers, Web Interface, and StoreFront.

2. Use PowerShell scripts to configure and administer the XenApp's infrastructure components.

3. Discover Citrix and community written tools to maintain a Citrix XenApp infrastructure.

Citrix® XenApp® 6.5 Expert Cookbook

Over 125 recipes that enable you to configure, administer, and troubleshoot a XenApp® infrastructure for effective application virtualization

Esther Barthel MSc   [PACKT] enterprise ⌗

Please check **www.PacktPub.com** for information on our titles

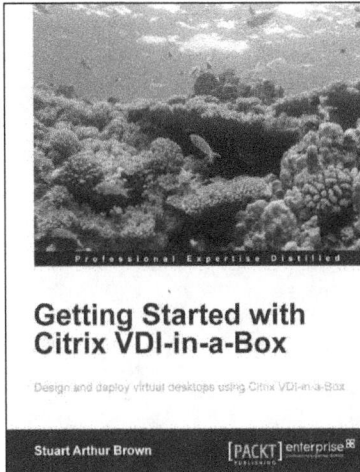

Getting Started with Citrix VDI-in-a-Box

ISBN: 978-1-78217-104-1   Paperback: 86 pages

Design and deploy virtual desktops using Citrix VDI-in-a-Box

1. Design a Citrix VDI-in-a-Box solution.

2. Get the budget for Citrix VDI-in-a-Box by building a case.

3. Implement a Citrix VDI-in-a-Box proof of concept and Citrix VDI-in-a-Box solution.

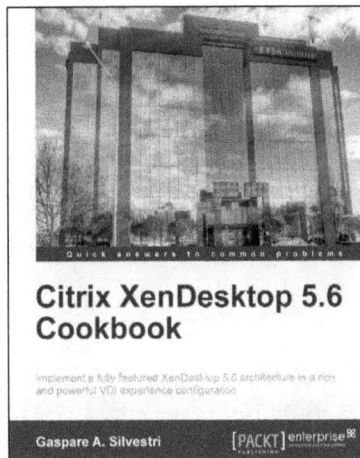

Getting Started with Citrix VDI-in-a-Box

Design and deploy virtual desktops using Citrix VDI-in-a-Box

Stuart Arthur Brown   [PACKT] enterprise ⌗

Citrix XenDesktop 5.6 Cookbook

ISBN: 978-1-84968-504-7   Paperback: 354 pages

Implement a fully featured XenDesktop 5.6 architecture in a rich and powerful VDI experience configuration

1. Real-world methodologies and functioning explanations about the XenDesktop 5.6 architecture and its satellite components used to perform a service-oriented architecture.

2. Learn how to publish desktops and applications to end user devices, optimizing their performance and increasing the general security.

3. Step-by-step guide on how to install and configure the XenDesktop 5.6 architecture to access and use the published virtual resources.

Citrix XenDesktop 5.6 Cookbook

Implement a fully featured XenDesktop 5.6 architecture in a rich and powerful VDI experience configuration

Gaspare A. Silvestri   [PACKT] enterprise ⌗

Please check **www.PacktPub.com** for information on our titles

www.ingramcontent.com/pod-product-compliance
Lightning Source LLC
Chambersburg PA
CBHW080139220326
41598CB00032B/5120